D1257509

THE HIDDEN GOD

International Library of Philosophy and Scientific Method

EDITOR: TED HONDERICH

A Catalogue of books already published in the
International Library of Philosophy and Scientific Method
will be found at the end of this volume.

THE HIDDEN GOD

A STUDY OF TRAGIC VISION IN
THE *PENSÉES* OF PASCAL AND
THE TRAGEDIES OF RACINE

by

Lucien Goldmann

translated from the French by
Philip Thody

ROUTLEDGE & KEGAN PAUL
LONDON AND HENLEY

THE HUMANITIES PRESS
ATLANTIC HIGHLANDS, NEW JERSEY

Translated from the French
LE DIEU CACHÉ

First published in England 1964
Reprinted 1976 and 1977
by Routledge & Kegan Paul Limited
39 Store Street
London WC1E 7DD and
Broadway House, Newtown Road
Henley-on-Thames
Oxon RG9 1EN

Printed in Great Britain by
Redwood Burn Limited
Trowbridge & Esher

ISBN 0 7100 3621 3

To
MONSIEUR HENRI GOUHIER

CONTENTS

CONTENTS

APPENDICES

PREFACE

When I began this work, I had two different but complementary ends in view.

The first was to develop a scientific method for the study of literary and philosophical works, and the second to contribute to the understanding of a particular set of texts which, in spite of considerable differences between them, did seem to me to be closely linked together.

The category of Totality, which is at the very centre of dialectical thought, prevented me from making any rigorous distinction between considerations of method and the actual process of research, since these are simply two aspects of the same question.

It seems to me, in fact, that the method lies wholly in the research itself, and that this research can be valid and fruitful only in so far as it becomes progressively more aware of its own progress and of the conditions which make such progress possible.

The central idea of this book is that facts concerning man always form themselves into significant global structures, which are at one and the same time practical, theoretical and emotive, and that these structures can be studied in a scientific manner, that is to say they can be both explained and understood, only within a practical perspective based upon the acceptance of a certain set of values.

Setting out from this principle, I have shown the existence of one of these significant global structures—the tragic vision—which has enabled me to bring out and understand the essence of several theological, ideological, philosophical and literary phenomena, and also to analyse relationships between these phenomena that had not been noticed before.

Thus, in my attempt to bring out the principal features of the tragic vision (Part One), and to use this vision to study Pascal's *Pensées* and Racine's tragedies, I have also been led to show that it is one of several elements that make up the common essence shared by the movement and ideology of 'extremist' Jansenism (Part Two), of the *Pensées*, of Kant's critical philosophy (Part Three) and, finally, of Racine's theatre.

The reader must judge for himself to what extent the present work has in fact enabled me to fulfil these two initial complementary aims.

I should like now to use this preface to forestall two possible objections. I have, naturally, read a number of works both on the tragic vision and on the nature of the scientific study of literary and philosophical works, and have concentrated especially on the ideas expressed by Marx, Engels, Georg Lukàcs and on the view of tragedy put forward by Hegel (particularly in his *Aesthetics*, and above all in the outstanding chapter on the Ethical Order in *The Phenomenology of The Mind*). The fact remains, however, that even in the case of Lukàcs, there was too much difference between what I was trying to do and the views expressed by these authors to enable me to discuss them in any detail. Thus, in order to avoid complicating the issue, I have studied the early writings of Lukàcs only in so far as he is concerned with tragedy, and not at all from the standpoint of his theories on a science of philosophy and literature.

I may also, in my attempt to express dialectical ideas in a terminology which is not yet used to them, have made remarks which appear contradictory. Thus, I have written both that it is impossible to elaborate a 'scientific sociology', an objective science of facts concerning man, and that we must try to achieve 'a definite and scientific knowledge' of such facts. And, for want of a better word, I have even called such knowledge 'sociological knowledge'. Similarly, I have stated that the *Pensées* were not written 'for the free-thinker', but that, among their potential audience, we do find free-thinkers etc., etc.

There is in fact no real contradiction between these various statements. Unlike the facts discovered by physics and chemistry, facts concerning man cannot be found out impersonally, from the outside, and by methods which exclude value judgements and practical considerations. These facts must, however, be of an equally certain and reliable nature, and, from this point of view, there is no contradiction between a refusal of 'scientism' and the desire to attain a scientific, historical and sociological knowledge of facts concerning man, a knowledge quite opposed to speculation and belletristic essay writing.

Similarly, Pascal did not write the *Pensées* 'for the free-thinker' in the sense that he was developing an *argumentum ad hominem* which he himself did not accept and which he did not believe was valid for the believer. Nevertheless, like all philosophical works, the *Pensées* are addressed to everyone who does not think as their author does, and this necessarily includes free-thinkers.

In every case, these contradictions are merely apparent ones which I could have avoided by making up an abstract language that was suited to the immediate needs of the situation, but which would have also been obscure and unintelligible for the lay reader. Too much clarity darkens, wrote Pascal, and I have preferred genuine clarity to any purely formal and apparent clarity.

I should like to conclude by thanking all those who have helped me by their advice, their comments, their criticisms and their objections, and, above all, Monsieur Henri Gouhier, who has watched. over the writing of this work in all its stages.

'Tragedy is a game . . . a game which is watched by God. He is nothing more than a spectator, and he never intervenes, either by word or deed, in what the actors are doing'.

GEORGE LUKÀCS, *The Metaphysics of Tragedy*, 1908.

'The Bishop of Nantes, in his wisdom, taught me a saying of Saint Augustine's which has greatly comforted me: that he who is not satisfied with God alone as a witness to his actions is too ambitious'.

MOTHER ANGÉLIQUE DE SAINTE-MADELEINE,
Letter to Arnauld d'Andilly
on January 9th 1623.

PART ONE

The Tragic Vision

I

THE WHOLE AND THE PARTS

THIS book forms part of an overall philosophical undertaking. Although scholarship is essential to the development of any serious philosophical thesis, I have set out to write neither a work of pure scholarship nor an exhaustive study of certain aspects of French literature in the seventeenth century. Both philosophers and historians are concerned with the same facts,[1] but they approach them from different points of view and with different ends in mind.[2]

The historian whose main concern is with scholarship remains on the level of the abstract empirical phenomenon, which he tries to analyse in the minutest detail. He thus does something which is not only useful in itself, but which is also indispensable to the historian whose concern is with philosophical ideas, and whose aim is to set out from the same abstract empirical phenomena in order to discover their conceptual essence.

Thus, the two types of research are complementary, since scholarship provides the philosophically minded historian with the facts that he needs, while his speculations guide scholarship in the tasks which it is to undertake, and indicate the greater or lesser importance of the innumerable facts which constitute the inexhaustible mass of available information.

Unfortunately, over-specialisation encourages a one-sided view of the matter, so that the importance of one of these two branches of research is often neglected: the scholar considers that the only thing which really matters is the establishment of a particular point about

[1] And they should, of course, have as good a knowledge of these as possible, bearing in mind both the general state of the knowledge available and the time and energy at their disposal.

[2] Needless to say, it is possible for one man to be at one and the same time a scholar and an enquirer into philosophical matters.

what the author in question did or said, while the philosopher looks with a certain contempt at the man who does nothing but accumulate facts without trying to decide on their relative importance and general meaning.

I will waste no time over this problem, and will state that I hold the following two propositions to be axiomatic: the only possible starting-point for research lies in isolated abstract empirical facts; the only valid criterion for deciding on the value of a critical method or of a philosophical system lies in the possibility which each may offer of understanding these facts, of bringing out their significance and the laws governing their development.

The problem remains, when the facts under discussion concern the nature and activity of man, of deciding whether or not this can be done except by making these facts concrete by a dialectical conceptualisation.

I set out in this book to try to solve this problem by studying a number of texts which, for the historian of literature and ideas, are a clearly defined unit of empirical facts: the *Pensées* of Pascal and four tragedies by Racine, *Andromaque*, *Britannicus*, *Bérénice* and *Phèdre*. I shall try to show how both the subject matter and construction of these works are more clearly understandable when they are analysed from a materialistic and dialectical standpoint. I need not add that this is a limited and partial undertaking which is in no way intended to constitute, by itself, a proof of the validity of the method adopted. The value and limitations of such a method can finally be decided only by a whole series of such works, some of which have already been written by the various materialistic historians who have followed the example of Marx, many of which still remain to be written.

Although scientific knowledge is built up step by step, we can still hope that each result which is definitely acquired will enable us to move forward more quickly. I am myself certain that this work of scientific investigation is, like human knowledge and awareness in general, a collective phenomenon which requires the co-operation of innumerable individual efforts. I therefore hope to contribute both to the fuller understanding of the work of Pascal and Racine, and to the elucidation of our knowledge of the structure of consciousness and its expression in literature and philosophy. Needless to say, any contribution which I make will be both completed and transcended by further work carried out along the same lines.

I should, however, like to insist that the above statement of the limitations of my ambitions is not merely the expression of personal modesty. It is part of a definite philosophical position, characterised by the rejection of any analytical philosophy which accepts the existence of rational first principles or starts with the recognition of the absolute validity of sense experience. Both rationalism, by assuming the existence of innate and immediately accessible ideas, and empiricism, by its reliance upon sensation or perception, pre-suppose that at any moment in a particular investigation there is a certain amount of definitely acquired knowledge, from which scientific thought moves forward in a straight line, admittedly with varying degrees of certainty, but without being normally and in-evitably [1] obliged to keep returning to problems already solved. Both rationalism and empiricism are thus opposed to dialectical thought, for this affirms that there are never any absolutely valid starting-points, no problems which are finally and definitely solved, and that consequently thought never moves forward in a straight line, since each individual fact or idea assumes its significance only when it takes up its place in the whole, in the same way as the whole can be understood only by our increased knowledge of the partial and incomplete facts which constitute it. The advance of knowledge is thus to be considered as a perpetual movement to and fro, from the whole to the parts and from the parts back to the whole again, a movement in the course of which the whole and the parts throw light upon one another

On this point, as on many others, Pascal's work marks the great turning-point in Western thought, the moment at which it began to abandon the atomistic approach of rationalism and empiricism, and to move towards dialectical reasoning. Pascal himself was aware of this, and noted it in two fragments which throw particular light upon the radical difference between his own philosophical position and that of any kind of rationalism or empiricism. In my view, these fragments provide the clearest possible expression both of Pascal's own attitude and of that of any dialectical thinker, whether one of the great representative figures like Kant, Hegel, Marx or Lukàcs, or someone such as myself, whose aim is to write only a more modest, partial and limited work like the present book.

I shall now quote these fragments, pointing out that I shall come back to them in the course of the work, and also stating that it is from the point of view which they express that we can and should try to understand both Pascal's work as a whole and the meaning of Racine's tragedies.

> If man were to begin by studying himself, he would see how in-capable he is of going beyond himself (*passer outre*). How could it be possible for a part to know the whole? But he may perhaps aspire

[1] Rational or empirical thought does in fact quite often go back over results already acquired, and there is certainly no *a priori* reason for it not to do so. Such an activity, however, does not form an essential part of its nature, and therefore remains accidental and, in principle, avoidable.

to a knowledge of at least those parts which are on the same scale as he himself. But the different parts of the world are all so closely linked and related together that I hold it to be impossible to know one without knowing the others and without knowing the whole (fr. 72).

Thus, since all things are both the result and the cause of causes, both helpers and receivers of help, both mediately and immediately linked together by a natural and imperceptible chain which connects together things most distant and distinct from one another, I hold it to be equally impossible to know the parts without knowing the whole, and to know the whole without having a particular knowledge of each part (fr. 72,[1] E.390).

Pascal is aware of how sharply such a concept sets him apart from the rationalist position of Descartes, who held that although we cannot grasp the infinite, we can at least base our ideas upon reliable starting-points or obvious first principles. Descartes did not see that we meet the same problem when we study the parts as we do when we try to understand the whole, and that in so far as one fails to know the part, so it is also impossible to know the whole.

But infinity in small things is much less visible: all the philosophers have attempted to achieve knowledge of it, and all have fallen down on this point. It is this which has given rise to the titles which we find so often: *Of the Nature of Things*, *Of the Principles of Philosophy*, and others which are just as pretentious in fact even if less so in appearance, like the one proposed by the man who dazzled us with his ambitions when he wrote: *De omni scibili* (fr. 72, E.390).

It is in the context of this way of looking at things that we must take absolutely literally and give its full meaning to fragment 19: 'The last thing one discovers when writing a work is what one should put first' (E.8).

This means that no study of any problem can ever be finally completed, either as far as the whole or as far as the individual details are concerned. Even if we were to begin writing the book again, we should still have to wait until we had finished before finding what ought to have been put first. Moreover, what is true of the whole is also true for each of the parts taken separately: though none of these is a primary element, each is a relative whole when taken by itself. Thought is a constantly living endeavour in which progress is real without ever being linear, and in which it can never be said to have come to an end and be finally completed.

[1] Pascal's *Pensées* are quoted in the Brunschvicg edition by Monsieur Goldmann in the original French version of this work. In translating them into English, I have made occasional use of the Everyman translation by John Warrington, and have also added the reference number to the different order—that of the Lafuma edition—which is observed in the Everyman translation. This number is indicated by a capital E.

It should now be clear why, apart from any subjective reasons, it is impossible for epistemological considerations to look upon this study as anything but a stage in the study of a problem, a contribution to an undertaking which can neither be carried out by one individual nor ever hope to achieve final completion.

The main concern of any philosophical investigation is man, his behaviour and his knowledge of himself. In the final analysis, every philosophy implies an anthropology, a complete view of the nature of man. It would clearly be going outside the scope of this work to define the whole of my own philosophical position; however, since I shall be concerned with philosophical and literary questions, I will give a brief account of my own view of human consciousness in general and of literary and philosophical creation in particular.

I set out from the fundamental principle of dialectical materialism, that the knowledge of empirical facts remains abstract and superficial so long as it is not made concrete by its integration into a whole; and that only this act of integration can enable us to go beyond the incomplete and abstract phenomenon in order to arrive at its concrete essence, and thus, implicitly, at its meaning. I thus maintain that the ideas and work of an author cannot be understood as long as we remain on the level of what he wrote, or even of what he read and what influenced him. Ideas are only a partial aspect of a less abstract reality: that of the whole, living man. And in his turn, this man is only an element in a whole made up of the social group to. which he belongs. An idea which he expresses or a book which he writes can acquire their real meaning for us, and can be fully understood, only when they are seen as integral parts of his life and mode of behaviour. Moreover, it often happens that the mode of behaviour which enables us to understand a particular work is not that of the author himself, but that of a whole social group; and, when the work with which we are concerned is of particular importance, this behaviour is that of a whole social class.

The multiple and complex phenomenon of the relationship which each individual has with his fellows often separates his daily life as a member of society from his abstract ideas or his creative imagination, so that the relationship which he has with his social group may be too indirect for it to be analysable with any degree of accuracy. In cases such as these—which are numerous—it is difficult to understand a work if one comes to it through a study of the author's life. What he intended to say, and the subjective meaning which his books had for himself, do not always coincide with their objective meaning, and it is this which is the first concern of the philosophically-minded historian. For example, Hume was not himself a thorough-going sceptic, but the empiricism to which his work gave rise does lead to

7

an attitude of complete scepticism. Descartes believed in God, but Cartesian rationalism is atheistic. It is when he replaces the work in a historical evolution which he studies as a whole, and when he relates it to the social life of the time at which it was written—which he also looks upon as a whole—that the enquirer can bring out the work's objective meaning, which was often not completely clear for the author himself.

As long as one remains on the level of the expression of personal ideas, the differences between the Calvinist and Jansenist doctrines of Predestination remain real but scarcely visible; it is when we pass to the study of the social and economic behaviour of the various Jansenist and Calvinist groups that the differences stand out with absolute clarity. The Calvinist groups studied by Max Weber practised self-denial but remained active in society, thus making an outstanding contribution to the process of capital accumulation and to the rise of modern capitalism. The extreme Jansenist groups, on the other hand, refused to take part in any worldly activity of any kind, whether social, economic, political or even religious. It was this difference in outlook which expressed itself in the hostility which the Jansenists felt for the Calvinists, which was a real and fundamental hostility that cut across the apparent similarities between the two doctrines. Racine offers us a similar example, for while a study of his personal life does not greatly help us to understand his tragedies, these can nevertheless be partially explained by a comparison with Jansenist ideas and by a study of the social and economic position of the legal profession under Louis XIV.

Thus, the historian of literature or of philosophy begins with a series of empirical facts consisting of the texts which he is going to study. He can approach them in one of three ways: by methods of textual analysis which I shall call 'positivistic'; by intuitive methods based upon feelings of personal sympathy and affinity; or, finally, by dialectical methods. Leaving aside for the moment the second group, which in my view is not properly scientific, there is only one criterion which enables us to separate the dialectical from the positivistic approach: the two methods consider the actual texts to be both the starting-point and the conclusion of their researches, but whereas one method offers the opportunity of understanding the more or less coherent meaning of these texts, the other does not.

The concept already mentioned of the relationship between the whole and the parts immediately separates the traditional methods of literary scholarship, which frequently pay insufficient attention to the obvious factors revealed by psychology and by the study of society, from the dialectical method. The actual writings of an author, in fact, constitute only a sector of his behaviour, a sector

8

depending upon a highly complex physiological and psychological structure which undergoes great changes during his life.

Moreover, there is an even greater though similar variety in the infinite multiplicity of the particular situations in which an individual can be placed during the course of his existence. Certainly, if we had a complete and exhaustive knowledge of the psychological structure of the author in question and of his daily relationship with his environment, we should be able, if not wholly then at least partially, to understand his work through his life. The acquisition of such knowledge is, however, both for the present and in all probability for the future, a Utopian dream. Even when we are dealing with people alive at the present day, whom we can test and examine in the laboratory, we can only achieve a more or less fragmentary view of any particular individual. This is even more the case when the man we are trying to study has been dead for a long time, and when the most detailed research will reveal only a superficial and fragmentary image of him. At a time when, thanks to the existence of psycho-analysis, of Gestalt psychology, of the work of Jean Piaget, we have a better awareness than ever of the extreme complexity of the human individual, there is something paradoxical in any attempt to understand the work of Pascal, Plato or Kant by a study of their life. However great the apparent rigour with which research is conducted, any conclusion is bound to remain extremely arbitrary. We must certainly not exclude the study of biographical details, since these often provide extremely useful information. However, it will always remain merely a partial and auxiliary method which must never be used as the final basis for any explanation.

Thus, the attempt to go beyond the immediate text by incorporating it into the author's life is both difficult and unlikely to provide reliable results. Should we therefore go back to the positivistic approach, and concentrate on everything implied by a 'complete study of the text'?

I do not think so, for any purely textual study comes up against obstacles which cannot be overcome until the work has been fitted into the historical whole of which it forms part.

First of all, how is the 'work' of an author to be defined? Is it everything which he ever wrote, including letters, notes and posthumous publications? Or is it only the works that he himself completed during his lifetime and intended for publication?

The arguments in favour of one or the other of these two attitudes are well known. The principal difficulty lies in the fact that not everything which an author writes is equally important for an understanding of his work. On the one hand, there are texts which can be explained by personal and accidental circumstances, and

9

which consequently offer at most a biographical interest; on the other, there are essential texts, without which his work simply cannot be understood. Moreover, the historian's task is made all the more difficult by the fact that an author's letters and rough notes may contain some of the really essential texts, while certain sections of his published work may have little more than an anecdotal interest. This brings us face to face with one of the fundamental difficulties of any form of scientific investigation: the need to distinguish the essential from the accidental, a problem which has preoccupied philosophers from Aristotle to Husserl, and to which we must find a genuinely scientific answer.

There is a second difficulty which is no less important than the first. It is that, at first sight at least, the meaning of some texts is by no means certain and unambiguous. Words, sentence and phrases which are apparently similar, and in some cases even identical, can nevertheless have a different meaning when used in a different context. Pascal was well aware of this when he wrote: 'Words arranged differently compose different meanings, and meanings arranged differently produce different effects' (fr. 23,E.944).

> Let it not be said that I have said nothing new: I have presented the matter in a different way. When men play tennis, they both use the same ball, but one places it better than the other.
> I would just as much prefer people to say that I have used old words —as if the same ideas did not make up a different body of discourse when they are differently arranged, in the same way as the same words present different ideas when they are differently arranged (fr. 22, E.4).

From a practical point of view, it is impossible to discover what place a particular set of words occupies in a 'body of discourse' until one has succeeded in distinguishing essential from accidental elements in the work as a whole.

All this is more or less obvious. However, there are many historians who still continue, in a quite arbitrary fashion, to distinguish certain elements of a work for the purpose of comparing them with analogous elements of another and completely different work. It is this which gives rise to the widespread and persistent legends about the 'romanticism' of Rousseau and Holderlin, to the parallel between Pascal and Kierkegaard, as well as to the attempt (which I shall discuss in detail later) made by Laporte and his school to assimilate Pascal's position with the completely different one of Descartes.

Exactly the same process is used in each one of these cases: certain partial elements of a work are taken out of context and transformed into independent and autonomous wholes; the existence of similar

10

elements in the work of another author is then noted, and a parallel is established; a wholly factitious analogy is then set up, which either consciously or not fails to take account of the context in which these elements are originally to be found, and which gives them a completely different and even contradictory meaning to the one which they originally had.

Rousseau and Holderlin certainly do have a certain affective sensibility, a strongly subjective streak and a love of nature which, when taken in isolation and removed from their context, make them apparently similar to the Romantics. However, we need only recall the *Contrat Social*, the idea of the General Will, the absence of any idea of an élite contrasted to the general community, the slight importance which both authors accord to the Middle Ages, and the enthusiasm of Holderlin for Greek civilisation to see how completely different from the climate of romanticism their work really is.[1]

Similarly, we can find both a positive and a negative attitude towards reason in Pascal. But the positive element brings him no closer to Descartes than the negative element does to Kierkegaard. The two attitudes exist permanently side by side, and we cannot even start to talk about them separately unless we have already decided to approach the *Pensées* from a Cartesian or a Kierkegaardian point of view. For Pascal himself, there is really only one position which he regards as valid: that of the tragic dialectic which replies both 'Yes' and 'No' to all the fundamental problems created by man's life and by his relationship with the universe and his fellows.

A large number of other examples could be given. But these are two problems which confront any purely philological positivistic method and to which, since this method lacks any objective criterion that might enable it to judge the importance of the different texts and their meaning for the rest of the work, it can find no satisfactory solution. These difficulties are, in fact, a particularly visible sign of the general impossibility, in the realm of our knowledge of man, of understanding empirical and abstract phenomena without linking them to their concrete conceptual essence.

The way suggested by the dialectical method is different. The difficulties presented by the relationship between an author's life and his work, far from suggesting that we should go back to simply studying the text, encourage us to keep moving forward in the original direction, going not only from the text to the individual, but from the individual to the social group of which he forms part. For when we look at them more closely the difficulties raised both by a

[1] Kant, who admired Rousseau while at the same time rejecting the enthusiastic and excessively emotional aspects of his thought, saw this quite clearly.

11

consideration of the text and by a study of the author's life are basically the same and have the same epistemological basis. For since the individual facts which we encounter are inexhaustible in their variety and multiplicity, any scientific study of them must enable us to separate the accidental from the essential elements in the immediate reality which presents itself to our experience. Leaving on one side the problem presented by the physical sciences, where the situation is different, it is my contention that, in the study of man, we can separate the essential from the accidental only by integrating the individual elements into the overall pattern, by fitting the parts into the whole. This is why, although we can never actually reach a totality which is no longer an element or part of a greater whole, the methodological problem, as far as the humanities or the science of man is concerned, is principally this: that of dividing the immediately available facts into relative wholes which are sufficiently autonomous to provide a framework for scientific investigation.[1] If, however, for the reasons that I have just given, neither the individual work nor the personality of the author are sufficiently autonomous wholes to provide such a framework, we still have the possibility that the group, especially if studied from the point of view of its division into social classes, might perhaps constitute a reality which could enable us to overcome the difficulties met with either on the plane of the individual text or on that of the relationship between the author's life and his work.

It is more convenient to reverse the order in which the two original difficulties were first mentioned, and begin by asking: how can we define the meaning either of a particular text or of a fragment? The reply is provided by our earlier analysis: by fitting it into the coherent pattern of the work as a whole.

The word to be stressed here is 'coherent'. The real meaning of a passage is the one which gives us a complete and coherent picture of the overall meaning of the work—provided, of course, that the work has such a meaning.[2] If it has not, then for reasons which I shall explain later, the text in question has no fundamental

[1] As far as the humanities are concerned, dialectical thought has so far concentrated principally on the critique of the traditional fields of university study: law, political history, experimental psychology, sociology, etc. In my view, none of these disciplines is concerned with a sufficiently autonomous subject matter to enable phenomena to be understood in a genuinely scientific manner. It is too frequently forgotten that *Capital* is not a treatise on political economy in the traditional sense of the word, but, as its title indicates, a 'critique of political economy'. (For further discussion of this point, cf. Lukàcs, *History and Class Consciousness* (Berlin, 1923).)

[2] This coherence is not, however, except perhaps for works of rationalist philosophy, a logical coherence. (Cf. Lucien Goldmann, *Sciences humaines et philo-*

literary or philosophical interest. Pascal was aware of this when he said:

A person can be handsome only if all the contradictory features of his appearance are harmonised together, and it is not sufficient for us to harmonise a series of features which already agree without at the same time fitting together the contradictory ones. In order to understand an author's meaning, we must resolve all the contradictions in his work. Thus, if we are to understand the Scriptures, we must find a meaning which reconciles all the contradictory passages. It is not enough to have one meaning which fits a number of passages that already agree with one another; we must have one which reconciles even those that are contradictory. Every author either has a meaning which fits all the contradictory passages in his work, or he has no real meaning at all. This is not true of the Scriptures and of the Prophets, for they were certainly too wise to allow such a thing to happen. Thus what we must try to discover is a meaning which brings all the different passages together (fr. 684, E.491).

The meaning of a particular passage depends upon the coherence of the work as a whole. A statement of belief in the infallibility of the Scriptures has neither the same meaning nor the same importance in Saint Augustine, Saint Thomas Aquinas, Pascal or Descartes. It is, I agree, an essential feature of the attitude of the first three of these thinkers—although its significance differs very widely from one to another—and it is accidental and quite unimportant in the case of Descartes. Fichte was probably right, in the famous Debate on Atheism, to insist on his own personal faith, but his opponents were also right when they maintained that this faith was a purely accidental and subjective element in a system which, taken as a whole, led objectively to atheism. Similarly, in the famous fragment 77 (E.1001), Pascal showed a much deeper understanding of Cartesian philosophy (and of its subsequent development in Malebranche) than does Laporte in the whole of his extensive work, where his interpretation is often based on texts which are accidental rather than essential in nature.

However, even though the criterion of coherence is an important and even a decisive factor when it is a question of understanding a particular, isolated text, it goes without saying that it is only in fairly rare instances that it can be applied to the author's work as a whole, and even then only when we are concerned with a work of quite exceptional importance.

---

sophie (P.U.F., 1952).) There, Monsieur Goldmann explains that representative great writers are, in his opinion, those whose work comes nearest to be the complete expression of the way a particular class looked at the world, cf. especially p. 47.

The fragment 684 (E.491), giving Pascal's views on the infallibility of the Scriptures, deals with a text of this nature, and one which, for a believer, has no parallel. For Pascal, the Scriptures can contain nothing accidental: they must fit together down to the last word and the last syllable. The historian of literature or of philosophy, however, is placed in a more complex and less privileged position: he must recognise from the outset that the text which he is studying was written by an individual who was not always at the same level of consciousness and creative power, and who was constantly more or less exposed to external and accidental influences. In most cases the criterion of coherence can be applied only to those texts which are considered essential to the work as a whole, and this brings us back to the first of the difficulties which any purely textual study must face: that of determining which particular texts it should analyse.

The historian of art or literature has an immediate and direct criterion: that of aesthetic value. Any attempt to understand Goethe's work can leave on one side minor texts such as *The Citizen General*, and any attempt to understand Racine's work can dispense with studying *Alexandre* or *La Thébaide*. But apart from the fact that, once isolated from any conceptual or explanatory framework, the criterion of artistic validity is arbitrary and subjective,[1] it has the additional disadvantage of being quite inapplicable to works of philosophy or theology.

It thus follows that the history of philosophy and literature can become scientific only when an objective and verifiable instrument has been created which will enable us to distinguish the essential from the accidental elements in a work of art; the validity of this method will be measured by the fact that it will never proclaim as accidental works which are aesthetically satisfying. In my view, such an instrument is to be found in the concept of the *world vision*.

In itself, this concept is not dialectical in origin, and has been widely used by Dilthey and his school. Unfortunately, they have done so in a very vague way, and have never succeeded in giving it anything like a scientific status. The first person to use it with the accuracy indispensable to any instrument of scientific research was

[1] And this is also true for reasons which are to a very great extent social. At any one historical period the sensibility of the members of any particular social class, and also of the intellectuals in general, is more receptive to some works than to others. It is for this reason that most studies written at the present day on Corneille, Hugo or Voltaire are to be read with a certain amount of caution. This is not the case with irrationalistic or even with tragic texts, whose aesthetic value can be clearly perceived by the modern intellectual even when their objective meaning is only imperfectly understood.

Georg Lukàcs, who employed it in a number of works whose methods I have tried to describe elsewhere.[1]

What is a *world vision*? It is not an immediate, empirical fact, but a conceptual working hypothesis indispensable to an understanding of the way in which individuals actually express their ideas. Even on an empirical plane, its importance and reality can be seen as soon as we go beyond the ideas of work of a single writer, and begin to study them as part of a whole. For example, scholars have long since noted the similarities which exist between certain philosophical systems and certain literary works: Descartes and Corneille, Pascal and Racine, Schelling and the German romantics, Hegel and Goethe. What I shall try to show in this book is that similarities can be found not only in the detail of the particular arguments put forward but also in the general structure of texts as apparently dissimilar as the critical writings of Kant and the *Pensées* of Pascal.

On the plane of personal psychology, there are no people more different than the poet, who creates particular beings and things, and the philosopher, who thinks and expresses himself by means of general concepts. Similarly, it is difficult to imagine two beings more dissimilar in every aspect of their lives than Kant and Pascal. Thus, if most of the essential elements which make up the schematic structure of the writings of Kant, Pascal and Racine are similar in spite of the differences which separate these authors as individuals, we must accept the existence of a reality which goes beyond them as individuals and finds its expression in their work. It is this which I intend to call the *world vision*, and, in the particular case of the authors to be studied in this book, the *tragic vision*.

It would be wrong, however, to look upon this world vision as a metaphysical concept or as one belonging purely to the realm of speculation. On the contrary, it forms the main concrete aspect of the phenomenon which sociologists have been trying to describe for a number of years under the name of collective consciousness, and the analysis which I shall now undertake will enable us to reach a clearer understanding of the notion of coherence.

The psycho-motor behaviour of every individual stems from his relationship with his environment. Jean Piaget has broken down the effect of this relationship into two complementary operations: the assimilation of the environment into the subject's scheme of thought and action and the attempt which the individual makes to accommodate this personal scheme to the structure of his environment when this cannot be made to fit into his plans.[2]

[1] See Lucien Goldmann, 'Matérialisme dialectique et Histoire de la philosophie', in *Revue philosophique de France et de l'étranger*, 1948, No. 46, and op. cit.
[2] Marx said the same thing in a passage from *Das Capital* which Piaget re-

The main error of most psychological theories has been to concentrate too frequently on the individual as absolute and sole reality, and to study other men only in so far as they play the part of *objects* in the individual's ideas and activities. This atomistic view of the individual was shared by the Cartesian or Fichtean concept of the Ego, by the neo-Kantians and the phenomenologists with their idea of the 'transcendental Self', by Condillac and his theory of the animated statue and by other thinkers. Now this implicit concept of man primarily as an isolated individual, which dominates modern non-dialectical philosophy and psychology, is quite simply wrong. The simplest empirical observation is enough to reveal its inaccuracy. Almost no human actions are performed by isolated individuals for the subject performing the action is a group, a 'We', and not an 'I', even though, by the phenomenon of reification, the present structure of society tends to hide the 'We' and transform it into a collection of different individuals isolated from one another. There is indeed another possible relationship between men apart from that of subject to object, and the 'I' to the 'you'; this is the communal relationship which I shall call the 'We', the expression which an action assumes when it is exercised on an object by a group of men acting in common.

Naturally, in modern society every individual is engaged in a number of activities of this type. He takes part in different activities in different groups, with the result that each activity has a greater or lesser influence on his consciousness and behaviour. The groups to which he belongs, and which may perform communal activities, can be his family, his country, his professional or economic association, an intellectual or religious community and so on. For purely factual reasons that I have expressed elsewhere,[1] the most important group to which an individual may belong, from the point of view of intellectual and artistic activity and creation, is that of the social class, or classes, of which he is a member. Up to the present day, it is class, linked together by basic economic needs, which has been of prime importance in influencing the ideological life of man, since he has been compelled to devote most of his thought and energy either to

[1] Cf. Lucien Goldmann, *Sciences humaines et Philosophie*.

produced in his latest work: 'Primarily, labour is a process going on between man and nature, a process in which man, through his own activity, initiates, regulates and controls the material exchanges between himself and nature. He confronts nature as one of her own forces, setting in motion arms and legs, head and hands, in order to appropriate nature's productions in a form suitable to his own wants. By thus acting on the external world and changing it, he at the same time changes his own nature' (Part Three, Chapter Five, Eden and Cedar Paul's translation in the Everyman edition, 1930).

finding enough to live on or, if he belonged to a ruling class, to keeping his privileges and administering and increasing his wealth.

As I have already said, an individual can doubtless separate his ideas and intellectual aspirations from his daily life; the same is not true of social groups, for as far as they are concerned, their ideas and behaviour are rigorously and closely related. The central thesis of dialectical materialism does nothing more than affirm the existence of this relationship and demand that it should be given concrete recognition until the day when man succeeds in freeing himself from his slavery to economic needs on the plane of his daily behaviour.

However, not all groups based on economic interests necessarily constitute social classes. In order for a group to become a class, its interests must be directed, in the case of a 'revolutionary' class, towards a complete transformation of the social structure or, if it is a 'reactionary' class, towards maintaining the present social structure unchanged. Each class will then express its desire for change—or for permanence—by a complete vision both of what the man of the present day is, with his qualities and failings, and of what the man of the future ought to be, and of what relationship he should try to establish with the universe and with his fellows.

What I have called a 'world vision' is a convenient term for the whole complex of ideas, aspirations and feelings which links together the members of a social group (a group which, in most cases, assumes the existence of a social class) and which opposes them to members of other social groups.

This is certainly a highly schematic view, an extrapolation made by the historian for purposes of convenience; nevertheless, it does extrapolate a tendency which really exists among the members of a certain social group, who all attain this class consciousness in a more or less coherent manner. I say 'more or less', because even though it is only rarely that an individual is completely and wholly aware of the whole meaning and direction of his aspirations, behaviour and emotions, he is nevertheless always relatively conscious of them. In a few cases—and it is these which interest us—there are exceptional individuals who either actually achieve or who come very near to achieving a completely integrated and coherent view of what they and the social class to which they belong are trying to do. The men who express this vision on an imaginative or conceptual plane are writers and philosophers, and the more closely their work expresses this vision in its complete and integrated form, the more important does it become. They then achieve the maximum possible awareness of the social group whose nature they are expressing.

These ideas should be enough to show how a dialectical conception of social life differs from the ideas of traditional psychology and sociology. In a dialectical conception the individual ceases to be an atom which exists in isolation and opposition to other men and to the physical world, and the 'collective consciousness' ceases to be a static entity which stands above and outside particular individuals. The collective consciousness exists only in and through individual consciousnesses, but it is not simply made up of the sum of these. In fact, the term 'collective consciousness' is not a very satisfactory one, and I myself prefer that of 'group consciousness', accompanied in each case, as far as that is possible, by the description of the group in question: family, professional, national, class. This group consciousness is the tendency common to the feelings, aspirations and ideas of the members of a particular social class; a tendency which is developed as a result of a particular social and economic situation, and which then gives rise to a set of activities performed by the real or potential community constituted by this social class. The awareness of this tendency varies from one person to another, and reaches its height only in certain exceptional individuals or, as far as the majority of the group is concerned, in certain privileged situations: war in the case of national group consciousness, revolution for class consciousness, etc. It follows from this that exceptional individuals can give a better and more accurate expression to the collective consciousness than the other members of the group, and that consequently we must reverse the traditional order in which historians have studied the problem of the relationship between the individual and the community. For example, scholars have often tried to determine to what extent Pascal was or was not a Jansenist. But both those who said that he was and those who said that he was not were in agreement as to how the question should be asked. Both agreed that it had the following meaning: 'To what extent did his ideas coincide with those of Antoine Arnauld, Nicole and other well-known thinkers who were universally acknowledged to be Jansenists?' In my view, the question should be asked the other way round: we must first of all establish what Jansenism was as a social and ideological phenomenon; we must then decide what are the characteristics of a consistently 'Jansenist' attitude; and we must then compare the writings of Nicole, Arnauld and Pascal to this conceptual prototype of Jansenism. This will enable us to reach a much better understanding of the objective meaning of the work of each of these three men, each with his own particular limitations; we shall then see that on the literary and ideological plane the only really thorough-going Jansenists were Pascal and Racine, and perhaps Barcos, and that it is by reference to what they wrote that we should judge to what extent Arnauld and Nicole were Jansenist thinkers.

18

Is this not an arbitrary method? Could we not do without the Jansenism of Nicole and Arnauld and the idea of the 'world vision'? I know of only one reply to this objection: 'By their fruits Ye shall know them.' Such a method is justified if it enables us to reach a better understanding of the particular works in question: the *Pensées* of Pascal and the tragedies of Racine.

This takes us back to our starting-point: any great literary or artistic work is the expression of a world vision. This vision is the product of a collective group consciousness which reaches its highest expression in the mind of a poet or a thinker. The expression which his work provides is then studied by the historian who uses the idea of the world vision as a tool which will help him to deduce two things from the text: the essential meaning of the work he is studying and the meaning which the individual and partial elements take on when the work is looked at as a whole.

I will add that the historian of literature and philosophy should study not only world visions in the abstract but also the concrete expressions which these visions assume in the everyday world. In studying a work he should not limit himself to what can be explained by presupposing the existence of such and such a vision. He must also ask what social and individual reasons there are to explain why this vision should have been expressed in this particular way at this particular time. In addition, he should not be satisfied with merely noting the inconsistencies and variations which prevent the work in question from being an absolutely coherent expression of the world vision which corresponds to it; such inconsistencies and variations are not merely facts which the historian should note; they are problems which he must solve, and their solution will lead him to take into account not only the social and historical factors which accompanied the production of the work but also, more frequently, factors related to the life and psychological make-up of the particular author. It is in this context that these factors should be studied, for they constitute elements which, although accidental, should not be ignored by the historian. Moreover, he can understand them only by reference to the essential structure of the object under investigation.

It must be added that the dialectical method just described has already been spontaneously applied, if not by historians of philosophy, then at least by philosophers themselves when they wanted to understand the work of their predecessors. This is true of Kant, who is perfectly aware, and says so in so many words, that Hume is not a complete sceptic and is not consistently empirical in his outlook, but who nevertheless discusses him as if this were the case. He does so because what he is trying to do is to reach the philosophical doctrine

19

(what I have called the 'world vision'), which gives its meaning and significance to Hume's position. Similarly, in the dialogue between Pascal and Monsieur de Saci (which, although a transcription by Fontaine, is probably very close to the original text) we find two similar examples of a deformation of another writer's ideas. Pascal doubtless knew that Montaigne's position was not that of consistent and rigorous scepticism. Nevertheless, for exactly the same reasons that Kant slightly distorts Hume's position, he does treat him as if this were the case: because what he is trying to do is discuss a specific philosophical position and not analyse the actual meaning of a text. Similarly, we also see him attributing to Montaigne the hypothesis of the malign demon—a mistake from a strictly textual point of view, but one that can be justified on philosophical grounds, since for its real author, Descartes, this hypothesis was merely a provisional supposition whose aim was to summarise and carry to its logical conclusion the sceptical position that he wants to refute.

Thus, the method which consists of going from the actual text to the conceptual vision, and then returning from this vision to the text again, is not an innovation of dialectical materialism. The improvement which dialectical materialism makes upon this method lies in the fact that by integrating the ideas of a particular individual into those of a social group, and especially by analysing the historical function played in the genesis of ideas by social classes, it provides a scientific basis for the concept of world vision, and frees it from any criticism that it might be purely arbitrary, speculative and metaphysical.

These few pages were needed to clarify the general characteristics of the method which I intended to use. I should now merely add that since a 'world vision' is the psychic expression of the relationship between certain human groups and their social or physical environment, the number of such visions which can be found in any fairly long historical period is necessarily limited.

However many and varied the actual historical situations in which man may find himself can be, the different world visions that we encounter nevertheless express the reaction of a group of beings who remain relatively constant. A philosophy or work of art can keep its value outside the time and place where it first appeared only if, by expressing a particular human situation, it transposes this on to the plane of the great human problems created by man's relationship with his fellows and with the universe. Now since the number of coherent replies that can be given to these problems is limited[1] by

[1] Although we are, today, very far from having indicated with any degree of scientific precision where such a limit might lie. The scientific elaboration of a typology of world visions has scarcely even begun.

the very structure of the human personality, each of the replies given may correspond to different and even contradictory historical situations. This explains both the successive rebirths of the same idea which we find in the world of history, art and philosophy and the fact that, at different times, the same vision can assume different aspects; it can be sometimes revolutionary, sometimes defensive, reactionary and conservative, and sometimes even decadent.

This statement is, of course, true only so long as the concept of the world vision is considered in the abstract, as an attempt to solve certain fundamental human problems and to give each of them its own importance. As we move away from the abstract idea of the world vision, so we find that the individual details of each vision are linked to historical situations localised in place and time, and even to the individual personality of the writer or thinker in question.

Historians of philosophy are justified in accepting the notion of Platonism as valid when it is applied to Plato himself, to Saint Augustine, to Descartes and to certain other thinkers. The same thing is true of mysticism, empiricism, rationalism, the tragic vision and other expressions of the 'world vision', as long as the following condition is held in mind: that setting out both from the general characteristics shared by Platonism as a world vision and from the elements which the historical situation of fourth-century Athens, sixth-century Carthage and seventeenth-century France have in common, historians try to discover what was peculiar to each of these three situations, how these peculiarities were reflected in the work of Plato, Saint Augustine and Descartes, and, finally, if they wish to present a really complete study, how the personality of each of these thinkers expressed itself in his work.

I will add that, in my view, the principal task of the historian of art or philosophy lies in describing the nature of the different world visions which may exist; that once he has done this, he will have made an essential contribution to any truly scientific and philosophical view of man; and that this is a task which has scarcely even begun. Like the great systems in the world of the physical sciences, it will be the eventual achievement of a whole series of particular studies whose own individual meaning it will then make clearer and more precise.

This examination of the tragic vision in the work of Pascal and Racine is intended to be one of these individual preparatory studies. This is why I shall now try to define more exactly what I mean by the idea of the tragic vision, the instrument I intend to use to study the works under consideration.

II

THE TRAGIC VISION: GOD

'However small man may be, he is still so great that he cannot, without injustice to his own greatness, be servant save of God alone' (Saint-Cyran, *Maximes*, 201).

IN order to describe the conceptual scheme of the tragic vision in its entirety, we should need to bring out the elements common to Shakespeare, Racine, Kant, Pascal, to certain of Michelangelo's statues and probably to a number of other works of varying importance. The present state of our knowledge, however, does not ·make this possible, with the result that the idea of the tragic vision, such as I have examined it in a number of earlier studies, applies only to the writings of Kant, Pascal and Racine. I hope eventually to be able to develop it to the point where it can be used to analyse the works mentioned above, but all that I can do at the moment is to describe this instrument of research at its present state of development, maintaining that in spite of all its imperfections it will enable us to reach a better understanding of French and German literature and ideas in the seventeenth and eighteenth centuries.

I should add that a fairly well-developed version of this concept can be found in the final chapter of Georg von Lukàcs' *The Soul and its Forms*,[1] the chapter entitled 'The Metaphysics of Tragedy'. I shall be quoting from this book, but with one important modification: for reasons which I cannot wholly understand—perhaps the lack of settled opinions in a writer of only twenty-five—Lukàcs talks both of 'plays' and 'tragedies', although his intention is to discuss solely the tragic vision. Thus, when I quote him I shall always use the terms 'tragic' and 'tragedy' instead of 'drama' and 'dramatic', maintaining as I do so that I am not distorting his meaning. I should also add that at this period of his life Lukàcs was still under the influence of Kant, and that he analysed the tragic vision without reference to

[1] Cf. Georg von Lukàcs, *Die Seele und die Formen* (Berlin: Essays Fleischel, 1911).

any historical context, concentrating on the works of the little-known writer Paul Ernst. I shall myself try to follow out the ideas later developed by Lukàcs himself, and to make his analysis clearer by linking it to a number of specific historical situations; I shall also be studying writers of greater importance than Paul Ernst, that is to say Pascal, Racine and Kant.

I shall be faithful to my own method if, attempting to describe the tragic vision in seventeenth- and eighteenth-century France and Germany, I begin by situating it by reference to the world view which preceded it (dogmatic rationalism and sceptical empiricism), as well as to that which followed and went beyond it (dialectical idealism in the case of Hegel, dialectical materialism in the case of Marx). However, the statement that rational or empiricist individualism is followed by the tragic vision, and that this in turn is followed by dialectical thought, needs to be justified by a few preliminary remarks.

I have already said that the different world views—rationalism, empiricism, tragic vision, dialectical thought—are not empirical realities but conceptualisations whose rôle is to help us in understanding individual works such as those of Descartes or Malebranche, Locke, Hume or Condillac, Pascal or Kant, Hegel or Marx. I will add that this succession of 'schools of thought' just mentioned is itself a conceptual schematisation of what actually happened; that its rôle is to enable us to understand events, and not to provide a complete account of them.

Pascal and Kant, the two principal tragic thinkers, were each of them preceded by a great writer—Pascal by the rationalist Descartes, Kant by the sceptic Hume—and it is most important to note how each defined his own work with reference to that of his predecessor. Paraphrasing the title of a recent work, we could write two most instructive books entitled respectively *Pascal, reader of Descartes and Montaigne*, and *Kant, reader of Leibniz-Wolff and Hume.*[1] But this in no way means that the appearance of the tragic vision was immediately followed by the disappearance of rationalism and empiricism as active and creative forces. On the contrary, while the disappearance of the *noblesse de robe* in France and the development of the bourgeoisie in Germany soon destroyed the social and economic foundations of Jansenism and of Kantian philosophy, rationalism and empiricism, as ideologies of the Third Estate which created modern France and even, although in very different conditions, modern Germany,[2] are still alive today. Rationalism, in particular,

[1] Cf. Léon Brunschvicg, *Descartes et Pascal lecteurs de Montaigne* (New York-Paris: Brentano's, 1944).
[2] Cf. Lucien Goldmann, *La Communauté et l'univers chez Kant* (P.U.F., 1948).

23

has always remained alive in France, although it is a descendant rather than an ascendant course which can be traced through the work of Malebranche, Voltaire, Anatole France, Valéry and—if one wishes to go on to the present day—Julien Benda.[1] Similarly, empiricism begins to play a rôle in French thought only a long time after Pascal's death, in the eighteenth and nineteenth centuries. The situation is similar in Germany, where Fichte comes after Kant and where the neo-Kantians used Kant's name in order to cover their retreat from his original position.

How, then, can the historical schematisation I have adopted be justified?

There are two complementary ways of looking at the history of philosophy: the first is concerned with the relationship between trends of thought and the concrete historical situations which enabled them to be born, develop and be expressed in literature and philosophy; the second, which I myself consider equally essential, studies the relationship between thought and between the immediate human and physical realities which form its subject-matter and which it tried to understand and explain.

Using two terms whose meaning will have to be further elaborated, we can say that the first of these two methods is concerned with the meaning of a set of ideas, while the second is interested in their relative truth. This immediately raises the question of what criterion should be used to establish an order of precedence as far as the relative truth of these ideas is concerned, since, as I have already said, mere chronological succession is not enough. It is a complex problem which I have tried to discuss elsewhere.[2]

I will merely point out that, in my view, the principal criterion lies in the extent to which a philosophical position is capable of taking into account both the coherence and valid elements of another position and its limitations and insufficiencies, while at the same time also managing to integrate the positive elements of the position it is studying into its own substance.[3] Kant and Pascal, for example, both

---

[1] One way of studying the evolution of French rationalism from Descartes to the present day would be by considering the relationship between thought and action. For while this is implicit in Descartes and explicit for Voltaire, it becomes, for Valéry, impossible to achieve. In Descartes thought changes man, in Voltaire it is a way of changing the human world, but in Valéry it has no practical relevance either to man or to the external world. We can thus find rationalism developing according to the following curve, itself related to the economic, social and political history of the French third estate: beginning as an end in itself, it becomes a means to an end and then takes on the value of an attitude of intellectual resignation to which is added a poetry that relies mainly on physical imagery.

[2] Cf. Lucien Goldmann, *Sciences humaines et philosophie* (P.U.F., 1952).

[3] The final point is, in my view, especially important: two sets of ideas can understand each other as coherent visions, can see each other's defects and

24

understood the internal coherence and positive elements of rationalism and empiricism, and were capable of integrating the positive
elements of these philosophies into their systems; at the same time,
however, they remained well aware of the limitations and insufficiencies which rationalism and empiricism contained.

Their success in doing this can be contrasted with the complete
failure of most rationalists, from Malebranche to ,Voltaire and
Valéry, to understand the value of the tragic position, and with the
inability of the neo-Kantians to perceive the real spirit infusing
Kant's thought.

If we want to find a criticism of the tragic position which both
understands it, goes beyond it and incorporates it in a higher
synthesis, then we need to go to the great dialectical thinkers, Hegel,
Marx and Lukàcs.

It is the manner in which the tragic vision incorporates and goes
beyond the findings of rationalism and empiricist individualism, and
in which it is itself then incorporated and transcended by dialectical
thought, that provides us with the historical pattern that I shall use
in the following pages. Such a pattern is based upon the idea that
each really valid philosophy contains an increase over its predecessors
in the amount of truth which it represents.

What was the general condition of science and philosophy in the
years during which Pascal wrote the *Pensées*? It was characterised
by the triumph of philosophical rationalism and of the scientific
and mechanistic attitude which accompanied it. This mechanistic
rationalism had not appeared suddenly on the intellectual scene like
Athene issuing ready armed from the head of Zeus, but owed its
triumph to a long struggle against two scientific and philosophical
positions that were still alive in the seventeenth century: the Aristotelian and Thomist concept of physics and philosophy, and the
animistic philosophy of nature. In 1662, the year of Pascal's death,
Thomism still dominated the teaching in most of the Schools, while
Aristotelian physics was retreating only slowly before the findings of
Galileo, Toricelli and Descartes.[1]

Thomistic Aristotelianism, the animistic philosophy of nature and
mechanistic rationalism constitute three stages in the development of

[1] The excellent studies of Father Lenoble on Mersenne, and especially of
Monsieur Koyré on Galileo, have thrown much light on the concrete aspects of
this evolution.

limitations, and yet each still remain unable to integrate the positive elements of
the views which it criticises. This is true, for example, of empiricism and
rationalism, and can be explained by the fact that they are complementary, at the
same time as neither can go beyond the other in the amount of truth which it
contains.

Western bourgeois thought, stages which it has successively transcended to reach the irrational tendency which characterises it today.

In the thirteenth century Thomism was the ideological expression of a movement of deep social change. The Third Estate had succeeded in inserting an urban and administrative section governed by 'reason' and secular law into the completely rural and decentralised hierarchy of the feudal system of the ninth and tenth centuries. The relationship between reason and faith in Thomism reflects and expresses both the real relationship between the Third Estate and the feudal nobility, on the one hand, and between the Church and the State on the other. At the end of the fifteenth century in Italy and Germany, after the discovery of America, and in the second half of the sixteenth century and the first half of the seventeenth in the other countries of Western Europe, the towns, the Third Estate and, later, the central state administration itself, all became sufficiently powerful to challenge the supremacy of the Church and of the feudal nobility. It was then that the Thomistic edifice, with its subordination of philosophy to theology and of reason to faith, and Aristotelian physics, with its subordination of the sublunary to the celestial world, were overthrown to make way for the Monistic and Pantheistic world of natural philosophy. But, as Monsieur Koyré has very intelligently pointed out, natural philosophy did not replace Thomism by a similarly precise and stable system. It abolished the miraculous intervention of the divinity by integrating it into the natural world, but once the possibility of supernatural interference had been destroyed, everything became both natural and possible. Nature had lost her rights, and the criterion which had enabled men to distinguish truth from error, fact from fiction, and the possible from the absurd, gradually became more difficult to discern. The man of bourgeois society, drunk with enthusiasm by the discovery of the external world, saw no limits to the future possibilities which lay open before him.

In the course of the sixteenth and seventeenth centuries the monarchical state gradually became firmly established and the bourgeoisie became the economically ruling class, and at least the equivalent in power of the nobility, which tended to lose its real social functions and fall from being *noblesse d'épée* to being *noblesse de cour*; the bourgeoisie then organised the production of wealth and elaborated the doctrine of rationalism on the two fundamental planes of epistemology and of the physical sciences. At the time when Pascal was writing the *Pensées* both Aristotelianism and neo-Platonic animism had been put out of date; the development of capitalism had transcended them on the economic and social plane, while on the intellectual level they had been rendered completely unimportant by the work of a whole collection of more or less rigorous and scientific thinkers such as Borelli, Torricelli, Roberval and Fermat, and above all by that of the great precursors of modern science such as Galileo, Descartes and Huygens.[1]

In his youth Pascal had played an active part in the attempt to abolish one of the central pillars of Aristotelian physics: the idea that nature 'has a horror of the vacuum'. This makes it even more interesting to note that while the *Pensées* occasionally refer to Aristotelian physics, they in fact assume the struggle to have been won, and attribute very little importance to Aristotelian or neo-Platonic ideas. In fact, the only positions which Pascal thinks worth discussing are those of the two ideologies which have just triumphed: scepticism and the mechanistic rationalism whose foremost representative was Descartes. It can be added that throughout this controversy Pascal never attempts to separate physics from morality and theology. He is not concerned with limited and partial experiments, but with world visions. Descartes is a worthy adversary, and even as he fought against him Pascal never ceased to respect him. The dialogue is conducted between minds of equal power.

What, in fact, had rationalism done? In the first place it had destroyed the two closely connected ideas of the community and the universe, and had replaced them by the totally different concepts of the isolated individual and of infinite space. In the history of the human mind this represented a twin conquest of immense importance: on the social plane the values to be recognised were those of justice and individual liberty; on the intellectual plane the system recognised as valid was that of mechanistic physics.

There were, however, other consequences: the triumph of the Third Estate replaced a hierarchical society in which each man knew and recognised the value of his own place compared to that of other people, by the concept of a collection of free, equal and isolated individuals, whose relationships were largely those of buyers and sellers.

It was, of course, a slow evolution, which had begun towards the end of the eleventh century, continued during the twelfth and thirteenth and was to be finally developed only during the nineteenth century, but which did, nevertheless, find a powerful

---

[1] Monsieur Koyré has also shown not only the important rôle played by the development of the animistic philosophy of nature in dealing the final blow to Aristotelianism but also—and this is more important—the long endeavour of thinkers in the field of mathematics and mechanics to constitute an image of the world which would be wholly free of any psychic or animistic element. One of the greatest pitfalls lay in the idea of attraction, which thinkers in the field of mechanics refused to accept because they saw it as a reversion to animism and to the attribution of psychic qualities to matter.

intellectual, scientific, literary and philosophical expression in the seventeenth century. After the value of the individual had been affirmed in the now stoic, now epicurean, now sceptical but always individualistic work of Montaigne, both Descartes and Corneille affirm, in the seventeenth century, that the individual can be self-sufficient.[1] Long before the time of Adam Smith and of Ricardo, Descartes was already writing to Princess Elizabeth of Bohemia that:

> God has so established the order of things and has joined men to-gether in so close a society, that even if every man were to be concerned only with himself, and to show no charity towards others, he would still, in the normal course of events, be working on their behalf in everything that lay within his power, provided that he acted prudently, and, in particular, that he lived in a society where morals and customs had not fallen into corruption.[2]

It was again Descartes who, this time on a philosophical plane, formulated the first great manifesto of revolutionary and democratic rationalism: 'Common sense is the most evenly distributed thing in the whole world . . . the ability to judge correctly, and to distinguish truth from error—which is what men properly call common sense or reason—is naturally equal in all men.'

The line which takes us from Descartes to the *Monadology* of Leibnitz, from *Le Cid* to that literary monadology to which Balzac gave the title of *La Comédie humaine*, as well as to Fichte, Voltaire and Valéry, is sinuous and complex, but nevertheless real and unbroken.[3]

Thus, as Western bourgeois and capitalist society developed, the intellectual and affective value of the community gradually became less important as far as men's actions and ideas were concerned, and was replaced by a self-centred attitude which allowed considerations

---

[1] The poet and playwright insist, as is natural, on the truth of this as far as action is concerned; the philosopher on its consequences in the realm of thought.

[2] Letter of October 6th, 1645.

[3] It goes without saying that a general statement of this nature can never do more than bring out one particular aspect out of a multitude of others. The important thing is to avoid any misleading perspective. Thus, we know very well that although the windowless and doorless Monad represents a continuation of the Cartesian ego, the fact that these Monads are organised in a hierarchical system constitutes a slipping backward from the democratic system of Descartes. This regression can, moreover, be explained by the fact that the German bourgeoisie was much less advanced than the middle class in France. (Cf. Lucien Goldmann, *La Communauté humaine et l'univers chez Kant* (P.U.F., 1949).) However, it is natural that in a work devoted primarily to Pascal and Racine any reference to other thinkers, such as Descartes or Leibnitz, cannot hope to give even a schematically complete image. All that can be done is to refer to certain features or elements of their work which may enable us to understand the authors immediately under discussion.

of communal interest to play only a small part by the side of private and personal ones. The social and religious man of the Middle Ages was replaced by the Cartesian and Fichtean Ego, the doorless and windowless monad of Leibnitz, and the 'economic man' of the classical economists.

This change of social attitudes was naturally reflected on the plane of ethics and religion. Expressed crudely, it meant that when individualism carried its own principles to their logical conclusion, ethics and religion ceased to play an independent part in determining human actions. The great seventeenth-century rationalists, Descartes, Malebranche and Leibnitz, certainly still talk about morality, and, with the possible exception of Spinoza, they still believe in God. But their moral and religious attitudes are merely old bottles which their new vision of the world has filled with completely new wine. This is so much the case that we no longer find—as we do at other periods in history—that new religious and moral emotions and ideas have merely been substituted for old ones. This time, the change is far more radical, and Pascal was perhaps the only thinker of this generation to be completely aware of it. What happened was that the older ethical and Christian forms were filled with a completely amoral and irreligious substance. This is obvious in the case of Spinoza, whose ideas have been well described as a form of theological atheism, and who still uses the word 'God' in order to express a complete refusal of any really transcendental attitude, as well as giving the title of 'Ethics' to a work in which all considerations of human behaviour are based upon the *conatus*, upon the egoism of the modes which tend to persist in their own being.[1]

This change is equally visible if we limit ourselves to a study of French thinkers. Descartes believed in God and Malebranche was a priest: however, the 'God of the philosophers' is no longer very real when placed by the side of man's reason. The Cartesian God intervenes in the rational mechanism of the world simply in order to keep it going once it has been first started. As Pascal remarked, his only function in Cartesian philosophy is to 'give a little tap to start the world off', after which he has nothing else to do. Even if we are

---

[1] This is, naturally, only a partial and one-sided view of this philosophy. For if, by its refusal of any transcendence, Spinoza's philosophy marks the logical conclusion of Cartesian rationalism and individualism it nevertheless also represents, by the introduction of the idea of totality, a move beyond this rationalistic individualism and a return to a genuinely religious mode of thinking.

One of the most urgent—and the most difficult—tasks confronting the modern historian of philosophy is to explain in comprehensible terms this co-existence in the seventeenth century of an extreme individualism and a form of pantheism within a philosophy which admits only one real substance. (Goethe indicated that such a problem existed in the famous scene between Faust and the World Spirit.)

more just to Descartes and point out that his God establishes the laws of the world at the same moment that he brings it into being, and that he then proceeds to maintain it in existence, we can still see that Pascal was quite right to ignore this arbitrary creation of the eternal truths, since it goes against all the other principles of Cartesian rationalism. We can see that this is the case from the example of Malebranche, the most important and faithful of Descartes' disciples, who fifty years after his master's death took notice of this fact and abolished this function of the Cartesian divinity. For him, the idea of order comes before the creation of the world, and is necessarily identical with the very will of God. As Arnauld very rightly observed, Malebranche retains miracles and the particular instances of the will of God merely as vague acknowledgments of the Biblical texts from which they cannot be removed. Grace itself is made to fit into the rational system of immediate causes.

Although his book speaks of God from the first page to the last, Spinoza draws the final consequences of this change by dispensing with the creation of the world and with its deliberate maintenance in existence by God. The name of God still lingers on, but the content has entirely disappeared.

In the same way there is no room in any consistently individualistic mode of thought for a God who still retains any real functions, there is likewise no room for any system of genuine morality. Like any other world vision, both rationalistic and empiricist individualism can still retain certain rules of conduct which it may refer to as moral or ethical norms. But in fact, whether its ideal is one of power or one of prudence or wisdom, any thorough-going individualism will still need to deduce these rules either from the individual's mind or from his heart, since by very definition individualism has abolished any supra-individual reality capable of guiding man and offering him genuinely transcendent norms.

This is not simply a verbal quibble: happiness, pleasure or wisdom have nothing at all to do with the criteria of good and evil; they can be judged only by the qualitatively different standards of success and failure, knowledge and ignorance, etc., and neither these qualities nor the standards by which they are judged have any specifically moral significance. Actions can be judged as good or evil only by reference to an independent system of ethical criteria which transcends the individual and exists independently of him. These criteria may be theological or they may be social, but in either case there is something—God or the community—which stands outside and above the individual. It is the characteristic of rationalism, however, to abolish both God and the community, and it is this which explains why the rise of rationalism was accompanied by the disappearance of any external norm which might guide the individual in his life and actions. Good and evil become, in a rationalist context, merely a question of what is reasonable and what is absurd, moral virtue becomes the *virtù* of the Renaissance man, and this in turn changes into the prudence and *savoir-vivre* of the seventeenth-century *honnête homme*.

The rationalism which, when carried to its logical though extreme conclusion, sees men only as isolated individuals for whom other men exist only as objects, also carries out a similar change in man's way of looking at the external world. On the human level, it destroys the idea of community and replaces it by that of an infinitely large collection of reasonable individuals who are all equal and all inter-changeable; on the level of the physical sciences, it destroys the idea of an orderly universe and replaces it by that of an infinite space which has neither limits nor individual qualities, and whose parts are both absolutely identical and completely interchangeable.

In the Aristotelian concept of space, as in the Thomistic idea of the community, each thing had its own place in the order of nature and tended to return to it: heavy bodies fell in order to reach the centre of the earth, light bodies rose because the natural place for them was above. Things were spoken to and judged by space, were told what to do and where to go, in exactly the same way as men were judged and directed by the community, and the language of space was, basically, the language of God. Cartesian rationalism changed the world, with the result that, as Henri Gouhier pointed out, 'the physics based upon clear ideas blew away all the "animal souls", "powers", and "principles" with which the scholastics had peopled nature: mechanistic physics offered man the means of conquering the world both by his intellect and by his technical skills, giving the scientist a universe that was intelligible and the artisan a universe subjected to the action of his tools'.[1] Both men and things became instruments, objects on which the thoughts and actions of the rational and reasonable individual could exercise their influence. The result was that once men, space and physical nature were reduced to the level of objects, they began to behave as objects. When confronted with the great problems of human existence they remained dumb. And God, deprived of the physical universe and of the conscience of man, the only two instruments by which He had been capable of communicating with man, departed from the world where He could no longer speak to the person He had made in His own image.

From a rationalist standpoint, there was nothing grave or dis-turbing about this. The man of Descartes and Corneille, like the

[1] Cf. H. Gouhier, *Introduction aux 'Méditations cartésiennes' de Malebranche*, p. xxvii.

man of the empiricists, needed no help from outside. He would have had no use for it. The rationalist was quite willing to see God as the author of the eternal truths, the creator and preserver of the world, and as the being who could—at least theoretically—perform infrequent miracles; but it was only on condition that this God did not interfere with the way men behaved, and, above all, that he refrained from casting doubt upon the absolute validity of human reason in the realms of both ethics and epistemology. Voltaire himself was prepared to build a chapel to a God who remained within such modest limits.

As far as their daily life was concerned, the rationalists were all the more ready to accept the God who manifested himself through the rational order and general laws of the world, since, during the seventeenth and eighteenth centuries, He also came to perform a very useful service: that of controlling the 'irrational' and dangerous reactions of the 'ignorant masses' who could neither understand nor appreciate the value of the consistently selfish and rational activity of economic man and of his social and political creations.

However, if in Descartes' time and in the course of the three centuries which followed him, victorious rationalism found no difficulty in eliminating the idea of the community and of specifically moral values from the economic and social behaviour of the individual, this was because, in spite of all the potential dangers which this involved, individualism had not yet revealed its final consequences.

As it gradually destroyed social life from the inside, rationalism was nevertheless still affecting a society which remained deeply imbued with values that men continued to respect emotionally and even to observe in practice, in spite of the way in which they contradicted the new ideas which were beginning to prevail. For a long time, the surviving remnants of Christianity and humanistic idealism continued to hide the dangers of a world which had no real moral values, and allowed man to celebrate the triumphs of scientific thought and technological progress as if these presented no problems. God had indeed left the world of men, but only a very small minority of the intellectuals in Western Europe realised that He had gone.

It is only in our own day that we have become conscious of this absence of valid ethical norms and of the terrible dangers which it involves. For if—in defiance of the God of enlightened rationalism—the ignorant masses have used political and trade-union action in order to impose some measure of control on the excesses of individualism in economic life, the absence of ethical forces capable of directing the use of scientific discoveries and of using them for the benefit of a genuine human community threatens to have un-imaginable consequences.

Rationalism continued to grow and develop in this way in France until the twentieth century, but in the seventeenth it stood at a turning-point. It had then, thanks to the work of Descartes and Galileo, found a philosophical system and a system of mathematical physics which were unmistakably superior to the old Aristotelian framework. It was against this background that, in connection with other factors, the Jansenist attitude which found its most coherent expression in the great tragic works of Pascal and Racine was developed.

The nature of the tragic mind in seventeenth-century France can be characterised by two factors: the complete and exact understanding of the new world created by rationalistic individualism, together with all the invaluable and scientifically valid acquisitions which this offered to the human intellect; and, at the same time, the complete refusal to accept this world as the only one in which man could live, move and have his being.

Reason[1] is an important factor in human life, one of which man is justly proud and which he will never be able to give up; however, it by no means constitutes the whole man, and it should not and cannot be taken as a sufficient guide to human life. This is true on every plane, even on that of scientific research, where reason seems so pre-eminently at home. This is why, after the amoral and a-religious period of rationalism and empiricism, the tragic vision represents a return to morality and religion, of religion in the wider meaning of faith in a set of values which transcend the individual. However, the tragic vision never actually reaches the stage of offering either a set of ideas or an art which are capable, by offering a new community and a new universe, of taking the place of the atomistic and mechanistic

[1] Here I should like to point out a terminological problem which confronted both Kant and Pascal and which still makes the translation of philosophical works from German into French, and vice versa, very difficult.

From Descartes to the present day, rationalism has recognised the existence of only two aspects of the mind: on the one hand, the imagination and the ability to feel emotion; and, on the other, the power of reasoning. For any tragic or dialectical thinker, however, what the rationalist understands by 'the power of reasoning' is a partial and incomplete faculty which is subordinated to a third, synthesising faculty. Such thinkers have thus been compelled to adapt the established vocabulary to their own purposes, Pascal by using the word 'heart'—and thereby opening the door to a large number of subsequent misunderstandings—while Kant kept the word '*Vernunft*' while giving it the meaning of 'synthesising faculty' that was entirely different from the one which the word '*raison*' had in the tradition of Cartesian rationalism. This makes the task of translators very difficult at the present day, for they can scarcely write 'l'entendement de Descartes ou de Voltaire' or 'Die Cartesianische oder Voltair'sche Vernunft'.

universe set up by individual reason and, from this point of view, it must be considered as essentially a transitional phase. It accepts that the world of rationalist and empirical thought is definite and unchangeable—although it perceives the ambiguity and confusion which lie behind its apparent clarity—and can offer as a challenge to it only a new set of demands and a new scale of values.

However, the tragic vision is incapable of seeing itself in this historical perspective. It is essentially unhistorical, since it lacks the principal dimension of history which is the future. Refusal, in the radical and absolute form which it assumes in tragic thought, has only one dimension in time: the present. As Barcos pointed out:

> Thoughts of the future are a dangerous and clever temptation of the Evil One, contrary to the spirit of the Gospel, and capable of ruining everything if not resisted; they must be rejected without even a first glance, since God's word tells us not only to take no thought for the morrow in things temporal but also in things spiritual, and it is these which hang much more on His will.[1]

Rationalist thought and the tragic vision share a common way of looking at the problems of the community and of the universe—or, rather, of the problems raised by the absence of any true community and universe, that is to say the problems raised by society and by space. Both see the individual as unable to find either in the universe or in society any guiding or transcendant principle; and, for both of them, if harmony and agreement do exist in the realm of things and the society of men, this is merely the result of the automatic interplay of wholly rational and selfish considerations, in which each man consults only his own interests. The difference between them lies in the fact that while rationalism is prepared to accept this state of affairs and indeed regards it as basically desirable—it shows its truly a-religious nature by considering human reason as capable of discovering genuine truths, if only on the plane of mathematics—the tragic vision is intensely aware of the inadequacy of such a world view. It cannot accept a concept of human society and of physical space in which no human value has any necessary and non-contingent foundation, and in which all non-values are both equally possible and equally probable.

Mechanistic rationalism had, with Descartes and Galileo, replaced the false and imaginary concepts of Aristotelian physics with a far more accurate notion of space, which it looked upon as wholly valid; it was this concept that was to make possible all the immense technological progress of the future, and Descartes himself considered that it would be possible, in a few years, to increase the span

[1] Cf. Martin de Barcos, *Pensées* (B.H.F., fr. 12.988), pp. 351–2.

of normal life. Good and evil had no part to play in this concept, and the only problems with which it confronted man were those of success or failure on a purely technical and scientific level. It was, indeed, of the concept of space first elaborated in the seventeenth century that Poincaré rightly said that we must, in order to understand it, make a clear distinction between statements in the indicative and statements in the imperative. This kind of space no longer had any limits because it had lost all possible human characteristics.

It was this same concept of space, whose very infinity seemed to the rationalists to be a sign of the greatness of God, since it revealed the existence of an infinity which human reason could not grasp, that inspired Pascal, as he foresaw both the immense possibilities and the immense dangers which it contained, and saw the incompatibility between such a concept and the existence of God, to cry out in a phrase of equal accuracy and power: 'The eternal silence of these infinite spaces casts me into dread' (fr. 206, E.392).

This remark is linked to the most important scientific discovery of seventeenth-century rationalism, that of geometrically infinite space, and it places by the side of it the silence of God. In the infinite space of rational science God falls silent, because in elaborating this concept man has been obliged to give up any genuinely ethical norm. The central problem which tragic thought and the tragic mind had to face, a problem which only dialectical thought can solve on both the moral and the scientific plane, was that of discovering whether there still was some means and some hope of reintegrating supra-individual values into this rational concept of space, which had now replaced for ever the Aristotelian and Thomist universe. The problem was whether man could still rediscover God; or, to express the same idea in a less ideological but identical form, whether man could rediscover the community and the universe.

Although it appears to speak solely of cosmological matters, fragment 206 (E.392) in Pascal's *Pensées* also has a moral content; or, rather, it deals with the gulf that lies between physical and cosmological reality, on the one hand, and human reality on the other. It was this content that Lukàcs reformulated when, without in any way referring to Pascal, but nevertheless speaking of tragic man, he wrote:

> He hopes that a judgment by God will illuminate the different struggles which he sees in the world before him, and will reveal the ultimate truth. But the world around him still follows the same path, indifferent to both questions and answers. No word comes from either created or natural things, and the race is not to the swift nor battle to the strong. The clear voice of the judgment of God no longer sounds out above the march of human destiny, for the voice which once gave

35

life to all has now fallen silent. Man must live alone and by himself. The voice of the Judge has fallen silent for ever, and this is why man will always be vanquished, doomed to destruction in victory even more than in defeat.[1]

God's voice no longer speaks directly to man. This is one of the fundamental points of tragic thought. 'Vere tu es Deus absconditus,' quotes Pascal. The hidden God.

However, this fragment also calls forth another remark which is valid for a large number of Pascal texts. It is that we should always give their exact and literal meaning to everything that Pascal writes, and should never try to whittle down the meaning of his *Pensées* in order to make them more accessible to Cartesian common sense. We must not allow ourselves to be held back by the fact that Pascal sometimes took fright at his own boldness, and tried to tone down the paradoxical nature of his ideas by writing a second version. (For example, he began by saying of Descartes—with complete accuracy —that 'too much light darkens the mind'. He then changed it to 'too much light dazzles the mind'.[2])

Deus absconditus. The hidden God. It is an idea which is funda- mental in tragic thought in general and in Pascalian thought in particular. It is a paradoxical idea, in spite of the fact that certain fragments of the *Pensées* seem, at first sight, capable of being inter- preted in a perfectly logical way. For example, fragment 559 (E. 319) could be interpreted as meaning: God has hidden himself from the sight of most men, but He is nevertheless visible to those to whom He has accorded Grace to see Him, since it reads:

Had there never appeared any sign of God, then this eternal priva- tion would be ambiguous, and could just as well be caused by the complete absence of any Divine Principle as by man's unworthiness to know it; but since God shows himself intermittently but not always, then all ambiguity disappears. For if God has once appeared, then he must always exist. From which we are forced to conclude that God exists, and that men are unworthy of Him.

This interpretation would, however, be unfaithful to Pascal's thought as a whole, since this never says 'Yes' or 'No' but always 'Yes' *and* 'No'. For Pascal, the hidden God is both present and absent, and not sometimes absent and sometimes present. He is always absent and always present.

Even in fragment 559, the essential argument lies in the words 'if God has once appeared, then He must always exist', or, as an earlier

[1] Georg von Lukàcs, *Die Selle und die Formen*, pp. 332–3.
[2] In fragment 72. Cf. Brunschvicg's edition of the *Pensées et Opuscules*, note 6 to p. 353.

and much stronger version put it: 'The eternal Being is for ever if He once has been.' What, then, is the meaning of the expression 'once appears' in fragment 559? For tragic thought, this represents an essential but constantly unrealised possibility. For at the very moment that God appears to man, then man ceases to be tragic. To see and hear God is to go beyond tragedy. For the Pascal who wrote fragment 559, God always exists but never appears, and this in spite of Pascal's own certainty—which I shall study when discussing the argument of the wager—that God can and may appear at every moment of man's life, although He never actually does so.

Even now, however, we have still not reached the real meaning of the hidden God. Always to be without ever appearing is, as far as Cartesian common sense is concerned, a logical and acceptable attitude, although common sense never actually goes so far as accepting it. But we must add that for Pascal, and for tragic man in general, this hidden God is present in a more real and more important way than any empirical and perceptible being, and that His is the only essential presence that exists. That God should be always absent and always present is the real centre of the tragic vision.

In 1910, again with no thought of Pascal in mind, Lukàcs began his essay in the following manner: 'Tragedy is a game, a game of man and of his destiny, a game which is watched by God. But God is nothing more than a spectator, and he never intervenes, either by word or deeds, in what the actors are doing. Only his eyes rest upon them.'[1] Lukàcs then went on to discuss the central problem of any tragic vision: can a man still live when the eye of God has lighted upon him? Is there not an unbridgeable gulf between human life and the divine presence?

For a rationalist, such a question is meaningless and absurd, for in the view of Descartes, Malebranche and Spinoza, God exists to guarantee the existence of order and the eternal truths, and to offer man a world open to his ideas and accessible to his instruments. This is why, full of confidence in man and human reason, these thinkers are also certain that God is present for the human soul.[2] The only difference lies in the fact that the God of the rationalists has no longer any personal reality for man, since all he does is to guarantee

[1] Loc. cit., p. 327.

[2] On this particular point rationalism marks a renewal of a genuine Augustinian tradition, and this in spite of the fact that it transforms it completely by making spirituality become mathematical reason. Jansenism, on the other hand, in spite of the protestations that its representatives made of Augustinian orthodoxy, constituted a break in the tradition. The Church, which always has had a remarkable flair for detecting heresy, was acting in a perfectly logical manner when it both condemned Jansenism and affirmed at the same time the orthodoxy of Saint Augustine.

the harmony existing among the different monads or between human reason and the external world. He is no longer man's guardian and his guide, no longer the person that he can turn to for advice; he has become a general and universal rule which guarantees man's right to free himself from any external authority, and to follow where his strength and reason may guide him. But, at the same time, he leaves man alone in the face of a silent and static world of things and individuals.

The God of tragedy, the God of Racine, Pascal and Kant, is a wholly different being. Like the rationalists' God, he does indeed bring man no help from outside; but, unlike the rationalists' God, he offers man no guarantee of the validity of his own strength and powers of reasoning. Far from offering man anything, the God of tragedy judges man and makes demands on him; he forbids the slightest degree of compromise, and constantly reminds man—who lives in a universe where life is made possible only by approximations—that a true calling is one devoted to the quest for wholeness and authenticity. Or, to speak as Pascal does, this God demands that man should devote himself to the only true life, which is a life of absolute justice and absolute truth, a life which has nothing to do with the relative truth and relative justice of ordinary human existence. He is a God, in Lukàcs' words,

> whose cruel and harsh tribunal knows neither pardon nor prescription, who mercilessly punishes the slightest hint of infidelity towards the quest for Essence; a God who, with blind rigidity, sweeps from the ranks of men all those who have, by the slightest gesture, made in the most fleeting and forgotten moment of time, shown that they are strangers to the world of Essences; a God whose merciless judgment can be softened by no riches and no splendid gifts offered by the soul, and in whose sight a long life, filled with the most glorious actions, is as nothing. Yet, at the same time, he is a God so full of smiling compassion that He forgives all the sins of daily life on the one condition that these have not offended against the innermost centre. Indeed, it would be wrong even to say that He forgives such sins; they pass unnoticed before His eyes, and His glance slips over them without being affected.[1]

He is a God whose judgments and scale of values are wholly different from those of everyday life, and Lukàcs writes, speaking of the tragic man who lives in the gaze of such a God, that 'many things disappear which earlier seemed to be the very pillars of his existence, while others, before scarcely visible, become his rock and resting place'. It was on a similar thought that Pascal concluded the *Mystère de Jésus*, writing that 'we must perform little things as if

[1] Cf. Lukàcs, *Die Seele und die Formen*, pp. 338–9.

they were great ones because of the majesty of Christ Jesus who does them in us and who lives our life; and we must do great things as if they were simple and easy, because of His omnipotence'.

Or, again, as Lukàcs writes,

Daily life is a confused and many-coloured anarchy, where nothing attains its perfect essence, and no clear dividing line separates the pure from the impure. Everything flows, everything is broken or destroyed, and nothing attains authenticity. For men love everything which is hazy and uncertain in life, and adore the soothing monotony of the Grand Perhaps. Everything clear and unambiguous makes them afraid, and their weakness and cowardice lead them to embrace every obstacle set up by the world and every gate that seems to bar their path. For what lies behind each rock too steep for them to climb is the unsuspected and ever unattainable paradise of their dreams. Their life is made up of hopes and desires, and everything which prevents them from fulfilling their destiny is easily and cheaply transformed into an internal richness of the soul The man who leads an ordinary life never knows where the rivers which carry him along will lead to, since where nothing is ever achieved everything remains possible.

However [he adds], when a miracle occurs then something real is achieved. . . . A miracle is both the result and the starting point for a number of definite actions; in an unforeseeable manner, it forces itself into a man's life and makes it into a clear and unambiguous sum of things achieved. . . . It strips the soul of all the deceitful veils woven from brilliant moments and vague feelings rich with meaning; and, as the soul then shows itself with every feature carefully picked out, and with its most naked essence visible to the eye, it stands alone before God.

And before God, only the miracle is real.

We can now see the meaning and importance for the tragic thinker or writer of the question: 'Can a man still live when the eye of God has lighted upon him?' And we can also see what is the only possible reply that can be given.

III

THE TRAGIC VISION:
THE WORLD

It is from our separation and absence from the world that is born
the presence and feeling for God (Saint-Cyran: *Maximes*, 263).

THERE are two distinct but complementary planes on which
philosophical thought considers the relationship between man and the
world: that of historical progress, and that of the ontological reality
which both conditions this progress and makes it possible. Thus, men
do not see the world as an unchanging unreality given once and for
all, since we cannot know what the world is like 'in itself', when not
seen through the categories of the human mind. There is only one
reality which we can gradually come to know through our historical
researches, and only one possible starting-point for philosophical
investigation: it is the succession of ways in which men have, in the
course of history, seen, felt, understood and, above all, changed the
world in which they lived, felt and thought. It is only when he studies
the way in which different social worlds and different world views
have followed one another in history that the philosopher can begin
to discover what is common to all the different relationships which
man has had with the world and with his fellows. It is this common
element which made it possible for these different world views to
follow one another in a manner comprehensible to human reason.[1]
Yet, even as we attempt to discover the basic and objective element
common to all forms of social organisation, we must always remember that we see this in a human and consequently subjective manner;
we should therefore resist the strong and permanent temptation to
consider our own social world as the world (ontologically speaking),

---

[1] Marx sketched out certain elements of this type of knowledge of the foundations of history in his *Theses on Feuerbach* and his preface to his *Critique of
Political Economy*.

and to look upon it as the one with which men have always been confronted.

This problem, however, goes beyond the immediate limits of this study. What I am here trying to do is to gain a knowledge of a parti-cular historical[1] world, which is paralleled by the particular form of the tragic vision found in seventeenth-century France and eighteenth-century Germany. I shall call the tragedy which forms an essential part of this vision the tragedy of refusal, in order to distinguish it from other forms of tragedy which are based upon fate or upon illu-sion. Yet in spite of its obvious limits, the study of this particular form of the tragic vision should, if it is valid and in so far as it is historical, be a step towards a solution of the ontological problem of man's relationship with the world; it is also inevitable that, studying the world of the tragic mind, we shall also be led to consider whether or not the vision associated with it offers valid insights into the human predicament, and whether or not it marked a step forward in man's progress towards consciousness and liberty.

I have already pointed out the limitations that prevent us from making out an overall picture of the tragic vision which would include both Greek and Shakespearian tragedy and the tragedy of refusal found in Pascal and Racine. It is nevertheless a fact that all forms of tragic vision have one feature in common: they all express a deep crisis in the relationship between man and his social and spiritual world. This is obviously true of Sophocles, who is the only one of the Greek playwrights who can, without any shadow of doubt, be called 'tragic' in the now accepted sense of the word. For Aeschylus still wrote trilogies, and the only complete one that we possess ends with the resolution of the conflicts described. We also know that *Prome-theus Bound* was followed by a *Prometheus the Torch-Bearer*, which described the reconciliation between Prometheus and Zeus. Moreover, in so far as the word 'classical' indicates the idea of a union between man and the world and thus, by implication, the idea of immanence,[2]

[1] Historical not in its content but in its reality. One of the most important characteristics of the content of tragic thought is precisely the non-historical character of its world, since history is one of the ways in which one can go beyond and transcend tragedy.

[2] If we define the classical spirit by the unity between man and the world and the substantial character of the latter, and the Romantic spirit by the complete lack of any satisfactory relationship between man and the world, and by the fact that man places essence and thereby substantial values in a reality that lies outside our world, we can still look upon Aeschylus, like Homer and Sophocles. as a strictly classical author, in spite of the fact that his work is already dominated by the threat of a split between man and the world, which thus makes it foreshadow Sophoclean tragedy.

Moreover, when Hegel in his *Aesthetic* reserves the term classical for Greek art and gives the name of romantic to any art which, since the coming of Christianity,

Aeschylus is still classical in the precise meaning of the word. For in spite of the fact that his immanence is threatened in his work, and that he needs a whole trilogy in order to re-establish the balance which has been disturbed by the hubris of both Gods and men, he still remains a writer of radical immanence. What he deals with is the hubris of both Gods and men, and if, in his work, man is never superior to the Gods and to the world, neither are the Gods and the world superior to man. Both Gods and men live within the same

---

has placed real values elsewhere than in this world, he does nevertheless express a valid idea. We are, admittedly, surprised at a classification which places Shakespeare, Racine and Goethe among Romantic writers, but we must nevertheless consider that, since the unity of man and the world does in fact imply that values are radically immanent, any mind which accepts the existence or possibility of intelligible or transcendent values is romantic in the widest meaning of the word. However, we must try to go beyond this global distinction, and remember that, within the art and philosophy that have been created since the Greeks, there are currents which go in the direction of immanence and others which resolutely turn away from the real and concrete world.

Thus, I shall call the first classical and the second romantic, using the first word in a wider and the second in a narrower sense. Thus, when we bear in mind the fact that even when it aims at being wholly *a priori* and directed towards a universal and intelligible truth, rational thought is still an attempt to understand the real world, it will not be incorrect to use the word classical in its widest sense to describe all literary or philosophical works which aim at a rational understanding of things, and romantic all those which turn away from reason to seek refuge in the passions and the imagination. Thus, in the narrower and more exact sense of the word, Bergson, Schelling, Novalis and Nerval will be romantics, but, in the widest possible sense of the word, Descartes, Corneille and Schiller will be romantic as well. The great writers of Greece, on the other hand—Homer, Aeschylus, Sophocles—will be classical in the narrower and more precise sense of the word, while in the wider sense Aquinas will be classical when compared to Saint Augustine. Shakespeare, Pascal, Racine, Descartes, Corneille and Goethe will be classical in comparison with all other literary or philosophical writers of the post-Christian era, and, finally, dialectical thinkers will be classical in the strictest and most exact meaning of the term.

What, however, from this point of view is the place of tragic art and thought?

On this particular point, I am entirely in agreement with Lukàcs, who sees tragedy as one of the two peaks of aesthetic expression (the other being the epic, with its representation of the natural, complete and straightforward unity between man and the world). One could thus define tragedy as a universe of agonising questions to which man has no reply. Lukàcs, in contrast, defined the world of the epic as the world where all replies are already given before man's intellectual development or the progress of history have enabled the questions to be formulated. It must nevertheless be added that—still according to Lukàcs—only the works of Homer are true epics. Tragedy expresses those moments when the highest value, the very essence of classical humanism, the unity between man and the world, comes under a threat, so that its importance is felt with a peculiar and urgent acuteness. From this point of view the works of Sophocles, Shakespeare, Pascal, Racine and Kant are, together with those of Homer, Aeschylus, Goethe, Hegel and Marx, peaks in the history of classical thought and art.

42

world where, in Saint-Evremond's perceptive phrase,[1] they form 'a society', and are subject to the same laws of fate. Xerxes is punished because he wanted to rule over nature, to enchain the sea and stretch

[1] Saint-Evremond did not like tragedy; in Greek thought he approved of Plato, and in the quarrel over the relative merits of Corneille and Racine he resolutely sided with the supporters of the former.

Nevertheless, he was fully aware of what constitutes the basic feature of the plays both of Racine and of Corneille when they are compared to classical Greek tragedies: the absence of God. Thus, we see him writing that: 'The Gods, by their hatreds and protective preferences, brought about all the extraordinary happenings in the theatre of the ancients; and, in the midst of so many supernatural occurrences, the people found nothing incredible or remarkable in the idea that *Gods and men should form a society.* [Here, as later, Monsieur Goldmann's italics.] The Gods almost always acted through the medium of men's passions; men undertook nothing without the Gods' advice, and achieved nothing without their aid. Thus, in this mixture of divinity and humanity, nothing was unbelievable. Today however, we find all these marvels fabulous and unbelievable. *We lack Gods and are lacking to the Gods in our turn*' (Saint-Evremond, *Oeuvres*, Vol. 1, p. 174, of the three-volume edition published by René de Planhal, Cité des Livres, Paris, 1927).

I should add that Saint-Evremond, who is a remarkably perceptive critic, saw quite clearly the non-Christian nature of Corneille's *Polyeucte*. He quite correctly observes that the hero is lacking in Christian humility and that he is wholly self-sufficient. However, his hostility to religious drama in general, linked with his admiration for Corneille, nevertheless leads him to exaggerate the importance of the non-Christian characters in the play: 'The spirit of our religion is entirely opposed to that of tragedy, and the humility and patience of our saints are at the furthest remove from the virtues expected of a hero in the theatre. Consider the zeal and strength that the heavens inspire in Néarque and Polyeucte. . . . Unmoved by prayers and entreaties, Polyeucte is more eager to die for God than other men are to live for themselves. Nevertheless, the subject which would have made an excellent sermon would make a very poor tragedy were it not for the fact that the conversations between Pauline and Sévère, both characters being inspired by other feelings and other passions, had maintained for our author the reputation which the Christian virtues of our martyrs would otherwise have taken from him' (op. cit., p. 175).

Similarly, Saint-Evremond has a very clear perception of what we might term the 'non-civic' character of tragedy, the conflict between tragic awareness and a wholehearted commitment to the life of the State. 'When we consider the normal impression that tragedy made on the souls of the spectators in ancient Athens, we can see that Plato was more justified in his condemnation than was Aristotle in his approval; for since tragedy consisted of excessive feelings of fear and pity, the theatre then surely became a school of terror and compassion, where men learned to be afraid of every danger and to weep over every misfortune.

'I find it difficult to believe that a soul accustomed to be terrified at the sight of other people's misfortunes would be capable of dealing adequately with its own. It was perhaps in this manner that the Athenians became so ready to feel fear, and that the spirit of terror, inspired with so much art in the theatre, became only too natural in the army.

'In Sparta and Rome, where the public showed the citizens only examples of valour and constancy, the people were no less proud and bold in battle than firm and unshakeable in the calamities which beset the Republic' (loc. cit., p. 177).

his authority beyond its valid limits, thereby ruling not only over the forces of nature but also over the Greek world, and especially Athens. Yet when the Erynnies themselves overstep the bounds of moderation they are judged by a human tribunal and made to submit to the laws of the city, in spite of the fact that they are divine. Similarly, when Prometheus is chained to the rock and in torment he still remains stronger than the King of the Gods, since he knows what is going to happen in the future and Zeus does not. This is why, in spite of the bitter conflict that divides them, they are inseparable, and, since neither can conquer or destroy the other, they finally achieve a reconciliation.

Authentic tragedy, on the other hand, makes its first appearance with the work of Sophocles. In my view, the basic meaning of his work is to be found in the expression which it gives of the unbridgeable gulf which now separates man—or, more accurately, certain privileged and exceptional men—from the human and divine world. Ajax and Philoctetes, Oedipus, Creon and Antigone all express and illustrate the same truth: the world has become dark and mysterious, the Gods no longer exist side by side with men in the same cosmic totality, and are no longer subject to the same rule of fate or the same demands of balance and moderation. They have cut themselves off from man and taken it upon themselves to rule over him; they speak to him in deceitful terms and from afar off, the oracles which he consults have two meanings, one apparent but false, the other hidden but true, the demands which the Gods make are contradictory, and the world is ambiguous and equivocal. It is an unbearable world, where man is forced to live in error and illusion, and where only those whom a physical infirmity cuts off from normal life can stand the truth when it is revealed to them: the fact that both Tiresias, who knows the will of the Gods and the future of man, and Oedipus,[1] who discovers the truth about himself at the end of the tragedy are both blind is symbolic of this. Their physical blindness is an expression of the separation from the real world which inevitably accompanies a knowledge of the truth; only those who are blind, like the agèd Faust in Goethe, can really live in this world, since as long as they keep their physical sight they can see only illusion and not truth. For the others—Ajax, Creon, Antigone[2]—their discovery of the truth does nothing but condemn them to death.

[1] It goes without saying that this refers to *Oedipus Rex*, since *Oedipus at Colonnus* is, like *Philoctetes*, an attempt to go beyond tragedy.

[2] May I be allowed to formulate a suggestion? In the whole work of Sophocles *Antigone* occupies a quite exceptional position. In spite of all the important differences that I would not for a moment think of denying, Antigone is the character who comes nearest to the modern heroes of the tragedies of

In my view, certain of the Platonic dialogues are directed not only against the Sophists but also against Sophocles; for while Plato is obviously maintaining against the Sophists that objective truth does exist, he is also arguing against another opponent and maintaining that this truth is not only bearable to man but also likely to make him happier and more virtuous. It would thus seem probable that someone had tried to maintain that this was not the case, and such a view is certainly implicit in Sophoclean tragedy.

However, in spite of Plato's argument, the work of Sophocles nevertheless marks the end of a stage in the history of European culture. For when Plato discusses truth, he is not talking about our immediate experience of the external world. Socrates is not interested in truth of this kind, and for him as for the tragic thinker, the external world is illusory and ambiguous. Substance, the eternal values, goodness, happiness and truth are now to be found in an intelligible world which, whether transcendent or not, is opposed to the world of everyday experience. When we take a wider view, and consider philosophy as well as art, it would seem that the transition from the classical to the romantic consciousness which Hegel, basing himself solely on a consideration of art, placed at the beginning of the Christian era, ought really to be put between Sophocles and Plato.

However, this must for the time being remain merely a hypothesis, since in order to grasp the real meaning of a literary or philosophical work we need to situate it in the social and economic circumstances of the time that gave it birth, and our knowledge of classical antiquity is too flimsy to enable this to be done. The same is true of Shakespearian tragedy, which can also be seen as marking the end of the aristocratic and feudal world, and expressing the crisis of the Renaissance and the appearance of the individualistic world of the Third Estate. However, as I pointed out in Chapter II of this book

---

refusal. Like Junia and Titus, she knows the truth at the beginning of the play, and does not need to discover it; like them, she acts in a conscious and deliberate way in refusing compromise and accepting death. It is, moreover, this particular quality that has led modern thinkers like Hegel and Kierkegaard to pay special attention to her in their reflections on Greek tragedy. I myself, reading the play, was struck by two facts.

First of all, from a purely textual and dramatic point of view, the character of Creon is far more important than that of Antigone—he is on the stage much longer, and says much more than she does.

Secondly, Creon is exactly like the other tragic heroes in Sophocles—Ajax, Philoctetes, Oedipus—who live in illusion and discover the truth only at the end of the play, when it kills or blinds them. Would it be too outrageous to suggest that Sophocles began first of all by writing the tragedy of Creon, the man who, in his blindness, infringes the divine laws, and that he then found, in addition, the exceptional character of Antigone, whose novelty and importance he then very rapidly appreciated?

45

and also elsewhere,[1] we do possess another example of the appearance of the tragic vision: in seventeenth-century France and eighteenth-century Germany the rise of scientific thought and its inevitable concomitant of greater technological efficiency, together with the rise of rationalism and of individualistic morality, produced the alarum cry of Pascal's *Pensées* and the critical philosophy of Kant. Here, once again, it was tragic thought that denounced the symptoms of a deep crisis in man's relationship with the world and his fellows and pointed to the dangers produced—or, rather, about to be produced— by man's progress along a path which had seemed, and which still did seem to many, to be so rich and full of promise. Once again, the danger was avoided and the potential impasse surmounted. The Hegelian and, above all, the Marxist dialectic played the same rôle for the tragic vision of Pascal and Kant that Socratic and Platonic rationalism had played for Greek tragedy, and which modern rationalism and empiricism had played for Shakespearian tragedy: that of going beyond the tragic vision by showing that man is capable of achieving authentic values by his own thoughts and actions.

Naturally, such a parallel is valid in a very general sense, for there are inevitably great differences of detail between the three cases.

After the problems raised by the tragedies of Aeschylus and Sophocles, Socratic and Platonic rationalism based itself upon entirely new foundations, giving up any hope or even desire to rediscover immanent substantiality. In the place of the classical unity between man and the world, it substituted the idea of intelligible truth; it thus separated man from the world of immediate experience, and considered this world either as mere appearance or simply as a potential tool. It is this new attitude which not only explains why Plato refused to allow tragic and epic poets into his ideal state but also why the statement that truth is intelligible—and, implicity, that it can be transcendent—allowed later thinkers to make Platonism the basis for Augustinianism, one of the three[2] great streams of Christian thought in the Middle Ages. Another aspect of Platonism also enabled it to become the basis for one of the two great currents of modern individualism, the rationalism of Descartes and Galileo. It would not, therefore, perhaps be wrong to say that Platonism remained one of the basic positions of Western thought until it was transcended by the first philosophical position which gave up the

---

[1] Cf. Lucien Goldmann, *La Communauté humaine et l'univers chez Kant* (P.U.F., 1949).

[2] I say three, because in addition to Thomism and Augustinianism there is a third eschatological current whose importance is not diminished by the fact that it was partially condemned by the Church: it is represented by the Eternal Gospel of Joachim de Flore, and the spiritualist tendencies of the Franciscans.

attempt to seek for values in transcendence and intelligibility in order to return to a new immanence and a new classicism: dialectical materialism.

I do not know English culture well enough to do more than make a suggestion about Shakespearian tragedy:[1] however, it does seem to me that European rationalism and empiricism of the seventeenth, eighteenth and nineteenth centuries was the ideological expression of a class which, as it gained mastery over the physical world and built up a new social order based upon liberalism and respect for the individual, tended increasingly to ignore and pass by the problems raised by Shakespearian tragedy. Rationalism and empiricism had so pauperised man's view of the world that the richness of the Shakespearian universe seemed for a long time to be merely a barbarous creation, admirable or absurd according to the taste of the individual reader, but certainly both foreign and difficult to assimilate. One might possibly see a slender link between Shakespeare and Montaigne; there was nothing at all in common between him and Hume or Descartes.

The relationship between the tragedy of refusal, expressed in the work of Pascal, Racine and Kant, and dialectical thought is something very different from the hostility which separates tragedy and rationalism. I have said that dialectical thought is characterised by its ability to integrate and go beyond other positions, and it is a fact that both Hegel and Marx both accept and integrate into the very substance of their ideas all the problems raised by the tragic attitude

[1] Readers may perhaps be surprised to find in a work devoted to seventeenth-century tragedy both such an incomplete hypothesis about Greek tragedy and a straightforward confession of ignorance as far as Shakespearian tragedy is concerned. A follower of the analytic method would doubtless have preferred to refrain from any remarks on these particular subjects, and to restrict himself to the immediate field of his research.

For me, such a restriction would have contradicted the very principles of my method. Convinced that the meaning of any element depends upon its relationship to the other elements and on its place in the whole, and that, consequently, research can never go directly from the parts to the whole or from the whole to the parts, I hold that it is very important to avoid the illusion that the study of any partial reality could be self-sufficient in a relative manner, or that general syntheses could dispense with detailed analyses of particular facts.

Research progresses by a constant movement from the parts to the whole and from the whole back to the parts again. This nevertheless implies that we must always point out the immediate aspects of any subject for which we do not have sufficient knowledge, and the points which, by being clarified, could either complete or modify the provisional results obtained. No study of tragedy will ever be complete until we have taken into account the three great forms of tragic awareness and creation that I have indicated—and this without mentioning the fact that tragedy cannot, as a whole, be understood without the study of the psychic forms which it replaced and of those which, in turn, sublated and transcended it.

which preceded them. For example, they share its critique of rationalist and empirical philosophy, of both hedonistic and utilitarian dogmatic morality, of the present condition of society, of any form of dogmatic theology and so on. Where they differ from it, however, is in replacing the tragic wager on eternity and a transcendent divinity by an immanent wager on man's future in this world. It is this wager which, for the first time since Plato in the history of Western thought, shows a deliberate break with intelligibility and transcendence, and re-establishes the unity of man with the world, thus raising the hope that we may return to the classicism abandoned since the Greeks.

The fact remains that the tragedy of the seventeenth and eighteenth centuries—and, for the rest of this book, the words 'tragedy' and 'tragic', except when otherwise stated, will indicate the tragedy of refusal characteristic of these two centuries—does, like other forms of tragic creation and awareness, express a crisis in human relationship between certain groups of men and the cosmic and social world.

I have already said that the central problem of this tragedy is that of discovering whether a man can still live when the eye of God has lighted upon him. This is a real problem, since to live means necessarily to live in this world—a fundamental and universal truth of which phenomenology and existentialism have merely made us more conscious. However, the fact that our attention did need drawing to this truth does indicate that the degree to which we are conscious of it can vary from one historical period to another. These variations cannot, at the present state of our knowledge, be known and studied in detail, but one preliminary observation can be made which will take us to the very centre of the problem we are studying: all forms of consciousness express a provisional and mobile balance between the individual and his social environment; when this balance can be fairly easily established and is relatively stable, or when it can pass fairly easily from one form to another, men tend not to think about the problems raised by their relationship to the external world. On a social as well as on an individual plane, it is the sick organ which creates awareness, and it is in periods of social and political crisis that men are most aware of the enigma of their presence in the world. In the past, this awareness has tended to find its expression in tragedy. At the present day it shows itself in existentialism.

These considerations should help us to see what view the tragic mind takes of the world. Briefly expressed, it is that the world is at one and the same time both nothing and everything. It is nothing, because tragic man lives for ever with God's eye upon him, because he can demand and accept only completely clear, absolute and unequivocal values, because for him 'only miracles are real', and because, measured by these standards, the world is essentially confused, ambiguous

48

and therefore non-existent. As Lukàcs writes, the problem of tragic consciousness is

> 'the problem of the relationship between being and essence—that of knowing whether everything that exists already is by the very fact that it exists. Are there, for example, different degrees of being? Is being a universal property of all things, or is it a value judgment which separates and distinguishes them? . . . Mediaeval philosophy expressed the problem with absolute clarity when it said that the *ens perfectissimum* is also the *ens realissimum*.[1]
> In order to enter the universe of tragedy [he continues] men must reach a very high threshold of perfection; anyone who does not reach this level simply does not exist. But everything that does reach it is always both present and absent to the same degree.[2]

It is, in short, because tragic man is aware neither of degrees nor of a transitional plane between nothing and everything, because for him anything which is not perfect does not exist, because he can see no possibility of bringing absence and presence together, that the eye of God makes everything which is not clear and unambiguous, and which does not reach the level of what the young Lukàcs calls 'the miracle', completely absent and unimportant. This means that tragic man finds the world as it normally is both non-existent and inauthentic, and that he lives solely for God, finding nothing in common between Him and the world. As Pascal wrote, illustrating Lukàcs' thesis in advance:

> The conditions which are most bearable according to this world are the most difficult to endure in the sight of God. For as this world judges, there is nothing more difficult than the Christian life; but in the sight of God, there is no life easier to live than that which keeps His law. For this world, there is nothing easier than to perform great functions and possess great wealth; yet there is nothing more difficult than to live in this world according to God's commandment and without taking love and care for the things it contains (fr. 906, E.705).

Many other fragments could be quoted from the *Pensées* in order to express this idea, but this one extract will be enough to show us how the tragic mind views this world. The only condition we must observe is that, in this as in every other case, we must give Pascal's words their fullest possible meaning, even if this means, in this particular instance, extrapolating to the point of saying that everything which God demands is impossible in the eyes of the world, and that everything which is possible when we follow the rules of this world ceases to exist when the eye of God lights upon it.

[1] Cf. Lukàcs, *Die Seele und die Formen*, pp. 335–6.
[2] Idem, p. 336.

However, this denial of the reality of the world only presents one aspect of the problem, and the Pascal text which I have just quoted gives us the other complementary but contrasting aspect: for, as I have said, the tragic mind sees the world as nothing and as everything at one and the same time.

The God of tragedy is a God who is always present and always absent. Thus, while his presence takes all value and reality from the world, his equally absolute and permanent absence makes the world into the only reality which man can confront, the only sphere in and against which he can and must apply his demand for substantial and absolute values.

Many forms of religious and revolutionary consciousness have insisted upon the incompatibility between God and the world and between values and reality. Most of them, however, have admitted some possible solution, if only that of an endeavour which can be made in this world to achieve these values, or, alternatively, of the possibility for man of abandoning this world entirely and seeking refuge in the intelligible and transcendent world of values or of God. In its most radical form, tragedy rejects both these solutions as signs of weakness and illusion, and sees them as being either conscious or unconscious attempts at compromise. For tragedy believes neither that the world can be changed and authentic values realised within the framework it provides nor that it can simply be left behind while man seeks refuge in the city of God. This is why tragic man cannot try to spend his wealth or fulfil his duties in the world 'well', nor pass over these duties and abandon his wealth completely. Here, as elsewhere, tragic man can find only one valid attitude: that of saying both 'Yes' and 'No', of being in the world but not of the world, as 'taking neither love nor care for the things which it contains'. Living in this world means accepting, in the full sense of the word, that it exists; being in it without being of it means refusing to accept that it has any real existence.

This is the coherent and paradoxical attitude which tragic man must adopt towards the world and towards anything that is in it. It is an attitude which is all the more coherent because of its paradoxical nature and one which, if we understand it correctly, will enable us to dispose of a false problem that has confronted a number of Pascalian scholars. This problem has, in the past, consisted of trying to reconcile two apparently contradictory facts about Pascal's thought. On the one hand, he did not think that 'knowledge of the machine'—that is to say, of the reality of the physical world—'was worth an hour's trouble', and said as much in a letter to Fermat on August 8th, 1661. 'To be quite frank with you,' he wrote, 'I consider geometry to be the highest exercise of the mind, but at the same time hold it so useless that

50

I would make little distinction between the man who is a geometer and nothing more and one who is a skilful artisan. Thus, while I call it the finest occupation in the world, it is but an occupation and nothing more; and I have often said that it is useful as a field in which to try out our strength, but not one in which to give it full employment; so that, for my own part, I would not as much as walk down the street for geometry's sake'.[1] On the other hand, however, this same Pascal never ceased, at the very time that he was writing his letter, to be interested in the life of this world, and especially in problems of geometry, and to devote a large amount of his time to their solution.[2] It is my contention that, looked at correctly, this paradox is not one which either can or should be solved; and that Pascal's attitude is exactly the coherent though paradoxical one which is characteristic of the tragic thinker.

No clearer definition could in fact be given of this dual attitude, which says '*Yes*' and '*No*' at the same time, than the famous passage, written either by Pascal or by someone closely influenced by his ideas, called *On the Conversion of the Sinner*. 'On the one hand,' writes this author, 'the presence of visible objects touches the soul more than does the hope of those invisible; while, on the other, the firmness of those invisible touches it more than the vanity of those visible. So that the presence of the first and the firmness of the second fight for its love, and the vanity of the first and the absence of the second excite its aversion'.[3]

Or again, if we want to gain a clearer picture of how the world presents itself to the tragic mind we must once more quote Pascal and once more give his words their full force. His letter to Fermat tells us that he sees 'little distinction' between a man who follows 'the finest occupation in the world', thus devoting himself to 'the highest exercise of the mind', and one who is merely an 'artisan'. What Pascal's letter tells us is that for the tragic mind there is so such thing as degrees, transitions or approximations; that this mind passes over the concept of 'more' or 'less' and concentrates solely on that of 'All' or 'Nothing'; and that when a man who has tragic vision sees 'little distinction' between two things, then this means, when we take what

---

[1] Letter of August 10th, 1661.

[2] The letter inviting solutions for the problem of the cycloid dates from June 1658; the *Histoire de la Roulette* from October 1658. A letter from Sluse to Pascal dated April 24th, 1660, mentions that the latter had written to him recently on the subject of the diagrams in Descartes's *Traité de l'Homme*. The document setting up the 'carrosses à cinq sous' dates from November 1661, and there is a letter from Huyghens to Hook indicating that the idea of organising the production of spring-type watches was being entertained in 1660.

[3] I have deliberately not quoted the rest of the passage, which I shall be analysing further in a subsequent chapter.

he says to its logical conclusion, that he sees no difference at all between the highest and humblest forms of worldly—and therefore relative—forms of existence and activity.

Yet in spite of this, the absence of God deprives tragic man of any right to remain ignorant of the world or to turn his face from it; his refusal remains within the world, both because it is this world that he rejects and because it is only by this movement of rejection that tragic man can know himself and understand his own limits and value. For if the world is too narrow and too ambiguous for man to devote himself to it entirely, and to 'give full employment' to his strength in it, it still remains the only place where he can 'try out his strength'. Thus in every possible aspect of human life, however minute, the reply of both 'Yes' and 'No' remains the only valid attitude for the man who has become aware of tragedy.

However, this analysis merely introduces us to one of the main difficulties of the subject under discussion: if we try to insert this idea of a simultaneous '*Yes*' and '*No*' into a coherent vision, then we must do so by linking it with practical and theoretical positions that provide an accurate justification and foundation for it. For the complete refusal of a world which offered the chance of achieving authentic values would show just as complete a lack of coherence as the acceptance of a world which was completely absurd and ambiguous. The decision, in Pascal's words, to 'try out our strength' in this world should therefore be neither wholly absurd nor wholly meaningful; or, to be more accurate, it should be both absurd and meaningful at one and the same time, an 'attempt' which is real in the fullest sense of the word, but one which, by its very nature, can never reach the level of a calling, in the sense of an activity which absorbs all our faculties.

For if we refuse the world absolutely and unilaterally, then we deprive it of any possible meaning, and reduce it to the level of an abstract anonymous obstacle, without form or qualities. Only an attitude which places itself within the world in order to refuse the world can, without abandoning anything of the absolute character of this refusal, still allow tragic man to know the world on which he passes judgment and thus justify his refusal of it by keeping his reasons for doing so constantly in mind. It is these characteristics of extreme rigour and extreme coherence that we find in the expression given to tragic awareness in Racine's *Phèdre*, Pascal's and Kant's philosophical writings and the text from Lukàcs that I have just quoted. It is a paradoxical attitude and one which is very difficult to describe, but it is, in my view, only by reference to it that we shall succeed in understanding the works under discussion.

Before continuing this analysis of the tragic mind, however, I shall now discuss a position which is important both for sociological and historical reasons, and also for an understanding of Pascal. It is a less radical position than the one just describéd, but one that not only represents a step towards complete coherence but also possesses a relative coherence which renders it autonomous in its own right. I shall call this position—which found its expression in the ideas of most of the more extreme Jansenists—one of complete and unilateral refusal of the world and consequent appeal to God; and I shall contrast it with the attitude to be found in Pascal, which consists of a refusal of the world from within the world and the decision to wager that God exists rather than to call on His presence as something established. The difference between the two positions is the one which lies between Junia and Titus, on the one hand, and Phèdre, on the other, or between Barcos and Mother Angélique and the Pascal who, during the last years of his life, was both discovering the area traced out by the cycloid, creating the first omnibus service and writing the *Pensées*. The importance of this intermediate position can be seen from the fact that, if *Phèdre* and the *Pensées* had not been written, it is the one which we should be tempted to consider as providing the coherent expression of Jansenist thought. It was, indeed, to a very extent the one which Molière made fun of in *Le Misanthrope*, but which also manifested itself in literary works as important as Racine's first three tragedies.

I shall deal with this position in greater detail in Chapter VII when I study Jansenist thought. It should be noted, however, that these two positions do not represent wholly different and autonomous visions. There is a link between them whose existence is proved not only by history—Pascal and Racine both come from Port-Royal— but also by textual analysis. For if the Jansenist doctrine of Grace is carried to its logical conclusions, what we find is the paradoxical notion expressed in the *Pensées* and in *Phèdre*: that of the just man to whom grace has been refused, that of the just man in a state of mortal sin.

Thus, there is an ideological as well as an historical link between Barcos, Pavillon, Singlin, Mother Angélique, on the one hand and, on the other, the Pascal of the *Pensées* and the Racine of *Phèdre*. There is also, in addition, a contrast between them which has found its expression in actual texts. The first time this happened was when Gilberte Pascal tried to explain away her brother's activity in the last years of his life, and the second when Pascal, in a famous fragment of the *Pensées*, reproved the Jansenists for not having 'made profession of two opposites'.[1]

[1] Cf. fr. 865 (E.947): 'If there ever is a time when one should profess both con- traries, it is when one is being accused of omitting one. Thus both Jansenists and

Gilberte Pascal was indeed faced with a problem when she had to provide a hagiographical account, consistent with Jansenist orthodoxy, of the way in which, in the last years of his life, Pascal returned to science and to life in this world, and came to accept the authority of the Church. In her *Life* she scarcely mentioned the problem of his submission to Rome, talked of his attempt to start the first omnibus service merely as an instance of his concern for the poor of Blois, and explained his return to science by a legend whose naïvety is equalled only by that of the commentators who have accepted it without question as an established fact. It is the story of how Pascal undertook to solve the problem of the cycloid in order to take his mind off his toothache; to which—since this toothache could scarcely explain why Pascal should then publish his solution—she added the account of a 'person as distinguished for his piety as for the qualities of his mind' to whom Pascal 'owed all kinds of deference both through respect and gratitude' and who 'concerned only for the glory of God, considered it fitting that my brother should use his solution as a challenge to his rivals and then have it printed'.[1]

It would, in my view, be quite wrong to interpret the change in Pascal's attitude towards the end of his life, his substitution of an attitude of '*Yes*' and '*No*' towards the world for one of absolute refusal, his acceptance of the authority of the Church and his consequent disagreement with Arnauld as to the signing of the *Formulary*, as an indication that he has returned both to the world and to the Church and completely given up Jansenism. What in fact he did was to accept a much more radical and a much more coherent position. Indeed, as Gerberon pointed out, he became 'more Jansenist than the Jansenists themselves',[2] and, I would myself add, more Jansenist than even the most radical and extreme among them. For the Jansenists, far from 'professing two opposites', simply refused the world, remained outside of it and abolished any link between it and men; or, to be more accurate, they recommended that any such link should be abolished, and called upon God to be the sole judge in these matters. But, for them, the existence of a God who watched all their actions was a certainty, a fixed and immovable point in their intellectual and spiritual make up; the element of doubt, the need to make a decision, the Pascalian idea of the 'wager' came only afterwards, when the problem arose of whether or not this God had granted the grace to persevere, of whether a particular person was simply a just man, or

---

[1] Cf. Brunschvicg edition of the *Pensées*, p. 24.
[2] Cf. Gerberon. *Histoire du Jansenisme* (Amsterdam, 1700), Vol. II, p. 515.

Jesuits are wrong to disguise them; but the Jansenists are more to blame, for the Jesuits have better professed both.'

'a just man to whom grace has been refused', or a just man who had been damned and had fallen into a state of mortal sin. Pascal carried Jansenism to its logical conclusion when he ceased to wonder whether a particular individual was damned or saved, and introduced doubt as to whether or not God himself really exists. By deliberately choosing the paradoxical position of the 'just to whom grace has been refused', by giving up the attempt to be an angel in order to avoid becoming a beast, Pascal, 'more Jansenist than the Jansenists themselves', became the creator of dialectical thought and the first philosopher of the tragic vision. For by wagering that God is both continually and permanently absent and present, he transformed the abstract and absolute refusal of the extreme Jansenists into a refusal within the framework of this world. He thus made it a total and concrete refusal of the world by a tragic and absolute being.

I shall discuss the position of the other Jansenists in Chapter VII.[1] For the time being, I am studying the extremist position, such as it is expressed in *Phèdre* and in *Pensées*.

I have already said that tragic man lives permanently with God's eye upon him, and that for him 'only the miracle is real'. I have also argued that he confronts the fundamental ambiguity of the world with his own equally fundamental demand for absolute and unambiguous values, for clarity and for the absolute essence of things. Prevented by the presence of God from ever accepting the world, but prevented at the same time by His absence from abandoning it altogether, he is constantly dominated by a permanent and fully

---

[1] Let me offer a brief outline of the three principal currents which showed themselves in seventeenth-century Jansenism. Each of them, naturally, contained every imaginable form of mixture and variation, but they nevertheless must be distinguished if we wish to understand the social and intellectual phenomenon of Jansenism.

Thus we have:

(a) The non-tragic current made up of those who could be called 'moderates'. The principal representatives of this group are, to a certain extent, Saint-Cyran, and especially Arnauld and Nicole. It is to the views of this group that we must link the *Mémorial* and the *Lettres Provinciales*. (A more detailed study should distinguish, within this current, those who were concerned with the spiritual life—the Pascal who wrote the *Mémorial*, Mother Angélique, etc.—and the intellectuals—Arnauld, Nicole, and the Pascal who wrote the *Provinciales*.)

(b) The extremists—Barcos, Pavillon, Singlin, Mother Angélique, Gerberon, etc. Their position tended to be that of the tragic but onesided refusal of the world, and the direct appeal to God. It is to the views of this group that we should link *Andromaque*, *Bérénice* and *Britannicus*.

(c) Those who carried Jansenism to its highest degree of coherence, to the position of tragic paradox represented by the refusal of the world from within the world, and the wager on the existence of God, to whose tribunal the final appeal is made. To my knowledge, this position was attained only by the Pascal who wrote the *Pensées*, and the Racine who wrote *Phèdre*.

justified awareness of the radical incongruity between himself and everything around him, of the unbridgeable gulf which separates him both from any real values and from any possible acceptance of the immediate reality of the ordinary external world. The situation of tragic man is paradoxical, and can be explained only by paradoxes: for he is in the world and conscious of it from within, but at the same time he refuses the world because of its inadequate and fragmentary nature; yet at the same time as he both refuses it and lives in it, he also goes beyond it in an immanent transcendence and a transcendent immanence.

This is why his awareness is first and foremost an awareness of the two complementary inadequacies which (for the historian who studies the mind of tragic man if not for tragic man himself) are mutually self-conditioning and self-reinforcing: man is inadequate and insufficient, he is at one and the same time a king and a slave, a beast and an angel; the world is inadequate because it is ambiguous and unsatisfying, and yet at the same time it is the only realm where man can both try out his strength and yet never put it to use.

'The wisdom brought by the tragic miracle is a wisdom of limits,' writes Lukàcs, and Pascal expresses the very essence of tragic awareness when he asks: 'Why is my knowledge limited? Why is my stature what it is, and the span of my life one hundred and not one thousand years? Why did nature give me this span of life, choosing it rather than any other from out of the infinite number available, where no compelling reason imposed on her this choice rather than another?' (fr. 208. E.385).

This is why—as I shall explain later—Lukàcs writes that 'tragic life', life dominated exclusively by the divine presence and by the refusal of the world 'is the most exclusively terrestial of all lives'.[1]

It is, however, precisely this 'Yes' and this 'No', both equally complete and equally absolute (the 'Yes' in so far as tragic man remains in the world to demand that values be achieved, the 'No' in so far as he refuses this world because it is entirely inadequate and offers no scope for the achievement of real values) which allow the tragic mind to achieve, on the plane of knowledge, a degree of accuracy and objectivity of a type never before attained. The man who lives solely in the world, but who remains constantly detached from it, finds that his mind is freed from all the current illusions and limitations which beset his fellows, with the result that the art and ideas which are born of the tragic vision become one of the most advanced forms of realism.

Tragic man never gives up hope, but he does not put his hope in

[1] Op. cit., p. 345.

this world; this is why there is no truth either about the structure of this world or about his place in it which can cause him to be afraid. Since he judges all things according to the scale of his own demand for the absolute, and since he finds them all equally wanting, he can look without fear upon their own nature and limitations and upon the limits which beset him personally when he tries out his strength in this world, either in the realm of action or in that of knowledge. Since it seeks only what is necessary, the tragic mind can meet, in this world, only what is contingent; since it acknowledges only the absolute, it will find in this world only what is relative. But as it becomes more aware of these two limitations (both its own and those of this world) and as it refuses to accept either of them, it saves human values and goes beyond both this world and its own condition.

What, however, is the concrete meaning of the expression: to refuse this world? The human mind sees the world as a demand for a choice among a number of different possibilities which are all mutually incompatible but none of which is wholly satisfying. To refuse the world while remaining within it means refusing to choose and refusing to be satisfied with any of the possibilities which it offers; it means making a clear and unrestricted judgment of their inadequacy and limitations, and setting up against them a demand for real and unambiguous values; it means setting up against a world composed of fragmentary and mutually exclusive elements a demand for totality that inevitably becomes a demand for the reconciliation of opposites. For the tragic mind, authentic values are synonymous with totality, and any attempt at compromise is synonymous with the complete fall from grace and honesty.

This is why tragic man, torn between 'Yes' or 'No', will always scorn those who choose an intermediary position, and will remain instead on the only level whose value he recognises to be adequate: that of saying both 'Yes' and 'No', of attempting to realise a synthesis. Man is 'neither beast nor angel', and that is why his real task lies in trying to create the whole and complete man who will bring the two together, the man whose body will be immortal as well as his soul, the man who will unite in his own person the extreme intensities of reason and passion, the man who, on this earth, can never become a reality.[1]

[1] There is no worse mistake than to interpret Pascal, basing oneself on the appearance of certain texts, as recommending a 'golden mean' between two extremes, a sceptical position frequently adopted by Montaigne but one which is the complete denial of any tragedy and any dialectical thought. Similarly, the God of the wager (like the God of Kant's practical postulate) is not a God whose existence is probable, but a God who is certain and necessary. However, this certainty and necessity are practical and human, certainties of the heart and not

It is from this that spring the two paradoxical elements of the tragic mind ('elements' in the sense that they have to be artificially separated for the purpose of analysis): its extreme realism and its demand for absolute values. Faced with an ambiguous and fragmentary world, the paradoxical nature of the tragic mind becomes a demand for the reconciliation of opposites, a demand in which the two elements reinforce each other. For what the tragic mind accepts as its first absolute value is that of truth, and this demand is inevitably accompanied by the realisation that all the possibilities offered by this world are limited and inadequate.

The fundamental philosophical problem is that of the relationship between value and reality, between what is rational and what can be perceived, between meaning and individuality and between the soul and the body; on this plane, the tragic mind resembles dialectical thought by the fact that it can recognise as valid only the reconciliation of opposites, the individualisation of essence and the identification between meaning and individuality. Thus, Kant places at the very centre of his epistemology the demand for 'integral determination' by the individual being, and Pascal writes, in the *Mystère de Jésus*: 'Behold, I have shed these drops of blood for thee' (fr. 553, E.739).

As the tragic mind becomes aware of the limits prescribing both it and the external world—and the most important of these limits is death—it sees everything in clear and unambiguous outline, even its own paradoxical character and the fundamental ambiguity of the world.[1] And, at the same time, it confronts this ambiguity with its own demand for extreme individuality and extreme essentiality.

Neither tragic nor dialectical thought can accept the idea that clarity should reside solely in ideas while reality remains ambiguous, and that values should not go beyond the stage of being demands and ideas; both reject the idea that the 'for itself' should remain empty and the 'in itself' blind, and that reality should be foreign or even opposed to value. In this, they are both philosophies of incarnation,

[1] Here again, we are in presence of a paradox: the tragic mind sees the world's ambiguity as clear and unambiguous.

---

of the reason (or, what is the same thing in Kant, certainties of the reason and not of the understanding).

In an article which, in spite of a number of errors and omissions, nevertheless had the merit of first indicating the dialectical quality of the *Pensées* and the relationship between this dialectic and paradox as a literary form, Professor Hugo Friedrich gave an excellent analysis of this difference between the notion of 'middle' (milieu) in Pascal and Montaigne. (Cf. Hugo Friedrich, *Pascals Paradox. Das Sprachbild einer Denform. Zeitschrift fur Romanische Philologie*, LVI Band, 1936.)

not, it is true, in any religious sense, but because both demand that values and meaning should become reality in the real world.

However, while dialectical thought considers that this can come about in the real world of historical experience, tragic thought eliminates this possibility from the world and places it in eternity. It therefore follows that, as far as this world is concerned, tragic thought merely poses the problem of a tension between a radically unsatisfactory world and an individual self that demands absolute authenticity. It does so, as Lukàcs writes,

> with a strength that eliminates and destroys everything until this extreme affirmation of the self, when it reaches the peak of its authenticity, endows everything it meets with a hard, steel-like autonomy; it then goes beyond itself, and in its final tension transcends everything which is purely individual. Its strength has consecrated things by raising them to the level of destiny, but in its great struggle with the destiny it has itself created, the tragic soul rises above itself and becomes a symbol of the ultimate relationship between man and his fate. (loc cit., p. 344).

'Death,' continues Lukàcs, 'which is an absolute limit, is for tragedy a constantly immanent reality indissolubly linked with everything that the tragic soul experiences', and he adds that it is

> for this reason that the tragic mind is a realisation of concrete essence. With complete assurance and certainty, it solves the most difficult problem of Platonism: that of discovering whether individual things have their own Idea and their own Essence. And the reply which it gives reverses the order in which the question is put, since it shows that it is only when what is individual—that is to say, a particular living individual—is carried to its final limits and possibilities that it conforms to the Idea and begins really to exist.
>
> The universal [he concludes] without form or colour, is, in its generality, too weak to become real. It is too much bound up in itself to possess real being, and to say that it is identical with itself is merely tautological. Thus, as it goes beyond Platonism, tragedy replies to the condemnation which Platonism had earlier laid upon it (loc. cit., pp. 347–8).

And, I will add, it re-opens the way towards the immanent and classical thought which Platonism had abandoned.

With his demand for clarity and for the absolute, tragic man stands confronted with a world that is the only reality against which he can set this demand, the only place where he could live if he were never to give up this demand and his effort to achieve it. But the world can never satisfy him, and this is why the eye of God compels man, for so long as he lives—and for as long as he lives, he lives in the world—never to 'love and care for it'. Tragic man is absent and present in the world at one and the same time, exactly as God is simultaneously absent and present to man. Even if the smallest and most imperceptible ray of light—of real truth or real justice—were to become visible, tragedy would disappear, and man would be linked with God in a world made humanly habitable. But there stretches before tragic man only 'the eternal silence of infinite space'; not even of the narrowest and most insignificant sector human life can a completely clear and unequivocal statement be made without the opposite and contradictory statement being immediately added; the only answer to every problem is both 'Yes' and 'No', and paradox is the only valid expression of reality. And, for tragic man, paradox is a constant source of scandal and concern: to accept paradox, to accept human weakness, the ambiguity and confusion of the world, its 'sense and nonsense' as Merleau-Ponty puts it, means giving up any attempt to endow life with meaning. Man is a contradictory being, a mixture of strength and weakness, greatness and poverty, living in a world which, like himself, is made up of opposites, of antagonistic forces that fight against one another without hope of truce or victory, of elements that are complementary but permanently unable to form a whole. The greatness of tragic man lies in the fact that he sees and recognises these opposites and inimical elements in the clear light of absolute truth, and yet never accepts that this shall be so. For if he were to accept them, he would destroy the paradox, he would give up his greatness and made do with his poverty and wretchedness (*misère*). Fortunately, however, man remains to the very end both paradoxical and contradictory, 'man goes infinitely beyond man', and he confronts the radical and irredeemable ambiguity of the world with his own equal and opposite demand for clarity.

Before continuing this analysis of the tragic mind, however, I should like to make one more point: it is that, as we can see from the popularity of Jean-Paul Sartre and Maurice Merleau-Ponty, the idea of the ambiguity of the world, its 'sense and nonsense' has, like that of man's inability to find a clear and unequivocal line of conduct, become once again one of the principal themes of philosophical thought. And, especially when we read their minor works, it is also easy to see what social and historical conditions have led them to the conclusions which they express: once again, the social forces that in the nineteenth century enabled man to go beyond tragedy by using dialectical and revolutionary thought have, for reasons too complicated to analyse here, led to the sacrifice of value to efficiency. And, once again, the most honest thinkers have been compelled to recognise the existence of the dichotomy which had already struck Pascal between justice and force, between man's hopes and the human predicament.[1]

It is also our present historical situation which has not only made us more aware of the ambiguity of the world and of the inauthentic nature of daily life, but which has also revived our interest in the tragic writers and thinkers of the past.

I should like to conclude this chapter by stressing one point: that in spite of the greater interest that we now feel for tragedy, and for the themes of anguish and suffering in Pascalian thought, none of the modern existentialist thinkers can really be linked with Pascal, Hegel and Marx, or to any classical tradition in either the wider or narrower meaning of the term. For it is precisely the fact that it does not accept ambiguity and, instead, keeps alive the demand for reason and clarity, that makes tragedy what it is, and also institutes the essence of the classical spirits. For example, Merleau-Ponty says 'sense and nonsense', just as Pascal did before him and as do all the dialectical thinkers who follow Pascal; but they, unlike Merleau-Ponty, insist upon the fact that we must not accept such a universe but rather, if we are men, strive to transcend it. There is a wide gap between these two positions, and I can see no way of bringing them closer together.

[1] This was written in 1952. Since then, the historical situation has changed, and both Sartre and Merleau-Ponty have modified their respective ideological attitudes—in opposite directions, it may be added.

IV

THE TRAGIC VISION: MAN

'That, if we hope, it is against hope.' Nicolas Pavillon, Bishop of Alet: letter to Antoine Arnauld in August 1664.

I HAVE in fact already begun the study of tragic man, and I shall be continuing it in one form or another throughout the book. For it is impossible to make a clear distinction between the three elements that I have described as forming the tragic vision—God, the world and man—since each can exist and be defined only by reference to the two others. In itself, the world is not contradictory and ambiguous, and not every mind sees it with these qualities. It only becomes contradictory and ambiguous when a man lives wholly in order to achieve absolute and impossible values. Even then, however, a distinction has to be made, for we must realise that tragic vision occurs only when the two elements of the paradox are both carried to their final conclusion. Thus, a man can live for absolute values, and yet do nothing more than vaguely desire them in his thoughts and dream. He thus becomes a Romantic character, and such an attitude is completely opposed to any genuine tragedy. Or, on the other hand, a man can spend his life in an attempt to achieve those relative values which are accessible to mankind. His attitude towards experience may then be that of rationalism or empiricism if he does not believe in God, or of Thomism if he is a Catholic. Or, again, if he is a revolutionary he may accept the viewpoint of dialectical materialism. But whatever he does, he will not be a tragic character.

Similarly, not every world view sees God as both absent and present at the same time. It is only the man who is supremely conscious both of the demand for absolute values and of the impossibility of ever satisfying this demand in the real world who sees the paradoxical nature of the tragic God.

Finally, even if, in the tragedy of refusal, there remains no common element between God and the world—except, perhaps, the fact that

62

they are mutually exclusive—they still, thanks to the presence of man as a mediator, remain part of the same universe. And, in the case of Pascal, to the supreme mediation of the God who becomes man. For man, who is a paradoxical being, 'goes infinitely beyond man', and joins together in his own nature all possible opposites: he is beast and angel, wretched but great, cursed with radical evil but blessed with the categorical imperative; he has a dual nature, both divine and worldly, noumenal and phenomenal, and it is because of this that he sees the world as contradictory and paradoxical. The God who is absent from the world when He is looked at from the standpoint of man's wretchedness becomes present in the world when seen from the standpoint of His greatness, and of man's demand for justice and truth.

There are two essential characteristics of tragic man which should be noted if we are to see him as a coherent human reality: the first is that he makes this absolute and exclusive demand for impossible values; and the second is that, as a result of this, his demand is for 'all or nothing', and he is totally indifferent to degrees and approximations, and to any concept containing the idea of relativity.

It is this rejection of any notion of progression or of degree which distinguishes the tragic mind from spirituality or mysticism. For if we leave on one side the question of pantheistic mysticism, which is obviously incompatible with any type of tragic vision, we shall see that nothing is more important for the mystic than the idea of the soul gradually detaching itself from the things of this world and gradually moving towards God. When the qualitative change finally occurs which transforms spiritual into mystical experience, and the conceptual awareness of God is replaced by the ecstacy of His presence, then this is a result of a journey which the soul has made through different stages on its path.[1]

The tragic mind can neither conceive nor recognise the existence of such an experience. However detached a man may be from the world, he still remains just as *infinitely distant* as ever from any authentic awareness, until the moment suddenly arrives when, without passing through any intermediary stage, his inauthentic consciousness enters the realm of essences. He then leaves the world—or, rather, to use Pascal's phrase once again, he 'has no love or care for it'—and enters into the universe of tragedy.

Thus, even though spirituality often precedes mystical experience,

[1] And this without taking into consideration the separation so often described by the psychologists of mysticism between the 'fine point' and the other faculties of the soul; a separation which is completely foreign to the tragic soul, for whom only what is essential has real existence and yet which also sees everything existing as equally essential.

and is in fact one of the paths leading to it, there is only one way of entering the world of tragedy: by conversion. Tragic man suddenly becomes aware, by a movement which, strictly speaking, is outside time, of the contradiction between the imperfect values of man and the world and the perfection of those to be found in God. It is an event which is difficult to describe, but one which must be understood if we are to study either the tragic characters of Racine—Berenice or Phaedra, for example—or the real life of the nuns and solitaries of Port-Royal.

The most important features of the tragic conversion are that it takes place outside time and independently of any psychological or temporal preparation;[1] and that, whether it be the effect of an intelligible choice or of divine grace, it nevertheless remains entirely foreign to the actual character or the particular will of the individual. We only need to read the letters of Mother Angélique to realise that, for her, conversion is not something which takes place at a particular moment in time. For we constantly see her asking her correspondents to 'pray for her conversion',[2] which thus appears as an event that she has doubtless already experienced, which has nevertheless still to be requested of God. God can always call this conversion into question again, and man is always in danger of losing the grace which made it possible.

The fact remains, however, that 'conversion' is also something that does take place at a particular moment in time, and that it does mark a stage in a particular individual's life. But even from this point of view, it can neither be the result of a decision that any person makes

[1] This is the most complex aspect of the tragic mind, and the one which has given rise to the most misunderstanding. For us, and for any historian, psychologist or sociologist, tragic conversion is the final stage in a whole temporal and psychic evolution without which it would be quite incomprehensible. But its content is the absolute negation of such a process or evolution. Everything temporal or psychological forms part of this world, and has therefore no existence for the tragic mind, which has moved out of time and into eternity and life in the eternal instant.

A psychologist with whom I once discussed the characters of Bérénice and Phaedra made a remark which I shall quote precisely because it illustrates the most dangerous form of misunderstanding, and one that one must avoid at all costs. 'Racine,' he said, 'left out any description of the way in which the two "conversions" were prepared in the psychology of the individual because this was not necessary to the structure of the play; what the critic must do, however, is to supply the description of how these two conversions came about, and thus restore the individualistic psychology neglected by Racine.' In my view, this would involve altering the psychology of these two characters, or, rather, attributing to them a psychological development that completely destroyed their tragic nature.

[2] See the letters of June 3rd, August 14th, August 17th and November 9th, 1637, November 15th, 1639, April 1644 (to Antoine Arnauld), March 16th and May 14th, 1649, September 24th, 1652, etc.

nor the outcome of a series of accidental events and encounters in an individual's life. People we meet or things that happen to us can only be the occasion for divine grace to manifest itself, an occasion which is quite trivial and unimportant when compared to the real significance of the event.

'The first thing that God inspires in the soul on which He deigns to lay His hand in a true and veritable manner,' writes the author at the beginning of the text *On the Conversion of the Sinner,* 'is an extraordinary knowledge and awareness by which this soul looks upon both itself and the world in a totally new way.' Lukàcs also points out that

> This moment is both a beginning and an end. It gives man a new memory, and a new concept of what is just and good. . . . Both the occasion and the revelation, the revealer and the revealed, stand face to face, too foreign to each other even to be enemies. For what the occasion reveals is indeed something quite foreign to its own nature, since it is higher and comes from another world. And the soul which has at last found itself looks with a different and a foreign eye upon the life preceding its moment of conversion. This life now seems wholly incomprehensible, quite inauthentic and foreign to the realm of essences; and the soul can do nothing more than dream that it was once other than it is now, for its real existence is the one which it now enjoys. All else is but as the dreams dispersed by the chance ringing of a lone and morning bell.
>
> Now [continues Lukàcs] the soul stands naked and speaks alone with its naked destiny. Both the soul and its destiny have been stripped of all chance and accidental features, and all the many and different relationships which existed in everyday life have disappeared. . . . Everything vague and uncertain, everything hazy and shaded, has ceased to exist, and there remains only the pure and transparent air which now hides nothing. What we see now are the final question and the final answers (op. cit., pp. 333–8).

In spite of the rather flowery language of the young man of twenty-five who wrote this passage, the central idea is nevertheless clear: worldly existence changes into tragedy and into the universe of the hidden God, who is at one and the same time both absent and present; and, as an inevitable result of this change, tragic man ceases to be able to understand the life that he led before his moment of conversion, and sees that all his earlier values have been overthrown. What was previously great now seems infinitesimally small, and unimportant has now become essential'. (See also the comparison between the last lines of *The Mystery of Jesus*, and the corresponding passage from Lukàcs already quoted on page 38 of Chapter II.) Lukàcs continues: 'Man can no longer tread the paths that he walked before, since he can no longer see which way he should go. With the ease and grace of a bird he now soars up to previously unscaleable heights, and with sure and certain steps crosses unfathomable gulfs' [op. cit., p. 338, compare fr. 306 of the *Pensées* (E.204)].

It is this instant of conversion which Lukàcs calls the miracle. Its central characteristic is that it transforms the essential ambiguity of man's life in this world into an unambiguous awareness and an unflinching desire for clarity. An anonymous Jansenist text expresses it in the following way:

> There is in our heart so deep an abyss that we cannot sound its depths; we can scarcely make out light from dark or good from evil; vices and virtues are so curiously compounded, and sometimes so apparently similar in feature, that we cannot know which we should avoid and which we should ask of God, nor how we should make our prayers for that which we do require. But the affliction that God, in His infinite mercy, sends down upon us is like a two-edged sword that enters into the very depths of our hearts and minds. There, it cleaves our human thoughts from those which God causes to rise up in our souls, and the spirit of God can then no longer hide itself. We begin to have so clear a knowledge of this spirit that we can no longer be deceived.
>
> It is then that, needing no further demonstration, we behold the extent of our sins and groan in the sight of God. For then we see that His rod, though it smite us hard, smites us rightly; and we see how greatly we need His help and how He is our sole salvation. It is then that we find it easiest to detach ourselves from the things of this world, whose nothingness we now see clearly set before us, and finding no rest here on earth turn to seek it in our Saviour: *Inquietum est cor nostrum donec requiescat in Te.*[1]

This passage, a defence of their faith by the nuns of Port Royal, is an equally good illustration of two things: the essential nature of Jansenist conversion, together with the transition which this implies from complete darkness to absolute clarity; and, with the *Requiescat in Te*, the difference between this conversion and the attitude of Pascal in the final years of his life.

For if the fundamental characteristic of tragic man is his demand for absolute truth, then this involves consequences of which only Pascal, among the Jansenists of seventeenth-century France, expressed fully in his work. These consequences concern the problem of certainty. This is, it is true, primarily a theoretical concept; yet any purely theoretical certainty runs the risk of being shown to be

[1] In the *Défense de la foi des religieuses de Port-Royal et de leurs directeurs sur tous les faits alleguez par M. Chamaillard dans les deux libelles*, etc. . . ., 1667, p. 59.

illusory, and any piece of abstract reasoning may, when judged by the light of experience, reveal flaws not noticed by the abstract thinker.

In spite of this, there is no conviction, however powerful, which can lead to absolute certainty so long as it depends solely upon practical or emotional considerations and has not found a solid theoretical basis.[1] Placed between a silent world and a hidden God, tragic man lacks any completely trustworthy theoretical foundation on which to base his certainty that God exists. Reason, which is for Pascal what the understanding is for Kant, the ability to think, cannot say with certainty either that God does or that He does not exist. This is why, carried to its final conclusions, Jansenist thought does not lead to the *Requiescat in Te* but to the phrase in the *Mystery of Jesus*: 'Jesus is suffering the torment of death until the end of the world. We must not sleep during all that time.'

But even though it is not a theoretical certainty, God's existence is nevertheless concrete and real; indeed, it does have a kind of certainty, that which depends upon will and value and which Kant calls 'practical' certainty. With greater accuracy, Pascal uses a word which indicates that theory and practice have been synthesised and transcended: 'certainty of the heart'. Now, practical or theoretico-practical considerations are not proofs or demonstrations but postulates and wagers. Both these words indicate the same idea, and Lukàcs expresses it in other terms when he says: 'Faith affirms the existence of this relationship (between empirical reality and essences, between facts and miracles) and makes its permanently unprovable possibility the *a priori* basis for all existence' (op. cit., p. 335).

I shall devote one of the chapters in Part III to Pascal's 'argument of the wager', but we are already in a better position to understand why God, who is made the '*a priori* basis for all existence', is eternally present but also eternally absent: it is because the fundamental clarity of the tragic mind never allows it to forget that, in God, absence and presence are indissolubly linked together. God's absence, and the paradoxical nature of the world, exist only for a mind which cannot accept this state of things, both because of the permanent demand for the unambiguous and the unequivocal, and because of the constant awareness of being under the eye of God which characterise it; on the other hand, this presence is only a 'wager' and a 'permanently unproveable possibility'. This is why the tragic mind is constantly haunted by both hope and fear, why it is always full both of fear and trembling and of hope, and why it is forced to

[1] It is the problem of the *Fidens quarens intellectum* from the *Prosologion* of Saint Anselm to the *Theses on Feuerbach*. I shall come back to this point in the chapter devoted to Pascal's epistemology.

live in uninterrupted tension, without either knowing or accepting an instant of repose.

But the absolute demand for theoretical and practical certainty also implies a second consequence: that man is alone, placed between a blind world and a hidden and a silent God. For there is no possible link or dialogue between tragic man, who can accept only what is certain and absolute, and the ambiguities and contradictions of the world. The languages of authenticity and inauthenticity, of clarity and ambiguity, are not only mutually incomprehensible but mutually inaudible. The only person to whom tragic man can address his words or ideas is God, but this God, as we know, is dumb and absent and never replies. This is why the only possible means of expression for tragic man is the monologue—or, more accurately, since this monologue is addressed not to himself but to God—what Lukàcs calls the 'solitary dialogue'.

Scholars have often wondered what reader Pascal had in mind when writing the *Pensées*. Finding it difficult to understand how a Christian thinker can use the argument of the wager to defend a position which other Christians—and even other Jansenists—find unacceptable, most scholars have maintained that Pascal was addressing himself to free thinkers. I shall try to show why this interpretation is wrong, and there is, in fact, one obvious reason for rejecting it: the free thinker would simply refuse to make the bet. But scholars are nevertheless right when they argue that the *Pensées* could not have been written for the believer—since he would not need to wager—and it is not really probable that Pascal simply wrote them for himself. In my view, the real solution is quite different: recognising that any dialogue with the world is quite impossible, Pascal addresses the only listener who can still remain, the silent and hidden listener who allows no restrictions, lies or prudence, but who nevertheless never replies. The *Pensées* are a supreme example of one of those 'solitary dialogues' with the hidden God of the Jansenists and of tragedy, one of the dialogues in which everything counts, in which each word is just as important as the next, in which the scholar should neglect nothing on the grounds that it is exaggerated or expressed in excessive language, a dialogue in which everything is essential because man is talking to the only being who can understand him, but by whom he will never really know whether or not he has been heard.

Certainly, the words of the 'solitary dialogue' are also addressed to men, but it does not matter whether these men are Christians or unbelievers; or, rather, we can say that the dialogue is potentially addressed to both classes, but really to neither. The tragic thinker addresses all men in so far as they, understanding him, might achieve essential existence, and 'go beyond man' in a sincere quest for God. But if there were a single human being in the world who could understand the words of tragic man and reply to them, then there would be a possible human community in the world, tragedy would be transcended and the 'solitary dialogue' would become a real dialogue.[1] But all that tragic man finds before him is the 'eternal silence of infinite space'. And it is when he becomes aware of his true situation that he feels that he is going beyond loneliness, and is drawing close to Him, who, in an exemplary and superhuman manner, has fulfilled the function of the tragic mind and has become a mediator between the world and the realm of supreme values, a mediator between the world and God.

I have already made the statement that I shall now repeat: that the *Pensées* mark the end of any purely speculative theology, and that there no longer is and never again can be, for Pascal, any solid theoretical proof of God's existence. But it is precisely by becoming aware of the implacable character of this situation, of the absolute silence of space and of the world, and of his own fatal demand for justice and truth, of the fact that man goes infinitely beyond man, and also of his own suffering and loneliness, that Pascal achieves the sole certainty which is open to him: the one which leads him, not to religion in general (for that is the task of the wager) but to Christianity in particular. For it is when he understands himself and sees his own limitations that he feels himself closest, not to Christ's divine nature but to His nature as a man, and to His suffering and sacrifice.

This description will, I hope, have enabled the reader to see the fundamental characteristics of tragic man and to understand their coherence and internal relationships. These are the paradoxical nature of the world, tragic man's conversion to essential existence, his demand for absolute truth, his awareness of the limitations of man and of the world, his refusal of any ambiguity or compromise, his loneliness and knowledge of the infinite abyss which separates him both from God and from the world, his wager that this God whose existence cannot be proved nevertheless does exist, and his decision to live wholly and exclusively for this God who is always absent and always present. The consequences which spring from this attitude are the absolute primacy accorded to morality over abstract

[1] There can, of course, be more than one tragic mind in real life and sometimes within the very same tragedy—Titus and Berenice, for example. But such minds do not come together to form a community. Berenice enters the universe of tragedy at the very moment that she leaves the world and cuts herself off from Titus. The Solitaries of Port-Royal—in principle at least—cut down their actual contact with one another to the absolute minimum. 'He has brothers who follow after the same star,' wrote Lukàcs in his *Die Theorie des Romans* (Berlin: T. Cassirer, p. 29), 'but never comrades or companions.'

theory or effectiveness, the abandonment of any hope of material victory or even of future life in this world and, at the same time, the certainty provided by eternity of the final moral and spiritual victory.

I shall conclude this chapter (and thus the first part of this book) by analysing two texts which are equally important both for the understanding of Pascal's work and for that of the tragic mind in general. They are the text *On the Conversion of the Sinner* and the *Mystery of Jesus*.

The first of these lies between the two sides of the balance of the tragic mind described in the preceding chapter: without arriving at the refusal of the world within the world and at the wager on God's existence, it nevertheless—by the structure of its argument rather than by its explicit content—goes beyond the simple rejection of the world and the appeal to God. Placed between the inadequacy of the world and, if not the silence of God, at least His distance from man, the soul becomes aware of the limits imposed both upon itself and upon the world only by a constant movement to and fro between the world and God, an oscillation which is both perpetual motion and absolute immobility.

We have already seen how the *Conversion of the Sinner* begins: the 'knowledge and quite extraordinary view' which God 'inspires to the soul' make it 'look on both things and itself in a quite different way' and 'separate it from the world'. The soul is thus made to feel 'concern in the midst of the repose which it used to find among the things that caused it delight. . . . In the midst of this delight, it struggles with a constant feeling of disquiet, and this new, inner view which it has of things prevents it from finding the accustomed sweetness in the things to which, in earlier days, it abandoned itself with a full and overflowing heart.'

However, the fact that it is now cut off from the world does not lead to the soul to be able to rest in peace; in fact, it finds no other presence or delights which can replace those that previously gave it happiness. This is why it 'finds more bitterness in pious exercises than in the vanity of the world'. For, 'on the one hand the presence of visible objects touches it more than the hope of those invisible, and, on the other, the firmness of the invisible touches it more than the vanity of the visible. Thus, the presence of the first and the firmness of the second fight over the soul's affections, while the vanity of the first and the absence of the second excite its hatred. So that the soul is full of disorder and confusion'.[1]

---

[1] At the level of coherence reached by this text the impossibility of choosing between God and the world still presents itself as 'disorder' and 'confusion', since the author has not yet arrived at the clear and unequivocal attitude of refusing the world while remaining part of it, and of the generalised paradox.

Here, the manuscript breaks off. It is possible, and even probable, that this was merely an accident. Yet it must be noted how in keeping with its general atmosphere this interruption appears. For, as we have seen, the tragic mind sees neither transitions nor degrees; and when the manuscript breaks off on the words 'disorder and confusion', it provides a direct rendering of the language of a soul now fully conscious of the universal limit constituting tragedy: death.

'Heroes predestined to tragic death,' writes Lukàcs, 'are dead long before they physically die' (op. cit., p. 342). And, elsewhere, he adds, insisting upon the timeless quality of the tragic world: 'the present becomes secondary and unreal, the past threatening and full of danger, the future already known and long since unconsciously experienced'. As the text of the *Conversion of the Sinner* puts it, the soul 'considers things which are perishable as already corrupt or falling into corruption' and adds that 'the soul takes fright when it clearly perceives the annihilation of all it loves'.

'Hence'—continues the same text—'comes the fact that the soul begins to consider as nothing everything which will return to nothingness, the heavens, the earth, its own spirit and body, its relatives, friends and enemies; both wealth and poverty, disgrace and prosperity, shame and honour, scorn or esteem, humbleness or greatness of station, sickness or health and life itself all appear to the soul as empty and void of all importance.'

This clear view of the nature of things nevertheless brings the soul back to the confusion of the present world. 'It begins to be amazed at the blindness in which it formerly lived; and, when it looks upon the great number of people who still live in this way . . . it once again enters into a great and holy confusion of mind, profiting greatly from this very amazement.'

As the soul thus moves from the disorder and confusion which characterised it when it was placed between the vanity and presence of the world and the reality and absence of God, it thereby gains a clear understanding of the nothingness of all corruptible things— which have, in its view, already fallen into corruption. Yet it once again beholds a world of confusion and ambiguity, before its own demand for the absolute and for eternity enable it to see death and the nothingness of all corruptible things as a limit imposed upon all men. For, as the text *On the Conversion of the Sinner* again says,

even when the things of this world do have some solid value, their accidental loss or death itself will inevitably one day deprive us of them; so that if the soul has laid up for itself treasures of any sort, either gold, knowledge or reputation, it will inevitably one day lose the objects of its delight. Thus, even though they may satisfy it for a time, they will

71

not do so always; and even though they may procure the soul a real happiness, they do not give it an eternal one, since such happiness is inevitably limited by the course of man's natural life.

It is this new knowledge which finally separates the tragic soul from the rest of mankind. 'God, by a holy humility,' writes the text *On the Conversion of the Sinner*, 'lifts the soul above pride, so that it thereby begins to rise above the common run of men; it condemns their behaviour, detests the principles they adopt, and weeps over their blindness.' And, in so far as it draws away from men, so does the tragic soul begin to live in the sight of God. 'It goes in search of true goodness and comes to understand that in this three things are necessary: that this goodness must endure for as long as the soul itself; that it must not be taken from the soul without the soul's consent; and that there should be nothing surpassing it in beauty and loveliness.'

With this new awareness, the soul nevertheless thinks once again of the world that it has forsaken, and sees that 'in the love which it bore the world, it found in its blindness that there was nothing more desirable than the world. But since it now sees that this world cannot last as long as the soul itself, then it knows that this world is not the sovereign good'.

This ends the first part of *On the Conversion of the Sinner*, the section dealing with the relationship between the soul and the world; the second part deals with the relationship between the soul and God.

Conscious now of its own essence, and living solely in order to seek out the supreme good, the soul knows that the things of this world 'will not satisfy it', and, consequently, 'looks elsewhere'.

And, knowing by a wholly pure light that this supreme good can be neither in itself nor outside itself, nor in the things which are set before it, begins to seek for it above.

This ascent is so eminent and transcendent that it does not stop at the heavens, since these cannot satisfy the soul; neither can it find what it seeks in any created thing, nor even among the angels or the most perfect beings. It goes beyond all creatures, and can halt the progress of its heart only when it arrives at the very throne of God, where it begins to find rest.[1]

---

[1] I must here briefly discuss the notes which Brunschvicg gives on this passage, since they illustrate two typical and striking examples of the type of misunderstanding most to be avoided.

The first of these is easily dealt with. On the phrase 'by a wholly pure light' Brunschvicg writes: 'This "pure light" has wholly intellectual connotations; it means that absence of any form of obscurity and of any reason for doubt which characterises the obvious nature of truth.' It is impossible to think of any interpretation that is more at odds with the meaning of Pascal's work. Human reason, human intellect, can never in Pascal's view offer clarity or self-evident truth, and

But the God which it seeks, whom it comes to know 'by reason helped by the light of Grace', and who is the only true good, remains deaf to its appeal.

For although the soul does not yet feel the delights with which God rewards consistent piety, it is nevertheless aware that there is nothing

---

especially when what is at stake is a religious conversion and the existence of God. It is, in my view, obvious that this 'wholly pure light' can come only from Divine Grace, which reveals itself not to reason but to that faculty of charity which surpasses the intellect, and which is not an intellectual light but an illumination of the heart. (A little later on in the same text Pascal himself speaks of 'reason helped by the light of Grace'.)

The second type of misunderstanding is less immediately obvious and therefore more dangerous. Speaking of the passage dealing with the elevation of the soul up to God, Brunschvicg speaks about 'degrees' and quotes two lines from, respectively, Voltaire and Leconte de Lisle: 'Beyond all Heavens, the God of Heaven dwells' and 'Unto the stars, unto the angels, unto God'.

I shall not deal with this rather odd way of bringing together Pascal, Voltaire and Leconte de Lisle, and shall deal directly with the problem created by this interpretation. The line from Leconte de Lisle does in fact express the idea of a gradation, since one definitely has the impression of passing upwards from one to the other of the three elements enumerated. Now, in my view, the same image has in Pascal an exactly opposite meaning, that is to say a complete absence of any idea of gradation. Instead, there is an absolute gulf between, on the one hand, created beings, who are all equally inadequate, and, on the other, God Himself, who is absolute and perfect. I shall try to analyse this difference in more detail.

The first thing to be noted is that Pascal (if, indeed, he is the author of the text) limits the idea of elevation to that of a purely spatial ascent. The soul, which has sought the Sovereign Good in those things which are 'in it, outside it and in front of it' has found this good neither 'in itself nor at its side'; thus, after having exhausted what we might call the horizontal directions, it moves towards the vertical, towards the idea of going up. Here, the image necessarily becomes dangerous and full of potential ambiguity. Ordinary language gives the idea of ascent not only a spatial but also an ethical sense. Those things which the soul encounters in its ascent—the heavens, angels, saints—are certainly beings that the believer conceives as existing in a certain spatial order, but also as being placed in this order precisely because of an ethical gradation. Did Pascal accept this idea? In my view, he did not, for this would not only amount to a complete contradiction of the ideas in the *Pensées* but would also go against the actual meaning of this text, which seems specifically to exclude it. Leconte de Lisle puts the same word in front of each of the members of his phrase, and thereby seems to assimilate them to one another. He thus gives them the same positive value, and even goes so far as to indicate the idea of an ascent which is total, spatial and human at one and the same time. Pascal, on the other hand, suggests exactly the opposite. Certainly, he assimilates the heavens, angels and the most perfect beings, but he does so in a purely negative manner, indicating that they are all equally devoid of value and contrasting them with the only real value, which is God. Thus he writes that the soul 'can find what it seeks . . . neither in any created thing, nor even among the angels or the most perfect beings'; that it 'does not stop at the heavens' but halts 'only when it arrives at the very throne of God'.

This is not all. Pascal here tells us why the heavens, the angels and the most perfect beings are inadequate, and he does so in the very same words that he had

73

more loveable than God'. The soul is conscious of the abyss which cuts it off from God. 'Thus it reduces itself to nothing, and, since it can neither conceive a sufficiently low idea of itself nor a sufficiently high idea of this sovereign good, it tries yet again to bring itself down to the final depth of nothingness, by looking upon God as living in immensities of space whose extent it never ceases to multiply.[1]

The soul chooses to live eternally in the eye of God and 'to be eternally grateful to Him'. It is also 'full of shame at having formerly preferred so many vain things to this divine Master; and, in a spirit of repentance and regret, it appeals to His pity to prevent His anger'.

It asks God 'that He may be pleased to lead it to Him and to show it by which path to come'. For the soul which now lives only in and for the quest of God 'aspires to reach Him only by means which comes from God himself, since it would have Him alone as its way, its aim and final end'.

Conscious of the vanity of the world, of the unbridgable gulf which separates it from Him, the soul understands at one and the same time both the exclusive value of God and the fact that it cannot reach Him by its own strength. And since God remains hidden and never speaks openly to the soul in an explicit manner, it will never know whether God will help it and come to its aid, whether He will guide its steps, or whether He has already condemned it to damnation. The text concludes with the following words:

> The soul then begins to know God, and seeks to arrive in His presence; but since it does not know which path to take, nor if it is acting through a sincere desire to know Him, then it acts as someone who has lost his way: it seeks counsel from those who have passed this way before, and who have a perfect knowledge of it. . . .
>
> It thus recognises that it should worship God as one of His creatures, give thanks to Him as a man endebted, satisfy Him as guilty, and pray to Him as poor.

[1] Which immediately reminds us of the passage in fragment 72 (E.390) on the two infinities.

---

used to explain the vanity of the world. He even uses them in a more definite and radical manner, writing that the things of this world 'will not always satisfy the soul' that even the heavens 'cannot satisfy the soul', and indicating that this is even now the case. Would it not therefore be forcing the text to make it put the heavens higher than this world?

I should add, in conclusion, that the words 'begins to find rest', used to speak of the soul that has now arrived before the throne of God, seem to me to express the idea that the soul had found nothing earlier than might satisfy it, and also to suggest that it has still not yet finally achieved repose.

This is all really a continuation of what I have already said: the tragic mind recognises only the categories of 'all or nothing', with no degrees or intermediary stages, and therefore is completely opposed to any idea of mysticism and spirituality.

'The wisdom of the tragic miracle,' wrote Lukàcs, 'is a wisdom of limits'. The final words of the text *On the Conversion of the Sinner* are, as we have seen, that the soul knows itself as 'endebted, guilty and poor'. There is a clear similarity between the two texts, but what I find still more remarkable in the text which I have just analysed is the constant movement to and fro, which nevertheless seems motionless and outside time, the dialectic of the thesis and antithesis which makes the converted soul turn to the world, find it unsatisfying, turn again from it towards the only true god, understand the essential qualities of this, turn again to the world to see that these qualities can never there be realised or brought together and, understanding the radical and unacceptable inadequacy of all that is earthly and perishable, rise up again to the throne of God. And, once it is there, the soul again becomes aware of the equally impassible chasm that separates it from its only value, of the fact that God is permanently absent in his continual presence. It is for this reason that the soul finds its only rest in uncertainty and its only satisfaction in perpetual seeking. The constant relationship between tragic man and the absent and present God of tragedy is expressed in the words which, because of their extreme importance, I have kept to the very end: 'to desire God is indeed to possess Him'.

Few more perfect expressions have been given to the nature of tragic tension, of the perpetual movement from being to nothingness and from presence to absence. It is a movement which, because it is eternal and instantaneous, never goes forward, since it is outside time, the only realm in which there is progress and retreat.

In addition to the content of the different passages (whose meaning, like that of any other tragic text, is relatively autonomous) the very structure of *On the Conversion of the Sinner* throws much light upon the nature of the tragic mind. I hope that this analysis will enable us to reach a better understanding of the other great tragic text of Pascalian[1] literature, the *Mystery of Jesus*.

Before discussing it, however, I must deal with a possible objection which I have already encountered when talking with supporters of the traditional interpretation of Pascal's work.

In my view, the *Mystery of Jesus* should be read as the expression of the tragic mind. At first sight, however, it is a close textual commentary on the Biblical texts describing the passion and death of our Lord. Many passages which might otherwise be interpreted as an expression of the tragic vision are in fact only slightly modified

[1] I use this expression because it is not absolutely certain that Pascal is the author of the text *On the Conversion of the Sinner*. On the other hand, he certainly did write the *Mystery of Jesus*.

versions of the Biblical text. If this is the case, is it not wrong to attribute tragic characteristics to a text which is quite simply and straightforwardly Christian? Do we not distort Pascal's ideas in reading the *Mystery of Jesus* as a tragic text?

There is certainly something in this objection. There is no doubt that Pascal never wanted to be anything but a faithful and orthodox Christian, and that, far from being merely an outer garment for his thought, Christianity is intimately linked to its very essence. What we must ask, however, is: Exactly what kind of Christianity was it in which Pascal so sincerely believed? For from the standpoint of a scientific historian of ideas, there is no doubt that the Christian thought of Saint Augustine is essentially different from that of Saint Thomas, which, in its turn, is different from that of Molina, and so on and so forth. There are many kinds of Christian thought, and they can all, more or less, argue that they are faithful to the Christianity of the Church and of the Revelation. Certainly, by its idea of a God who dies but who is immortal, and by the paradox of a God made man, by its idea of mediation and by its insistence upon the folly of the Cross, Christianity is particularly susceptible to a tragic interpretation. It is still true, however, that for social and historical reasons, this interpretation has not occurred very frequently. It is also true that, although faithful to certain passages of the Scriptures, the tragic interpretation is nevertheless obliged to take these out of context and neglect a number of other texts, especially those which speak of the manifest presence of God.

This is why, in my view, Pascal was already putting forward a particular interpretation of the Scriptures, and was giving them a tragic meaning, by choosing to discuss the two passages in which Christ is supremely alone, the Garden of Gethsemane and the Cross. This is even more significant when we look at the actual passages on which Pascal chose to comment, and compare them with those that he left on one side. His text certainly conforms very closely to the two similar accounts given to us by Mark and Matthew, but it is worth noting that both Evangelists present us with texts that can be interpreted in a tragic manner. They differ in this respect from Luke —whose Gospel Pascal nevertheless used—in that Luke includes a passage which definitely contradicts any tragic interpretation, telling us (xxii. 43) that Christ was not alone on the Mount of Olives but that God sent a messenger to comfort him: 'And there appeared an angel unto him from heaven, strengthening him.' Most significantly, the *Mystery of Jesus* makes no mention of this transcendence of the tragic vision by divine intervention.

Similarly, we know that Pascal also used the Gospel according to Saint John to compose the *Mystery of Jesus*, since it is the only one of the four Gospels which he specifically mentions.[1] But whereas in John there is no tragic content in the account of the Agony in the Garden and of the crucifixion—he misses out the *lama sabachthani* of Matthew and Mark, and the forsaking of Christ by God which, in the *Mystery*, becomes his 'anger', and makes the solitude of the Mount of Olives a prayer which speaks constantly of the glory of Christ and of the blessèd nature of the disciples—nothing of this more comforting element appears in the *Mystery of Jesus*. In fact, we even find two texts which explicitly contradict it,[2] and we also notice that Pascal has selected the only fragment of Saint John's Gospel which, taken out of context, can have a tragic meaning, and has incorporated it in tragic form in one of the *Pensées* (fr. 906, E.705). Indeed, there is an obvious similarity between John xvii. 11 and the text of fragment 906, which demands that man should live in the world 'without love or attachment' (Cf. John xvii. 11–16).

All this seems to me to support my contention that the *Mystery of Jesus* is not a direct reproduction of the Gospels, but a tragic meditation on them.

However, before I begin the actual analysis of the text, I should like to clear up another problem which concerns not only Pascal but also the tragic mind in general. In fact, the tragic mind comes to think of God in two distinct ways: as God, and as Mediator. It sees God as a hidden reality, to whom the whole of man's life is devoted—'Whether I am alone or in the sight of man' writes Pascal in fragment 550 (E.748), 'God watches and judges all my actions, and to Him have I dedicated them all'—but with whom it has no immediate and direct relationship, and whose very existence it is unable to prove. As I have already several times remarked, the tragic mind sees God as a practical postulate or as a wager, but not as a theoretical certainty.

However, the tragic mind also entertains another and different relationship with the Mediator, a being who is absolutely alone, wholly true and wholly real, and who links God to man and man to God. Being both man and greater than man, the mediator both creates and affirms by his conscious faith, by his postulate and by his wager, the eternally unprovable nature of God. The human mind knows this mediator in the most certain and immediate fashion possible; indeed, it does more than know this mediator, it is him. Between the tragic mind and this mediator there is a relationship of complete participation and even of identity, whether the mediator assumes for the atheist the form of an incarnate idea or of an idealised

[1] John xxiii. 4.
[2] 'There is nothing in common between me and Jesus Christ the Righteous' (cf. E.739), and 'To Me be the glory, not to Thee, miserable worm of the earth'.

man, or whether he takes on for the believer the form and figure of the Man-God. This relationship, however, has nothing to do either with the idea of mystical participation, since, far from leading to ecstacy, it creates and maintains the clearest and most rigorous conceptual awareness, or with that of communion, since it enables man neither to transcend his loneliness nor to reduce the tension of the tragic mind. As an atheist, Lukàcs expressed this idea of the mediator by the image of the brothers, by the quest for the same stars by people who are nevertheless neither friends nor companions; as a believer, Pascal expressed it in the extraordinary text known as the *Mystery of Jesus.*

This relationship of sharing and identity makes it impossible for man, in so far as he really is a man—that is to say, as he goes beyond himself to live within the sight of God—to know himself except through his knowledge of the Mediator. 'Not only do we not know God but through Christ Jesus,' writes Pascal, 'but it is only by Christ Jesus that we know ourselves. It is only through Him that we know life or death, for outside Him we know neither what our life is, nor our death, nor God, nor ourselves' (fr. 548, E.602).

It is important to note, however, that while Christianity tends to bring together the two concepts of God and of the Mediator in the person of Christ, the tragic vision tends to separate them from each other. The tragic development of Pascal's own ideas also led him to make more of a distinction than we find in most Christian texts between these two characteristics of the person of Christ. We can see this in fragment 552 (E.752), which clearly separates the tragic, human figure of Christ on the Cross—a figure visible to all men— from the divine but hidden figure of Christ in the tomb,[1] which is visible only to saints. We also see it in the following passages from the *Mystery of Jesus*: 'There is nothing in common between God and man, or between Jesus Christ the righteous and my sin. But He was made sin through me and for my sake; all your stripes have fallen upon Him. He is more abhorred than I, yet, far from hating me, He is honoured that I should go to His help.

'But He has cured Himself, and thus will He certainly cure me.'

---

[1] Cf. *Tomb of Jesus Christ* (fr. 552, E.752). Jesus Christ died, but was seen to die, on the cross.

> He was buried by none but saints.
> He worked no miracles in the Tomb.
> None but saints enter into His tomb.
> It was there, and not upon the Cross, that Jesus took on new life.
> This is the last mystery of the Passion and of the Redemption.
> On earth, Jesus had no place to lay His head but in the tomb.
> His enemies ceased to persecute Him only in the tomb.

These lines contain, either explicitly or implicitly, all the elements which enable us to understand the relationship between the tragic mind and its exemplary incarnation, the Mediator. At the risk of seeming pedantic, I will now try to bring out these elements.

(i) The first words remove any possibility of confusion between God and the Mediator.

(ii) The Mediator closely resembles the tragic man, and He is in fact the hypostasis or underlying essence. By the existence of the human condition, the Mediator has become sin, and needs human help.

(iii) But the help that man can bring Him is naturally not immediate and direct. There are several sentences in the *Mystery of Jesus* which express this idea most clearly. "Christ will be in torment of death until the very end of the world. For all that time we must not sleep.' 'Christ tears himself from his disciples to enter into the agony of death; we must tear ourselves from those nearest and dearest to us if we are to imitate Him.'

'To imitate', 'to march under the same starry vault.' This is the only help, and the only kind of relationship, that can possibly exist between tragic minds, a relationship which, by laying stress upon their loneliness, enables them to transcend it.

(iv) However, this help which each tragic mind can offer its fellows while at the same time pursuing its own course in no way changes the fact that each soul can save itself only by its own endeavours. Christ 'cured Himself'.

(v) Lying behind the whole of the text is the implicit idea that, by healing himself, Christ will also heal men; but this cure will be at the same time just as much the result of each man's own efforts, the work of his own conscience and his own free will as of Christ's intercession. If there is a complete absence of any relationship between tragic man and Jesus Christ the Righteous, there is, on the other hand, a positive and symmetrical relationship—that is to say a mutual one—between tragic man and Christ crucified, between such a man and Christ suffering and dying to save humanity.

It is these five points which show us why no other text could offer us a better understanding of the tragic soul than the *Mystery of Jesus*. Tragic loneliness is not sought for or welcomed; on the contrary, it springs from the inability of the world even to listen to the sound of a voice speaking genuinely of essence.

'Christ prayed to men and was not answered.' 'Christ seeks at least some consolation from his three closest friends, but they are asleep; He begs them to watch a while with him, but they leave Him with complete indifference, having so little compassion that it cannot keep them even for a moment from their sleep. And thus was Christ foresaken, left alone before the anger of God.' 'Christ seeks company and consolation among men. This happens only once in His life, I think. But He receives no comfort for His disciples are sleeping.'

'This happens only once in His life, I think.' These words, from the *Mystery of Jesus*, are especially important in this context. Pascal knows that this is a unique and exceptional moment in the life of Christ as told in the Gospels. But this unique and exceptional moment is the only one which he, Pascal, can understand, because it is one which he himself lives and experiences at every moment in his life. When He feels himself alone and exposed to God's anger Christ is, in Pascal's view, living out the truth of the human condition at an exemplary level.

When Christ is 'alone and exposed to God's anger', when his disciples are sleeping and cannot hear Him, when those who can hear Him can help Him only by remaining awake and undergoing the same suffering. He is living outside time, cut off from both past and future. As I have already said, the tragic mind does not recognise the existence of time, and this is the true reason for the observance of the three unities in Racine's plays. Since the future is a closed door and the past has been abolished, the tragic mind sees only two possibilities before it, nothingness or eternity.

Since it has achieved its essence, the tragic soul can imagine no further change or transformation, for, in the world of tragedy as in the world of rationalism, essences are unchangeable. The only danger of which the soul is constantly afraid—but which, in so far as the soul is really tragic, will never become a reality—is that of leaving behind it the world of essences and going back to the ordinary, everyday world of compromise and of relative values.

The tragic mind lives so much outside temporality that Pascal, in the *Mystery of Jesus*, situates at exactly the same moment in time the two separate incidents which he takes from the Gospels: the desertion of Christ by his disciples, on the Mount of Olives, and the forsaking of Christ on the cross by God, the cry of *lama sabachthani*. This was in no way an arbitrary or an accidental identification: for the tragic mind, in fact, every moment in life mingles with one single moment, that of death. 'Death is an immanent reality, indissolubly linked with all the events of his existence,' writes Lukàcs of the tragic hero, and Pascal expresses the same idea in a different and more powerful way when he writes: 'Christ will be suffering the torments of death to the very end of the world; for all that time we must not sleep.'

In this eternal and intemporal moment which lasts to the very end of the world, tragic man remains alone, doomed to be misunderstood by sleeping men and exposed to the anger of a hidden and an absent God. But he finds, in his very loneliness and suffering, the only values which he can still have and which will be enough to make him great: the absolute and rigorous nature of his own awareness and his own ethical demands, his quest for absolute justice and absolute truth, and his refusal to accept any illusions or compromise.

Small and wretched by his inability to attain real values—wholly true truth and completely just justice—man is nevertheless great through his ability to think and be aware. It is this which enables him to detect all the inadequacies and limits of everything which is or might be in the world, to be constantly unsatisfied by any of them, and to accept no form of compromise. It is an idea which Pascal frequently repeats in the *Pensées*: 'Man's true vocation is clearly to think; for in this lies his whole dignity and worth. And his duty is to think correctly' (fr. 146, E.226). 'Man is but a reed, the feeblest in nature. But he is a thinking reed. And even if the universe were to crush him, he would still be nobler than what kills him, since he knows that he is dying and the universe knows nothing of the advantage which it has over him' (fr. 347, E.391).

It is in the light of these and many other texts expressing the same idea that we should interpret one of the most important sentences in the *Mystery of Jesus*: 'Christ is completely alone on earth, not only without anyone to feel His suffering or share it with Him, but alone also in his awareness of it. He and the heavens are alone in knowing that this suffering exists.'

In the perspective of tragedy, clarity means first and foremost awareness of the unchangeable nature of the limits placed on man, and of the inevitability of death. There is no possible future reality for man in history, and his greatness can lie only in the conscious and willing acceptance of suffering and death, an acceptance which transforms his life into an exemplary destiny. Tragic greatness transforms the suffering which man is forced to endure because it is imposed upon him by a meaningless world into a freely chosen and creative suffering, a going beyond human wretchedness by a significant action which rejects compromise and relative values in the name of a demand for absolute justice and truth.

In His passion, Jesus suffers the torments which men inflict upon Him. But when He undergoes the torments of death, He endures the sufferings which he inflicts upon Himself: *turbare semetipsum*. It is agony imposed not by a human but by an almighty hand and one must be almighty to bear it. . . .

He prays only once that this cup should pass from Him, and even

81

then He prays with submission; but twice He asks that it may come if it must. . . .[1]

When Christ prays, He does not know what the Father's will will be, and He fears death. But once He knows this will, he goes forward to offer Himself freely to it.

There is thus an absolute difference between the suffering undergone by a man who does not rise above the level of a brute beast, and the suffering which the Man-God both wills and accepts. For by this very act the Man-God saves the values and dignity of humanity.

> Christ is in a garden. Not of Eden where Adam sinned and was lost, and together with him all mankind, but in a garden of agony, where He saved both Himself and the whole of mankind.

The relationship of tragic man with other men is twofold and paradoxical. On the one hand, he hopes to save them to carry them with him, to keep them from sleeping and to raise them to his own level. And, on the other, he is aware of the great gulf which separates him from them and accepts it. He thus leaves them to sleep, since they do, after all, form part of that universe which, even if it were to crush man, would know nothing of what it did.

> While His disciples were sleeping, Christ accomplished their salvation. The same did He for all the just while they too slept, both in the nothingness which preceded their birth, and in the sins which followed it. . . .
>
> Christ, seeing that all men, and even those friends chosen to watch and pray, have forsaken Him, grows angry, not on His own account, but on that of the peril to which these men are thus exposed. And He warns them for their own good and for their own salvation, with a tenderness which is full of love for them in the midst of their ingratitude, telling them that the spirit is willing but the flesh is weak. . . .
>
> When He finds them sleeping yet again, and sees that neither His nor their own thoughts have kept them awake, He does not, in His goodness, disturb them again. But He leaves them to their rest.

In the last analysis, Christ's acceptance of reality, his '*Yes*' to fate extends not only to his own suffering and to his sleeping disciples, but also to the whole of the universe which crushes him.

> Christ sees in Judas not his enmity, but the order of God whom He loves and He so little notices Judas that He calls him friend. . . .
>
> If God were to give us masters with His own hand, then how willingly ought we not to obey them. Necessity and events are infallibly such masters.

[1] It is scarcely necessary to point out that there is a qualitative and not merely a quantitative difference between the 'once' and the 'twice'.

But whatever tenderness tragic man may feel for other men, the gulf between him and them has become unbridgeable. Tragedy, Lukàcs said, is a game played for one spectator, for God. And Pascal writes that:

> Christ tears Himself from His disciples to enter into the agony of death. We must tear ourselves from those nearest and dearest to us if we are to imitate Him. . . .
> Christ, seeing all His friends asleep and all His enemies awake, commits Himself entirely to His Father. 'Lord, I give you all.'

What, however, is this demand that tragic man can never satisfy in the world, and which causes him to place himself entirely in God's hand? What can he hope for from a silent and hidden God? As I have already said, this demand is for unity and for the synthesis of opposites. It is a demand for totality. This is why, in the *Mystery of Jesus*, the divine promise is expressed under the form of a promise to overcome a fundamental duality—for Christian ideas in general and, in the seventeenth century, for almost any set of ideas—between the soul and the body. Here, this separation becomes a symbolic expression of all the dualities and alternatives which make up human life in this world, and the answer proposed in the *Mystery of Jesus* is that they should be joined together in immortality.

Nothing on this earth, in fact, can prevent all physical things from dying, and this death is irredeemable. This is why tragic man can never accept existence in this world, for he can accept neither perishable things nor the partial values implied in the separation of the soul from the body. His life is meaningful only in so far as it is entirely devoted to the quest for total and eternal values, and it is only when he is striving to achieve these that his soul 'goes beyond man' and achieves immortality in this world. But the soul is immortal only in so far as it is wholly and completely human, and goes beyond man in its quest for totality. Which means, in fact, that the demand of the tragic mind is that the body would put on immortality. The tragic soul is great and immortal only in so far as it seeks union with passion and so on and so forth. Tragic faith is, above all, faith in a God who will one day bring into being the creature known as total man, having both a soul and a body which are immortal.

'Doctors will not heal you, for you will eventually die. But I will heal you and make your body immortal. . . .

'Endure the chains and slavery of the flesh. For in this world I will free you from spiritual bondage.'

The soul has now broken with the world and placed itself out of time, so that all it now knows is its own desire for the divine presence and the prayers which it makes. Thus, it thinks neither of the moment that has just passed nor of the moments to come. 'If you think that you will do such and such a thing which you have not done, you are tempting me rather than testing yourself. For I will do it in you if it comes to pass,' writes Pascal in the *Mystery of Jesus*. And the word 'future' occurs only once in the whole of this text, and then to express the idea that the future does not differ from the present and should not be distinguished from it: 'I must add my wounds to His and join myself to Him, and He will save me as He saves Himself. But I must not add to these wounds in the future.'

However, we must not misunderstand either the way in which tragic man breaks with the world or his total surrender to the will of God. This brings about neither a mystical ecstasy nor a feeling of repose comparable to that promised by a spiritual experience conceived on the Augustinian pattern. For if the soul gives itself over entirely to God this God never gives himself over entirely to the soul. This is paradoxically brought out in the highly significant text which Pascal wrote in order to express the idea of the total and universal presence of God: 'I am present for you through My word in the Scriptures, through My spirit in the Church, and through the inspiration that I have accorded; I am present by My power in the priest and by My prayer in the faithful.' For, in spite of Pascal's intention and apparent meaning, this text fits in with almost all those where he tells us that God is eternally absent in his perpetual presence.[1]

'I am present through My word in the Scriptures'—certainly, but we must be able to read and understand this word. And the Jansenists, Pascal among them, are more aware than any other Christian group that it is not enough to read the Scriptures—which are accessible even to the ungodly and to sinners—to be able to understand the divine voice and become one of the elect.

'Through My spirit in the Church.' But, here again, the Jansenists know that the real church, with its terrestial head, the Pope, does not always incarnate the divine spirit. Pascal himself once indicated his position, after the publication of the Bull in which Alexander VII condemned the 'Five Propositions' of Jansenius, when he said, in words which are terrible for any Christian or Catholic conscience, that the 'Disciples of Saint Augustine' were *'between God and the Pope'*.

'Through the inspirations that I have, and by My power in the

---

[1] This is one of the few texts which, taken out of context, might apparently justify the type of interpretation given to it by Monsieur Laporte. But Pascal is at the furthest possible remove from a Thomistic attitude. He never ceased to affirm the need—doubtless one condemned to remaining eternally unsatisfied—for an immediate and individual knowledge of truth.

priests.' This is a more serious and real—but, like the Church, the priest can claim divine inspiration only if he is a true priest, and does more than merely wear the habit and perform the functions.

To find God, we therefore need to distinguish the real meaning of the Scriptures, to identify the real Church and the real priests from the worldly clerics and time-servers. And the real tragedy of Pascal's position lies in the fact that the believer cannot rely upon his own powers of judgment to do this. No real Jansenist ever believed that he could find truth by trusting in his own reason or intuition, or by submitting himself wholly to the Church. The believer finds God 'through prayer', by the need which he has of God, and by his decision to devote the whole of his life to His service.

But—and the text *On the Conversion of the Sinner* has already shown this to be the case—the believer finds no joy through his prayer. God does not reward him for his piety, for if He were to do so He would be present by His rewards and not through the prayer of the believer. Moreover, the believer can never know whether the path he takes will lead him to God or whether it will bring Him back to the world. The only thing of which his prayer reassures him is of his own need, his own demand for the divine presence, and of the infinite distance which still separates him from God, and which, for the whole of his earthly life, will continue to separate him from the only Being for whom he really lives. The tragic believer lives constantly in hope and never in certainty. This hope, born of the clash between the demand for authentic values and the eternal silence of God and of the world, is, first of all, that the complete reversal of values which his tragic awareness has brought to his soul shall become a reality. Secondly, however, it takes a different and more important form and one which, because of the nature of the tragic experience, is essentially paradoxical. It becomes a confidence in God which can exist only in the form of man's anxiety and concern; and this anxiety is the only form of certainty open to the man who seeks faith and repose.

This is why I shall conclude the first part of this study by quoting two passages which are central to any understanding of the *Mystery of Jesus* and of Pascal's work as a whole. In their brevity, they contain the essence of the long analysis which I have just given of the nature of tragic man. The first expresses the relationship between tragic man—the man who, in Pascal's words, 'goes beyond man'—and the world. This world, we should remember, has become completely unreal and non-existent in his eyes, while at the same time remaining the only sphere in which he can act.

'We must do small things as if they were great ones because of the majesty of Christ Jesus who does them in us and who lives our life.

And we must do great things as if they were small and easy, because of His omnipotence.'

The second expresses the unique relationship between man and the God who is always present and always absent, the God of whom *On the Conversion of the Sinner* said 'to desire Him is to possess Him', and yet whose presence for the soul can be nothing more than a wager. The search for this God is permanent and permanently present in every thought and action of the soul, and this text of Pascal expresses the very essence of tragedy, the message which the soul thinks that it permanently receives from the voice of the hidden and invisible God. It is a message which, when the soul doubts, gives it certainty; when it is afraid, gives it hope; when it is wretched brings it greatness and when it is weary rest. A message which amidst the perpetual anxiety and anguish of the soul, is the only valid and permanent reason for confidence and hope.

'Be comforted. You would not seek me if you had not already found me.'

PART TWO

The Social and Intellectual Basis of the
Tragic Vision in Seventeenth-century
France

PART TWO

The Social and Intellectual Basis of the
Tragic Vision in Seventeenth-century
France

V

WORLD VISIONS AND
SOCIAL CLASSES

THIS second section will inevitably be very different from the first, both in its subject matter and in its greater aspiration to scientific accuracy. I shall therefore begin by explaining why I have not adopted one of the two traditional ways of studying literature and philosophy: that of separating the works from any discussion of their economic, social or political context, or, alternatively, of merely selecting certain arbitrary elements of this context and emphasising them in a spectacular manner. The aim of this chapter is to justify the existence of Chapters VI and VII, and to do so in the name of a scientific study of history and literature. The sole aim of these two chapters will be to indicate the enormous amount of information that we still need to collect if we are to base our knowledge of Pascal and Racine on a really firm footing.

My starting point is this: facts concerning man always present themselves in a significant pattern, and this pattern can be understood only by explaining how it came into being. Any genuinely scientific study of this pattern must be based upon a knowledge of this development.

In studying Pascal's argument of the water, as in studying Kant's practical postulates and Marx's socialism, I shall adopt this method for both theoretical and practical reasons. Theoretical because it seems to me to be the only one which enables us to see the facts as they really are; and practical because it enables us to justify science by showing how it has a human function. It will also help us to justify man by the image which so exact a knowledge gives us of him.

This is a truly Marxist starting-point, since it implies that practice and theory, sociology and ethics, cannot be separated. Indeed, there cannot, in Marxist thought, be a separation between ethics and sociology, for the simple reason that Marxist value judgments try to be scientific and Marxist science to be practical and revolutionary. It thus abolishes the false distinction between ethics, conceived of as existing outside social structures, and sociology, conceived of as dealing solely with ethically neutral social facts. Thus, when we come to a really scientific study of human life, it is misleading to talk of science, on the one hand, and ethics, on the other. What we must find is an attitude which understands social reality as a whole, in an organic unity which links together both values and actions.

In my view, this attitude can best be described by using the word faith—provided, naturally, that we dissociate it from any exclusively religious connotation. There is, in fact, no other term which so accurately indicates how values are embedded in reality and how many different layers and levels reality reveals when judged by reference to values.

It is certainly dangerous to use the word faith, since Marxist thought has, from the nineteenth century onwards, been strongly opposed to any revealed religious truth and has always, in spite of the fact that it has both integrated and sublated both Augustinianism and eighteenth-century rationalism, maintained a strongly rationalistic bias. Marxism is, in this respect, the inheritor of the development of the Third Estate, of its still recent revolutions and of its doubtless real opposition to Christianity.

This is why the use of the word faith in a Marxist context gives the impression that an attempt is being made to 'Christianise' Marxism or to introduce transcendental values into it. This is, however, a completely false impression. Marxist faith is faith in the future which men make for themselves in and through history. Or, more accurately, in the future that we must make for ourselves by what we do[1], so that this faith becomes a 'wager' which we make that our actions will, in fact, be successful. The transcendental element present in this faith is not supernatural and does not take us outside or beyond history; it merely takes us beyond the individual. This is sufficient to enable us to claim that Marxist thought leaps over six centuries of Thomist and Cartesian rationalism and renews the Augustinian tradition. It does not, of course, do this by reintroducing the same idea of transcendence, but by affirming two things: that values are founded in an objective reality which can be relatively if not absolutely known (God for Saint Augustine, history for Marx); and that the most objective knowledge which man can obtain of any historical fact presupposes his recognition of the existence of this reality as the supreme value.

[1] There is a considerable difference between the way in which the two ideas are formulated. 'Men make' implies that an attempt is being made to see human history from outside. 'We make' indicates the practical perspective implied by faith and action.

There is, however, yet another major difference between the two positions. The God of Saint Augustine exists independently of any human wish or action, whereas the future which we have in history is created by our actions and desires. What characterises Augustinianism is the certainty that God exists, whereas what characterises Marxism is the wager which it places upon the reality that we must create. Pascal's position lies in between the two: he wagers that God exists, and that He is independent of any human will.

The fact that Marxism begins with a wager and that it sees this as a necessary precondition for any knowledge should come as no surprise to anyone familiar with scientific habits of thought. Surely the physicist and chemist set out from the wager that the general physical laws do in fact apply to the particular sector of reality which they happen to be studying? And surely in the seventeenth century—and even more so in the thirteenth—this wager was a new and quite extraordinary thing?

Thus, any objection to the scientific use of the dialectical method must attack not the principle of the wager itself but the actual kind of wager used. There are two main differences between the type of wager adopted in the physical sciences and the type adopted in the sciences which study man. In physics and chemistry the initial wager belongs wholly to the realm of theory, and is linked to practice only in the subordinate domain of technological application. In the sciences concerning man, on the other hand, this wager belongs both to the realm of theory and to that of practice. The second difference is that, in the human sciences, this wager contains an element of finality which is not to be found in the physical sciences, where the initial wager may either give rise to a general law or simply to a number of statistical observations.

In view of the remarkable results obtained by the physical sciences, it is not surprising that the first attempts to conduct a scientific enquiry into social life should have imitated the example which they offered, and have made the same clear distinction between value judgments and empirical observations. However, it is by no means certain that this imitation is entirely valid, and the fact that these methods succeeded in the physical sciences only makes it more probable that they will be equally effective in the sciences of man. The final proof can only be found in the individual studies which are finally produced, but we can nevertheless begin by clearing the ground and dealing with certain prejudices.

All we need to do is to examine how the great tragic thinkers, such as Pascal and Kant, or the great dialectical thinkers, such as Marx and Lukàcs, go about their work. We note first of all that both Pascal and Kant begin by showing that no empirical observation can show that the initial wager is either right or wrong.[1] For example, they both set out from the problem of the existence of God, and both establish the fact that no scientific proof can be regarded as valid either way. Similarly, Marx and Lukàcs know that there is no empirical way of proving that progress existed in the past and that it will continue in the present, since the two fundamental values which they recognise—progress and socialism—are linked to specifically human actions and are dependent on them.[2]

'The question of whether human thought can discover objective truth is not a theoretical but a practical one. It is in what he does that man must prove truth, that is to say reality and power, what lies behind his thought. The discussion on whether thought is real or unreal remains a purely scholastic one as long as it is isolated from practice.' 'Social life is essentially practical. All the mysteries which divert theory towards mysticism find their rational solution in human activity and in the understanding of this practical reality.' 'Philosophers so far have merely interpreted the world. We must change it.'[3] It would be just as absurd for Pascal or Kant to deny the existence of God on empirical grounds as it would be for Marx to use the same criterion to assert or deny the validity of the idea of progress or of humanity's march towards socialism. In both cases the initial wager depends upon an act of faith, on 'reasons of the heart' in Pascal, or the validity of reason in Kant and Marx, a wager which goes beyond and integrates theory and practice.

Thus, no basis can be found in the physical sciences for affirming or denying the existence of God or of historical progress. All they can show is that the practising scientist does not need such concepts, unless, of course, he is talking about the history of physics or chemistry, for in that case he is dealing with human events.

The fact, however, that the validity of the initial wager in dialectical or tragic thought can be neither proved nor disproved does not of itself make this wager a necessary one to make. Could we not study man by the same methods as those used in the physical sciences?

It is here that, after having established that there is no contradiction between the idea of the wager and the findings of empirical science, the champions of tragic and dialectical thought can move on to the offensive. Pascal and Kant try to show that it is impossible to

[1] Cf. Kant, *Critique of Practical Reason*, Vol. V, pp. 120 and 146 of the German Academy edition. Cf. p. 224 and p. 227 of Lewis White Beck's translation, University of Chicago Press 1949.

[2] Whenever mention is made in this book of Georg Lukàcs as a Marxist thinker and theoretician, I am referring to the book which he published in 1923 on *History and Class Consciousness*, and that he now disowns and declares to be 'wrong and out of date'.

[3] Second, eighth and ninth of the *Theses on Feuerbach*.

give an account of human reality without assuming either that God exists or that the practical postulates are valid, while Marx and Lukàcs go even further. They argue two things: that any theoretical statement about the structure of reality implies an initial hypothesis, which may or may not be a wholly conscious one, and which I have called the wager; and that, in the human sciences, we come up against immediate contradictions if we make this wager the assumption that reality is governed by absolutely deterministic laws.

Thus, any discussion about methodology in the human sciences needs to clear up two points. First of all, accepting the idea that all sciences do set out from a wager, should we make this explicit, or should we leave it implicit and try to compose an objective and impartial study free of all value judgments? Secondly, if it is to be made explicit, which particular wager is most likely to lead to the most objective and adequate knowledge of human reality?

The answer to the first question would seem quite obvious, were it not for the fact that rationalists so frequently base their objections to any tragic or dialectical thought on the rejection of the notion that science is based upon a wager. When, in Pascal's imaginary dialogue, the free thinker reproached the believer with having made 'not this particular choice, but any choice at all; for the person who says "heads" and the person who says "tails" are both equally at fault. The correct thing to do is not to wager at all,' Pascal had his reply ready: 'Yes,' he said 'but you must place your bet. This is not something which you can choose either to do or not to do, for you are already embarked.' Similarly, in the *Theses on Feuerbach* Marx insisted on showing that any state of awareness must inevitably have some practical intention, and that 'we are embarked' from the very moment that we make the most insignificant act of perception: 'Feuerbach, not satisfied with abstract thought, also appeals to sensible perception, but does not look upon sensibility as such as forming part of the practical activity of man's senses.'[1] Now this linking up of intention

[1] Fifth thesis. It may perhaps be objected that if Marx is right this is valid not only for the humanities but also for chemistry and physics as well. Of course! And this is why I said earlier that any science sets out from an initial wager. However, the wager which lies at the basis of the physical sciences—the wager on the causal or statistical rationality of the sector of the universe which we are studying and which we can in no way influence, and on the technical utilisation of the laws governing it—is today universally accepted, and, moreover, has been confirmed by so many technical triumphs that only philosophers, who are at the periphery of such activity, ever think of calling it into question.

The comparison may appear rather a far-fetched one, but it might nevertheless be suggested that the person who would perhaps correspond to Pascal's unbeliever —that is to say, someone who doubted the rational and comprehensible character of the physical universe—no longer exists. It is therefore no longer necessary to write apologies to convince him.

with awareness always implies an end; or, as Piaget would say, aims at establishing a balance—which means, when this end becomes conscious of itself, either implicitly or explicitly accepting a scale of values.

As far as the second question is concerned, it should be noted that any wager that absolutely fixed but non-finalistic laws exist in the domain of the humanities or science is both contradictory and impossible. This is because in the humanities man is at one and the same time both the student and the object of study, so that any law discovered by the student must also be held partly to apply to the student himself. The denial of meaning and finality in the human sciences either involves the denial of the meaning and finality of scientific thought itself or the creation of an unjustifiably privileged status for the scientist. When we look at this problem from the point of view of action—and, as we have seen, all ideas are linked to action and, in the realm of the human sciences, are part of the action itself—we see that Marx's critique of determinism in the *IIIrd Thesis on Feuerbach* is equally valid for any purely scientific concept of man which sees him as bound by certain laws.

> The materialistic doctrine which maintains that men are the products of circumstances and education, and that, consequently, different men are the product of different circumstances and of a different education, forgets that it is men who change these circumstances, and that the educator himself needs educating. This is why such a doctrine inevitably tends to divide society into two parts, of which one is placed above society.

The coincidence between a change in circumstances and a change in human activity can be rationally understood only as an activity which effects a qualitative change in reality (*umwälzende Praxis*).

Thus, any general hypothesis about social life must include both the seeker himself and the kind of investigation he is carrying out. That is to say, it must imply: (*a*) man's practical activity; (*b*) the meaningful character of this activity; (*c*) the possibility that he may either succeed or fail. These three characteristics cannot apply to activity in the physical sciences, since not only is the seeker himself not part of the investigation or object he is studying, but this object is created by taking away everything which might be the subject matter of thought or action.

Thus, if we are to arrive at a scientific knowledge of man, we must begin by the wager, or assumption, that history has a meaning. We must, therefore, set out from an act of faith, and the phrase *Credo ut Intelligam* provides a common basis for Augustinian, Pascalian and Marxist epistemology, in spite of the fact that in each of these three cases the 'faith' is of a very different type. In the case of Augustine it is the certainty that God exists; in that of Pascal the wager on His existence; and in that of Marx the wager that history does have an immanent meaning.

As far as the method to be used by dialectical study is concerned, this initial presupposition implies certain consequences. One might, for example, presuppose that history is meaningful only when looked at as a whole, and that each individual series of events, taken by itself, appears meaningless. In that case we should be well advised to give up any hope of carrying out a scientific study of man. It is impossible for man to know history as a whole, both because his interpretation of the past always depends upon future events, and because he himself is inside history and therefore cannot achieve the 'objective' knowledge available to the physical scientist. Thus, if it is assumed that the elements which he is about to study are completely meaningless when abstracted from the whole movement of history, then it is impossible for him to gain any knowledge of them at all.

Thus, when we study man, we must assume both that history itself has a meaning and that individual series of events which constitute history are meaningful as well.

There are several different ways of considering such a relationship between the parts and the whole.[1] My initial assumption, however, is that as we fit the individual series of events into a wider context, we little by little improve our understanding both of the whole and of the parts. Any valid object of study in the human sciences has a complete though relative meaning which is brought out when this object is seen against a wider pattern.

However, this leads up to still greater problems. For even if this initial hypothesis is valid, we still cannot be certain that the events which we have chosen to discuss are in fact meaningful. We might have taken our slice of reality at a completely wrong level, and selected events which cannot be analysed except in terms of a causality applicable to the physical but unsuited to the human sciences. The only way to avoid this danger is to concern ourselves with events that we can see to possess an overall meaning, and it is the quest for this meaning which is the first concern of the scholar.

Thus, in my view, the greatest danger threatening serious scholarship lies in the uncritical acceptance of traditional fields of study, for

[1] The most important hypothesis would be that of a totality that was meaningful as a whole, and made up both of a certain number of relative wholes—among which would be historical research itself—and of a certain number of non-significant elements that do not form part of any relative significant whole. This is not only a possible but also a probable hypothesis. However, the choice between it and the one put forward in this chapter could be made only on the basis of a fairly large number of actual research projects completed.

these may eventually show themselves to be quite meaningless even after the most careful and painstaking examination. For example, Marx points this out in *Capital* when he gives it the subtitle of *A Critique of Political Economy*, and shows that this science falls into error and produces ideological deformations when it studies the production, circulation and distribution of goods instead of dealing with the production, distribution and circulation of exchange values. Similarly, most modern universities continue to study subjects which are really non-existent because they have been badly selected—as, for example, the histories of philosophy, of art, literature and theology, etc.

Take, for example, the history of philosophy, since it is essentially with philosophy that I am concerned. Most great philosophical doctrines are, it is true, significant wholes. But, when they are looked at together—or even in groups—they lose this character. This does not mean, however, that the historian of philosophy should simply limit himself to the admittedly useful task of describing the nature and significance of one philosophical system. Neither should he try to fit it into the unreal and badly conceived pattern known as the 'history of philosophy', and this is why I cannot but agree with the criticisms made by Monsieur Gouhier of the contradictory nature of the concept of 'the history of philosophy'.[1] The historian should always, in

[1] I refrain from quoting Monsieur Gouhier in the text because of a difference in our terminologies which might lead to misunderstanding. In the sense in which I speak of 'world vision', he keeps to the German terms 'Weltanschauung'. For him the expression 'world vision' is a conceptual tool which fulfils a different, though entirely legitimate, function. If I understand him rightly, he uses it to place a philosopher's or writer's work not in the context of the consciousness of a social class but in that of the individual's consciousness and biography. No doubt such a concept is indispensable. I have repeatedly said that when one is studying a set of particular facts, specifically in the form of a collection of texts, one has to place the facts in the widest possible number of significant wholes. A philosophical work should be interpreted and its origin explained as the expression both of the consciousness of a social class and the consciousness of the individual. There are, however, two points on which I differ from M. Gouhier. The first is a question of practice rather than principle, and may in the last resort be decided by the nature of the topic, the stage which the enquiry has reached and, above all, by the personality and aptitudes of the investigator. The question is whether it is easier to proceed from the individual and the individual's consciousness to the consciousness of the class, or vice versa. In principle, and subject to exceptions, the latter procedure is the one I think generally valid. Monsieur Gouhier, though he does not explicitly say so, seems to prefer the former. The second point seems to me to go deeper. M. Gouhier gives the word 'essence' a rationalistic and a-temporal meaning. This leads him to construct abstract essences with concrete particular facts. Accordingly, he distinguishes between, on the one hand, 'The history of philosophies', which can be either the description of several essences or the study of an essence, and, on the other, the history of individual world visions, which he rightly sees as a conceptual instrument for studying individual facts. This leads

my view, see any philosophy within the context of a significant whole made up either of a general current of ideas or of a relatively homogeneous social, economic or ideological group.

Organic analogies are very dangerous—and Marxist thinkers have always underlined this fact—but there is one which may be useful here to illustrate my meaning. A physiologist may study the brain merely as a biological structure, but so long as he remains on this level his research will be incomplete. Any continuation will involve extending the area of his investigations to include the whole of the nervous system of which this brain forms part. It is no use his just comparing this brain to a number of others, each of which is studied in isolation from the total organism of which it forms part. If he

---

him to write, in *L'Histoire et sa philosophie* (pp. 149–50), that: 'Continuity and essence belong to the same pattern of thinking, for in the philosophy of philosophy according to Dilthey, as in the phenomenology of Max Scheler, or in Marxist humanism, the Weltanshauungen represent types of essences: the concept of "world vision", on the other hand, has been defined in such a way as to provide a useful tool for studying a history without essences.'

'Thus the different problems raised by the history of philosophy,' continues Monsieur Gouhier, 'may perhaps be regarded as constituting really only one problem: is it legitimate to link together two types of research which differ so completely from each other and talk about 'The history of philosophy'? The two disciplines covered by the title seem to me to be sufficiently different to exist separately side by side.'

For dialectical thought, however, there is no opposition between essences and individual facts, since, by its very nature, an essence is an individualising concept. Essence is the insertion of abstract individual facts into a coherent whole, by a process of conceptualisation which makes them concrete; and, indeed, for the biologist and the psychologist, the individual is himself a relative whole having both structure and meaning. In order to go from the text to the individual author, Monsieur Gouhier feels the need for an instrument which is similar to the Weltanschauung: the individual world vision, which enables him to fit the individual element—the text—into the whole made up of one person's life and mode of thought. Like Monsieur Gouhier, I hold that the two forms of history—individual and social—must exist side by side and that they do in fact throw light on each other, but it does not seem to me that one can talk about a difference of nature between the two. If we give the word 'essence' a rationalistic and a-temporal meaning, then they are both 'histories without essence'; if, on the other hand, we give it a dialectical meaning they are both histories which try to incorporate essences, and which do so in so far as they succeed in transforming partial and abstract facts into concrete ones. Obviously I agree with Monsieur Gouhier in holding that, in the last analysis, there is no valid history either of 'philosophy' or of 'philosophies', and that we must combine the study of a particular set of ideas as an expression of one person's life and thought with an examination of the history of the society in which those ideas occurred, seeing them both as the product of one individual and of the degree of consciousness attained by a particular class. Any attempt at writing history presupposes the existence of significant structures, and these can be made up either of individuals, classes, particular philosophical systems or works of literature. Philosophy, however, is taken as a whole and in isolation, does not constitute such a structure.

does this, he will be concerned not with the brains as biological structures but simply as structures of a similar type. This is merely an example, since no serious biologist has ever thought of doing anything so absurd, but it does illustrate a number of weaknesses in the modern approach to the humanities. There are, in fact, a number of traditional historians of philosophy who do just this, and as long as they are concerned with just one philosophical system they are, admittedly, still dealing with a valid subject in a valid manner. But when such an historian goes straight from Kant to Hegel, for example, and makes no attempt to fit each philosopher into his artistic and literary environment—and, above all, into the social and economic circumstances in which he lived—then he is making the same mistake as the biologist who tries to study a series of brains without fitting any one of them to the body of which it formed part. He will fail to explain anything at all and will simply provide a series of more or less accurately described but nevertheless isolated and lifeless examples. This is why there are a number of very good histories of philosophy which tell us about the structure of each particular philosophical system taken individually, but very few—perhaps none at all—which show any organic link between the different systems. This is because, if this link does exist, it joins together not the philosophical systems as such, but the civilisations of which these systems were parts, and which must themselves be studied as social, economic and cultural wholes if this link is to be discovered.

However, the history of philosophy must always set out from what individual philosophers actually wrote. I have already said in Chapter I, and I shall again argue the point in the course of this book, that it is not every writer whose works can be looked on as constituting a significant whole. Only a very small number of highly privileged writers have this distinction, and it is precisely because their work has such a coherence that it possesses artistic, literary or philosophical worth. The concept of 'world vision' is an extremely useful one in any attempt to discover this meaning, and I shall here be using it to study the work of Pascal and Racine. However, in addition to actually describing their work, it is also very useful to discover in what circumstances this work came to be written. It is rarely sufficient to concentrate solely on the personal life of the writer in question, and the scholar must often deal first of all with the general climate of thought and feeling, of which the philosophical system or literary work provides the most coherent expression. This climate—which can be called group consciousness, or, in certain definite cases which I shall be describing later, class consciousness—can also provide an historical explanation as to why a particular work came to be written in its present form.

This climate does itself constitute a significant whole, but one which is among the least autonomous and the most difficult to describe. The historian must deal with it, but he must also go further: he must examine and elucidate this climate against the background of the wider economic, social, political and ideological life of which it forms part.

These are my reasons for maintaining that any scientific study of a literary work of a philosophical system must involve linking it with the social, economic and political life of the group whose world view or vision it expresses. Although a more precise definition of what constitutes such a group could be left to be determined in each particular case, it is nevertheless possible to make the following observation: any valid literary work of philosophical system takes in the whole of human life. It thus follows that the only groups whose world view is likely to find expression in such works or systems are those whose ideas or activities tend towards the creation of a complete vision of man's social life; and that, in the modern world—from the seventeenth century onwards—artistic, literary and philosophical works have been associated with social classes and closely linked with the consciousness which each class has of itself.[1]

It will now be clear that, in my view, any valid and scientific study of Pascal's *Pensées* or Racine's tragedies will be based not only upon a careful analysis of their structure but also upon an attempt to fit them into the intellectual and emotional climate which is closest to them. That is to say, they should first of all be studied as part of the whole movement of Jansenism, seen both as a spiritual and as an intellectual phenomenon, and then in relation to the economic and social life of the group or class which found its expression in the Jansenist movement. This book is thus a study of Racine and Pascal with special respect to the expression which Jansenism gave to the social, economic and political situation of the *noblesse de robe* in seventeenth-century France.

This study will consist of three stages, but these will not necessarily be presented in chronological order. In the first text will be seen as the expression of a world vision; in the second this world vision will be more closely analysed as constituting a whole made up of the intellectual and social life of the group; and in the third the thoughts and feelings of the members of the group will be seen as an expression of their economic and social life. It must be fully recognised, however, that this is a schematic view of a much more complex phenomenon, and that there are many other causes which contributed to the significant whole constituted by Pascal's *Pensées* and Racine's tragedies. The historian must never forget these, and he must remain equally

[1] Cf. Lucien Goldmann, *Sciences humaines et Philosophie*.

aware of the fact that the social, economic and political activity of the class he is studying can be understood only by reference to the social, economic and political activity of the whole of the society of which this class forms part.

There are, however, two contradictory qualities to this programme: dialectically, it is indispensable; from a practical point of view, however, it can never be carried out at the present moment, even if only a provisional degree of accuracy were required. In fact, as we go up the scale—from the work to the vision, from the vision to the class and from the class to society as a whole—the same difficulty keeps recurring: the facts to be taken into account become increasingly numerous, so much so that it is almost impossible for one man to deal adequately with them.

This difficulty is particularly important when the dialectical method is being used, since this method begins by rejecting any *a priori* principles. If we are to bring out the essential qualities of a meaningful structure, we must examine all the individual empirical facts[1] which go to constitute it. And it is only when these facts are known and assimilated that we can begin to see what kind of conceptual pattern they form. Of course, the scholar does not set out from an absolute zero, since not only the work itself, but also the climate of opinion which it reflects and the society in which it came to birth have already been analysed by earlier students. The main difficulty lies in the fact that their analyses have set out from a number of different points of view. And since very few of them reflect dialectical considerations, their usefulness is rather limited.

What I mean is this: the dialectical historian is trying to find the whole structural meaning represented by each of the individual wholes which I have mentioned—the text, the world vision, the social class. (Whether he finds it or not has nothing to do with the success or failure of his initial wager.) And it is a fact that, up to the present, most scholars have not given serious attention to this question, either with regard to the texts or to the intellectual and economic life of the society. This is particularly true of the traditional methods still used for studying the history of the seventeenth century, and which are in sharp contrast to those used by historians such as Mathiez, Pirenne, Lucien Febvre, Daniel Guérin for the period of the French Revolution. Thus, in studying Jansenism it has not been enough for me

---

[1] The research may, of course, subsequently lead to a modification of the actual subject matter and its reconstitution in a different form, from which certain original elements have been eliminated but to which others have been added. There is always a dialectical relationship—what Piaget called a 'return bounce'—between the activity of study and research and the object that the scholar began by examining.

simply to read a certain number of historical works and to think about their content. I have had to go back to primary sources and think out the whole question of the relationship between literature and society in a new perspective.

This was fortunately possible in so far as the texts were concerned, but was much more difficult when I was dealing with the intellectual and emotional climate of the various Jansenist groups under discussion.

It is important to note that my initial hypothesis that Jansenist sensibility existed as a significant structure did enable me to discover a set of facts and documents, now published elsewhere, which has changed our traditional picture of the 'Friends of Port-Royal'.[1] This discovery is not a decisive proof that my method is a valid one, but does nevertheless create a strong presumption in its favour. But even as far as this second level is concerned, there is still much to be done in the direction of a serious exploration of the life and thought of the Jansenist group.

Less progress, however, could be expected in the study of the link between the social and economic circumstances of the *noblesse de robe* and its ideas and feelings. Too much work still has to be done on this question, which is nevertheless essential to a real understanding of Pascal and Racine.

However, rather than simply neglect this problem or simply accept at their face value the results of the remarkable studies that already exist, but which have been written from entirely different points of view, I have devoted a chapter to it. It immediately follows this one, and is to be looked upon simply as a hypothesis based upon a number of facts noted in the work of other historians and in the *mémoires* of the seventeenth century. I will, however, make one or two remarks about the probable validity of this hypothesis, while insisting on the fact that it can be finally confirmed or rejected only by a detailed and thorough examination of primary sources.

It is based first of all on the fact that it provides an explanation for a whole collection of apparently unrelated facts. One should, it is true, always mistrust the apparent elegance which over-simplification offers in intellectual matters, but when an hypothesis offers a new explanation for a phenomenon it should perhaps first of all be appreciated for its possible fertility. Thus, if we take into consideration my contention that a change in the balance of power between the different social classes in seventeenth-century France did have repercussions in the field of theology and philosophy we shall very probably be able to see connections which earlier scholars have missed.

[1] Cf. *Correspondance de Martin de Barcos*, edited by Lucien Goldmann (P.U.F., 1955).

Moreover, if it brings together within the framework of a single significant structure a large number of facts taken from widely different sources, all foreign to the realms of the original hypothesis, then this hypothesis becomes worth noting and exploring. I have given a brief account of it in Chapter VI, and future dialectical historians will either confirm or invalidate it by looking further into the subject, if it interests them. As far as Chapter VII is concerned, this again is not intended as an exhaustive study, but, taken side by side with the correspondence of Barcos that I have published elsewhere, it does throw a certain light both upon the group of the 'Friends of Port-Royal', and, implicitly, upon the genesis of the *Pensées* and of Racine's tragedies.

I should like to conclude by answering a criticism made of one of my earlier books. I have been attacked for trying to fit Kant into a highly schematic and over-generalised conception of the history of Western bourgeois thought. My reply is that schematisation is an inevitable stage through which any serious dialectical study must pass, since the dialectical historian is compelled to fit any significant set of facts into a totality which he is obliged to sketch out in a schematic manner. If he had been fully acquainted with this totality, then he would have concentrated on describing it, but the problem would then only have been postponed and would have recurred at a higher level. But there is nothing contradictory or reprehensible about this, for this schematisation is by no means arbitrary. The dialectical historian sets out from the significant structure of the facts which he intends to study, and aims to fit this structure into another and more comprehensive one that will provide an historical framework for it. This, alone, limits the possible schematisations open to him, especially when one considers that he must constantly defer to the facts themselves, which have almost inevitably been brought to light by studies written from a completely different standpoint from his own. Any serious historical study must, in my view, have two starting-points: the facts themselves, and a conceptual schematisation intended to make them comprehensible. And it is in the very nature of dialectical thought that, as more facts are revealed, they will modify the original schematisation. This is an inevitable characteristic of any serious dialectical research, which must always be moving from the whole to the parts and from the parts back to the whole again. These are the principles governing the present work, and which provide a framework that, in the very nature of things, will always remain provisional, since the discovery of each new fact will inevitably modify the initial hypothesis.

VI

JANSENISM AND THE 'NOBLESSE DE ROBE'

THE hypothesis put forward in this chapter is based upon two main sources: a number of *mémoires* and first-hand accounts concerning events in the seventeenth century, and the conclusions reached by historians who have studied the subject for a long time.[1] However fragile

[1] Since I shall be making special reference to the work of Monsieur Roland Mousnier, I think it is my duty to point out that he himself—while admitting that there are several genuine problems that historical research should try to clear up —has expressed a number of reservations about the interpretation that I have given of these facts, and which I have tried to illustrate by quoting from his work.

The passages in question deal first of all with the relationship between the Royal Councils and the *Cours souveraines* under Louis XIV, with the discussions about the measure known as La Paulette at the beginning of the seventeenth century and with the variations in the price of the various legal charges in the course of the century. Except for certain detailed problems that I shall be discussing in the course of this chapter, Monsieur Mousnier's reservations seem to be concerned essentially with the following points:

(*a*) He does not consider that we can say definitely that royal absolutism grew in importance between the middle of the sixteenth and the seventeenth century, and he is particularly critical of the three stages of growth that I have tried to distinguish in a purely hypothetical manner; he does not accept that each of these marked an advance when compared to the previous one.

(*b*) He sees the statement that the alliance between the Crown and the Third Estate against the feudal Nobility was the main driving force in the evolution of the French state for several centuries as a gross over-simplification; he points out that the king often allied himself, according to occasion and opportunity, with the minor nobility against the more powerful nobles and against the towns, or with one particular vassal or clan against another.

(*c*) He denies that any specific relationship has been sufficiently established between Jansenism and the *Noblesse de robe* and points out that a large number of members of the *Cours souveraines* sided with the Jesuits, or at least were hostile to the 'Friends of Port-Royal'. For him, the fact that Jansenism developed among the legal profession results primarily from the fact that lawyers constituted, in seventeenth-century France, the most highly cultured section of society, and con-it might appear, this hypothesis has at least the merit of offering the

---

sequently the one whose members had the most intense intellectual and ideological interests.

I have too high an opinion of Monsieur Mousnier's abilities as a scholar not to have given very careful consideration to these objections. Moreover, if I continue to maintain that my hypothesis has something to be said for it, this is not because I claim to have as great a knowledge of the facts as a professional historian. On the contrary, I have just emphasised the extent to which Chapter VI, which takes in the widest totality that will be dealt with in this book, is necessarily a hypothetical sketch, based upon an inadequate empirical foundation.

However, it seems to me that the difference between Monsieur Mousnier and myself is essentially one of perspective. As far as the facts themselves are concerned, Monsieur Mousnier is certainly right. What we must do, however, is weigh the relative importance of these facts, and this raises the problem mentioned in the very first chapter of this book: that of the difference between abstract empirical facts and their concrete significant essence. I do not, of course, maintain that I have here managed to establish the concrete essence of a particular historical evolution, since I do not know enough to go beyond a mere hypothetical sketch. However, it does nevertheless seem to me that the following points are quite valid:

(*a*) The intensity of the conflicts between the *parlement* of Paris and the Crown (in so far as this can be deduced from the work of Monsieur Maugis) and the existence of the two civil wars of the Ligue and the Fronde do seem to me to justify the suggestion which I made as to the three stages of growth of royal absolutism.

(*b*) The occurrence in the middle of the seventeenth century both of the Fronde and of Jansenism seems to me to justify the suggestion that it was at this period that the conflict attained its maximum intensity.

(*c*) The very fact that the feudal nobility finally disappeared and became transformed into a *noblesse de cour*, while at the same time both the Crown and the Third Estate continued concomitantly to increase their power until the end of the seventeenth century, does seem to me to indicate that the alliance between king and commoners did constitute the essential phenomenon that should be distinguished from any alliances between the king and different goups of feudal nobles, and which thus remained, in the last analysis, purely secondary and episodic events.

(*d*) The interests of the legal nobility, and its relationship with the other classes in French society, do seem to me to make tragic Jansenism or active opposition into the only possible forms of consciousness available to it. Moreover, Jansenism seems to me to have constituted the only ideology that was peculiar to this nobility, since an attitude of active opposition corresponded, especially in the eighteenth century, to its tendency to follow in the wake of the Third Estate as a whole.

The fact that certain lawyers sympathised with the Jesuits does not, for me, constitute a decisive objection to my hypothesis, any more than the existence in our own days of numerous and powerful anti-Marxist trade unions proves the anti-proletarian nature of Marxist thought. An ideology never, in fact, affects more than a larger or smaller fraction of the particular class to which it corresponds, and it is often the case that this fraction is only a minority, and even a small one at that.

Finally, it seems to me that the following problem is to be found at the very basis of this difference of opinion between Monsieur Mousnier and myself: should one admit that everything is possible, or should we, on the contrary, set out from

only scientific[1] explanation for a number of political,[2] social and ideological events which deeply influenced French life, both materially
and intellectually, between 1637, the date at which the first 'solitary',
Antoine Le Maître, retired to Port-Royal (and 1638, the arrest of
Saint Cyran by Richelieu) and 1677, the date of the first performance
of *Phèdre*. In my view, these events are linked with the appearance
and development of an ideology which asserted that it is impossible
to live a valid life in this world—an ideology that constitutes a world
vision which I have called *tragic*.

Since men's awareness of what is happening always takes some
time to catch up with events, a further division can be made within
the period 1637–67. The social and political struggle goes from 1637
to 1669 (the date at which the *Peace of Clement IX* put a temporary
end to the struggles between the Jansenists and the Crown), while its
philosophical and literary expression goes from 1657 (the *Pensées*
were probably written between 1657 and 1662) to 1677.

There were, of course, other men who withdrew from the world
before Antoine Le Maître, but none who did so for such definite
reasons. Both he, and the many people who continued to follow his
example until 1669, not only refused any ordinary form of social life,
but any social function at all, even an ecclesiastical or a monastic
one.[3] It is for this reason that all the withdrawals from the world

---

[1] Explanations of a historical phenomenon by the 'pride' or 'obstinacy' of the
Jansenists, or by the 'resentment' or 'intriguing spirit' of the Jesuits or by a
'prolonged and general failure of the two sides to understand each other's point of
view', seem to me to be ideological explanations that are in complete opposition
to any scientific understanding.

[2] The word 'political' may give rise to a certain number of objections, since the
Jansenists always refused to take part in any activity in the 'polis'. But even when
we take this objection into account, this persecution still remains political when
one looks at it from the point of view of the authorities who attacked the Jansenist 'party'.

[3] 'I then saw,' writes Saint-Cyran, speaking of the conversion of Antoine Le
Maître, 'what advantage might accrue to me from this. So I did not trouble myself
with the fear of being too wise in the sight of God, not to say too timid, by

---

the hypothesis that social and historical structures always have a significance,
reject the idea of historical miracles and argue that Jansenism could not in any
case have occurred in sixteenth-century France because the necessary social and
economic infrastructure was lacking and that, consequently, if it appeared in the
seventeenth century, it was because such an infrastructure did then exist? I should
add that, even if this is the case, the only thing which can decide which is the
significant structure in any one particular case is empirical research.

I will, in conclusion, repeat what I have already said: that this chapter is only a
provisional hypothesis, which will doubtless be made more accurate, be modified
or even altered by subsequent investigations. Bearing in mind all these reservations, it still seems to be useful and even necessary to put it forward provisionally
in this book.

before 1638 are neither Jansenist nor tragic, and that, after 1677, no more authentic tragedies will be written until the end of the eighteenth century. There will, it is true, be grave, serious and sad plays, but none in which God alone is spectator, and it is only plays such as these that I shall call tragedies in this book. Between 1637 and 1677, on the other hand, there are innumerable examples of tragic vision in the history of the Jansenist group.

A problem thus arises for both the sociologist and the historian: what people formed this group and why? What was the economic, social and political infrastructure of the class from which the people came who made up what I am tempted to call the 'first Jansenism'—the Jansenism of Barcos, Mother Angélique, Pascal and Racine?

It has already been shown by most of the dialectical studies devoted to the history of ideas that cultural events of outstanding importance—such as the *Pensées* and Racine's tragedies—are rarely linked with obscure and secondary social movements. On the contrary, they are more frequently the expression of deep changes in the social and political structure of society, of changes which are therefore fairly easy to discover. Now, if we look at French society immediately before 1637 the first thing that we notice is the development of royal absolutism and of its most important instrument, the 'bureaucracy'[1] of royal agents closely linked to the central authority and completely dependent upon it.

The objection may, of course, be made that this growth of the king's power had been going on for a long time, and that it therefore cannot be used to explain a number of events which are as highly localised in time as those which concern us here. It should be remembered, however, that during the wars of religion in the sixteenth century the king's power had suffered a severe set-back, and that it had only just begun to regain ground after the coming to power of Henri IV in 1598. The first years of the seventeenth century thus form part of a development that had been going on for a long time, and

---

[1] I use the term 'bureaucracy' to describe all those who make an essential contribution to the running of a government or administration. The word thus implies no attempt to assimilate the members of the *Cours souveraines*, or the *commissaires*, to the bureaucratic apparatus of a modern state.

---

neglecting an important opportunity that was offered me of glorifying Him before the whole world, and thereby showing forth, by an authentic witness, that truth which I wanted to publish forth, in order to *show men of quality that there was, in the Church, a manner of conversion that differed from the one which they ordinarily followed* (Monsieur Goldmann's italics). And I considered that the means which God had offered me of teaching this truth to be so important that I would have thought myself a criminal not to have taken every opportunity to set up a public example of penitance in the person of a man whom everyone knew and esteemed in Paris' (*Oeuvres chrétiennes et spirituelles* (1679), Vol. III, p. 553).

which had just received a new lease of life. Moreover, the period 1637–77 constitutes the final, critical stage of a process that was to reach its highest point under Louis XIV, and then to decline under his successors.[1]

It is almost a commonplace to observe that the Capetian monarchy was transformed into the monarchy of the *ancien régime* by a continual struggle between the king and the feudal nobility. The king, however, had neither enough servants nor enough money and soldiers to fight against the nobility all by himself, and therefore had to depend upon the main ally that he could find: the Third Estate. The most important link between the king and the middle class was made up of the legal and administrative professions, whose members, living both in Paris and in the provinces, had originally belonged to the Third Estate and were still closely connected with it by family ties. They were faithful to the king by education, tradition and self-interest, and had—together, of course, with the army—become the essential administrative and governmental arm of the central monarchy. As a social layer, the legal and administrative profession represented the fusion between the Third Estate and the power of the king.

The extent of this fusion is indicated by the difficulty which historians have in describing the venality of legal offices during the sixteenth century. Were these offices actually sold, or were they merely exchanged for 'services rendered'? This is not, in fact, a very meaningful question, since one of the most useful ways of proving one's loyalty to the king was precisely to find him the money of which he always had such an urgent need. Moreover, even the sale of offices always took place within a fairly limited group of people who were faithful to the king, and was perhaps very similar to the system of recommendations and 'protections' essential to a modern bureaucracy. The sale of offices seems, in fact, to have become an economic institution only when it had also acquired a specifically political meaning, that is to say, when the alliance and solidarity between the king and his legal officers can no longer be taken for granted.

Similarly, the distinction between *officiers* and *commissaires*, which became essential in the seventeenth century, did not, in my view, present any real social antagonism in the fourteenth and fifteenth centuries, or even perhaps at the beginning of the sixteenth. (It is, of course, difficult to give any precise date where the whole process of development is so long and complex.) For example, there had been *Maitres de Requêtes* who, for a very long time, had gone on circuit

[1] Speaking of the reign of Louis XIV, Monsieur Méthivier wrote: 'The history of his reign is essentially characterised by the gradual taking over of power from the *compagnies d'officiers* by the *commissaires*, who were direct agents of the king' (H. Méthivier, *Louis XIV* (P.U.F., 1950), p. 50).

and who were obviously future *Intendants*. The important thing to discover is the date at which these judges became sufficiently numerous to form an organised body which opposed the activity of the *parlement*.

There are, in fact, as Monsieur E. Maugis has pointed out, three main stages in this development of royal absolutism.[1]

A. In the first the king was merely someone who happened to be more powerful than most of the other nobles (but not all of them), and also enjoyed the additional prestige which he drew from the support of the towns and of the Third Estate. At this stage the monarchy was indirect and feudal, and the system can be characterised in sociological terms by saying that there was no really dominant royal power.

B. In the second stage the king definitely acquires authority over the other nobles, basing it on the Third Estate and on the body of legal and administrative officers. This constitutes the limited monarchy of the *ancien régime*.

C. In the third and final stage the king becomes independent not only of the rest of the nobility but also of the Third Estate and of the *Cours souveraines*. He governs through his *corps de commissaires* by maintaining a balance of power between the different classes, especially between the nobility and the Third Estate, while at the same time justifying his power in the eyes of both classes by arguing the need for a central authority strong enough to put down popular revolts.[2]

---

[1] Cf. E. Maugis, *Histoire du Parlement de Paris de l'avènement des rois Valois à la mort d'Henri IV*, 3 volumes (Paris: Picard, 1913–16). On p. 12 of his preface, Monsieur Maugis, speaking of the functions of the *parlement* in the sixteenth century, writes: 'It was thus that this intermediary form of monarchial administration, which for a century and a half was to characterise the transition from the old, feudal royalty to the authoritarian type of government realised by Richelieu, was set up. Previously, the king had exercised his power indirectly, through the medium of the feudal system; now, he governed directly through the *Maîtres des Requêtes*, through what is known as government through office holders and through the *compagnies de justice et de finance*.'

[2] Monsieur Mousnier, *Histoire générale des civilisations*, Vol. IV. *Sixteenth and seventeenth centuries* (Paris: P.U.F., 1954), p. 160, observes that: 'peasant revolts, and even those of artisans organised in town guilds, were directed against the taxation system and not against the rich. Tax collectors are attacked, but not large town or country houses, and even when this does happen the properties which suffer most are those belonging to people who have made a rapid fortune out of the tax system. Revolts are directed against royal taxation.'

This is certainly correct. And it appears even more natural when one reflects that the absolute monarchy was based upon a policy of the balance of power, where no particular class was sufficiently attached to the Crown to be identified with it. In my view, however, these more or less permanent revolts by the people constituted a potential threat against every class which owned wealth—a threat which prevented these classes from carrying their opposition to the king too far.

The period 1637–77 is one characterised by the transition from stage A to stage B. Jansenism appears in its initial form during the transition from limited to absolute monarchy, when the king is in the process of transferring authority from the *officiers* and *Cours souveraines* to the *commissaires*. Thus, in order to understand how Jansenism was born and developed, we must study two particularly important features of the process: the organisation of the Royal Councils in the seventeenth century and the conflicts between the king and the *parlements*, especially the *parlement* of Paris. These features are not, of course, peculiar to the period 1637–67, since they form part of a historical process which went on for two centuries. What the historian and sociologist must do is to find some kind of order which governs the mass of information available to him—*édits bursaux*, creation of offices, remonstrances, *lettres de jussion*, registering of edicts on the king's express order, temporary or permanent commissions issued to his servants—and see what general principles govern it. The two features already mentioned provide a guide, and have been dealt with by a number of historians whose work I have consulted. These are, for the sixteenth century, the works of Edouard Maugis and H. Drouot; for the seventeenth century, and especially for the problems connected with the *Conseils du Roi*, those of Clément, Boislisle, Caillet, Chereul; and, above all, the excellent modern studies of Georges Pagès and Roland Mousnier.[1]

[1] I am also particularly indebted to the following works:

(*a*) E. Maugis, *Histoire du Parlement de Paris de l'avènement des rois Valois à la mort d'Henri IV*, 3 volumes (Picard, 1913–16).

(*b*) H. Drouot, *Mayenne et la Bourgogne*, 2 volumes (Picard, 1907).

(*c*) Pierre Clément, *Histoire de Colbert et de son administration*, 2 volumes (Paris, 1874); *L Police sous Louis XIV* (Didier, 1866).

(*d*) *Mémoires* de Saint-Simon, Ed. Grands écrivains de France, appendices by A. de Boislisle, Vol. IV, pp. 377–440; Vol. V, pp. 437–83; Vol. VI, pp. 477–513; Vol. VIII, pp. 405–45.

(*e*) Jules Caillet, *L'Administration de la France sous le ministère du Cardinal Richelieu*, 2 volumes (Paris: Didier, 1863).

(*f*) Adolphe Cheruel, *Dictionnaire historique des institutions, moeurs et coutumes de la France*, 4th edition (Paris, 1874).

(*g*) George Pagès, *La Monarchie d'ancien régime en France* (de Henri IV à Louis XIV) (Paris: Colin, 1928); *Les Institutions monarchiques sous Louis XIII et Louis XIV* (Paris: Centre de documentation universitaire, 1933). *Le règne d'Henri IV* (Paris: same publisher, 1934); *Naissance du grand siècle*; *La France d'Henri IV à Louis XIV* (collaboration with V-L. Tapié (Paris: Hachette, 1949).

(*h*) Roland Mousnier, *La Vénalite des Offices sous Henri IV et Louis XII* (Rouen: Maugard, 1946); *Les règlements du Conseil du Roi sous Louis XII* (Paris, 1949); *Sully et le Conseil d'Etat et des Finances, la lutte entre Bellièvre et Sully*. In *La Revue historique*, vol. 192 (1941); *Le Conseil du Roi, de la mort d'Henri IV à l'avènement du gouvernement personnel de Louis XIV*, taken from *Etudes*

Once the presupposition is granted that the intensity of the conflicts between king and *parlement* is an indication of the growth of royal absolutism, three main stages can be distinguished in the period leading up to 1637. They are: the reign of Louis XI; from Francois I[e][1] to Henri II; and from Henri IV to Louis XIII. Each successive advance of royal absolutism takes place on a level which is higher and qualitatively different from the preceding one.[2]

I shall pass over the reign of Louis XI, since the conflicts produced by his absolutism were not sufficiently important to disturb the peace of the kingdom.[3] The second two stages, however, each lead to a civil war: the struggle with the *Ligue*, and the conflict of the *Fronde*. Although these stages are similar, there are also important differences which must be borne in mind if we are to understand why only the latter gave rise to Jansenism.

During the religious wars of the sixteenth century the monarch came into conflict with a *noblesse d'épée* which was much more powerful than it was to become in the seventeenth century. While a majority had gone over to the Huguenots, there were still nobles—especially the more powerful ones—who joined the *Ligue*. At that time the monarchy was caught between two hostile camps, the first

[1] Maugis writes (op. cit., vol, I, p. 136): 'The reign of Francois 1[e] witnessed the first violent clash between king and *parlement*, but this had already been foreshadowed under earlier reigns. The first sign of rebellion against the exercise of arbitrary power occurred under Louis XI, and the conflict seemed to threaten to break out on a number of occasions under Louis XII. But neither side committed itself fully, the king being content to threaten and the *parlement* to give indications of discontent.'

[2] G. Pagès also refers on a number of occasions to the reigns of Francois I[e] and Henri IIe as periods that marked an increase in royal absolutism, an increase which was resumed, after the interruption caused by the wars of religion in the sixteenth century, under the second part of the reign of Henri IV. He writes that: 'Thus, once the wars of religion were over, Henri IV very quickly began to behave just as much like an absolute monarch as Francois I[e] or Henri II had done before him' (*Les Institutions Monarchiques*, p. 12). Cf. also *La Monarchie de l'ancien régime*, p. 3: 'One might say that no French king ever exercised more power than Francois I[e] or Henri II, and it was at the beginning of the sixteenth century that royal absolutism began to triumph.'

[3] As far as the great nobles and the aristocracy are concerned, their power, from the sixteenth century onwards at least, was too slight to enable them to constitute a threat to the monarch—as long, that is, as in the case of the wars of religion of the Fronde, they do not exploit a critical moment in the conflict between the king and the Third Estate or the king and his parlements.

d'histoire moderne et contemporaine (1947–48). *Histoire Générale des Civilisations*, Vol. IV. *Sixteenth and Seventeenth centuries* (P.U.F., 1954).

I have, of course, also studied a number of books on Europe in the seventeenth century. Since, however, these have been of a more general nature and have tended to concentrate more on foreign policy and military events, they have been of less immediate use.

made up of an alliance between certain sections of the middle class and a large part of the nobility, the second composed of an alliance between the urban middle class of several large towns and the more powerful of the rebellious nobles. On the other hand, the monarchy then found its natural allies in the *officiers* of the *Cours souveraines*, and a large number of bishops and episcopal officers who, since the Concordat of 1516, were one of the main sources from which the central royal bureaucracy was to be recruited.[1] By the time of the *Fronde*, however, the absolute monarchy had already made up its apparatus of *commissaires*, and transformed this into a separate social body, distinct from the *officiers* and in opposition to them. Moreover, since the idea of an absolute monarchy and of a balance of power between the different classes were practically synonymous, the king had, since the ascension of Henri IV, granted numerous economic and social advantages to the nobility, on the understanding, of course, that it would allow itself to be converted into a *noblesse de cour* and give up any attempt to be independent.[2]

This explains why the members of the *parlement* who, at the time of the *Ligue*, had been one of the main sources of support for the king, now began to turn against him. We can also understand why a section of the middle aristocracy, those who were to derive most profit from the king's new policy, adopted a much more passive attitude and even began to support the crown.

[1] I must mention the Concordat of 1516, which, by giving the king power to appoint bishops, marked an important step in the development of royal power. For a long time—and this was certainly still the case in Richelieu's day—the great ecclesiastical dignitaries, such as Sourdis, La Rocheposay, le Père Joseph and Richelieu himself, made up an important section of the apparatus of royal government. This enables us to understand (a) the determined and continued resistance of the *parlement* to the Concordat, and (b) the danger implicit in the Jansenist demand for a rigid separation between ecclesiastical functions, on the one hand, and any political, administrative or even social activity, on the other.

[2] According to H. Mariejol, *Henri IV et Louis XIII*, Vol. IV of Lavisse, *Histoire de France depuis les origines jusqu'à la Révolution*, the 16–17 million livres actually coming into the royal treasury in 1607 were shared out in the following manner:

(a) The royal household: 3,244,151.

(b) Pensions for the aristocracy (who are already acquiring the habit of living in this manner): 2,069,729.

(c) The army: less than 4 million.

In 1614–15, on the occasion of the last meeting of the Estates General before the Revolution, the actual royal income from taxation was 17,800,000 livres, and the pensions paid to the nobility 5,650,000 (cf. pp. 64 and 171).

According to d'Avenel, *Richelieu et la Monarchie absolue* (Paris: Plon, 1884), there were, between 1611 and 1617, nine great noblemen who, for themselves alone, received almost 14 million livres in the form of 'exceptional gifts', in addition to the money which they received for services rendered and for the maintenace of their soldiers (Vol. 1, pp. 407–8).

Both in the sixteenth and in the seventeenth century, the monarchy was saved by the divisions among its opponents, who were always much more hostile to one another than they were to the king. In peace-time it was these divisions which guaranteed the continued existence of the central authority—a fact which offers yet another proof of one of the most permanent of social laws: that the only difference between war and peace is to be found in the type of weapons used.[1]

As far as Jansenism is concerned, its birth round about 1637–38 coincided with the final stage in the advance of royal absolutism, that is to say the formation of the permanent bureaucratic apparatus which is essential to any system of absolute government. After a brief relapse—perhaps more apparent than real—at the time of the *Fronde* the formation of this bureaucracy led to the high-water mark of absolute monarchy in the reign of Louis XIV. Jansenism, born ten years before the *Fronde*, thus comes into being against a background of the decline in power and social importance of the *officiers*. Its birth also coincides with the period 1635–40, which marked a particularly acute stage in the relationship between king and *parlement*.

Two events of unequal importance for the historian took place during this period: the constitution of the small group of individuals who formed the first core of Jansenism, and the effect which this had in certain, easily definable sections of French society. Since so few people were actually concerned in the formation of this core—Saint-Cyran, Arnauld d'Andilly, the Bouthillier family, La Rocheposay and, perhaps, Antoine Le Maître—the first of these two events appears almost accidental and anecdotal, so much so that one is tempted to dismiss it as merely one of the many ideological incidents that accompanied the growth of state bureaucracy in France.

If, in fact, Jansenism sprang initially from certain legal circles, its first representatives—already listed above—actually formed part of a fairly narrow and clearly defined sector of the legal profession. They were what one might call potential candidates for the post of *grands commis*, potential political or ideological leaders of the central bureaucracy. This has been known for a long time, but new light has been thrown upon it by the excellent researches of Monsieur Orcibal and Monsieur Jacquard on Saint-Cyran.[2] Thus, we know now that Saint-Cyran and Arnauld d'Andilly were originally members of the

---

[1] Cf. Karl von Clausewitz: 'War is simply the continuation of policy by different means.'

[2] Cf. J. Orcibal, *Les Origines du Jansénisme*, Vol. II: *Jean Duvergier de Hauranne, abbé de Saint-Cyran et son temps (1581–1638)* (Paris: Vrin, 1947), and L. Jacquard, *Saint-Cyran, précurseur de Pascal* (Lausanne: *Editions de la Concorde*, 1944).

same group as Richelieu, Le Rocheposay, Bouthillier and, later, of
Father Joseph, who all intended to support one another in making
a political career in the world. Later on, for reasons which cannot be
clearly established (how, indeed, can one really distinguish jealousy
felt for a former friend who has moved far ahead of his contemporaries from the indignation felt by a Catholic on seeing the
Catholic king of France ally himself with the Swedish protestants?)
Saint-Cyran left Richelieu and went over to the opposition. He thus
became an ally of Bérulle, the Queen Mother, and the *Société du
Saint-Sacrement*, and a member of a group which, while in no way
denying that a Christian could take part in the life of this world,
simply supported a different policy from that of Richelieu, demanding an alliance with Spain and a determined fight against Protestantism both at home and abroad.[1] Thus, initially, and perhaps even up
to 1637–38, Saint-Cyran and Richelieu were divided not on the question of whether or not a Christian could take part in politics, but
simply on which particular policy he should support.

The death of Bérulle and the 'Journée des Dupes' led to the final
defeat of the 'Spanish' party. Nevertheless, Saint-Cyran remained
fairly close to Zamet, who was Bishop of Langres, the son of one of
the principal financial agents of Henri IV, and one of the leading
members of the *Société du Saint Sacrement*. It is true that, after the
death of Bérulle and the exile of the Queen Mother, the survivors of
the Spanish party were less concerned with offering an alternative
policy to that pursued by Richelieu and Louis XIII than with trying
to bring a Catholic and Christian influence to bear upon the internal
life of France.

Later, however—we do not know exactly when—Saint-Cyran began to adopt a different position, which was soon to give birth to the

[1] According to Monsieur Orcibal (op. cit., pp. 488–9), it was the influence of
Bérulle which played a decisive rôle in Saint-Cyran's life and the evolution of his
ideas. In my view, however, Monsieur Orcibal overestimates the importance of
the influence of Bérulle, and I prefer to consider Jansenism as having been born of
the third period in Saint-Cyran's life, during which he rejected any idea of any
valid participation of a Christian in the political life of this world. I also maintain
that, until 1662, Jansenism followed his example on this point. On p. 324 of the
work already quoted Monsieur Jacquard insists on the difference between Saint-
Cyran's views and those of Bérulle, and on the way in which the followers of
Arnauld tried to hide this difference in the edition which they prepared of Saint-
Cyran's letters.

In a private conversation Monsieur Cognet had indicated to me that, towards
the end of his life, Saint-Cyran came back to the idea that it was possible for a
Catholic to take part in political life and promote the interests of his faith. I find
this possible and even probable, but we shall have to wait for the publication of
the rest of Monsieur Orcibal's work before reaching a decision on this particular
question.

Jansenist movement. He argued that no true Christian, and certainly nobody in holy orders, could take part in political and social life.[1] (Here again, it is very difficult to discover whether this position was the result of the disappointment felt by Saint-Cyran when Bérulle's party was defeated, or whether it sprang from the influence of his nephew Martin de Barcos, who had become his secretary and collaborator in 1629.) However that may be, it was between 1635 and 1638 that the first important signs of what was to become Jansenism began to show themselves. In 1636 there is a split between the *Institut du Saint Sacrement*, grouped around Saint-Cyran and Mother Angélique, and its original creator and director Zamet. And, in 1637, Antoine Le Maître, a famous young lawyer who was already a member of the *Conseil d'Etat* and a protégé of the Chancellor Séguier, became the first of the *solitaires*. This was a spectacular event in itself, and was made even more so by the publicity which Antoine Le Maître gave to his friend's decision by writing an open letter to Séguier, copies of which were circulated in the various ecclesiastical and legal circles.

There is no better indication of Richelieu's political genius than the contrast between the relative indifference which he showed so long as Saint-Cyran remained a member of a hostile and probably unsuccessful group, and his concern when his opponent began to act in a different manner. Zamet and Séguier no doubt kept him informed of what was happening, and by 1638 Saint-Cyran was in prison in the Chateau de Vincennes. He was not to be released until after Richelieu's death.

Why was Richelieu afraid—for afraid he certainly was. This is indicated not only by his decision to have Saint-Cyran locked up and by his hesitation, in spite of the numerous interrogations of the prisoner by his best agents, Lescot and Laubardemont,[2] to bring him into open court, but also by his permanent interest in everything which Saint-Cyran did and thought, and his constant attempts to have him watched over by Arnauld d'Andilly and even by his own niece, the Duchesse d'Aiguillon.[3]

It was not, in my view, Saint-Cyran himself whom Richelieu feared,

[1] Cf. the remark in one of his letters (*Bibliothèque municipale de Troyes*, MS. 2. 173. Fol. 160): 'The true ecclesiastic has no greater enemy than the politician.'

[2] In 1634 Laubardemont was responsible for organising the trial of Urbain Grandier (in the course of which we also come across La Rocheposay, Bishop of Poitiers). Lescot was Richelieu's confessor.

[3] Cf. the very interesting book of L-F. Jacquard for further discussion of this point. Jacquard is a Protestant who, in spite of his admiration for Saint-Cyran, remains fairly hostile to Jansenism. He has thrown much light on the rather odd and more than slightly ambiguous rôle that Arnauld d'Andilly played during the whole of this period, being at one and the same time both Saint-Cyran's 'friend' and Richelieu's informer.

since he showed no concern at all when Saint-Cyran was one of Bérulle's followers and supporters. Saint-Cyran's opposition to the annulment of the marriage between Gaston d'Orleans and Marguerite de Lorraine, his views on the problem of attrition and contrition, mentioned every time this arrest is discussed and which seem, in fact, to have been suggested by Richelieu himself, are in my view purely minor factors which are in no way the real reason for this arbitrary arrest, with all the interest that it aroused. We are forced to recognise that what really worried Richelieu was this new ideology which showed itself in Saint-Cyran's attitude towards the *Institut du Saint-Sacrement* and in Antoine Le Maître's withdrawal to Port-Royal, and that he was afraid of it less on account of those it had already influenced than because of all those who might come under its sway. On this particular point, the historian who is in a position to judge events in perspective can only admire Richelieu's perspicacity, irrespective of the approval or disapproval that he may feel for the policies which Richelieu was following. For a while the Spanish party left no heirs, Jansenism exercised a deep influence on the social and intellectual life of France, and constituted one of the main currents of opposition to the monarchy of the *ancien régime*.

However, an ideology is never dangerous purely by itself, and it is here that the point which I made earlier becomes relevant. By itself, the third ideological position adopted by Saint-Cyran, and the influence which it might have on a number of individuals who were either potential or actual members of the central bureaucracy—Arnauld d'Andilly, the Bouthillier family, Antoine Le Maître—was just an incident. It became an important historical fact because of the ideological and political struggle to which it gave rise—and which was to last for two centuries—between the monarchical and ecclesiastical establishment on the one hand, and the Jansenists or 'Friends of Port-Royal' on the other. An ideology only becomes dangerous when it reflects the interests and aspirations of certain social groups, and it is the social origins of those who adopted the Jansenist position that we must now examine.

When certain omissions have been made—the clergy, because they came from all classes of society; Singlin, the son of a wine merchant, and Lancelot, because they are exceptions; the originators of the movement, who came both from the urban middle class and from the legal profession (and who had originally been candidates for the important posts in the central bureaucracy), because they remained few in number—the supporters of Jansenism came from two distinct social groups. On the one hand, there are a few members of the upper aristocracy, who find it difficult to accept the domestication involved by royal policy and who—especially after the failure of the *Fronde*—

are too weak and isolated to form an effective opposition. These include Mme de Longueville, the princesse de Guéméné, the dukes of Roannez, Liancourt and Luynes, the prince and princess of Conti, Mme de Grammont, etc. And, on the other, the *officiers*, especially those who are members of the *Cours souveraines*, and the *avocats*.

These two groups had very different relations with Port-Royal. However great the influence of Jansenism may have been on some members of the aristocracy, it is significant that no aristocrat ever entirely abandoned the world. Mme de Longueville—if we believe the *Mémoires* of Fontaine—may have wanted to do so, but came up against very strong opposition from Singlin, her director of conscience, who was in turn almost certainly following Arnauld's advice on this matter, as well, probably, as that of Barcos and Mother Angélique. Indeed, as Port-Royal was very well aware, there was a difference in nature between the conversion of Mme de Longueville and that of Antoine Le Maître, for example. The other members of the nobility either gave up Jansenism—like Mme de Roannez and Mme de Guéméné—or became friends of Port-Royal while remaining in the world.

This indicates that the link between Jansenism and the nobility was rather superficial, and the few important nobles who did join the movement did so because they were too weak to form an opposition of their own. This idea is supported by the fact that most of them drew nearer to Port-Royal after the *Fronde* had failed and any hope of an independent aristocratic resistance had disappeared.

The situation is very different when we look at the families of *officiers* and lawyers who joined or supported Port-Royal.[1] Not only did the Arnaulds come from a family of lawyers closely linked to the *parlement*, but many other members of the *Cours souveraines* and families of *officiers*—those of Pascal, Maignart, Destouches, Nicole, Bagnols, Tillemont, Bignon, Domat, Buzenval, Caulet, Pavillon—played a leading rôle in the life of the Jansenist group. Another important factor is that the *mémoires* of the time often show Port-Royal enjoying a considerable amount of sympathy in circles closely con-

---

[1] Monsieur Drouot, in his excellent book on *Mayenne et la Bourgogne*, has shown how, during the wars of religion, *avocats* and *officiers* made up the most dynamic factors of the opposing sides. Thus, the *Officiers*, grouped around the king in order to defend their privileges and social and political position, constituted the core of the 'political' party. The *avocats*, on the other hand, who were unable to pay the increasingly high prices asked for legal charges, took over the administration of the towns and became one of the most important social groups on whom the followers of the anti-royalist and ultra-Catholic 'Ligue' depended.

In the seventeenth century, in contrast, the building up of the royal bureaucracy tended to make the *officiers* less sympathetic to the king, and naturally made them side increasingly with the *avocats* and *procureurs*.

nected with the *parlement*, even among people who, like Molé, Lamoignon and Broussel, were far removed from any temptation to give up their office and retire into solitude.

Thus, in so far as any notion can be drawn from an insufficiently explored area of facts, everything seems to indicate that the relationship between Jansenism and certain members of the French legal profession is a fairly typical example of the general relationship between an ideological movement and the social group whose preoccupations it reflects.

The ideology is first of all elaborated outside the social group by a few professional politicians, and, essentially, by ideologists—in this case Saint-Cyran and Barcos. It is the circles which are outside the main group which combine to provide both the ideologues and the extremist leaders (Barcos, Singlin and Lancelot). However, shortly after the birth of the movement, it is the *élite* or vanguard of the group itself which takes control, providing the leaders for the main body of opinion, and offering the real resistance to the king's authority. What might, in modern times, be called the sympathisers or fellow travellers come from the *officiers* and in particular from the *Cours souveraines* and the *parlements*. It is thanks to them that the ideas of the *élite* produce the great effect which they do upon the rest of the country.

We must now answer two main questions: what particular instances can be quoted to support and illustrate this general picture? And why did the *noblesse de robe* act in this particular way? (The term *noblesse de robe* must, of course, be seen as a general sociological term which has nothing at all to do with whether or not certain individuals in the Jansenist group had or had not received patents of nobility as a result of their legal functions.)

I shall begin by trying to deal with the second of these two questions, since the only answer which I can give to the first consists of a number of isolated examples whose value depends upon the explanation given of the whole process. I have already said that the limited monarchy, based on the support of the middle class and of the *parlements*, became absolute in three successive stages. Each stage showed a marked progress over the preceding one, and each was linked with an attempt to create a centralised governmental apparatus completely dependent upon the king's authority. In the seventeenth century this apparatus consisted essentially of the *Conseils* and of the *Intendants*, and its creation aroused strong opposition from the Third Estate, from the *officiers*, who had been the backbone of the limited monarchy, and, in so far as its members were still strong enough to do anything at all, from the old nobility.

I have already noted that the Concordat of 1516 gave the king the right to appoint Bishops, and this marked an important step in the

formation of the royal bureaucracy.[1] The reigns of Louis XI, Francois I[e] and Henri II differed from those of Louis XIII and Louis XIV,
however, by the fact that until the seventeenth century this bureaucracy was recruited to a considerable extent from the *parlements* and
the *Cours souveraines*, and was still far from being fully constituted.
Thus the *Cours souveraines* remained the principal organ of government, so that however great their resistance may have been to
'arbitrary' royal measures (that is to say, acts which went against
legal tradition or the personal interests of the Court's members), they
still continued to support the king whenever the country was endangered by the quarrels or resistance of the different classes. Thus,
during the sixteenth-century wars of religion Henri IV was granted
strong support not only from the openly royalist *parlements* of Tours
and Chalons but also from those of Paris and Dijon, which were,
theoretically at least, on the side of the *Ligue*.

The situation changes during the reigns of Henri IV and Louis
XIII, when the *commissaires* begin to be recruited not only from
among the *officiers* themselves[2] but also from outside the *Cours
souveraines*.[3] The royal bureaucracy thus became a political and
social reality which was independent of these courts of law, and was
now in more or less permanent conflict with them. At the same time
the king began to pursue a economic and social policy which clearly
favoured the aristocracy, with the result that the nobles agreed to

[1] It is important to stress the fact that although I am primarily interested in the
relationship between Jansenist ideology and the *noblesse de robe*, it is improbable
that either Richelieu or Saint-Cyran initially foresaw the extraordinary success
that Jansenism was to have in legal circles. Saint-Cyran seems to have been concerned first of all with trying to revive the spirit of the primitive church and persuading members of the clergy, and especially bishops, to go back to the customs
of this church that had recently been re-established by the Council of Trent and
give up all political functions. As I have pointed out, the higher clergy did constitute an important part of the monarchical system of government, so that it was
natural for Richelieu to see the political danger implicit in Saint-Cyran's
doctrines. The fact that so many lawyers then began to support Jansenism had
the effect of exacerbating the conflict.

[2] The post of *Maître des Requêtes* at the *Hôtel du Roi* had become one of the
normal ways for the members of the *cours souveraines* to make their way into the
higher echelons of the royal bureaucracy. D'Argenson wrote that these posts
were 'a regular breeding ground for administrators' (Boislisle in the *Mémoires de
Saint-Simon* (G.E.F.), Vol. IV, p. 409). To occupy one of these posts meant that
one was on one's way to becoming one of the *grands commis*, the chief administrators in the bureaucratic system of Louis XIV. Saint Simon (*Mémoires*, Vol.
IV, p. 412) compares the *Maître des Requêtes*, who has not advanced any farther,
to an old page, an elderly spinster, or a middle-aged curate.

[3] In his article 'Le Conseil du roi', etc. (cf. note on p. 109), Monsieur Mousnier
points out that the *Maîtres des Requêtes* were important rivals with the members
of the *Cours souveraines* for posts in the King's Council, and gives figures (loc.
cit., p. 57).

become domesticated[1] and to be transformed into *noblesse de cour*. This policy was naturally accompanied by stern repression by the king of any attempt of the nobles to assert their political independence.

Thus, the policy of the central government gradually reduced the social and administrative importance of the *officiers*, both as compared with the nobility in general and with respect to the *Conseillers d'Etat* and *Intendants* in particular.[2] This fact is especially important when one considers that at the end of the wars of religion the *officiers* had looked upon themselves as the principal support and indispensable allies of the monarchy. They had thus hoped for a considerable increase in their power and importance, both as individuals and as a class, with the result that they were naturally highly dissatisfied when the king failed to act as they expected.

At first sight it might seem that the opposition between the new bureaucracy—represented by its apparatus of *commissaires* and *Maîtres des Requêtes*—and the *officiers* and members of the *Cours souveraines* would naturally lead the latter to oppose the king. In fact, however, events followed a much less simple pattern. There had, of course, always been a tendency for certain lawyers to link their cause with that of the Third Estate in general, as is shown by the example of Barillon and Broussel, and this was particularly noticeable at critical moments in the *Fronde* and during the second half of the eighteenth century. It illustrates the attraction exercised over the legal profession by the Third Estate, in which it eventually merged. In the seventeenth century, however, and especially between 1637 and 1669, the appearance and development of Jansenist ideology differing from that of the Third Estate indicate that the lawyers formed a social group that was fairly autonomous and independent. If they did not make up a social class as such they formed something very like it.

A real attitude of opposition which was openly hostile to a particular type of government could in fact spring only from a social class

[1] I have already mentioned this as an economic and social measure, and noted how the fact that loyal nobles received royal pensions can be used to explain the massive conversion of the Huguenot nobility to Catholicism during the seventeenth century. There remained, at the end of that century, very few Huguenot nobles indeed.

Although he offers a different explanation for what happens, Monsieur Emile Léonard (*Le Protestantisme français* (P.U.F., 1953)) also draws attention to the disappearance of a Protestant nobility in France during the years immediately before and after the Edict of Nantes.

[2] Georges Pagès also considers that the development of the institution of the *Intendants de Justice, Police et Finances* is a factor accompanying the transition from one type of monarchial government to another, different type (cf. op. cit., p. 89).

119

that enjoyed complete economic independence of this type of government, and which could therefore survive either its destruction or its radical transformation. (This was the case for the feudal nobility or the Third Estate, as it is today for the proletariat.) What always prevented the *officiers* of the *ancien régime* from becoming a genuine social class—although they came very near to being one in the seventeenth century—was the fact that their legal functions made them economically dependent, as *officiers*, upon a monarchical state whose growth they opposed from an ideological and political point of view. This put them in an eminently paradoxical situation—and one which, in my view, provides the infrastructure for the tragic paradox of *Phèdre* and of the *Pensées*—where they were strongly opposed to a form of government which they could not try to destroy or even to alter in any radical manner. This paradoxical situation had been made more intense by a brilliant decision of Henri IV. By introducing the tax known as *La Paulette*, he made it possible for the *officiers* to hand their charges down from father to son on the payment to the Crown of an annual sum of roughly 1½ per cent of their value. At the same time, however, this measure also made the *officiers* more dependent upon the king, for he could always threaten to rescind the right of any *officier* to pay this tax.[1]

I do not need to insist at any great length on the link between the economic and social position of the *officiers* of the *ancien régime* and the ideology of Jansenism. The *officiers* were dependent upon an absolute monarchy which they disliked intensely, but which had no means of satisfying their demands by any reforms conceivable at that time. The tragic teaching of Jansenism insisted upon the essential vanity of the world and upon the fact that salvation could be found only in solitude and withdrawal.

The brief sketch which I have given provides a sufficiently clear outline of my general hypothesis. This hypothesis is based upon four main contentions: that an antagonism existed, in the seventeenth century, between *officiers* and *commissaires*; that there was a particularly acute period of tension round about 1637-38; that the development of Jansenism parallels that of a central bureaucratic apparatus; and, finally, that there is a close link between the sections of society from which the *officiers* were drawn—particularly the *avocats* and members of the *Cours souveraines*—and Jansenist ideology.

I have already pointed out, however, that I cannot prove these assertions absolutely, but can merely produce arguments based upon a certain number of clues and presuppositions. These clues are to be

[1] Cf. Roland Mousnier, *La Venalité des offices sous Henri IV et Louis XIII*, pp. 308 and 557.

found either in contemporary texts or in the work of modern historians, and therefore both suffer from the same disadvantage: that a summary tends to distort them, and that it also omits certain apparently minor factors which are in fact essential to the communication and understanding of a general atmosphere. This is why, instead of referring to authorities that most readers will probably not consult, I shall illustrate my main contention by quoting fairly lengthy passages from recent historians as well as from contemporary sources.

It is difficult to deny that the birth and development of Jansenism coincided with the setting up of the central bureaucratic administration of the absolute monarchy. The three main events which marked the beginning of the Jansenist movement—the crisis in the *Institut du Saint-Sacrement*, the withdrawal from the world of Antoine Le Maître, and the arrest of Saint-Cyran—all took place between 1636 and 1638. The following passage from J. Caillet, whose work still remains, a hundred years after it was written, one of the best studies of the *ancien régime* monarchy, provides a remarkable commentary on this:[1]

> The establishment of *Intendants* of Justice, Finance and Police as permanent officials in every province was one of the most important events of Richelieu's administration. These new civil servants, largely of middle class origin, were appointed by the king and could be dismissed by him, with the result that their dependence on and devotion to the central power were both very great. It was they who made the most important contribution to the firm establishment of a centralised royal authority, and both provincial governors, powerful noblemen and *parlements* found that these new *Intendants* were energetic defenders of the royal prerogative. It is significant, in this respect, that when at the beginning of the *Fronde* the nobility and *parlements* were no longer held in check by Richelieu, they immediately directed their attacks against the *Intendants*. (Note: When the deputies of the four *compagnies* met together in the Salle Saint-Louis in order to discuss governmental reform, the first thing which they asked for was the abolition of the *Intendants* and of any Commissions Extraordinary which had not been registered as valid by the *Cours souveraines*. The Court then felt itself, in the words of the Cardinal de Retz, attacked *in its very eyeballs*, and tried to resist. Nevertheless, the *Intendants* were abolished except in Languedoc, Burgundy, Bourgogne, Provence, le Lyonnais, Picardy and Champagne. [Declaration of July 13th, 1648.] It is generally but wrongly believed that the *Intendants* were restored in these provinces only in 1654. However, as Monsieur Chaluel has shown in the third volume of his learnèd *Historie de Touraine*, eight months after July 1648 Denis de Héere, who had already been *Intendant* in Touraine from 1643 to 1648 received a new commission for this province which he continued to exercise until his death in 1656).

[1] Cf. J. Caillet, op. cit., Vol. I, pp. 56–7.

Most historians have given a very inaccurate account of the origins of this most important institution. One reads, for example, that the *Intendants* of Justice, Finance, and Police were established by Richelieu in 1635. This is not true, for there are several mentions of *Intendants* before 1624, the date at which Richelieu entered into the king's administration. What Richelieu did was to realise how useful such an institution could be in carrying out his plans, and therefore to give them permanent instead of temporary commissions in all the provinces. He did this gradually—not all at once as most historians allege—and from the first years of his 'reign' we see them following one another without intermission or interruption in certain provinces. But it was only from 1633, and, particularly, from 1637, that the systems of *Intendants* was applied to the whole kingdom (pp. 56-7).

Monsieur Caillet continues, several pages later in the same volume:

It was them [i.e. in 1637 L.G.] that Richelieu conceived the idea of establishing *Intendants* on a permanent basis in all provinces, with full powers for administering justice and controlling police and finance. He thus helped to create throughout the whole kingdom a body of devoted servants capable of offering effective resistance to the attacks of his numerous enemies. He was not disappointed, for from then onwards the *Intendants* began to bring all the provincial administration under the authority, and to destroy all the obstacles which the governors, the *Cours souveraines* and the *bureaux de finances* constantly tried to put into the path of the king's authority. The proof of this can be found in an unpublished document from the archives of the Ministry of War, Volume 42, number 257, entitled: *Commission granted to the Commissaires going out into the Provinces to enforce the payment of the tax imposed upon towns and boroughs for the maintenance and payment of troops*. This document, dated March 31st, 1637, contains the following very interesting remarks: 'We have decided . . . that it was fitting to send out to each of Our Provinces persons of quality and authority chosen from among the principal members of Our Council of State, and to endow these with full and complete powers an *Intendants* of Justice, Police and Finance' (p. 78).

Similarly, Omer Talon writes in his *Mémoires*, speaking of the *Intendants* on July 6th, 1648: 'It is fifteen years since they have been sent out on various occasions, and eleven whole years [i.e. since 1637] that they have been set up in all provinces.'[1]

It is, of course, a pure coincidence that Antoine Le Maître should have withdrawn from the world in the very same years that the decree was established setting up the machinery for sending *Intendants* to every province, since the two events could easily have taken place at two, three, four or five years distance. Both, however, are the result

[1] Cf. Omer Talon, *Mémoires*, Ed. Petitot and Monmerqué (Paris, 1827), Vol. LXI, p. 210. Cf. also, for the dates of these events, G. Pagès, *Institutions Monarchiques*, pp. 102-7, and *Naissance du Grand Siècle*, p. 134.

of two parallel processes of evolution, which strongly influenced each other. And what, in my view, was especially important as a factor relating these two processes was the influence which the setting up of the system of *commissaires* had had of the mentality of the *officiers*—and contrairiwise.

The other important tool of royal absolutism, the *Conseil du Roi* have been brilliantly analysed by Monsieur Roland Mousnier.[1] A reading of his work is sufficient to demonstrate the parallelism between the birth and development of the first Jansenist movement (1636–69), and the setting up of this essential organ of the royal government.

> It was between 1622 and 1630 [he writes] that the most important crisis took place in the growth of the *Conseil du Roi*. After the *règlement* of May 21st, 1615, which reorganised the commissions (which had the task of preparing reports submitted to the different members of the Council. The setting up of these commissions marks an important stage in its development), the *règlement* made at Tours on 6th August 1619 developed the other commissions attached to the *Conseil des Finances*. Four other commissions were each made responsible for several tax farms, spread out over the whole of France, and for several neighbouring *généralités* which formed two or three separate groups. . . . This organisation seems to have remained the same up to 1666.

The *Grand Règlement* of Paris (June 16th, 1627) appears to have set up ten other commissions for the whole of the *Conseil*, and temporary commissions were also established in addition to the permanent ones (pp. 51–2). On the problem of the respective status of the *Conseillers* and the members of the *Cours souveraines*, Monsieur Mousnier tells us that: 'the *Conseillers d'Etat* looked upon themselves as a *compagnie d'officiers*, and therefore rejected the pretensions of the members of the *Cours souveraines*, who tried to look upon themselves as superior to the *commissaires*'. The *Grand Règlement*, which he quotes, states that *Conseillers* have 'a permanent commission which gives them permanent and hereditary rank and dignity'. They have, continues the *Règlement*, 'all the emblems of the greatest *Officiers* of the Kingdom; their authority is laid down by the King's order, and sealed with the Great Seal; the choice which the King makes of their persons involves an inspection both of their moral worth and of their professional competence. And there is no limit of time imposed upon the exercise of their functions'. Moreover, the *Conseillers* had yet another reason to feel superior: they did not buy their charge. It thus followed that they should be accorded rank and quality outside the *Conseil*, and take precedence in the *Cours souveraines*, while the normal *commis* have no rank outside the limits of their commissions.

[1] Cf. Mousnier, loc. cit., in *Etudes d'Histoire moderne et contemporaine* (1947).

This superiority of the *Conseillers* over the *commissaires* was officially recognised by the king, since from 1616 he began to accord the Keeper of the Seals—who was originally merely a *commis*—the right to preside over the *parlement* as if he were Chancellor, and consequently a Crown Officer. The functions which the Keeper of the Seals there exercises as head of the *Conseillers* carries with it precedence and authority over the members of the *Cours souveraines* when he is out of the Council Chamber. The king also distributes, especially after 1632, letters patent of *Conseiller d'Etat* to the most faithful and experienced members of his Council, and these entitled their holders to take their seat and proffer advice in all the meetings of the *parlement*, including the secret council, and this without forfeiting the rank which they have in the *Conseil du Roi*. He thus indicates that the functions of *conseiller* involve a pre-eminence of rank which is everywhere valid. In May 1643 the Order in Council compels the *avocats* from the *parlements* who wish to plead before the *Conseil* to take a new oath in the presence of the Chancellor or of the Keeper of the Seals, in addition to the oath which they have already taken to the *parlement*, because the *Conseil* is 'a tribunal which is superior to the *parlement*'. The *Règlements* of April 1st, 1655, and May 4th, 1657, pronounce the decisive word when they define the *Conseil*, taken in its three sections of *Conseil d'Etat et des Finances, Conseil privé* and *Conseil des Finances*, as 'the first *Compagnie* in the Kingdom'. (Cf. Mousnier pp. 60–1.)

'The authority of these *Conseils*,' so runs the *Règlement*, 'is such as it pleases the King, for He and his ancestors have always desired that the decisions of Their Council should have the same authority as if they had been given in Their presence, and this They have always shown on all occasions.' The use of such terms clearly indicates that it is the whole of the *Conseil* which enjoys the king's authority. The *Cours souveraines* were thus forced to acknowledge that the *Conseil* had complete power over their decisions. Towards 1632 the *Conseil* began to maintain that, armed with the king's authority, it could declare nul and void any decisions of the *parlements* which went against royal ordinances and against royal authority generally, or against 'public interest' or against the rights of the Crown. 'It was difficult,' Monsieur Mounsier tells us, 'not to find a large number of such decisions which came under such a wide definition.'

Finally, in order to give a clear indication of what was happening, I shall quote Monsieur Mounier's conclusions *in extenso*:

> The other sections of the *Conseil* also assumed complete authority 'over the decisions concerning justice and police' of the *Cours souveraines*, and in certain cases carefully laid down by the *ordonnances*, these courts were not allowed to discuss the decisions of the *Conseil*

privé, and of the *Conseil d'Etat et des Finances*. Moreover, when objections were put forward on matters of fact or on damages undergone by one of the parties in a civil case, the *conseils* could suspend the decisions made in these courts. The *Maîtres des Requêtes* examined the case, and, if they found the complaint justified, ordered the court to reconsider its decision. The *Conseil* also had the right to assume jurisdiction in a case if requested to do so by one of the parties involved, if this party's opponent had friends or relations in the court in question (father, child, son-in-law, brother-in-law, uncle, nephew, first cousin), or if either the *présidents* or the *conseillers* had personal interest in the case, or if they had either given a written opinion or solicited on behalf of one of the parties. If any of these things had happened, the *Conseil* either gave judgment itself or sent the case to another court. When it was uncertain which court had the right to judge a case, the decision was taken by the *Conseil privé*. Finally, the *Conseil privé* had the right to confirm the seal placed upon letters of Office, because only the king had the right to choose and set up his own officers.

There could be no discussion about these rights, since they had been imposed by necessity, strengthened by custom, and finally consecrated by the *ordonnances*. Disputes arose, however, in cases where the *conseils* received requests in civil law on the grounds of error, and used their authority to annul decisions taken by the courts. They suspended execution of judgment when a request had been sent to the *Conseil*, while the *Conseil privé* also kept the cases that had been referred to it for a second opinion and decided them itself. The king used his own authority to give merchants, courtiers, rebellious nobles, protestants, towns or individuals who surrendered to him, the right to have all their cases judged by the *Conseil*. This was a far reaching decision, for we must remember that the *Cours souveraines* often used to give judgment in cases which we should now consider as routine administrative matters. The *Cours souveraines* were responsible for what we now think of as 'police' matters, and for everything connected with infringement of edicts and *ordonnances*. But, as the *Conseils* gradually transformed themselves into *Cours souveraines* on their own behalf, they deprived the official courts of their powers, and left them merely with an empty title.

The *Cours souveraines* did not accept this without protest, for they became more hostile to the growth of the powers of the *Conseil* and rebelled in 1648. On a number of occasions, in 1615, 1630, 1640 and 1657, the *règlements* of the *Conseil* sent back to the *Cours souveraines* and to the ordinary judges all disputed cases and judgments concerning private individuals. In 1644, Séguier very skilfully tried to obtain straightforward verification of edicts by sending back to the courts all the cases concerning the execution of edicts verified in the *compagnies*, unless these *compagnies* had introduced modifications which the *Conseil* had removed by decree. On many occasions, *règlements*, *arrêts* and *déclarations* promised that 'the decision given in the *Cours souveraines* can neither be annuled or postponed except by legal means provided for in the *Ordonnances*'—that is to say, by a formal proposition made in civil law and not by a simple request to the *Conseil*. This would have preserved the administrative authority of the *parlement*, and the *Assemblée de la Chambre Saint-Louis* once again demanded, on July 17th, 1648, that the Ordonnances of this point should be observed and obtained a promise to this effect in the *Déclaration* of October 24th, 1648.

All these efforts, however, were in vain, and the authority of the *Cours souverainès* was gradually whittled down. Already, in 1632, all the decisions given in all the *Cours souveraines*, except the *Parlement* of Paris, were annuled 'either in the *Conseil d'Etat ou privé*, although the King was not present'. The *Parlement* of Paris still enjoyed the priviledged position where its decisions could not be annuled except by the *Conseil d'en Haut*, and then after a hearing granted to its *Premier Président* and the *Gens du Roi*. But in 1645 the *Conseil des Finances* annuled a decision whereby the *Parlement* had forbidden the creation of an office of *Président* at Saint Quentin when requested to do so by the inhabitants, and the *Parlement* was unable to secure the annulment of this decision of the *Conseil des Finances* by the *Conseil d'En Haut*. The *Parlement*, supported by the other courts, grew obstinate. Even after the failure of the Fronde, the courts continued to fight, giving judgments that contradicted those of the *Conseil*, forbidding the execution of the decisions of the *Conseils du Roi*, and condemning anyone who disobeyed this injunction. But little by little they had to give ground, and, at the beginning of his reign, Louis XIV finally managed to defeat them. Each and every one of the *Cours souveraines* was obliged to acknowledge that the *Conseil* had supreme authority over their decisions, both as a body and in a general and universal manner.

The *Cours souveraines* also attacked both the commissions set up by the *Conseil* and entrusted by the king with the task of judging certain cases which concerned the state, and the sending out *Maîtres des Requêtes* and *Conseillers d'Etat* into the provinces with power to act as judges of appeal in final instance. The courts maintained that all matters which 'lay in dispute' and everything connected with the observation of edicts and *ordonnances* belonged to the ordinary judges on their first hearing and then to the *Cours souveraines* if there was an appeal, and that no commission, be it general, particular, collective or individual, could take this right from them. In 1617 the *Notables*, the majority of whom were members of the *Cours souveraines*, and the *Assemblée de Saint-Louis* in 1648, both proclaimed that these principles were valid, demanded that the commissions should be recalled, and received the promise that this would be done in a Royal Declaration on 24th October, 1648.

But Le Bret had explained that by article 98 of the Edict of Blois, the king had wished to make a distinction between private and public cases. The private ones could well be judged by the *officiers* under whose competence they fell, but this was not so 'when the matter at hand is of public concern and of interest to the state'. In such a case the king can 'appoint such persons as seem to Him most suitable to take cognisance'. These persons are superior to the *officiers* for as long as their functions last, since 'it is a principle of canon law that *Omnis delegatus est ordinario in re delegata*'. One of Colbert's secretaries adds that the *Ordonnance de Blois* and that of October 24th, 1648, had been 'extorted from the king by the violence of His people' and were therefore 'null and void'. The king, who before 1648 had maintained his commissions and *commissaires* against all and every protest, re-established them as soon as he could after that date.

By an irresistible process, these royal *commissaires*, the *Conseil* and the *Intendants*, created by the king and responsible to him, took over many of the functions of the ordinary judges. They thereby enabled the king to reassert his authority over the *compagnies* which had been weakened by the venality of offices and by the payment of an annual sum.

By 1661, we find that the conception of a number of different royal courts, all performing different functions under the overall but distant supervision of the king and a few chosen advisers—the king concerning himself largely with foreign affairs and war—had been replaced by a *Conseil* with a large number of political, administrative, fiscal and judicial tasks. This *Conseil* is superior to all the different individual courts, divided into sections whose work is much better organised, and made up of a much more intelligently trained and chosen personnel than in 1610, in spite of the fact that this personnel still remains the weakest part of the *Conseil d'Etat* (pp. 64–7).

The establishment of a framework of *commissaires* closely dependent upon the king, and entrusted with the main task of imposing his absolute authority, could clearly not remain an isolated phenomenon in French society. Once one important organ is changed in the body politic, the others must necessarily feel the effects. The studies made by Marxist historians showed a long time ago that a bureaucratic apparatus is rarely strong enough by itself to impose its own authority on society,[1] and that the workings of a bureaucracy can be understood only when it is seen and studied in relation to all the different social classes. The government of the limited monarchy depended upon the *officiers* and *Cours souveraines*, and therefore presupposed a close understanding between the king and the Third Estate. The government of the absolute monarchy depended on the *Conseils* and the *Intendants*, and therefore presupposed a balance of power between the different classes, between the nobility on the one side and the *officiers* and the Third Estate on the other. The development of

[1] This statement might turn out to be false as far as modern totalitarian states are concerned, although I do not think so. It is, in any case, correct in so far as it applies to what happened up to the end of the nineteenth century.

absolute monarchism thus involved—once Louis XIV had finally deprived the nobility of its independence by bringing it to Versailles —a policy of alliance between the Crown and the nobles. This brought with it the risk that the aristocracy would find its ways into the apparatus of government in the same way as the bourgeoisie had done when the king was allied with the Third Estate. The Crown therefore had first of all to see that this apparatus remained above all social classes, and secondly, to ensure that the *offices* remained the exclusive province of the middle class.

This seems to have been achieved by the measure known as *La Paulette*, which kept all such offices venal and prevented them from falling into the hands of the aristocracy. We cannot tell at the moment whether this was a deliberate intention or an accidental by-product of a measure whose primary aim was to make money, and no serious study has yet been made of how this measure was first introduced. However, Monsieur Mousnier has provided a most useful analysis of a number of ideological conflicts which accompanied both the adoption and the maintenance of the custom whereby *officiers* were enabled to buy their charges and keep them from year to year. These conflicts are, in my view, important for a study of Jansenism, and I shall therefore mention them here.

Two positions were adopted, though not both at the same time. The first, that of Bellièvre, appeared in 1604 and expressed the opposition of the *officiers*[1] themselves. The second, though attributed by Richelieu to Sully, does not, for Monsieur Mousnier, show itself until later. But, in any case, it was quite visible by 1614, since, remarks Monsieur Mousnier, 'it was mentioned by a large number of the pamphleteers who put forward arguments in favour of La Paulette at the Estate General of 1614, or at the *Assemblée des Notables* in 1617' (p. 561).

Now what Bellièvre represented was the attitude of the more powerful *officiers*, who, at the end of the religious wars, hoped to profit by becoming the mainstay of the country. Their central idea was that the king should appoint *officiers* as a return for fidelity or services rendered, and in exchange for a purely nominal sum. La Paulette destroyed this illusion, and Monsieur Mousnier sums up La Bellière's objection:

> The king would no longer be able to choose his *officiers* since he would be compelled to accept the candidate presented by the *officier* who had paid the annual rent. Thus corrupt or incapable people would

---

[1] There was, in fact, as Monsieur Mousnier pointed out, an aristocratic opposition to the sale and hereditary transmissibility of legal charges throughout the whole of the seventeenth century, but this expressed a wholly different attitude.

128

come to be office holders merely because of their money . . . and . . . the king would no longer be able to appoint a faithful servant or reward a magistrate by waiving payment of the tax. . . . The charges would become so expensive that gentlemen would no longer appoint sons as members of the *Cours souveraines*, or *Présidents* or *Conseillers du Parlement* appoint their children. The *parlement* would thus be filled with speculators, and justice would grow corrupt and fall into contempt.[1] . . . The *officiers* would no longer be *officiers* of the king but of their own purses.[2]

In fact, if the *officiers* were to remain the backbone of the administration, these objects were quite justified. But, on the other hand, they cease to be valid if the Crown is to set up its own administrative apparatus which deprives the *officiers* of most of their importance.

There is an interesting comment on the link between Bellièvre's position and the later development of Jansenism in the passage in his *Mémoires* where Arnauld d'Andilly comments on his own refusal to pay one hundred *livres* for the post of *secrétaire d'Etat* in 1622: 'Subsequent events,' he writes, 'showed that I had made a great mistake: yet I should be excused for this, on the ground that, having come to Court in the time of Henri IV, I had been brought up to believe that one's own efforts and fidelity were alone sufficient, without money, to secure a charge.'[3]

Those who defended the annual payment were first of all supporters of the central power, and later of the *officiers* themselves, when these had lost their early hopes of power and influence. They argued, quite rightly and very typically, that if the annual payment were abolished, 'then the nobles would beg the king to give the principal charges to those whom they recommended; thus the *officiers* will feel that they owe their position to the nobles and not to the king—a drawback which had already increased the confusion which prevailed at the time of the *Ligue*'. Alternatively, it is argued that 'the annual payment makes all the *officiers* immediately dependent upon the king, and therefore affectionate and grateful to him'.[4]

The argument that the nobles might influence the appointment of the king's servants would have been absurd when the Crown was linked to the middle class and opposed to the feudal nobility. It became increasingly valid as the absolute monarchy grew closer to the nobility, while at the same time the venality of the offices protected the

---

[1] Cf. Mousnier, loc. cit., pp. 210–11.

[2] Cf. *Bibliothèque Nationale* (Fonds français), No. 15.894.

[3] Cf. *Mémoires* of Messire Robert Arnauld d'Andilly, in the *Nouvelle Collection des Mémoires pour servir à l'Histoire de France*, by Michaud and Poujoulat, 2nd series, Vol. IX, p. 437.

[4] Cf. Mousnier, loc. cit., p. 561.

Crown from the danger that a new feudal class of *grands commissaires* might come into being. The whole process will have to be studied in detail one day, but its general lines stand out fairly clearly from the studies of Monsieur Mousnier.

If we now examine the position of the *officiers* we can see from any volume of *mémoires* that the reign of Louis XIII is filled with quarrels between the *parlements* and the central authority. I shall not insist on this, but shall merely pick out from the *Mémoires* of Omer Talon three points which seem to me to be particularly significant.[1]

(*a*) The years 1636–43 constituted a period of particularly intense struggle in this continual battle between the king and the *Parlement*, and contained two major disputes: the edict of December 1635 created twenty-four *conseillers* and a *président*, and thus provoked a crisis which lasted for three months, during which time the administration of justice was partly suspended, since the already existing *conseillers* were taken up with the struggle against the king, who exiled to the provinces five of those who seemed to him to be leading the resistance. The dispute was apparently settled in March 1636, when the king reduced the number of newly created offices from twenty-five to seventeen, and authorised the exiled *conseillers* to return to Paris.

However, this was not the end of the affair since on Tuesday, March 23rd, 1638, a decision of the *conseil* was presented by the *Procureur général*, whereby the king, 'learning how ill the *officiers* of his new creation had been received—their being given no cases to judge and being forbidden from expressing an opinion in the *chambre des enquêtes* and even from receiving fees—therefore orders' (Volume 60, pp. 175–6).

At this point an even more serious conflict breaks out, resulting from the emprisonment of those who, on Wednesday, March 25th, 1638, had organised a riot to 'protest against the failure to pay sums of money due on the interest of investments in the *Hôtel de Ville*'. Among those pursued was Pascal's father, who had managed to hide. Now, in the view of the *Parlement*, this affair came under its jurisdiction and not under that of the *Conseil*, and it maintained, moreover, that 'it was an extraordinary thing to pursue those who had merely made a little noise while demanding their own property'.

On Wednesday, March 31st, two *présidents*—Barilon and Charton —and three *conseillers* were exiled to the provinces. This time they were authorised to return only in 1643, after the death of Louis XIII.

All this gives a fairly clear picture of the legal background to the years which were decisive for the birth of the Jansenist movement. It may be added that in 1644 a similar conflict broke out when Anne of

[1] Cf. Petitot and Monmerqué, Vol. 60–3.

Austria and Mazarin wanted to send Antoine Arnauld and Barcos to Rome and the *Parlement* came to their defence.

(*b*) Either rightly or wrongly, Omer Talon has the impression that a turning-point has been reached in the relationship between the king and the *parlement*, and he defines it in the report which he gives of his own speech at the king's *lit de justice* on January 15th, 1648:

> Sire, it has always been an occasion of high ceremony, glory and majesty when our kings held a *lit de justice*. . . .

but, he adds:

> In former times, Your Majesty's forefathers gave the people the opportunity to hear how the great affairs of state were discussed and matters of peace and war were decided. They asked advice from their *parlements* and replied to their allies. Such events were not then what they are now—as merely the effect of a Sovereign Power which strikes terror everywhere—but as meetings for deliberating and taking counsel.

He then mentions the case of 1563, when:

> the refusal of the priests, under a religious pretext, to contribute money for a holy war for once rendered this novelty bearable. Yet this, which then passed for an exception, and was against established principles, has now become a thing of custom. And for the last twenty-five years, it has become practised in all public affairs, either through real or feigned needs of state . . . Sire, for ten years the *compagnie* has been undermined, peasants reduced to sleeping on straw (Vol. 61, pp. 114–18).

Thus we once again find mention of the same period, 1623–38, by one of the most typical representatives of the lawyers' discontent.

(*c*) Talon has nothing of the Jansenist about him, and even seems to reproach the followers of the movement—in the person of Bignon, for example (Vol. 60, p. 35), with being 'naturally timid, over-punctilious, afraid to make a mistake or to give offence'. He also accuses Bignon of being 'kept from going to extremes by fear of failing and being thus responsible before his own conscience for some unhappy event'. However, he also mentions the desire of certain *officiers* to react to royal absolutism by giving up their charge. Thus, he explains that his elder brother 'grew weary of the position of *avocat général* . . . since the carrying out of his functions was difficult, the government harsh[1] . . . and matters were ordered by authority rather than decided by discussion'. Similarly, he tells us that the king introduced what was to become a permanent innovation in a *lit de*

[1] It is true that Jacques Talon gave up the post of *avocat général* in order to become a *conseiller d'Etat*, and that Pascal's father, after having sold his office as *Président* at the *Cour des Aides* at Montferrand, and having been mixed up in the

justice in 1632, when he took the votes of the Princes and Cardinals before those of the *présidents* of the *parlements*, and notes that: '*Monsieur le Premier Président* was so astonished that he was on the point of asking the king to release him from his office and allow him to withdraw into private life' (loc. cit., p. 53).

This tension between the Crown and the *officiers* shows itself even in the price asked for various charges. Monsieur Mousnier provides the following essential figures: at Rouen, in 1593, a charge of conseiller was worth 7.000 *livres*; in 1622, 40.000; in 1626, 66.000; in 1628, 68.000; in 1629, 70.000; in 1631, 74.000; in 1633, 84.000; in 1634, 80.000; in 1636, 79.000; in 1637, 85.000; in 1640, 67.000; in 1641, 25.000; in 1642, 55.500; in 1643, 62.500' (loc. cit., p. 335).

In Paris, where the information is slightly less reliable, his results are as follows: 1597, 11.000; 1600, 21.000; 1606, 36.000; 1614, 55.000; 1616, 60.000; 1617, 67.500; 1635, 120.000; 1637, 120.000 (loc. cit., p. 336).

Thus, there was—within the framework, it is true, of a general crisis—a fall in the price of charges in Normandy from 1633, and in Paris a falling off after 1635 in the inflationary sums asked for the most popular charges. It is probable, I think, that there was a mutual influence—what Monsieur Piaget would call as 'return bounce'— between this failure of the prices to keep rising and the development of Jansenist ideology. The lawyers were disappointed because the value of their charges was not continuing to increase, and this turned them towards Jansenism; at the same time the growth of Jansenism among the legal profession led to a reduced demand for such charges.

When we turn to the relationship between the members of the *parlements* and the Jansenist movement it is obvious that as many cases could be quoted of individual *conseillers* who were for Port-Royal as of those who were against it. The difficulty lies in the fact that we cannot say what influence either side had on the mass of the *conseillers* whose opinions we do not know. Similarly, no precise figures can be given for those who were definitely friendly or hostile to Jansenism. What I shall therefore do, before discussing a number of those who were openly Jansenistic, is to mention four examples which seem typical both of their relative neutrality on the question of Jansenism and of their eminence in legal circles. There is Broussel, whose rôle in the *Fronde* is well known, Barillon, Lamoignon and Molé. None of them was really a Jansenist, and Molé is even considered to have been an opponent of Port-Royal. Each had a profes-

---

seditious disturbances of 1638, finally took a post in the bureaucracy of the commissaires. But the fact that certain individuals may move from one social group to another has never diminished the genuine antagonisms that have existed between these groups.

sional interest in not being linked with a persecuted group, and yet we see three of them, at certain moments in their career, openly supporting Jansenism.

Gerberon tells us in his *Histoire du Jansénisme*[1] that it was Broussel who, in 1649, accepted the task of presenting the report of the two 'Doctors belonging to the Party of Saint Augustine', and who supported them with all his authority against 'Monsieur Molé, the *premier président* whom the Molinists had strongly prejudiced against the disciples of Saint Augustine'. Similarly, Lamoignon was linked both with the Jesuit Rapin and other anti-Jansenist circles, and with the 'friends of Saint Augustine', notably with Hermant and with Wallon de Beaupuis.

As for Barillon, one of the principal leaders of the resistance of the *parlements*, he was closely linked with Henri Arnault, future Bishop of Angers—the *Bibliothèque Nationale* still has about four hundred letters addressed to him—who looked after Barillon's children when Barillon and his wife were exiled to Amboise.

Gerberon tells us that the Molinists had strongly prejudiced Molé against Jansenism, but he had in fact begun by being quite closely connected with it, especially with Saint-Cyran himself. It was the attitude of Barcos, who refused in 1643 to accept money from someone whose behaviour was so ambiguous, which, together, of course, with his own interests, threw him into the opposite camp.

The story of how Mathieu Molé either deliberately or accidentally came to the help of Mother Marie des Anges Sureau, Abbess of Maubisson and later of Port-Royal (and, it may be added, the daughter of an *avocat* from Chartres), throws more light on the relationship between Jansenism and the circles of the *parlements* than the brief summary of three or four other examples.

Since the Holy Mother thought only of pleasing God and serving Him, so did God also bend Himself to help and protect her. He gave her marks of this aid on all sorts of occasions, but here is one especially worthy of note. If we are fully to understand it, we must go back a little in time. The inhabitants of Pontoise had often had the idea of freeing themselves from the payment of the *droit de minage* (weighting tax) which the Abbey of Maubuisson had had on corn and other grains almost from its very foundation. They had never dared bring a suit against the Abbey as long as its Abbesses had been of an authority and condition where their friends and relations would come to their aid. However, since from father to son these people of Pontoise had kept this intention, they thought that they would be able to carry it into practice against Mother Marie des Anges, since they looked upon her as unlikely to receive any help. They began a great lawsuit, and

[1] Cf. *Histoire Générale du Jansénisme*, 3 volumes (Amsterdam, 1700).

THE TRAGIC VISION IN SEVENTEENTH-CENTURY FRANCE

since it was a town matter it was considered by the *Messieurs de Pontoise* (town councillors) in several meetings. In order to bring about the success of their enterprise, the people of Pontoise decided to appeal to the Cardinal de Richelieu; and, in order more easily to obtain his support, they suggested to him that he had the right to half the tax which the abbey of Maubuisson had acquired from the Governor of Pontoise, for the other half was a royal gift. The Cardinal entered willingly through this gate of self-interest into support of their cause. Speaking as Governor, he maintained that his predecessors had had no right to sell or otherwise dispose of this half of the tax, since it belonged to the King's Domain and that it was only the revenue and not the sum itself which belonged to the Governors during their time of office.

Moreover, the Merchants of the Town of Pontoise also claimed that they were not obliged to pay this tax when they bought their grain from the farmers who sold it outside the town. The Canons of Saint Mellon maintained that an eighth of the tax which had been given by the King to the abbey belonged to them, and therefore joined forces with the town. They all hoped that, with Richelieu's support, they would easily gain a victory over Maubuisson. And, indeed, as men see it, this could not fail to happen, and no one doubted that the Mother would be overwhelmed by the Cardinal's power, and obliged to give way to the other people involved.

This suit was long and very difficult to argue. It continued for two years, and there were always two inhabitants of Pontoise delegated by the town to apply pressure. They were for ever bringing up new incidents to confuse matters. Thus the abbey was obliged to produce new arguments in its defence, and this was a great labour for the Mother. However, it did not disturb her tranquillity, which had something unchangeable about it. The confidence which she had in God seemed to grow greater with each human reason which she had to be afraid. She found in the power of her enemies and in the small amount of credit which she possessed great reasons to hope for a happy issue out of all her afflictions, for she saw it all as an occasion for God to show forth His greatness and pity. This is why, when sister Candide, weary of all these legal details and chicanery, said to her: 'Mother, everyone says that we shall certainly lose, and the Gentlemen of the Town are as sure of this as if they held us in their hand', she would say to her in reply: 'Daughter, we must allow ourselves to be neither weary nor discouraged. We must do all we can, for such is our duty. Be not troubled by all these threats and rumours. God is all-powerful. It is true that our enemies are strong, but my hope lies in God who will come to our help. Goodness is on the side of the poor, and we ourselves are poor and without credit. These two reasons should make us hope for His help. We must not tire of praying for it.'

This prayer of faith and perseverance received help from Heaven. After two years of legal proceedings, the case at last came up for judgment. The town of Pontoise sent eight of its principal inhabitants

134

to solicit in its favour. The Cardinal's servants were also trying their best to influence their friends, and the canons of Saint-Mellon were also most active. The Holy Mother then began to solicit not men but Angels, Saints and God Himself. It then appeared that these Divine Helpers were stronger in her defence than her enemies were against her. For while she was deep in prayer, God so disposed matters that when her enemies began their solicitations against her, the Gentlemen of the *Parlement* went up to the Chamber to judge a very small matter and disposed of it very quickly; the Président Molé then asked if there was not another case ready to be judged. The clerk replied that there was only the Maubuisson affair, but that it was a very important and complicated one, meaning thereby to indicate that there was not now enough time to decide on it. The first *Président*, seeing that the *Rapporteur* was present in the Chamber, nevertheless said: 'No matter. Let us decide this little Abbess's problems.' The case was therefore heard and examined without soliciting on anyone's behalf. A decision was given that was so much in favour of Maubuisson for the maintenance of the taxation rights belonging to the abbey that nothing further could have been hoped for on its behalf. All the decisions given against private individuals over the last hundred years were confirmed in such a way that these persons could never again have the right to cause trouble. The *Procureur de Maubuisson*, Dom Paul, having gone to Paris to solicit the judges, went to see them and discovered to his immense surprise that judgment had already been given in favour of the Mother Superior. He immediately wrote to her to send her this good news.

In exactly the same manner as she had remained wholly calm throughout the two years that the case had lasted, without ever being disturbed either by her labour or by the fear of losing, so she was apparently unmoved when she learned, against all hope and expectation, that God had concluded the affair in her favour. She immediately went down on her knees to thank Him, and then said calmly to Sister Candide: 'My Daughter, our suit has been won; we must give thanks to God, but speak little of it'.

When the eight Gentlemen from Pontoise learned of the decision and came back from Paris in the greatest confusion, they were as amazed as anyone at how this had happened. Each one said publicly that it was a miracle; that, from a human point of view, the Mother Superior was bound to lose her case; and that God had secretly—or, rather, openly—intervened in her favour by making the judges act so suddenly.[1]

If we now turn rapidly to the *officiers* who did in fact go over to the Jansenist cause we unfortunately find only a few families for whom we have information concerning more than one generation: the

[1] *Relations sur la vie de la Révérende Mère Marie des Anges, morte en 1658 abbesse de Port-Royal, et sur la conduite qu'elle a gardée dans la réforme de Maubuisson, étant abbesse de ce monastère* (1737), pp. 120–5.

Arnauld, the Pascal, the Maignart des Bernières, the Thomas du Fossé and the Potier.[1] It is nevertheless fairly probable that these cases, taken all together, will give us a typical image of the way in which a fraction of the *officiers* went over to the ideology of Port-Royal. In two of these cases the normal rise of the family was, if not hindered, then at least made more difficult, by the fact that they did not have enough money to deal with the situation created by *La Paulette* and the constitution of the bureaucracy of *commissaires*. It was this shortage of money which led both the *avocat* Arnauld (father of Le Grand Arnauld) and Charles de Maignart to have recourse to certain fraudulent manoeuvres—an action which thus created a mental and spiritual state that later encouraged the development of oppositional tendencies. Thus, Arnauld, having to find openings for ten children (ten others having died in infancy), falsified the ages of his two daughters (the future Mothers Superior Angélique and Agnès) in order to obtain the Papal Bulls confirming them as Abbesses of Port-Royal and Saint-Cyran. It was this lie which later presented serious problems of conscience to the great Abbess of Port-Royal. Similarly, the failure of his eldest son Robert, who seemed destined to make a great career for himself in the world, was in part due to his inability to purchase, in 1622, the charge of *secrétaire d'Etat* that the king offered him at a price that was nevertheless a particularly favourable one. The second son, Henri, the future great Jansenist bishop, began by leading a more than mediocre existence, as Brulart's and later Mazarin's agent, and was often in serious financial difficulties. He became bishop only at the age of fifty. (The youngest son, Antoine Arnauld, enters into active life when his family has already become strongly Jansenist.)

As to Maignart des Bernières, son of a *président* of the *parlement* at Rouen, he was prevented by the sharing out of his father's fortune between himself, his brothers and his mother, from marrying Ann Amelot, daughter of Jacques Amelot, *Président* of the first *Chambre des Requêtes* at the Palais de Justice, since the latter asked for a fortune of commensurate size with that of his daughter's dowry. Charles Maignart therefore had to have recourse to a subterfuge: his mother, Françoise, née Puchot, gave him the necessary sum of money in exchange for an ante-dated I.O.U. We know that this caused a prob-

---

[1] The book by Besoigne, *Vie des quatre evêques engagés dans la cause de Port-Royal* (Cologne, 1756), is very interesting on the social origins. Leaving aside Henri Arnauld, we find that both Nicolas Pavillon, Etienne-François de Caulet and Nicolas Chouart de Buzenval came from families with a long connection with the law (Vol. II, pp. 3–4). The fourth, Nicolas Chouart de Buzenval, came from a family that had been disappointed in its ambitions to achieve high office in the diplomatic service by the rise of Mazarin (Vol. II, pp. 3–4).

lem after the death of Charles in 1662, since it is mentioned in the will of Françoise Maignart that bears the date of March 1655.[1]

With the Pascal family, their behaviour is all the more significant because it preceded the development of the Jansenist ideology. It was long before he came across the ideas of Saint-Cyran that Etienne Pascal sold his charge of *Président de la Cour des Aides* at Montferrand and withdrew into private life in Paris. We know that in 1638 he was one of the leaders of the demonstration against the arrears in payment of the sums lent for the construction of the Hôtel de Ville, that he was obliged to hide in spite of the energetic support which the 'seditious elements' received from the *Parlement*, and that he was able to recover favour only by accepting a particularly difficult—because *anti-parlementaire*—commission in the repression of the paupers' rebellion in Normandy. It is easy to understand that, in the Pascal family, the ground was ready for the encounter with Jansenism.

Finally, the case of Thomas du Fossé—in so far as one can trust the *Mémoires* of Pierre Thomas[2]—seems to have been specially invented to fit in with my hypothesis. I shall quote the text of these *Mémoires* at some length.

Pierre Thomas du Fossé's grandfather had two uncles, one of whom was a *Conseiller d'Etat*, and doyen of the *Secrétaires du Roi*, and the other a *Maître des Requêtes*. This grandfather came to Paris 'with the intention of improving himself as best he could', and, Pierre Thomas tells us:

> Towards the year 1589, the disturbances and barricades of Rouen took place, under the reign of Henri III. And my grandfather, having been chosen by the King's good servants as a person very attached to His Majesty's interests, and having been chosen to carry all despatches to His Majesty and to receive His orders, was made prisoner en route by supporters of the *Ligue*, stripped of everything and emprisoned under a very close guard. But in spite of this, he managed to escape and to complete his journey. He found the King at Blois, gave him an account of his errand, and returned to Rouen with despatches from His Majesty. He continued to use all his power to favour the interests of his lawful prince (pp. 5–6).

At the end of the civil wars the king rewarded him—as was right—for his devotion:

> This is why the King, after the end of the war, wishing to acknowledge his services, sent him for nothing, and free of all financial charge,

---

[1] Cf. Alex Fréron, *La Vie et les oeuvres de Charles Maignart des Bernières (1616–1662)* (Rouen, 1930), pp. 7–10.

[2] It may be that this is a distorted account of events, but if that is the case, then this very distortion supports the idea that an ideology of the type I am discussing did exist. These *Mémoires* were published by F. Fouquet, Rouen, in 1876.

the post of *Maistre des Comptes* of Normandy, which post he occupied for a long time, acquitting himself with much honour and honesty.

He had two children—'Anne, married to a *conseiller du Parlement* called Monsieur Déry, who before he died had become *conseiller à la Grande Chambre*, leaving as his heir Jacques Déry, *conseiller de la Cour*, at present *Doyen des Requestes du Palais*', and Gentien Thomas, the father of the author of these *Mémoires*, who was at Boulogne where he was studying law, and 'received in 1621, in his twenty-first year, the news of his father's death', and immediately returned to Normandy.

On his arrival in Rouen, he decided to apply for the post which his father had occupied and thus to set himself up. He married the daughter of a *conseiller du Parlement*. . . . His manner of living both maritally and in the exercise of his official functions was more that of a man of honour than of the true Christian which he later became . . . The life which he and his wife led made them stand out from the commonalty, so that it became normal to refer to them as Prince and Princess Thomas (pp. 11–14).

He shows himself brave and decisive in his struggle against the nobles, as can be seen from his conduct in the affair of the comte de Montgomery:

Everyone knows what sort of man the Count was, and how he had behaved in such a manner as to compel Louis XIII to give an Order in Council to the effect that Pontorson—the property of Montgomery and the seat of all the violent acts that he performed throughout the country—should be razed to the ground, and the moats be handed over to Monsieur Moran, whom the king wished to reward. When this order was sent to the *Chambre des Comptes* in Normandy, an officer had to be found who was ready to carry out such an order. The Count was greatly feared, and the threats which he had uttered on hearing of the king's command were such that they had terrified everybody. None could be found ready to take on the task, for each could see the way in which so hasty-tempered a lord would act if anyone came to demolish a place in which he found security and protection against any punishment for his crimes. They all foresaw that, unless force were used, he would have no respect for the officers of justice. Esquire Thomas, however, was naturally of great courage, and could not bear to see the authority of the King put at naught. Being also jealous for the authority and honour of his *Compagnie*, he said confidently that he was ready to accept the task, that he had nothing to fear so long as he was clothed in the king's authority. His offer was unanimously accepted. He made ready for his voyage, and set off accompanied solely by the officers who are necessary for such errands. The Count was warned of his approach, and learned at the same time what type

138

of man it was whom the *Compagnie* had entrusted with the task. Realising that threats and violence were no longer likely to achieve' their effect, he therefore chose to give way (pp. 14–16).

But Gentien Thomas is not always as enterprising as when it is a question of defending the honour of the Court against aristocrats who are rebellious against the king's authority. On the contrary, we see him show much more reticence when urged to become part of the new bureaucracy. What, in fact, he was afraid of in this context was entering into conflict with the *Cours souveraines*.

> He himself has told me [writes his son] that the reason for which he refrained from purchasing the charge of *Procureur Général* of his *Compagnie*, when urged to do so, was that he considered it impossible to perform these functions without making a large number of enemies for himself. Yet he was not lacking in courage. It was merely that he saw no necessity, and no particular compulsion, to assume an office which would raise him above others only by making him hateful to those who have no wish to be watched over. Besides, he had no interest in rising any higher, so that when his friends suggested that they might secure for him the title of *Conseiller d'Etat*—such a thing then being common—he did not even consider it.

This *officier*, so determined both in fighting against the rebellious nobles and in refusing to become part of the new bureaucracy, was as it were predestined to fall under the influence of Jansenist propaganda. The actual way in which this happened is, in itself, highly characteristic.

> We had at that time in Rouen as priest of our parish of Sainte-Crois-Saint-Ouen, a Father of the *Oratoire* called Father Maignart, a member of the family of Monsieur de Bernières to whom my father was related by marriage. Father Maignart . . . having heard speak of the abbé de Saint-Cyran, whose reputation was now spreading throughout every province . . . decided to go and consult someone who was so great a light about certain moral problems which were preoccupying him. . . . Having managed to talk to this very enlightened man . . . Father Maignart raised the question of the priesthood, of the vocation which men should have to take on ecclesiastical posts, and of the right conduct of souls. . . . He was thus led to reflect seriously on everything which concerned his inner conscience. He condemned everything which earlier had escaped from the light, and resolved to reform, by changing his behaviour, everything which might have been lacking in his earlier life. At the same time he decided to resign his living, which he placed in the hands of the Fathers of the *Oratoire*, in order that they might replace him by someone who would be more competent and worthy. He then chose a retreat where he could spend the rest of his days in penance (pp. 39–41).

As soon as my father heard of this decision [continues Pierre

Thomas] he was struck with amazement, *not as other people were* (my italics), but in a different and incomparably more intense manner. . . . So that he himself decided to go to Paris and look for the person whom he had lost. . . . Arriving in Paris, still full of grief at this loss, he went to seek out the abbé de Saint-Cyran, whom he held responsible for the loss of his priest (pp. 41–2).

He explained his grievances to Saint-Cyran, who 'let him talk for just as long as he pleased; for he could tell from the tone of his voice that it would be unfitting to stand out against him in his first passion . . .' after which, however,

he explained to him that there were occasions on which a priest might well fall into the same fear that had once afflicted even one of the apostles, and not the least of their number, of falling into sin after having preached on sin to other people; that the charge and conduct of souls was so great and dangerous a thing that men should not object if those who had perhaps failed at first to know its perils and importance then had recourse to a withdrawal from the world . . . For this was what Father Maignart had done, and no-one should fall into the danger of condemning the inspiration which he had received from the Holy Ghost to act in this manner; since Father Maignart had followed an Inner Light, and, although men had spoken to him, he had nevertheless listened to God rather than to them in deciding what he had done (pp. 43–4).

The result of this could be foreseen: Gentien Thomas emerged from this interview with Saint-Cyran a convinced Jansenist. He sent his wife to spend some time at Port-Royal, where she was received by Mother Angélique.

After she had as it were renewed her substance by a general confession, and had attained a sufficient knowledge of the duties which she owed both herself, her servants, and her children, she was told by Mother Angélique to return to her family.

Gentien Thomas's children are also sent to Port-Royal 'in order to be brought up', and Pierre Thomas rapidly concludes his account in these terms:

My father, on his return to Rouen, after having secured for us the very Christian education that we received at Port-Royal, judged that it also befitted him to free himself of everything that still attached him to the world. And with no consideration as to whether his charge stood at its full value, he immediately sold it—at a considerable loss compared to the prices later paid for similar offices (p. 136).

All these different and apparently disconnected facts seem to me to point in the same direction, and I shall conclude this chapter by summing them up as briefly as possible.

1. A tendency existed to set up a body of *commissaires* to whom would be transferred a large number of the tasks and prerogatives of the *officiers*. This tendency was particularly marked in the first half of the seventeenth century, and especially from 1620 to 1650.

2. The years 1635–40 constituted a particularly intense crisis in the relationship between the Crown and the *Cours souveraines*. This showed itself both in the conflicts between the king and the *Parlement de Paris* and in the final establishment of *Intendants* as a general institution. It can also be seen in the temporary halt in the rise in prices of the different venal charges open to purchase by the *officiers*.

3. The discontent of the *officiers* gave rise, within a small group which I shall call the *avant-garde*, to two different reactions: the withdrawal from the world of the Jansenists, and the attitude of active opposition adopted by men such as Barillon and Broussel.

4. The great mass of *officiers*, however, remained vaguely discontented and did not adopt a particular ideological attitude. They either tried to secure posts as *Maîtres des Requêtes* or else they tried to become *commissaires* themselves.

5. We find in addition:

(*a*) That legal circles played a decisive rôle in the history of the Jansenist movement.

(*b*) That there were close contacts between the Jansenists and leaders of the active opposition movement such as Barillon and Broussel.

(*c*) That the Jansenist movement could depend upon a reasonably favourable attitude on the part of the great mass of *parlementaires*, and that on occasions it received unexpected support from important members of the *parlements* who otherwise were either indifferent or hostile to it (cases of Molé and Lamoignon).

6. That before their conversion, a number of important Jansenists were either frustrated themselves or saw the frustration of their relatives, in their attempt to make a career in the central royal bureaucracy.

I should like to emphasise once again that there is not, as yet, enough evidence to support a definite theory about the economic and social infrastructure of the Jansenist movement. Nevertheless, I do consider that the facts which I have outlined in this chapter justify the insertion of this hypothesis, in spite of the fact that much research will have to be done before it can be finally accepted or rejected.

VII

JANSENISM AND THE
TRAGIC VISION

I

I TRIED in the preceding chapter to give a general picture of the
effect which a certain aspect of the evolution of royal absolutism in
France had upon legal circles, and in particular upon lawyers closely
connected with the *parlements*. I suggested that this evolution gave
rise to an attitude of reserve towards social life and the State—'the
world'—but that this attitude was free from any element of active
political or social opposition to the monarchy. It was this attitude
which in my view, provided the background of ideas and feelings
against which Jansenist ideology developed.

In studying the relationship between this background and the work
of Pascal and Racine—the person whose work provides the most
important philosophical and literary expression of this ideology—
we must distinguish between features common to Jansenism as a
whole and those peculiar to the two trends—moderate and extremist
—to which in my view the work of these two men is linked.

The Jansenist movement as a whole had a number of general
characteristics: defence of Jansenius himself against the accusations
made against him, anti-Molinism, concept of the rôle of efficacious
grace in man's state of fallen nature, refusal of the 'God of the
philosophers', etc. Here, however, I shall be concerned with two
main features that are particularly important for Pascal and Racine,
and which in the case of the latter are expressed in largely non-
religious terms: a refusal both of the world and of any desire to
change it historically; and an attitude of indifference if not of hostility
towards mysticism.[1] These characteristics are, of course, to be found

---

[1] There are, of course exceptions, especially as far as the hostility to mysticism
is concerned, since Mother Agnès, for example, who was rather unstable and
ecletic in temperament, did have leanings in this direction. However, it is always

142

in other Jansenists, but they are not the same in each of the different tendencies which together constitute the whole set of attitudes to be found in the 'Friends of Port-Royal'.

Certainly, people as different from one another as Arnauld d'Andilly, Gilbert de Choiseul, Bishop of Comminges, Antoine Arnauld, Nicole, Jacqueline Pascal and Barcos all agree that the world is evil and that no human action can change or radically alter it before the Last Judgment. But Choiseul and Arnauld d'Andilly both lived in the world, the first for all his life and the second for most of his, and neither seemed to reject all possibility of compromise or of coming to terms with it. Arnauld and Nicole recognise that, in the world such as we know it, there is a fight between goodness and evil, truth and error, the City of God and the City of Satan, holiness and sin. They consider that the Christian should fight the good fight, although—here I am extrapolating, but I think justifiably—they see this struggle as something permanent and not likely to be concluded either way here on this earth. They, too, probably accept the need for compromises, but only reluctantly and as a means to an end, and in so far as such an acceptance will help to defend goodness and truth without compromising these values. Jacqueline Pascal, on the other hand, gives up the world completely. She demands absolute truth and absolute holiness, knowing that no victory can be won and refusing to compromise in the vain hope of obtaining one. Similarly, Barcos not only refuses any compromise but also any fight to achieve goodness and truth, both in the world itself and—to the extent that the Church is of the world—in the Church Militant. And, unless he is absolutely compelled to do so, he even refuses to proclaim the truth in the face of a world incapable of hearing or understanding it.

There are, in fact, four positions here, which I am doubtless over-simplifying but which all go to make up the Jansenist movement. The first involves reluctantly coming to terms with the sins and lies of the world; the second fighting for the goodness and truth which have a real but limited place in the world; the third proclaiming goodness and truth in a world which can only misunderstand and persecute them; and the fourth keeping silent in an irredeemably deaf and hostile world. What they have in common is the fact that they all condemn the world without putting forward any hope of transforming it in and through history.

Scholars would be less likely to agree that Port-Royal was consistently anti-mystical. Few, it is true, would try to maintain that

the case that, in any ideological movement, there are members who remain faithful to its general tendencies and even play a leading rôle in its activities, while differing from the dominating ideology in some of their ways of thinking and feeling.

there were important mystical tendencies in Arnauld d'Andilly, Antoine Arnauld, Nicole or even Jacqueline Pascal. Moreover, the abbé Brémond has insisted on the general anti-mystical attitude of Port-Royal. Nevertheless, there are a number of individuals— Saint-Cyran, Mother Agnès, Barcos, Pascal—about whom doubts have been raised, and, more important, there are two texts, the *Mémorial* of Pascal and the *Sentiments de l'abbé Philérème sur l'oraison mentale* of Barcos, which are given a mystical interpretation by certain authors.

I have already given my views on Mother Agnès. Similarly, it is probable that Saint-Cyran did have periods of mysticism, although it would be interesting to see just how long these lasted. However, neither of these two figures is particularly important for my thesis.[1]

The case of Pascal and Barcos, especially of the two texts that I have mentioned, is much more important.

I do not know enough about mysticism to pronounce judgment on the case of the *Mémorial*. For a long time I was prepared to recognise certain mystical features in this text, and see in it signs of an incoherence that was most surprising in a thinker of Pascal's calibre, but which was nevertheless there. However, the recent analysis of this text by Monsieur Gouhier has changed my mind, and I will merely refer the reader to his study.[2]

In the case of Barcos, however, I consider his text not as the expression of an actual mystical experience, but as a doctrinal pamphlet belonging to the history of religious ideas. Some historians have seen it as a mystical text, but I think they are wrong. Since it is very important both for the history of Port-Royal and for the sociology of Pascal's *Pensées* and of Racine's plays, I will explain why I hold this view.

We can dismiss the opinion of H. Brémond from the start, for he admits that he has never actually read the text by Barcos, and says that he could not even find a copy of it.[3] Since, in fact, no one has ever published his reasons for looking upon it as an expression of a

---

[1] Saint-Cyran did, it is true, enjoy quite exceptional prestige, but he died in 1644, long before the works of Pascal and Racine were written. And, as I have argued in my book *Sciences humaines et Philosophie*, the posthumous influence of any writer is something which we need to explain, and such never take as a principle of any explanation. And, as we see from Lancelot's *Mémoires* (Vol. II, pp. 36–44), the Saint-Cyran who was admired by Port-Royal had very little of the mystic about him.

[2] Cf. the article 'Le Mémorial est-il un texte mystique?' in *Blaise Pascal, la vie et l'œuvre* (Paris: Editions de Minuit, 1955).

[3] Cf. *Histoire du sentiment religieux en France*, Vol. IV, pp. 479 and 494. It is an even more remarkable statement when one considers that, at the time Brémond was writing, there were several copies at the Bibliothèque Nationale.

mystical experience, I shall not discuss other people's opinions but shall concentrate on the text itself.

It is obvious, to begin with, that Barcos's *Réflexions de l'abbé Philérème*—a commentary on a work entitled *Philagie* by Mother Agnès—are intended *first and foremost* as an attack against Nicole's anti-intellectualist tendencies and the influence which these have had on Mother Agnès. But it would be wrong to assume, as some scholars have done, that an anti-intellectualist text is *ipso facto* a mystical one.[1] In my view, it may well be an eschatological text, or, in the terms of the present study, a *tragic one.*

Let us define our terms. A mystical text is one which somehow or other describes the immediate and perceptible presence of God—either to the intelligence or to the emotions—or expresses the idea that it is in man's power to draw near to such a state. In that case, it describes the soul's journey towards unity and identification with God. Henry Gouhier, in an unpublished lecture, has distinguished three essential features of mysticism: intuitive knowledge of God, the passivity of the soul during this experience and the disinterested love of God.

Now Barcos criticises both the intellectualist ideas which Nicole had rather inadequately communicated to Mother Agnès, and her own mystical and spiritual experiences. Like all tragic and dialectical authors—Pascal, Kant, Hegel, Marx, Lukàcs—Barcos fights on two opposite fronts: against both intellectualism and mystical spirituality.

Thus, he vigorously denounces any idea that God can be directly experienced or perceived, or even that the human soul can draw near to Him in this way. Man's fallen nature is such that only in prayer can he approach God (or, more exactly, the Holy Ghost). The infinite difference which separates him from God, the absence and need for God which he experiences, cut him off from any state of blissful contemplation. Only prayer corresponds to man's true condition.

Prayer is certainly, in Barcos's own words, 'the work of the Holy Ghost, and not of other men, who can bring only human and natural things into the soul' (p. 19). But this action of the Holy Ghost is completely different from the immediate and intuitive perception of God implied in any version of mysticism. It is not a full and satisfied being who prays, but a soul which is poor, empty and a beggar, seeking what it does not possess. Thus, for Barcos, the vision which the

---

[1] The term 'spiritual' may lead to a certain confusion. But since the word 'mystical' has so many associations with the ideas of ecstasy and identification with the Divine Being, I had to choose another term that would indicate the idea of a movement towards such a state. I thus use the word 'spirituality' in order to express the idea of the soul journeying towards the ecstatic union with God by the inner life.

blessèd have of God when they are in heaven eliminates any need for prayer.

> The Blessèd can see and gaze upon the mysteries and truth of God far more clearly than we can, and their love for him is therefore incomparably more fervent and more strong. But since they no longer groan in anguish, and have nothing further to ask or desire of God, they do not, according to all the Fathers, continue to pray, and we do not pray for them. They pray only for us, as we pray for ourselves (pp. 3–4).
>
> Prayer properly so called [writes Barcos in a later passage] is not the elevation of the spirit to God or a familiar conversation between the soul and Him; for when one's spirit is raised up to Him and when the soul does speak familiarly with Him, one does not pray: for one has nothing further to ask of God (p. 75).

The texts show that for Barcos prayer is not disinterested: one prays in order to ask for something.

There is also another very important text which confirms this idea. It was a common notion at Port-Royal that the life of the nuns and solitaires, the life of a Christian, was a play acted out under the sight of God. Mother Agnès gives an indication of her basic spiritual attitude when she sees no incompatibility between praying to God and possessing Him (or being possessed by Him). Like all mystics, she holds that one can pray for what one already possesses, and writes: 'Lord, I long for but one glance of Your eyes, and I shall desire nothing ever more.' This provokes Barcos's comment that: 'This is a very free interpretation of the Psalmist's words. The sacred text does not say that the Prophet wants God to look upon him, but that, on the contrary, he wishes to gaze upon the face of God.'

The text in which Barcos rejects any idea that God can be immediately felt and experienced makes up almost a third of the volume.

Here are a few examples:

> Philagie (Mother Agnès): 'After having put yourself in the presence of God'.
>
> Philérème (Barcos): 'To feel the presence of God, or to feel God present, means to look upon everything which one does in the light of goodness and truth, for God is nothing but Goodness and Truth. Any other presence of God can only be deceitful, and be shared by virtuous and evil people alike'.
>
> Philagie: 'Doing everything possible to make yourself worthy to speak to God face to face, in so far as one can do this in this life'.
>
> Philérème; 'One does not, in the sacrament of Holy Communion, behold God face to face. His presence is there covered by a veil that cannot be penetrated by any creature. Only faith can look through it, and the mystery of how this is done is more obscure here than anywhere else. His Divinity is much more present to us when it compasses

us about on every side and is wholly within us, than is His body, when it is contained in a little space and is outside us. And yet we cannot say that we see God face to face anywhere in this world, for He is always covered by so many veils which hide Him from our sight' (pp. 33–4).

Similarly, Barcos rejects any idea of either a natural or a supernatural knowledge of God which would either enable us to approach Him or enter directly into His presence.

All ways of knowing do not bring us nearer God, neither does mere ignorance take us from Him. Only sin and corruption take us from Him, even as only groaning and weeping with love and with the Holy Ghost take us towards Him, and not knowledge of any kind (p. 14).

We must have a low opinion not only of the truths which we discover through our own minds, but also of those which God gives us by His divine light. For this light is not the perfect gift of which the Scriptures speak, to which we should cling and which we should both ask for and desire. For these truths can be given both to the wicked and to the good, both as a punishment and through His mercy.

This is why those who would keep on the path and not stray do not cease to strive when these truths are vouchsafed to them, for they believe that God is merely testing them. They do not hope for these truths, and do not pray God to grant them (pp. 10–11).

Barcos also insists on the need for action, so that his advice once again shows how he differs from the exponents of any mystical conception of man's relationship with God such as Monsieur Gouhier defines it.

'The light which the Saints ask of God in their prayers,' he writes, 'is not the knowledge of the divine mysteries and truths; it is the ability to distinguish between good and evil, in order to be able to follow the one and shun the other' (pp. 8–9).

This analysis could be continued, but I have said enough to prove my point: that it is wrong to look upon the anti-rational characteristics of Port-Royal and of Jansenism as an indication of its links with the mystical tendencies of the Counter Reformation—or with Berullian spirituality. Mother Agnès and Saint-Cyran remain, after all, peripheral figures, and there is no question of finding mystical tendencies in Arnauld or Nicole. Thus, Barcos and the group that followed him—Singlin, Guillebert, Mother Angélique and, to a great extent, Lancelot—are the only people who can be quoted as illustrating the 'mysticism' of Port-Royal. And, as I have tried to show, Barcos has none of the characteristics of mysticism such as Monsieur Gouhier defines it—intuitive knowledge of God, passivity and the purely disinterested love of God.

This is an important question for the history of Port-Royal and especially for the understanding of Pascal and Racine, for, in my view, mysticism is incompatible with tragedy and, from a literary standpoint, with the theatre in general. If it is pantheistic in tendency it leads to the absorption of the individual in the cosmos; if it is theocentric, to his total identification with God. It can thus be expressed only in lyricism or in songs of praise.

The theatre, on the other hand, needs accurately and closely defined characters. Thus, although a mystic can be presented on the stage as long as he is seen from the outside, it is not possible to write an aesthetically valid mystical drama. This difficulty is even greater for the tragic vision, since this involves an acute and painful awareness—on a theological and philosophical, as well as on a literary plane—of the existence of limits and of the impossibility of transcending them. Port-Royal produced no lyric poetry, and its two greatest literary expressions were in drama and tragedy. It would thus have been surprising to find a great mystic among those who formulated its doctrines.

If Barcos and those who shared his opinions really had been mystics, then we should have had to choose between two explanations which both seem equally difficult to maintain: either we could look upon the *Pensées* and Racine's four tragedies as purely 'miraculous' historical events, completely dissociated from any intellectual or social background; or, since they can be scarcely linked to the rationalism of the 'middle of the road' thinkers such as Arnauld and Nicole, we should have to interpret them in the light of Barcosian mysticism, and this could scarcely be supported by the actual text. In fact, we do not have to make this choice. Whatever differences separated Barcos from Arnauld and Nicole—and such differences did exist—all these thinkers are equally opposed to any real or potential mysticism. It is probably this fact which made Port-Royal into one of the principal centres of French seventeenth-century classicism, and enabled its views to be expressed both in the rationalism of the *Lettres Provinciales*, the tragic philosophy of the *Pensées*, and the tragic theatre of Racine.

II

There were four main streams in seventeenth-century Jansenism of which two—the 'third party' of Monsieur Orcibal and the non-tragic extremists represented by Jacqueline Pascal and Le Roi—found no important literary or philosophical expression. Almost all the works of Racine and Pascal are linked to what might be called the dramatic centralism of Arnauld and Nicole or the tragic extremism of Arnauld and his group.

There is nothing surprising about this, since both Orcibal and Jacqueline Pascal were on the periphery of the 'Friends of Port-Royal' and had, in any case, too few followers to give rise to any important literary or philosophical works. On the other hand, it was the ideas of Arnauld and Barcos which, at least from 1650 to 1669, provided the essence of Jansenism. After 1661 the persecution of Port-Royal strengthened the followers of Arnauld, who clearly dominated the movement round about 1669, and were almost completely identified with it when persecution resumed after the ending of the so-called 'Peace of the Church' or 'Peace of Clement IX'.

I shall try to show that the *Provinciales* and the sacred dramas of *Esther* and *Athalie* are fairly closely linked to the Arnauldian tendency; that the near-tragedy of *Andromaque*, like Racine's first two real tragedies, *Britannicus* and *Bérénice*, are, on the other hand, linked to the extremist attitude of Barcos; that *Phèdre* and the *Pensées* express a much less radical positions than that of Barcos, but must nevertheless be interpreted in the light of his ideas; and that the plays of Racine where the action takes place wholly in this world—*Bazajet*, *Mithridate* and *Iphigénie*—reflect the mistrust and hesitation which Racine felt towards the Peace of Clement IX at a time when his own attitude, in his literary work if not in his actual life, was one of tragic extremism.

Thus, Pascal, between 1654 and 1662, moves from the centralist intellectualism of the *Provinciales* to the tragic extremism of the *Pensées*, while Racine, between 1666 and 1689, goes from this extremism to dramatic centralism. Looking at the dates, we can see that the evolution of both thinkers closely followed historical reality. While Pascal started out from the world of social life and science, and only gradually came to accept the most radical aspects of the Jansenist movement, Racine, who had been educated at Port-Royal, followed the later and opposite direction of the movement.

The difference between Racine's hesitation in accepting Arnauld's position—a hesitation visible in his three 'worldly' dramas—and his close identification with this same position in *Esther* and *Athalie* needs to be explained. In fact, Arnauld's centralism showed itself in two ways at two different times: between 1669 and 1675 he was prepared to compromise with the powers that be, since this was the period of the Peace of Clement IX .during which these powers did seem ready to serve the cause of justice and truth; after 1675 his opposition to the people who then resumed the persecution of the 'Disciples of Saint Augustine' was much stronger. In fact, it was not he who had changed but the king and his ministers, for it was they who first of all began by persecuting Port-Royal, stopped doing so and finally resumed their persecution. These apparent changes have no importance

F

for Pascal, since he continued to support Arnauld until 1657, and then began to adopt an extremist attitude. However, he died in 1662, before the Peace of Clement IX was signed. These changes do nevertheless throw light upon the way in which Racine's plays evolve from tragedy to drama as Racine himself moves from an extremist to a centralist position: as long as a compromise with the temporal powers seems possible, Racine's attitude towards Arnauld is one of suspicion; when Arnauld's centralism is later persecuted, Racine's support for him becomes much stronger. I shall try to show this when I deal with Racine's plays in the fourth part of this book.

III

I still have to clarify the position of Arnauld and Barcos, and show how the first is linked with the *Provinciales* and Racine's dramas, and the second to the *Pensées* and Racine's tragedies. I shall do this by referring to three main problems: on the theological plane, that of the attitude adopted towards Grace by the 'new Thomists'; on the social and political plane, that of the attitude which the Christian should adopt towards the state and the powers that be; and on the philosophical plane, that of the value to be accorded to rational knowledge of the real world. I shall try to show how the followers of Arnauld defended an active concern with the problems of this world, while Barcos and his supporters argued in favour of a tragic refusal of the world and a withdrawal into solitude.[1]

I shall point out to begin with that I am not concerned with the doctrinal differences on the problem of Grace which separated the 'Disciples of Augustine' from the views actually held by Saint Thomas or defended by his disciples in the seventeenth century. The important thing here is to discover how Arnauld's and Barcos's followers interpreted the position of the 'New Thomists', and not whether their interpretation was right or wrong.

In fact, the only divergence between the two Jansenist groups on the relationship between the views of the 'New Thomists' and the doctrine of Saint Augustine seems to have been that Arnauld's followers stressed the similarities while Barcos emphasised the differences. To my knowledge, no one in the Arnauld group over-explicitly denied that the 'New Thomists' had a completely new doctrine concerning the state of the angels and of man before the Fall, nor that they used a completely different terminology as far as the state of fallen nature was concerned. Barcos, on the other hand,

[1] I could have illustrated this further by giving examples of the various issues on which the followers of Arnauld became engaged. However, this would have been out of place in what is primarily a philosophical work.

insists most of all on the importance of the terms used and on the difference between the state of the angels and that of Adam before his fall. Thus, the quarrel between Barcos and the followers of Arnauld is concerned not with the nature but with the extent of the difference between the Augustinian doctrine and that of the 'New Thomists'.

Barcos defines these differences in the following manner and, in his *Exposition de la Foi touchant la Grâce et la Prédestination*,[1] makes these remarks about the state of Adam and of the angels:

> According to this Saint (i.e. Augustine), Adam had the power to persevere of his own free will (p. 41).
>
> What difference is there then between the grace accorded to Adam and that of the Angels?
>
> None at all, and Saint Augustine makes no distinction between them (p. 41).
>
> Do all theologians agree that the Grace accorded to the Angels and that given to the first man was a Grace subordinated to man's own free will?
>
> No, for the disciples of Saint Thomas maintain that the Grace accorded to the Angels who did not fall was a predetermining Grace, which is completely contradictory to the principles of Saint Augustine. These theologians also reason similarly concerning the first man, maintaining that he was lacking in that efficacious and determining Grace which they say was necessary to him in the very state of his innocence (pp. 42–3).

Concerning the state of nature, Barcos says:

> The new Thomists mean by sufficient Grace a Grace which is never efficacious in any particular instance, but which is purely sufficient. Which means that it always needs another Grace which will be efficacious, so that the will may work even for the smallest beginnings of goodness and the slightest desires (p 176).
>
> If we take sufficient grace in the third sense of the word (that of the 'New Thomists') it is more difficult to understand its workings. However, since what seems to be meant by this Grace is simply the power by which nature, although corrupted by sin, is still capable of good, we will agree to accept it, in order to avoid any further dispute (pp. 177–8).

We must be under no illusions about this. Barcos 'agreed to accept' this grace in those who defended it, and refused to argue with them. But he always contested the use of this terminology of the 'New Thomists' when it was used by the 'Disciples of Saint Augustine'.

We still have to discover why these differences between the 'New

---

[1] Cf. *Instructions sur la Grâce selon l'Ecriture et les Pères*, by M. Arnauld (Cologne, 1700).

Thomists' and the 'Disciples of Saint Augustine'—especially those concerning the grace accorded to Adam—appeared so important to Barcos and so slight to Arnauld and his followers.[1] The reason for this seems fairly clear when we remember the distinction already made: Arnauld maintained that the *present* task of man lay *in* the world and *in* the Church Militant; within this Church the true Christian should always defend goodness and truth, but without expecting them to prevail. Any distinctions concerning the first state of man before his fall had no relevance to his present sinful state. They had no importance simply because they were unlikely to have any practical influence upon his conduct.

Similarly, there is more than a purely verbal distinction between the statement that men now enjoy *sufficient* grace and the Jansenist position. The fact is—as Barcos observed—that some call 'sufficient Grace' what others call 'the fallen state of man'. These are real differences of opinion, and not mere terminological distinctions. The 'New Thomists' call this Grace 'sufficient' because it characterises the state of man both before and after the Fall. Thus, man cannot hope for a state which is radically different from his present condition. For the Jansenists, on the contrary, the Fall establishes a qualitative difference between a state where man was free and a state where his every act needs a medicinal Grace. This Fall was a historical event, but the process will be reversed—for the Elect—at the end of time at the Last Judgment. But for Arnauld, all these are purely doctrinal difficulties which have no practical importance.

It is this which explains why both the first two and the final letters of the *Provinciales*—which all three support Arnauld's position—maintain that what separates the 'New Thomists' and the Jansenists is merely a question of terminology, put forward solely for reasons of ecclesiastical politics and empty of all real importance.[2]

Barcos sees the problem completely differently, for the extremist position which he adopts refuses all the relative values of the visible world and even of the Church Militant. He declares that man's will has been wholly corrupted by original sin, and that since man cannot achieve absolute values radically different from those of the world, he should retire into solitude. For him, the notion that the absence of free will should be linked not to the nature of man but to the particular historical event constituted by the Fall is therefore an im-

---

[1] The same difference in attitude shows itself in the fact that the *Instructions sur la Grâce* of Arnauld do not mention Adam, and begin by 'the state into which sin has reduced man', probably in order to avoid talking about the differences between the doctrine of Saint Augustine and that of the New Thomists. The Exposition of Barcos, on the other hand, devotes 53 out of its 277 pages to this subject.

[2] Cf. 2nd and 18th *Lettres Provinciales*.

portant one. If there was a state of man which differed wholly from his present one this may happen again, and it is therefore right and proper for man to strive after values which are absolute and not relative. The idea of the fall of man and of the memory which he has of his own past greatness is also essential to the *Pensées*, another extremist text, since it is the ontological basis for man's present aspiration towards the true greatness of those who seek for God without having found him.

Finally, this is why Barcos 'agreed to follow' other men when they called the present state of men who have not efficacious Grace 'sufficient', when these men are not of the Elect. But we can also see why he is infuriated that such terminology—acceptable in an Arnauldian perspective—should be used by the 'Disciples of Saint Augustine'.

The later evolution of Arnauld and Nicole towards positions that are increasingly Thomist in content as well as in word is merely the natural development of ideas implicit in their original position. Thus, Monsieur Dedieu seems to me to be wrong when he attributes this evolution to the influence of Pascal, especially as Pascal himself seems, between 1657 and 1661, to have moved steadily away from the almost implicit Thomism of the *Provinciales*.[1]

As far as social and political ideas are concerned, Arnauld and Nicole recognise that there can be good kings and ministers or bad ones—the latter, in Nicole's own words, being those who do not pray and who thereby betray their function. A king or minister who was not also a good Christian would be a bad king or a bad minister— that is, he would not be a real king or minister at all—but Nicole recognises no necessary contradiction between the Christian life and active participation in social and political life. People who adopted Arnauld's or Nicole's position would, in fact, be very good citizens. Indeed, their insistence that society should live according to its explicit code of morality would range them among the best, for they would demand that its religious beliefs should be genuinely put into practice. There are innumerable quotations which show that both Arnauld and Nicole neither recommend the Christian to refuse the exercise of political authority nor try to stand apart from it

[1] According to Nicole, Pascal expressed the desire, towards the end of his life, to revise his earlier books, in order to reduce them 'to a perfect conformity of expression' and to cross out any 'signs of weakness and half measures'. The fact that this took place at a period when Pascal was at odds with the moderate group at Port-Royal, that Nicole gives very few details, together with a reference to the actual terms which he quotes Pascal as using, all indicate that the latter was in fact striving to give up any connection with Thomism. (For an opposite view, see Jean Dedieu, 'Pascal et ses Amis de Port-Royal', *La Table Ronde*, December 1954 pp. 84–88).

themselves, but that they do genuinely argue in favour of the application of moral principles to social and political life.

For example, at the beginning of the *Traité de la Prière*, Nicole
sums up his own position admirably when he writes:

> Thus, one must say that a Christian prince is one who prays and who
> rules over a state; that a Christian general is one who prays and leads
> an army; that a Christian magistrate prays and administers justice to
> the people; that a Christian artisan prays and works at his craft. . . .
> Prayer enters into all vocations and sanctifies them all. Without
> prayer, they are merely profane, pagan, and often sacrilegious oc-
> cupations: but with prayer they all become Christian and sanctifying.[1]

His essay on *Grandeur* contains the following lines directed against
the tragic position of Pascal:

> These principles will help us to solve the problem put forward, that
> of knowing by what means great men are to be considered worthy of
> respect. It is neither by their riches, their pleasures nor their pomp,
> but by the share which they have in God's royalty. It is by this that we
> should judge them worthy of honour, and by the order in which God
> has placed them and that He has disposed by His providence. Thus
> when we submit to something really worthy of respect, we should do
> so not merely by outward forms but in our heart of hearts, and should
> thus show forth our acknowledgment of a true greatness and super-
> iority in those whom we honour. This is why the Apostle recommends
> Christians to submit to the powers that be not only for fear of punish-
> ment but also for reasons of conscience: *Non solum propter iram, sed
> etiam propter conscientiam.*[2]

> Thus those who have said that there are two sorts of greatness, the
> one natural and the other created by custom, and that we should
> esteem and submit in our minds only to those possessing natural great-
> ness, giving but the outward show to those whose greatness comes
> solely from custom, should add, if they would have their ideas be
> wholly true, that this outward show should body forth an inner feel-
> ing, by which we recognise that the great men of this world do possess
> true superiority. For since, as I have said, this state shows that they
> participate in God's authority, so should it be worthily and inwardly re-
> spected. It is wrong to say that the great ones of this world can demand
> only an outward and empty show of obedience. Rather should we say
> that they can demand this show only in order to implant in men's
> minds the right feelings which they should have for people in their
> station. It will result from this that when the rulers are sufficiently
> well acquainted with certain of their subjects to know that their feel-
> ings towards them are what they should be, then they can dispense
> them from observing those external signs of obedience, for these have
> now lost their aim and utility.

[1] Nicole, *Traité de l'Oraison*, Preface, p. 13.
[2] Nicole, *Œuvres Philosophiques* (Paris: Hachette, 1845), p. 392.

It is true that the respect which we owe to the great should not corrupt our judgment of them, nor give us a high opinion of qualities in them which are not worthy of esteem. The respect which we show can be reconciled with the knowledge we have of their failings and defects, and in no way prevents us from preferring those who have true goodness and natural worth. But since the common run of men have not sufficient wisdom to condemn the failings without despising those in whom they are found, we must show the greatest care in speaking of the great and of all those to whom honour is due. The words of the scriptures 'Speak not ill of the Prince of your people' apply to all our superiors, both lay and ecclesiastical, and indeed of all those who share God's authority. Thus the liberty which the common run of men assumes in criticising those who govern the state is very contrary to true piety; for not only do they speak too boldly and in error, because they are never sufficiently informed, but they also speak unjustly. For by speeches of this kind one leads another to assume a disposition contrary to that which God instructs us to have towards those whom He uses to govern us.[1]

Nothing, indeed, could be clearer.

Because of his preoccupation with theology and morality, Arnauld doubtless mentions political life less frequently than Nicole, but whenever he did so it was in a similar vein. For example, in his *Instruction sur la Grâce selon l'Ecriture et les Pères* he gives a number of examples of actions which are 'good in themselves' but which become sinful when performed by the unfaithful.

Helping the poor, granting justice to those who ask for it, governing a state well, courageously serving one's country, and performing similar duties that can be considered as worthy of approval and praise in themselves, without our seeking to penetrate into the mind of the person performing them.[2]

Similarly, in a document as important as his *Testament Spirituel*, Arnauld twice mentions his fidelity to Louis XIV, and tries to exonerate the king from so evidently blameworthy an activity as the persecution of the 'Disciples of Saint Augustine'.

After expressing the hope that God will praise him for the calumny which he had to undergo because of his fight against the lax morality of his time, and remarking that since God inspired him with His Grace and will therefore, in His goodness, take account of this when Louis appears before him, Arnauld continues:

I say the same of the suspicions which people have tried to implant about me in the mind of him whom You have placed above us, and towards whom You command us to have an unshakeable fidelity. For

[1] Loc. cit., pp. 394–5.
[2] Arnauld, *Instructions sur la Grâce*, etc.

155

a while they have tried to present me as a man of intrigue and cabals; you alone know, O God, what my real feeling was for this great Prince; what vows I made every day for His sacrèd person, what passion I have to serve Him, and how far removed I am from any desire to stir up trouble in His State. Nothing, indeed, seemed to me further removed from the state of a true Christian, and especially from one whose life is devoted to Your service. For such a man should concern himself only with the affairs of Your kingdom.

A little later in the same text, speaking of the persecution of the 'Disciples of Saint Augustine', Arnauld continues:

But even the best Princes can be deceived by those who have gained their confidence, and especially in Church matters where these Princes may not perhaps be quite so enlightened. Since they know it is their duty to forestall the evils which might spring from a new heresy, they often find themselves performing, because of their great zeal, and because of the care which they have for the well-being of their subjects, actions which they would never commit if they were better informed of the matters incorrectly reported. What is good in this is their intention, and this belongs to the Princes themselves; what is bad is the persecution of the innocent and the scandal which this brings upon Your Church, and these should be attributed solely to those who have misled Princes by their counsels.[1]

It is a position similar to these that we find in the *14th Lettre Provinciale*, which concerns itself in passing with problems of the state and of justice considered as human institutions.[2]

One would certainly have much more difficulty in finding texts by Barcos expressing the principles which shóuld govern the Christian's attitude towards authority and towards the State. The case is the reverse of what we found earlier: if moderate thinkers were reluctant to discuss the problem of the Grace accorded to Adam lest they might draw too much attention to what separated them from the 'New Thomists', Barcos is reluctant to deal in a general manner with the problem of the State, because he is afraid of slipping into an attitude which is foreign to him, that of active opposition. In his view, the true Christian, withdrawn into solitude, knows nothing of the State and of the world, and speaks of them only when compelled to dó so, and then only on the particular matter under discussion. Thus, in his *Exposition de la Foi touchant la Grâce et la Prédestination*, he gives the following actions as being 'good in themselves'.

[1] Cf. Arnauld's *Testament* (written September 16th, 1689).
[2] The point at issue is the permission which the Jesuits seem to give people who consult them about the justification for duelling. In so far as they justify the taking of life, they seem to Pascal to be going against both man's natural moral instinct and God's law. Cf. 14th *Lettre Provinciale*.

Giving alms, helping a person in danger of death, defending the innocent, bearing all manner of evil rather than commit an injustice (p. 113).

The actions he mentions no longer presuppose, as did those enumerated by Arnauld, the active participation of the Christian in society. Similarly, as I have shown elsewhere,[1] Barcos was very reserved both about the visit which Arnauld d'Andilly paid to Louis XIV (and we know that Antoine Arnauld paid the king a similar visit after the signature of the Peace of Clement IX) and about the true nature of Marie de Gonzagues, Queen of Poland, who was the epitome of all the virtues of the Christian monarch and a great friend of Port-Royal.

Finally, the position of the *Pensées* is similar to that of Barcos, in so far as it implies that the Christian should adopt a somewhat reserved attitude towards social and political life, and should refuse to acknowledge that laws and institutions have any real and unambiguous value. However, in so far as Pascal developed this extremist attitude to its conclusion by transforming Barcos's straightforward refusal of the world into a paradoxical refusal of the world by a person who remained within it, he also worked out a theory of the relationship between justice and force in social life. Barcos himself, because of his complete rejection of the world, had no need of such a theory.

On a literary plane, we find the contrast between the moderates and extremists recurring in some of Racine's tragedies: on the one hand, we have Pyrrhus, Néron, Antiochus and Theseus, and, at the other extreme, Titus, who is 'banished within the empire'. We also have the kings of the dramas—Mithridates, Agamemnon and Assuérus, whose attitude is more or less valid from a human point of view.

Finally, on the third of the planes on which the difference between the moderates and the extremists can be studied we find a similar contrast between Arnauld and Nicole, on the one hand, and Barcos, on the other.

Arnauld considers that there is a field in which reason is perfectly valid, and can operate without the help of feeling or of religious faith. Certainly, there are differences between his attitude and that of Nicole, or between both these thinkers and Pascal as he was before April 1657, as far as the value which they attribute to the knowledge derived from experience and the knowledge derived from reason is concerned. The differences, however, are not relevant here. Whether this knowledge comes from reason and experience or purely from

[1] Cf. *Correspondance de Barcos, abbé de Saint-Cyran, avec les principaux personnages du groupe janséniste* (P.U.F., 1955).

reason, it is human knowledge and, in spite of its limitations, is perfectly valid within certain limits. In fact, as far as epistemology and not ethics is concerned, Arnauld's position is quite close to that of Descartes, as is shown by the following examples.

Like Descartes, he makes 'rules which we should bear in mind when seeking the truth'.[1] The first of these 'is to begin with the clearest and simplest things, of which we can attain certain knowledge if we pay sufficient attention'. The second is 'not to confuse clear knowledge by confused notions which men would have us use to make it more explicit. For this would be to throw light on knowledge by darkness.' And there are five other principles, of which the fourth is explicitly derived from Descartes. Arnauld's Cartesian leanings are also evident in the titles of his works—*Logique de Port-Royal*, *L'Ecrit géométrique sur la Grâce générale*, etc. Similarly, the whole distinction made between questions of right and questions of fact assumes that the natural faculties of sense and reason have a field in which they are valid.

Pascal adopts exactly the same position in the seventeenth and eighteenth *Lettres Provinciales*.

This is why God guides the Church, when decisions are taken on points of faith, by the help of His spirit, which cannot err. But in matters of fact, the Church is allowed to act by reason and by the senses, for these are the natural faculties of judgment in such matters. For only God could instruct the Church in matters of faith; while we only need to read Jansenius to know whether or not the five propositions are in his book. It is for this reason that it is heretical to oppose the Church on matters of faith, for this would be to set up one's own mind against the spirit of God. But there is no heresy—though there may be boldness—in not believing certain particular things: for this simply involves setting up one's reason, which is capable of clear understanding, against an authority which may be great but which is not infallible in these matters.

How then shall we learn whether the facts are true or false? Through our eyes, Father, since these are the rightful judges in these matters, even as reason is of natural and intelligible things and faith of things supernatural and revealed. For since you force me to point this out, Father, I will tell you that in the opinion of the two greatest Doctors of the Church, Saint Augustine and Saint Thomas, each of the three principles on which our knowledge is based, the senses, faith and reason, has its particular subject matter and is valid in that field. And that since God has decided to use the senses to provide an entry for faith: *Fides ex auditu*, then faith is as far from destroying the certainty of our senses as it would be destructive of faith itself to cast doubts upon the faithful evidence of these senses.[2]

[1] A. Arnauld, *Des Vraies et fausses idées*, Chapter I.
[2] Pascal, 17th and 18th of the *Lettres Provinciales*.

Barcos, on the other hand, explains to Mother Angélique how little trust should be placed in human reason:

> Allow me to tell you that you are wrong to apologise for the disorder of your speech and thought; for if they were otherwise, they would not be in order, above all for a person of your profession. For even as there is a wisdom which is folly in the eye of God so also is there an order which is disorder; so that there is a folly which is wisdom and a disorder that shows true order. It is these which the followers of the Gospel should love, and it pains me to see how they depart from them, seeking unworthy ornaments and niceties which disturb the symmetry of God's spirit and lead to a visible disproportion and deformity in the rest of their lives. For they cannot follow at one and the same time both the simplicity and childishness of the Gospel and the cares and curious preoccupations of this world. Thus, Reverend Mother, I like both the matter and the style of your letter, for the ease with which you allow your mind to wander from the laws of human reason, placing no other limits upon it but those of charity, which has no limits when it is perfect and yet too many when it is weak.[1]

Similarly, in a letter probably addressed to Pascal in 1657, Barcos explains to him that 'the obscurities of faith descend upon all things, so that there is nothing that is not obscure'. He tells him that we should 'restrain our curiosity and the temerity of our judgments . . . by considering how narrow are the limits of our thoughts and minds, which can never rise to the subject in hand but which the slightest thing can halt and cast into disorder', and that 'the infinite number of natural things that visibly surpass our reason should teach us not to think it capable of following God's wisdom in the height of His ways'.[2]

Every time that he mentions them, Barcos refuses to admit that reason and the natural faculties have any validity at all. He naturally wrote no philosophical treaties, for this would have been self-contradictory, but his position is nevertheless easy to define. Although he had neither sufficient interest in the problem to write a 'Critique of Reason' nor even to state explicitly his doubts on the validity of rational statements, he everywhere insists on the slight importance which the Christian should give to rational truths.

The internal link between the moderate and extremist Jansenists, which shows itself in their attitude towards the 'New Thomists', towards political and social life and towards the truths of reason and experience, is too obvious to need stating. The two sets of thinkers differ, however, in that the moderates consider that the Christian can

---

[1] Letter written by Barcos to Mother Angélique on December 5th, 1652.
[2] Letter probably addressed to Pascal in 1657.

try to achieve moral values in the world and can thus serve God's will, while the extremists adopt the more radical attitude of insisting upon the difference between God and the world, and between God and certain aspects of the Church Militant. They therefore come to condemn any participation by the Christian in political and social life.

IV

This contrast between the followers of Arnauld and those of Barcos does not, of course, exhaust the schematic analysis of the Jansenist movement. For although I have pointed out the similarities between the ideas of Barcos and those expressed in the *Pensées*, there are also differences between Barcos and Pascal. For example, fragment 865 (E.947) is obviously directed against Barcos and his friends, and Pascal frequently asserts not only that man cannot do without reason but that social privileges do have a real value in the expression which they give to the possession of wealth or power. In short, wherever Barcos says 'No', Pascal replies both 'Yes' and 'No', and it is this which leads us on to the most important and difficult problem for the student of Jansenism: that of the paradoxical being *par excellence*, the *juste pécheur* (righteous sinner).

We should look in vain for this righteous sinner in the writings of the 'Friends of Port-Royal'. The Church had condemned the idea of such a person as an essential element of the Jansenist heresy, and all the thinkers of Port-Royal, in their desire to remain orthodox at any price, did everything possible to avoid mentioning it. Arnauld himself condemned the idea by saying that it came near to Molinism on the plane of ethics and to Calvinism on the plane of theology.[1] It was, however, if not the absolute essence then at least the permanent temptation and the final limit of extremist Jansenism—so much so that without it we should not be able to understand the two most important works that have come down to us from Port-Royal: *Phèdre* and the *Pensées*.

Arnauld's attitude was fairly simple, and contained no element of paradox even when pushed to its logical conclusion. The world is divided into the Elect and the Damned, the righteous and the sinners. The Damned sin naturally as a result of original sin, and the Elect owe their virtues and perseverance to the Divine Mercy, which gave them freely, without weighing their merits, the help of efficacious Grace. Moreover, although this Grace works here and now, there is

[1] See his criticism of the book by Bourdoille, *La Théologie morale de Saint Augustin*, in letters written in 1687 and published in 1700 as *Deux Lettres de Messire Antoine Arnauld, docteur en Sorbonne.*

no reason to think that God might not suddenly take it away. The same man can be, successively, both Saved, a sinner and Saved Again. The rôle of the just man in this world is to fight against sin for the sake of goodness and truth, especially since he can know them either through his own reason or through the revelations of the Bible or the wisdom of the Fathers of the Church. On the moral plane, difficulties can arise only when it is doubtful whether a particular act should be included under the moral law, but even then these are exceptional and not unsurmountable. Thus, there is no place in Arnauld's thought for the paradox of the righteous sinner. The theme of the hidden God, the fundamental tendency of Jansenism to insist on the difference between God and men, recurs implicitly in his polemic against the two theories of the vision of God of Malebranche and of Father Lamy and against Nicole's theory of General Grace. He argues that we see nothing in God, that God does not always accord us His light, but that He has given us the means to know the essential truths through the Scriptures and through our own reason. If we happen not to know them it is either through our own wickedness—as in the case of certain free-thinkers—or because of a historical accident—as in the case of the pagans. Certainly, Arnauld sees the Christian attitude in the same way Pascal and Barcos do, as composed essentially of hope and trembling. But while uncertainty reigns everywhere for Pascal and Barcos, it is limited, for Arnauld, to the realm of the future, of perseverance, and of sin.[1]

Although he avoids paradox and the idea of the righteous sinner, Barcos sees the problem quite differently. While this paradox simply did not exist for Arnauld, it constitutes for Barcos a fundamental danger that must be avoided. If God hides himself, then in Arnauld's view it is because He does not choose to reveal to man how He assures the victory of truth, and never allows man to discover, in this life, whether he will be able to persevere in the path of goodness and truth. Man must act, and if he has Grace, then his actions will fit into God's plan without his knowing exactly how. But man does know—through the Bible, through the Christian tradition, through his own reason and conscience—whether the particular act which he is performing is good or bad.

For Barcos, God is more completely and radically hidden. He has abandoned the world and even—to the extent that it forms part of the world—the Church Militant itself. If a man wants to live as a Christian in the world, if he wants to speak and act in the Church—otherwise than by administering the sacraments if he is a priest or by

---

[1] Although this uncertainty still remains genuine as far as the difficulty of arriving at a full knowledge of a person's intention is concerned, and also in cases of subsuming certain problems under a general law.

praying to God if he is simply a faithful believer—he will find no certain guide, even for the immediate acts that he is going to perform. In the world a man can only be either a reprobate cast off from God or a righteous sinner. Certainly, Barcos is deeply aware of the need to avoid this second idea, since he can find it explicitly stated neither in the Bible nor in patristic literature. But he succeeds only by asking the Christian to live outside the world and to take no part in any of the struggles or efforts of the Church Militant. Or, if he is not strong enough for that, to give up the responsibility for his own actions and become a monk. And it is highly significant that the only occasion in his life when Barcos was forced to leave his solitude and adopt a demand to sign the *Formulary*, he replied—scandalising the logically minded Arnauld—that he submitted to the Papal constitutions which demanded a signature, but that he refused to sign.

In my view, he adopted a coherent position, and this is confirmed by the fact that it is the same position which we find in literary works of the value of *Andromaque*, *Britannicus* and *Bérénice*. But it is one which, in certain circumstances, leads to the most extreme tragic position, to the paradoxical idea of the righteous man fallen into sin. In the case of Pascal, this sprang from a philosophical attitude and in the case of Racine from an actual historical event—the Peace of Clement IX in 1668. The first concentrated upon the life of the Christian in the world and the second transposed the idea into a pagan setting, but they both arrived, like Barcos, at the same concept of the righteous man fallen into sin.

Barcos could avoid this paradox, because it never occurred to him that one could doubt the existence of God and the consequent need to withdraw from the world into solitude. But if one carried the idea of a hidden God who allows no certainty as to His existence to its final conclusion, and arrived at the concept of faith as a wager, then one would reach a general attitude based on paradox, where the man must remain in the world while at the same time refusing the world, and must see himself as a righteous person fallen into sin. Barcos does not finally accept this idea, and he also shares with Arnauld the belief that God always grants every prayer which is sincere, although, in man's fallen state, this can only be through the healing power of His Grace. The difference lies in Barcos's view that such a prayer can be made only by someone who has withdrawn from the world into solitude.

It is here, in my view, that the position of Pascal in the *Pensées* and Racine in *Phèdre* makes the position of the 'Disciples of Saint Augustine' into an even more radical one. The wager that God exists, the refusal of the world by the man who remains in the world and the idea of the righteous fallen into sin all imply the idea of a sincere prayer which is not granted. What would remain of *Phèdre* if we ceased for one moment to believe that her solitary dialogues with the sun were wholly authentic? Merely a drama of adultery in high places. And in the *Pensées* the notion of those who seek God without finding Him—who seek him with groans and anguish (*en gémissant*) —recurs again and again throughout the book. Is this really Jansenism? Theologians such as Arnauld or Barcos would certainly make a number of reservations, but the Church has stated in its very condemnation of the doctrine that such is the nature of Jansenist belief. The sociologist who studies Jansenism as a historical phenomenon agrees with the verdict of the Church, though of course for purely profane reasons. In my view, this is quite natural, for one rarely if ever finds the sides taking part in a great social and ideological struggle failing to recognise the essential nature of their opponents' ideas, however much they may distort these for propaganda motives. And, in my view, the Church saw truly the doctrine behind the five propositions which she condemned in the *Augustinus*.

PART THREE

Pascal

VIII

THE MAN. THE MEANING
OF HIS LIFE

I HAVE hesitated for a long time before writing this biographical section. In fact, it will be difficult to give it any truly scientific accuracy, and we must remember the principle common to Pascalian epistemology and to any dialectical thought: that it is impossible to know the parts without knowing the whole, and impossible to know the whole without knowing the parts. This means that any non-dialectical approach, whether synthetic, analytic or eclectic, is fore-doomed to failure and hides more than it reveals. The task of the dialectical method—and, in my view, this is the only method which can be called scientific as far as the study of man is concerned—is gradually to bring out the essence of the phenomenon. This essence determines both the global structure of the phenomenon and the meaning of its parts, and is in fact nothing but the union between the structure and the parts. (For any structure is meaning, and every meaning is structure.)

This method is a difficult one to apply, but has made considerable progress both in the study of valid literary, philosophical or artistic works and in the realm of historical, social or economic facts. However, the difficulty is of a different kind when what is being studied is an individual life. In the first two cases the facts present themselves in real or potential 'forms', and thereby render the student's task easier. The reality of an individual life, on the other hand, has generally so little structure that the very notion of essence loses practically all meaning, with the result that the student's task is much more difficult.

A great work of art, or an historical movement such as the French Revolution or the Crusades, always has a coherent meaning and structure. But while the biographer can discover whether the man he is studying did or did not perform a particular act at a particular moment (although he cannot always say whether it was a real act or merely remained a gesture), this gives him no information at all about the meaning which such an act—getting married, making a scientific discovery, publishing a book—had in his subject's life. It is, in fact, generally easier to find out the meaning, place or importance which this discovery or publication had in the history of science or literature than what it meant in the life of its author.

In spite of the difference between the two men, there are essential facts which are common to the scientific activity of Descartes and Pascal, and which it is possible to study historically. And as long as he bore these differences in mind, an historian could study them both together in a book about French scientific thought in the seventeenth century. It may be, however, that as far as the lives of the two men are concerned, there are no such common elements. A book which treated them both, for example, from the standpoint of the 'rôle of science in the life of the scientist' might give no useful information at all. In the sentence 'Pascal, *like* Descartes, devoted much of his life to science', the word '*like*' might be relatively true for the historian of science, but completely wrong for Descartes's or Pascal's biographer.

One might say that this is not a real difficulty, and that nothing is needed but the transference into the field of biography of the methods already used to bring out the meaning of events in the realms of science, politics and religion. However, in addition to the fact that history presents fewer and therefore more easily classifiable types of event than does the study of individual lives, more progress has been made in forging valid instruments for dialectical research in the historical sciences. These are lacking in biographical studies, and it is therefore understandable that the best representatives of dialectical thought—Marx, Engels, Lukàcs—have most frequently preferred simply to give a dialectical analysis of the content and style of the works they have examined, linking them with the general economic and social realities of the time, rather than take the risk of studying the author's life. They may occasionally have done so, but only when the polemics aroused by their studies concerned immediate political struggles.

It would, of course, be possible to do this when studying Pascal's *Pensées* or the plays of Racine. The *Pensées* are a completely coherent work which can be analysed in both content and form without any reference to the author's life, and I will admit that I have been tempted to do this. But in the case of Pascal, the possibility of illustrating the life by the work, and vice versa, seemed so strong that I have decided to write this chapter. For in spite of its complexity, Pascal's life does have a perfectly structured form, and therefore seems capable of revealing an essence. However, I shall not attempt a complete biography, but shall merely make a number of suggestions.

The one great sin which all dialectical thought must avoid is that of saying definitely either 'Yes' or 'No'. Engels once said that to write 'Yes, Yes' or 'No, No' was to go in for metaphysics—and this was not intended as a compliment. The only way to discover human reality—Pascal realised this two centuries before Engels—is to say both 'Yes' and 'No', and to bring the two opposite extremes together. This is confirmed in a particularly striking fashion when one studies Pascal's life, especially as far as the famous problem of his various 'conversions' is considered. Every time one of his biographers insists on the importance of these conversions, the dialectical student must underline the unity and continuity of Pascal's life. Similarly, when an attempt is made to show that these conversions were not radical (and God himself knows how untrue this is), and that Pascal continued to live in the world and to pursue his scientific activity, the same student will argue that the real unity of Pascal's life lies in his uninterrupted and impassioned quest for a transcendent reality, with all the conversions that this necessarily implies. Pascal's life was not only a perfectly coherent and unified whole which contained radical conversions; it was also a life whose unity was created only by the power of an absolute quest for truth which was entirely subordinated to its object, and which therefore ignored any purely subjective considerations of external and formal unity. Similarly, his conversions are only as radical and serious as they are because they always set out from the same quest for wholeness and transcendence. What makes up the unity of Pascal's life is the uninterrupted tension, the permanent effort to go beyond himself whose various, qualitatively different turning-points have been called 'conversions'. Similarly, it is the uninterrupted continuity of his quest which made these qualitatively different turning-points necessary.

However, this statement of the dialectical relationship between Pascal's conversions and the continuity of his life does not exhaust the problem, for nothing seems further from the concrete reality of his life than the standards by which most historians have judged it.

Most of them, in fact, have envisaged the 'conversion' as a swift transition from a life of free thought or loose living to a life of religion.[1] In fact, there is less difference between the early and late

---

[1] I have myself dealt with it to a very great extent from this point of view in Chapter IV of this present book. However, I was then concerned less with studying real 'conversions' from a psycho-sociological point of view than with trying to bring out the importance which conversions had for the tragic mind. In actual fact, nothing takes place out of time; and, moreover—to my knowledge at least— Pascal was never either an agnostic or free-thinker in the modern sense of the

Pascal than between the Pascal of the *Pensées* and his collaborators Arnauld and Nicole, and this in spite of the fact that, when he wrote the *Provinciales*, Arnauld and Nicole were his close collaborators.

Thus, it is not surprising that these critics failed to realise what was the real guiding thread of Pascal's life and were also unable to see the real turning-point in it. The *Memorial* is certainly far too important a text for any life of Pascal to be written without taking the night of November 23rd, 1654, as one of its turning-points. However, it is surprising that almost no one should have seen that the night was obviously the culmination of a long crisis which began, at the latest, with the death of Etienne Pascal in 1651 and reached its height in 1653 with the dispute over Jacqueline's dowry and the discussions as to whether or not one should submit to the *Constitutions* of Innocent X. What is even stranger is that most of his biographers should have mentioned only two conversions, those of 1646 and 1654, and have ignored the one which most influenced his life and thought.

In my view, the slight importance attributed to the crisis of 1657[1] is one of the most glaring examples of the influence which implicit values or mental categories can exert over the approach to a subject. Before March 1657 Pascal collaborated with Arnauld, and Nicole wrote the *Lettres Provinciales*—which, in the last analysis, are rationalistic in approach—and fought for the triumph of truth in the Church and the world. In 1662 he died a radical and intransigent Jansenist, refusing to countenance any signature of the Formulary while at the same time professing his submission to the Church. He had already, with similar paradoxicality, proclaimed the vanity of science and the world while at the same time solving the problem of the *roulette* and organising the competition connected with it. He had also abandoned any hope in the world or the Church, but set up the plan for the first omnibus service and written, in the *Pensées*, the first expression of tragic philosophy in the history of thought. This means

[1] In the original French edition of *Le Dieu Caché* a long footnote examines the views of writers who, like François Mauriac, Mademoiselle Russier and Jean Mesnard, consider Pascal to have undergone only one real conversion, that of 1654. Monsieur Goldmann points out that both François Mauriac and Mademoiselle Russier were prevented by their own intellectual attitude from understanding the tragic paradox of Pascal's last years, in which he pursued scientific activity while nevertheless considering that, like all worldly activities it was completely valueless, and argues in favour of a 'second conversion' in 1657–58.

word. The turning-points which are called 'conversions' took place, in Pascal's case, within the framework of a profoundly religious existence, and it is for this reason that the biographer should try to understand them from the point of view of the events of this life and of Pascal's reaction to certain specific situations. They should be seen as the psychologically and intellectually necessary results of a dialogue between Pascal and reality.

that in the course of the eight years which followed what is usually called Pascal's 'final' conversion there was a complete and coherent change in his position, a change which affected his philosophy, his style, his attitude towards the Church and towards other Jansenists, his behaviour in the world and even his conception of God. Unless we examine this change—and most of his biographers have studied these eight years as if they were a single unit—it is almost impossible to understand not only his life but also his work. Pascal himself marked the beginning of the crisis which led to this change when he wrote, in 1657, these words whose accuracy and controlled power make them into some of the most shattering ever penned by a believer who still looked upon himself as belonging to a religion and a Church: 'the anguish of seeing oneself torn between the Pope and the Church'.[1] When their implications were finally developed, these words led to the manuscript of the *Pensées*.

II

I have no new facts to offer about Pascal's life, although the recent research of Monsieur Mesnard has shown that there are still discoveries to be made. What I shall do is try to look at some of the already known facts in a new light. My approach will differ from that of the historians who have looked upon Pascal as a seventeenth-century scientist, a representative of the Counter-Reformation, or as a Christian thinker in general. I see him as the first of a long line of thinkers who go beyond—and integrate—both the Christian tradition and the achievements of rationalism and empiricism and create a new moral attitude which is still valid today. For me, Pascal is the first modern man.

Now this means something different if it is said by a rationalist or by a Marxist. If one sees the *Discours de la Méthode* rather than the *Theses on Feuerbach* as the great manifesto of modern man, then one's ideal is the enlightened scientist, advancing courageously and unreservedly towards the conquest of truth. One's hero is then the traditional image of Galileo, Copernicus or Descartes; and, although we really know little about them, this image is probably a fairly accurate representation of the essential qualities of the men who, in the waning of the Middle Ages and the dawn of the Renaissance, created modern experimental science and in particular mechanistic physics. There is a definite link between Descartes and Brunschvicg, and I have already said that the line joining the two together comes fairly close to the *Provinciales* and to Voltaire and Valéry.

[1] Cf. Brunschvicg edition of the *Œuvres Complètes* of Pascal, Vol. VIII, p. 174.

Monsieur Gilson has even shown that the origins of modern rationalism go much farther back, and that it really began in the thirteenth century when Thomistic Aristotelianism took the place of Augustinianism as the guiding philosophy of the West. This seems a correct analysis, as long as we do not fail to see that there is a qualitative difference between Thomism and extreme rationalism, and between Aristotelian and mechanistic physics. It is, moreover, confirmed by the findings of historical materialism, in so far as this links both thirteenth-century Thomism and the rational and empirical thought of the Enlightenment to the continued development of the bougeoisie within feudal society and the monarchy of the *ancien régime*.

The term 'modern man', however, means something else in addition to 'scientist', for from its first manifestations dialectical thought has always refused to recognise the autonomy of conceptual thought, and, implicitly, to see the scientist as the ideal human type.

The philosophy of rationalism reaches its highest point in the generation immediately after Descartes, with Malebranche, Leibnitz, Spinoza and—with some delay—in Germany with Lessing. But Pascal was already anticipating the ideas of the German thinkers who followed Kant—Hegel, Goethe and Marx—and elaborating a new vision of man. This took into account the genuine achievements of rationalism and empiricism, but transcended the self-centred quality of conceptual thought. Thus, in certain of its essential aspects this passed through the 'natural philosophy' of the fifteenth and sixteenth centuries and rejoined the great tradition of Augustinianism.[1]

It just so happens that we have, in Goethe's *Faust*, a classic literary expression of this new vision of man, and this can help us greatly in our understanding of Pascal. Certainly, I do not want to develop striking but superficial analogies, and I know how wide a gulf is set between a real man and a character in fiction. Nevertheless, there do seem to be a number of valid analogies, especially since Goethe's imagination, when he created Faust, was structured by a world vision that was essentially similar to that of Pascal.

The first similarity lies in the fact that, like Pascal's, Faust's life had a deep unity composed of his continual quest for transcendence but also punctuated by three conversions. This similarity goes deeper when we examine the first part of the play, in which the figure of the

---

[1] Since all types of misunderstanding are possible, I should like to underline the fact that although Marxist thought implies a faith in the future, it naturally denies any idea of the supernatural or of revelation. It is, certainly, a religion, but a religion with no God, a religion of man and of humanity. In the epistemology which we find in common between the *Theses on Feuerbach* and Augustinianism, it is man's faith in eternity or in the future of humanity which decides the existence, not of truth, but of the possibility of knowledge.

ageing scientist in his study provides a brilliant literary expression of
the clash between the new dialectical mode of thought and what was
best in the old rationalism. Thus, we can easily recognise the World
Spirit as an expression of Spinoza's philosophy, but we also need to
realise that, until the curtain rises, Faust represents, in the universality of his knowledge—medicine, law, theology—the ideal man of
the Enlightenment: he acquires knowledge freely and without preju-
dice, and places it fully at the service of mankind at times of danger
or epidemic, and it is both his knowledge and his devotion to others
which have gained him the esteem and admiration of his fellow-citizens.

The play begins, however, when Faust realises how vain all this
knowledge is as long as it remains constantly on the surface and does
not lead to anything 'beyond', anything which might enable him to
understand 'How secret elements cohere, and what the universe
engirds'.[1]

It is here that he passes from the ideas of rationalism and of the
enlightenment to the world of dialectical thought, from the atomistic
attitude which is satisfied with the accurate, scientific knowledge of
'phenomena' to the quest for essence and totality. And, fatally (I say
'fatally' because Goethe is a very great writer), Faust meets the two
forms under which religion can still offer itself to a thinker of the age
of Enlightenment: on the one hand, Spinoza, and, on the other, the
traditional, spontaneous belief of the people.

Spinoza was, in fact, the only rationalist thinker to have achieved a
complete vision of cosmic totality, and to have promised, in the
amor Dei intellectualis, the knowledge of the third degree, the possibility of going beyond purely intellectual understanding.

Both Goethe's admiration for Spinoza and the rôle which he
played in enabling Spinozism to penetrate into Western thought are
well known. Goethe always said that he was a pantheist, and it is
therefore even more important to recall the reproach which Faust
addresses to the World Spirit. It exactly defines the difference between the pantheism of Spinoza and that of Hegel and Goethe: 'O
endless pageant—but a pageant still.'

In Spinoza's universe there is no place for human freedom and
activity. The most that man can do is to understand the universe; he
cannot act and change it.

We can thus see why Faust turns towards the Earth Spirit who

> With weaving motion
> Birth and the Grave,
> A boundless ocean,

[1] Here, as elsewhere, Goethe's *Faust* is quoted in the Penguin translation by
Philip Mayne.

ceaselessly giving
Weft of living,
Forms unending
. . . works . . . on the whirling loom of time,
The life that clothes the deity sublime.

But, even when he has understood and felt the need to go beyond rationalism, there is still an unbridgeable gulf which separates the scientist, the man of the Enlightenment, from the reality of life and action. When Faust cries out enthusiastically to the Earth Spirit:

How near akin our natures seem to be,

the Spirit replies:

You match the spirit that you comprehend, Not me.

Thus, at the very beginning of the play Faust is in the same position as the man so frequently described in the *Pensées*: he who seeks God but does not find Him. His position is that of the tragic man, and he can see only one way out: death.

What characterises the dialectical vision, however, is precisely the fact that it goes beyond tragedy. Thus, at the very moment that he is going to take poison, Faust hears the Easter bells. He cannot respond to their call because it still comes in an archaic form which he, as an enlightened thinker, has long since outgrown, but precisely because he has also gone beyond purely intellectual rationalism, he can see in it a real and valid essence, one which is doubtless difficult to attain, but which is nevertheless still accessible to man. He therefore replies to it in two ways: he gives up the idea of suicide, but he also cries out: 'I hear but lack the faith, am dispossessed.'

Although he cannot go back to the old, outworn religion that still lives on among the people, he still hears, in the Easter bells, the transcendent call of a God whom he can and must reach by new and clear paths, paths which will both integrate and transcend the religion of the people and the rationalism of the Enlightenment, and which will thereby bring together the intransigent criticism of reason and the unshakeable certainty of faith. The theme of the play is thus announced: the progress of Faust towards God both through and thanks to the pact with the Devil.[1] This is why the sound of the bells

---

[1] The idea of a pact with the Devil as the only way which leads to God (the ruse of Reason in Hegelian philosophy) is one of the points which separate the tragic attitude of Pascal from dialectical thought properly so-called, in spite of the fact that here again tragic vision marks a transitional phase between rationalism and the dialectic.
Basically, it is the problem of good and evil, which since the Middle Ages has

and the renewal of contact with the people will enable him (in the next scene, outside the city gates) to translate the sacred text of the New Testament into a new language, that of his own people and of his own time, and into that of the future.

When he gives the only valid translation now possible of the begin-

---

found its literary expression in the theme of the 'man who has sold his soul to the Devil'.

From a schematic point of view, five stages can be distinguished in the development of this theme.

(a) For the Christian thinkers of the Middle Ages good and evil were clearly and distinctly separated from each other. Sin and virtue were complete opposites, sin leading to hell and virtue to heaven, except in cases where, as in the divine intervention of the Virgin in the case of Theophilus—cf. *Le Miracle de Théophile* by Rutebeuf—the sinner can be saved at the last moment.

(b) With the Renaissance, the legend of Theophilus becomes that of Faust. He is a disquieting but nevertheless attractive figure, who tends progressively to lose any idea of sin. This is because, with the Renaissance, the age of individualism begins, and with it the abolition of the heavens and of the conflict and contrast between good and evil. More and more, things happen solely on this earth, where the only criteria are success and failure. Mediaeval virtue becomes the *virtù* of Machiavelli's Prince, and ceases to be incompatible with crime.

(c) With the rationalism and empiricism of the enlightenment, this revolution is carried to its logical consequences. In what appears to be an increasingly ordered and rational world, virtue becomes pleasure or enlightened self-interest, and this becomes impoverished and merely schematic. However, it still retains this characteristic of efficiency which makes good and evil into subordinate and secondary characteristics.

With material progress, even the dangers of the legend seem to disappear. Whereas in the original legend Faust confronted a real Devil and ran the real risk of losing his immortal soul, Lessing's Faust realises that all this is simply a dream, since the Devil does not exist.

(d) The appearance of the tragic vision marks the reappearance of good and evil as genuine realities that determine a man's existence. But we are no longer confronted with the type of sin which, in the Middle Ages, was clearly visible and easy to distinguish from virtue. Evil still remains totally opposed to goodness, but the two are now inseparably linked together.

Even the most virtuous action, which has perhaps never been carried out, Kant tells us, is merely the action which conforms to the categorical imperative and is not one which necessarily achieves supreme goodness. Both the moral law and radical evil are part of man's nature, and Pascal tells us that man is 'neither angel nor beast' and that 'he who would be an angel becomes a beast', since we 'have goodness and truth only in part, inextricably mingled with evil and falsehood' (fr. 385, E.298).

Thus, since good and evil are inseparable in man's conscience and cannot be reconciled, the tragedy which transforms God into a silent spectator does the same thing with the Devil. The theme of Theophilus and of Faust has never found tragic expression.

(e) The theme nevertheless reappears with the dialectical vision, with Goethe, Hegel and Marx. Initially, they see the problem in the same terms as the tragic thinkers do, and recognise that, for the individual, good and evil are at one and the same time both real, in conflict, and inseparable. However, they all admit that

175

ning of the Gospel according to Saint John—'In the Beginning was the Deed'—Faust now finds by himself the word that, two scenes previously, in the presence of the Earth Spirit, he could not understand. He can now finally set out, and therefore speaks directly to the person who will enable him to reach heaven—to the Devil, to Mephistopheles.

However, before Faust meets Mephistopheles, and before he translates the Gospel, the man of rationalism and of the Enlightenment appears once again in the person of his disciple Wagner. For Faust, Wagner now represents the type of man whom he himself has already outgrown. As soon as he hears him arrive, he cries out:

> Damnation, that will be my Servitor!
> My richest hope is in confusion hurled:
> He spoils my vision of the spirit world,
> This lickspittle of learning at my door.

Wagner enters in his dressing-gown, with a nightcap on his head and a lighted candle in his hand, and provides his own definition of himself when he says:

> I've learnt a deal, made books my drink and meat,
> But cannot rest till knowledge is complete.

He is the 'rational man' of the Enlightenment, and the whole scene is certainly satirical in intention. But we should be wrong if we looked at it as the expression of Goethe's own subjective attitude. It is an objective account, by one of the greatest realists in universal literature, of the meeting between two world visions, one of which has outgrown the other. For Goethe's attitude towards Wagner is by no means a simply negative one. He always had the greatest admiration for scientific work, and devoted much of his own time to research into mineralogy, biology and botany. Moreover, the caricature of Wagner in this scene in Act One as the apprentice who remains on the surface of things, who seeks for the truth in books and strives most of all after respectability and general esteem, is largely corrected in Part II. We there learn that, after Faust's departure, Wagner has proved a worthy substitute for his master, and that his fellow citizens think even more highly of him than they did of Faust himself. Wagner, however, is not taken in by his own success, and still venerates Faust in exactly the same way. Despising purely external achievements, he

---

the 'ruse of reason', the March of History, will transform individual evil into the very vehicle of a progress which will bring about the good as a whole. Mephisto describes himself as the person who 'always strives after evil but always achieves the good', and it is he—against his own wish, of course—who allows Faust to find God and to reach Heaven.

devotes himself entirely to research in his laboratory, where he achieves remarkable success in making an artificial man. Once created, however, this man escapes Wagner's control. Moreover, it is not simply a fantasy on Goethe's part which brings Faust back to Wagner's laboratory, but the need which Faust has of his disciple in making his way to heaven.[1] For only on the first and third stages of his way to heaven—love and human relationships (Marguerite), and revolutionary action—can Faust be helped by Mephisto. To make contact with Helen of Troy—who symbolises culture—he needs Wagner and his inventions. For in action, and even in human relationships, 'he who would become an angel becomes a beast', and the criticism which both Hegel and Goethe made of the 'Fine Soul' is sufficiently well known not to need repeating here.

To return to the first meeting between Faust and Wagner in Act One.[2] Wagner is strongly and deliberately satirised, but there is an objective basis for Goethe's attack: in spite of his respect and admiration for him, Wagner cannot understand what Faust is saying, and this is obvious throughout the scene. He has been woken up by what critics will insist on calling Faust's 'monologue'—and which is in fact a solitary dialogue between Faust and a silent and absent transcendence—and enters in his nightcap:

> Beg pardon, Sir, but I heard you declaiming—
> Some tragedy, I'll warrant, from the Greek?

He makes two mistakes: convinced that no one talks to himself, and not even suspecting the existence of any transcendence, he says that Faust is 'declaiming'. And, as a true 'humanist', he thinks that no one can 'declaim' except from a book, and a Greek one at that. And all this is crowned by the word *gewiss*, certainly.

I could analyse the scene at greater length, but must return to Pascal. I shall merely remark that Wagner begins by esteeming knowledge for its own sake, but then values it because it enables him to help, convince and guide his fellow citizens.

This apparent digression on Goethe is in fact the shortest and simplest way of showing how Pascal looked upon science both before 1654 and after March 1657. In considering how science took up most of his time before 1654 and continued to preoccupy him after 1657,

[1] I will recall that at the end of his life, at the very moment when he was writing the *Pensées*, Pascal also resumed his mathematical work.

[2] It must be added—and it is an additional proof of the realism and the genius of Goethe—that the satire in Act I was aimed solely at Wagner's pretensions at understanding history and social life through the medium of reason and of books. The satire completely disappears when Wagner is treated as a chemist and a biologist. Goethe's only reservation is then concerned with Wagner's inability, even in these fields, to retain mastery over his own results.

we should be careful to distinguish his activity from that of Wagner. The correct comparison is with the dialectical activity of Faust, not with the rationalism of his disciple.

One example will suffice to show this: towards the end of his life, Pascal looked back over what he had done and recalled both the general inadequacy of science and his feeling of dissatisfaction with his own scientific activity. 'I had spent a long time in studying the abstract sciences,' he wrote in *pensée* 144 (E.756), and continued: 'and the small amount of communication that can be derived from them had made them extremely distasteful to me'.

The similarity with what Faust says at the beginning of the play is obvious, in spite of the fact that Pascal is possibly not talking about how he actually felt in 1643 or 1648. His later development shows, however, that he might even then have realised that he was looking for something else, something whole and transcendent, and which science could not give him, and which, in this *pensée*, he calls 'communication'.

Léon Brunschvicg, the best editor of Pascal and a brilliant student of his scientific and mathematical work, confirms this view when he writes:

> It seems that, for Pascal, the value of science should lie not only in itself and in the truths which it enables us to attain, but beyond itself, in the life of man, in what it brings with it, in what Pythagoras and Plato saw as the inner communion of minds. And history offers us no career in which this hope of the wide influence and 'communication' of science was satisfied earlier. Pascal was still a child, Mme. Périer tells us, when his genius 'burst forth'. From the age of thirteen, she tells us, he regularly attended the lectures in Paris where the cleverest men assembled, and she adds that the brother 'held his own among them'.

However, as Monsieur Brunschvicg points out, he came up against the lack of understanding shown by Father Noël, and even Roberval and Descartes.

In spite of the extremely high regard which I have for Léon Brunschvicg both as a thinker and as a scholar of Pascal, I do nevertheless think that, like Voltaire and Valéry, he was prevented by his own rationalist approach both from accepting and understanding Pascal's life and work. Everything which he has written on Pascal's scientific texts is perfectly valid for the historian of science, but is highly misleading to anyone studying Pascal's life. Similarly, he is almost always right about the *Provinciales* and wrong about the *Pensées*.

For example, he is not only surprised by Pascal's remark that the value of science 'should lie beyond the truths which it enables us to attain', but also fails to find the right parallel which would enable him to understand the word 'communication'. Instead of seeing it as linked with the quest for transcendence characteristic of the Augustinian thinkers of the Middle Ages, or with the movement through thought to action typical of Marxism, he places it by the side of the legend of Pythagoras or of Plato's *Republic*. He thus completely misinterprets what Pascal actually says, and maintains that, in his youth, he did find that science provided this 'communication'. In explaining Pascal's later disappointment by the criticisms of Father Noël or his discussions with Roberval and Descartes, Brunschvicg is failing to understand Pascal in exactly the same way as Wagner failed to understand Faust.

Fragment 144 (E.756) is one of the most important biographical texts written by Pascal, and, as Brunschvicg saw, the word 'communication' means to a great extent 'communion and understanding with other men'. What the famous author of *Le Progrès de la Conscience Occidentale* failed to see was that Pascal meant something different from the rationalist concept of general and universal truth. Neither was Pascal talking about the agreement which two scientists may have about a particular result or the degree of understanding shown by a number of men who accept the same scientific law. He was referring to something much larger, to the whole community of men as men, which is the fundamental category of both Christian and dialectical morality. This category is present when men believe either in the promise of a Kingdom of Heaven at the end of time or in the eventual creation, by their own efforts in history, of a socialist society. When it is absent, then we have tragic thought and tragic literature.

We should be grossly underestimating Pascal if we saw the origins of his disappointment in science either in the hostility of Father Noël or in the failure to understand him of Roberval and Descartes. All scientific thinkers who make any progress have always met with difficulties such as these, and, when not actually persecuted, have always borne them philosophically. We should be taking Pascal for an innocent choirboy if we attributed him with the starry-eyed belief that all new scientific truths will be immediately and enthusiastically accepted by everyone.

Brunschvicg is right, however, but from a rather special point of view. The failure of Noël, Descartes and Roberval to see the validity of Pascal's conclusions about the Toricelli experiment did contribute to his disillusion and disappointment, but only in so far as it was yet another proof of man's inescapable insufficiency and inadequacy. Contrariwise, the admiration which other scientists had for him, and all the fame that he achieved in the world through his scientific

179

PASCAL

activity, were meaningless for Pascal because they completely failed to take account of the real nature of things.

One more remark must be made about this fragment. The word 'communication' implies not only communion with other men—a meaning which it derives solely from the context—but also 'the communication of science and truth to other men by study', an activity to which Pascal had devoted so much of his time. For Pascal himself, as for any dialectical thinker, these two meanings are complementary and inseparable, for truth alone establishes communion between men, and no true communication can be established except through truth.

Pascal writes elsewhere (fr. 221, E.337) that 'Atheists must express perfectly clear ideas'. What he means by this is that no one has the power to express perfectly clear ideas, and that therefore no one can be an atheist. No one conscious of his condition and of the absolute need to communicate truth to others can reduce the essence of man to science and reason alone.

III

Towards the end of his life, as fragment 144 (E.756) shows, Pascal realised that until 1654 he had sought in the abstract sciences, and after 1654 in the science of man, something which these sciences were incapable of giving him. It is true that he did not repudiate either his scientific work or the *Lettres Provinciales*, but he knew that they both implied the illusion that man could at least progress towards real values in this world, even though he could not finally achieve them. By the time he wrote the *Pensées* he no longer believed this.

Like any Christian, Pascal himself gave the name of God to this reality which he spent his life trying to find. A rationalist would call it truth and fame, and a socialist the ideal community. They would each one of them be right, and there are many other ways of expressing this reality which men try to achieve. The general word which I shall use is that of totality, or wholeness, because these words are, at the moment, free from any ideological connotations.

It is traditional—and correct—to speak of Pascal's life as divided up into different periods. Scholars have, however, distinguished these periods by very different criteria, and the most important starting-point for any research is to find a way of dividing Pascal's life which follows the real course that it actually took. In my view, the best division distinguishes the following periods:

(*a*) From his first intellectual activity to November 23rd, 1654. During this period Pascal consistently subordinated reason to revelation and things natural to things supernatural. Nevertheless, he also looked for totality in the realm of nature and of reason, and saw it as scientific truth and purely human glory.

(*b*) From November 23rd, 1654, to March 1657. During this period the realm in which Pascal sought totality had shifted from nature and reason to the Church and Revelation. Pascal hoped to bring both lay and Christian society closer to the original Christian ideal from which they had lately fallen away, and wrote the *Provinciales* in order to further this end.

(*c*) From after March 1657—the exact date is difficult to determine —to the end of his life. Pascal now expects nothing further either from the world or from the Church Militant. His demand for totality changes into a radical refusal of any compromise with the powers that be, both lay and ecclesiastical, and this refusal shows itself in tragedy, paradox and the direct appeal to God. At the same time, however, he submits externally to the powers that be, and continues to live in the world and pursue his scientific activity.

Clearly, I do not attribute any great importance to the conversion of 1646, although, according to François Mauriac, it was the only important one in Pascal's life. In fact, it did not radically affect either his ideas or his behaviour. Both before and after 1646 he held the same doctrinal beliefs (that man could know nature through his senses and through reason, but that revelation and the supernatural were nevertheless superior to the findings of human reason) and behaved in the same way (devoting most of his energy to science and practical matters). His encounter with Jansenism merely enabled him to find expression, within an already existing system of belief, for the longing for the absolute and the transcendent which, in my view, had already been the more or less conscious basis for his early work.

By speaking directly to man through revelation, God has given him an absolute value by the knowledge thus vouchsafed to him of supernatural truths. However, he has also placed him in nature and society, and given him the wit and reason to understand and dominate them. In the realm of nature and of the mind, man can attain the two values of truth and reputation, and although he continued to recognise the primacy of revelation, Pascal devoted most of his time to these two values until 1654.[1] His life was thus deeply divided: in theory, he recognised the absolute primacy of religion; but in practice, he continued to live in the world. During the last few years leading up

[1] It may be that scholarly research will one day solve the problem of whether or not Pascal did go through a 'worldly' period and whether he did write the *Discours sur les passions de l'amour*, but it does not seem to me that this will seriously call into question the validity of this general pattern. For from the point of view of the tragic attitude which Pascal finally reached, both his early scientific work and his invention of the calculating machine were eminently 'worldly' activities. Cf. also Appendix.

to the crisis of November 23rd, 1654, this contradiction grew steadily greater, and was accompanied by a certain number of significant events: the quarrel over the dowry due to his sister on her entry into Port-Royal, his suggestion—mentioned by two reliable sources—that the Jansenists should resist the *Constitutions* of Innocent X and appeal to the Council, and also his letter to Christine of Sweden in which he places such great insistence on the superiority of the mind but never even mentions the question of Grace.

The fact that this contradiction disappears in November 1654 is the most significant indication of the great importance which his 'second conversion' had for his life and thought. What it did not do, however, was effect any qualitative change in his ideas. It merely brought them into harmony with a life that was henceforth devoted to the struggle for the triumph of truth within the Church and for the victory of religion within society. Moreover, during the final months leading up to his new 'conversion', Pascal seems to be increasingly committed to the same course of action. He interprets the miracle of the Holy Thorn as a sign sent by God to show not only the general rightness of the Jansenist cause but also the particular rightness of the Pascal family in taking part in the struggle against the Jesuits. At no other times was he so close to the position of Arnauld and Nicole, and so far from that of the extremists such as Barcos, Singlin and Mother Angélique, who all held back from and disapproved of such polemics.

And yet, at a date which cannot be exactly determined, Pascal sent Barcos twelve questions on miracles and asked for his opinion on the problems of Justice and Divine Providence. Although apparently concerned only with general matters, these questions did have an immediate practical significance: What should be the reaction of the true Christian to the Bull of Alexander VII, and to what extent had the miracle of the Holy Thorn really proved that Pascal was right to publish the *Provinciales*? The real problem which Pascal's biographer has to face is this: why should Pascal send these questions to Barcos, whose position he knew and whose answer he could consequently foresee? There is no text which tells us what importance Pascal attributed to Barcos's reply. However, it does seem clear to me that the many fragments of the *Pensées* which state the uncertainty of religion, like his return to what he now saw as the vanity of science and of worldly activity, and his statement to Beurrier that he submitted to the Pope's decisions—although he never ceased to find them unjust— provide us with the elements of an answer to this problem.

Until 1654 Pascal looked for truth in the natural world and in the

---

[2] It is difficult to believe that Pascal did not, before 1657, consider the possibility that Jansenius might be condemned and think of how he himself would then react.

abstract sciences; from 1654 to 1657 he hoped that truth would triumph in the Church and religion in the world, and played an active part in trying to bring this triumph about. But towards the end of his life he learned that man's true greatness can lie only in his awareness of his weakness and limitations, and saw the uncertainty which characterises any human life, both in the natural world and in the Church Militant. He realised that, without faith, reason is incapable of understanding the smallest natural object, and that faith cannot genuinely penetrate a man's life except by the rational attitude of the wager. He went further than Barcos, who never thought that faith and tradition needed any rational support, and further even than Saint Augustine (cf. fr. 234, E.353), whose authority was immense in all Jansenist circles. In doing so, he discovered tragedy, the complete and certain uncertainty of all truth, paradox, the refusal of the world by a man who remains within it and the direct appeal to God. It was by extending paradox to God himself, and making Him both certain and uncertain, present and absent, that Pascal was able to write the *Pensées* and thus open a new chapter in the history of philosophical thought.

IV

In both the decisive turning-points in Pascal's life—that of November 1654 which gave birth to the *Mémorial* and that which began in March 1657 and led to the writing of the *Pensées*—his sister played an important rôle. It is therefore essential that we should understand what his relationship was with Jacqueline, but nevertheless curious that most scholars have failed to examine its true nature. It was more than the close union between two members of the same family who are deeply attached to each other and who suffer deeply whenever they do not agree about matters which both find extremely important; what is really essential is the meeting of two minds, each of which expressed in his highest and most intense form a particular moral attitude, or, rather, a particular world vision.[1]

Jacqueline had a weaker personality than her brother and was, to a considerable extent, his own moral and intellectual creation. This explains why the differences which came between them assumed such an importance in Pascal's eyes on the two occasions when, faced with the extremely difficult and complex problems put to him by reality, he found himself in danger of making concessions and of betraying his own values. On both occasions the choice which Jacqueline finally makes is, judged by Pascal's standards, an easy because a unilateral

[1] One might say, somewhat anachronistically, that on both occasions Jacqueline acted in a Cornelian manner and Pascal in a Racinian one. This does not, of course, imply that I consider Jacqueline to have been influenced by Corneille.

one. These choices were nevertheless based, for all their unacceptable one-sidedness in Pascal's eyes, on a principle which he himself had always recognised as valid. For example, when she wanted to enter the convent of Port-Royal in 1652 she was following Pascal's own precept that one should give oneself wholly to God; and when she began by maintaining that one should not sign the Formulary she was observing his own principle that one should always confess the truth in its entirety. This is why, on both occasions, Pascal finds her attitude both wrong and yet completely valid: wrong because one-sided, but valid because it states something which he has never doubted, and insists upon a duty which must be integrated and transcended but which can allow no compromise or concessions. The meaning of Pascal's own life, long before he himself became conscious of it in the last years of his life, was always the same: the quest for totality. And no one has given a better expression of what this word totality really means than Pascal himself, when he wrote in fragment 353 (E.229): 'One does not show one's greatness by being at one extreme, but by touching them both at the same time, and by filling up all the space between.'

The practical difficulties of anyone who tries to base his life on this maxim are obvious: he will always be tempted, when he sees the difficulty or even impossibility of 'touching them both at the same time', to accept the middle way between the two extremes. On both occasions in Pascal's life when he faced this temptation he came up against the example of his sister: in 1652, when he had to choose between the world (in the best sense of the word, that of fame and success in science) and his duty towards God; and in June 1661, when he had to choose between the defence of truth and the unity of the Church. On each occasion Jacqueline reminded him that neither God nor truth can admit of concessions or compromises, and it is not merely because she was his sister and because he loved her so dearly that her words struck so deeply into his conscience. Both lived at a level where even the strongest and deepest human affections are never the deciding factor. What Jacqueline's heroic behaviour offered to Blaise was the result of his own teaching, the lessons which she had learned either from him directly or through the intermediary of Saint-Cyran, whose authority he recognised. Pascal had never doubted these values, but he was in danger of neglecting them in order to observe other, opposite values, which were equally important for him but which meant almost nothing to Jacqueline. In 1652 Pascal held the views which he continued to hold until 1657: that the truths of natural science and those of revelation belong to two separate and complementary fields of experience; and that, whereas one uses one's reason and senses in the first, one submits to authority in the second. He had always looked upon the truths of science as inferior to those of revelation, but until 1654 he considered that he, Blaise Pascal, the man who had invented the calculating machine, conducted the experiments which successfully disproved the idea of nature abhorring a vacuum, written the essay on conic sections, had his own task to perform in the field of science. In order to do this, he needed money, and he was not a rich man. Jacqueline knew this, but she also feared —quite justifiably—that her brother's principles of subordinating reason to revelation and fame to holiness might not actually be observed in a life devoted primarily if not entirely to scientific research and worldly aims. It is this which explains the dispute over her dowry in 1651 and the means which she thus acquired—either consciously or unconsciously—to intervene decisively in her brother's life.

If Monsieur Mesnard is right in fixing Jacqueline's share in the family inheritance at about 40,000 *livres* the final arrangements about her dowry seem to have been a kind of compromise. Jacqueline herself probably shared the views of Port-Royal, who asked for no money from the novices admitted to become nuns, but who nevertheless maintained that a Christian owes everything to God and nothing to the world. Faced with the need to choose between her desire to give everything to the convent and the worldly demands of her brother and sister, Jacqueline seems to have compromised. She gave half her wealth to her brother in the hope that he and Gilberte would give her the remainder in cash so that she might donate it all to the convent. She did this, however, in rather a complicated way, for while she gave more than 23,000 *livres* to her brother, she received no guarantee that he would give her the rest of the money before she took her vows. She thus put herself quite deliberately at the mercy of Blaise and Gilberte.

It is difficult to believe that she herself found this a normal thing to do, and the proof of this can be found in the letter which she wrote on June 10th, 1653, to the Prioress at Port-Royal-des-Champs. There, she tells how she thought for a moment that she might fail to carry out her wishes, and was filled with regret at not having acted differently:[1]

> One of the things which most worried me [she writes] was the fear that I might have used my money wrongly. For when I still had possession of it, I had made gifts to various people of money which might have been distributed with more charity. And although I then thought that I had sufficient both for these gifts and for the other projects that I had in mind, I very greatly fear that I had acted with excessive haste.

[1] Cf. *Œuvres*, Brunschvicg edition, Vol. III, p. 74.

185

However, in spite of this moment of anxiety, Jacqueline seems to have gained a greater victory over her brother over the question of her dowry than she did over the problem of the Formulary in 1661. What she was asking of Blaise was merely that he should act according to his own conscience, and she seems to have been completely successful. Not only does Blaise agree to give the convent much of what Jacqueline had previously asked of him, but the actual crisis brought on by this decision was destined to have further results. What he in fact had to do was choose between continuing his scientific career and allowing his sister freely to follow her chosen vocation. The decision which he took, on June 4th, 1653, to give Jacqueline's share of the inheritance to Port-Royal, made him keep thinking about the choice which should be made between God and the world. As was natural with a man of Pascal's quality, what had begun as a purely external question of how one should use one's money becomes the much more important one of deciding how one should dispose of one's whole life. He found an answer to this problem only seventeen months later, on the celebrated night of November 23rd, 1654, when he had the experience which led to the writing of the *Mémorial*.

In reality, however, Jacqueline's triumph was less complete than it appears, for the apparently similar paths trod by brother and sister led them to very different positions. From 1650 onwards, Jacqueline had rejected the world and given herself wholly over to God. In 1653 she became a nun, fully aware of all that this involved in the way of renouncing the world for prayer and charity, of giving up the body for the soul, and abandoning any attempt to act in the world and in the Church, even in the cause of truth itself. Jacqueline adopted this position quite finally and definitively in 1653, and never changed.

Pascal, on the other hand, never gave up either the world, or the body, or the demand for effective action, and this for religious reasons. He was only half aware of these between 1654 and 1657, but completely aware in the last years of his life. Although he fully realised it only at the end of his life, Pascal never looked upon God as representing the 'good' part of the world in contrast to the 'evil' part; he never saw the Church apart from the world, the soul apart from the body or reason apart from instinct and feeling. For him, God was universal and nothing could or should escape Him. God was Totality in the fullest meaning of the world, that is to say both the opposition and contrast of extremities and what links them together and divides them. Psychologically, this is even more remarkable, since between 1652 and 1657 Pascal the philosopher and scientist held the theoretical view that there were separate but distinct fields of experience: on the one hand, there was God, revelation, authority and positive theology; and, on the other, human and physical nature, science, critical judgment, reason and the senses. Nevertheless, on the day when Pascal finally chooses God, after the crisis set in motion by the affair of Jacqueline's dowry, he is perhaps farther from her than ever before. When Jacqueline chose God she became a nun and left the world behind her; but when Pascal made the same choice he wrote the *Provinciales*, an attempt to fight the good fight and conquer the world for God. Thus, although Pascal the theoretician continued to maintain until 1657 that it was possible to divide life and knowledge into separate, hierarchically arranged spheres of activity—something which he later denies in the *Pensées*—the living, acting and struggling Pascal never accepted such a separation as valid. This illustrates one of the fundamental laws governing human life, and the fundamental principle of historical materialism: that man becomes aware of the moral, intellectual, aesthetic and religious values which correspond to his actions only after these actions have been performed. The time which individual men may take to achieve this awareness will obviously vary, but the awareness follows and does not precede the action. As far as the individual's mind is concerned, modern psychologists, and in particular Jean Piaget, have discovered exactly the same law experimentally.

As to the crisis of 1661, this both repeated and went further than that of 1652. From 1654 onwards, both Pascal and Jacqueline live only for God, albeit in ways that are wholly dissimilar. Neither can be tempted by any of the forms which the world may assume, and on the advice of Mother Agnès Jacqueline gives up poetry, the worldly activity to which she was most attached. And although Blaise does not give up all activity in this world, he at least replaces scientific research by the struggle against the Jesuits, and apparently ceases to envisage the possibility that the problem of the reunion of opposites might again present itself to him.

Nearly all thinkers actively engaged in trying to achieve a particular set of values tend in fact to suffer from an illusion which would deserve close study by psychologists and which is the same in every case. From the medieval masters of the spiritual life to Marx, Engels, Lenin and Lukàcs, all such thinkers tend to overestimate the changes of success and to underestimate the opposition of reality. They all continue to think that victory is just around the corner at the very moment that reality comes and destroys their illusions. The reign of the spirit no more came in the middle or at the end of the Middle Ages than the German revolution in 1848 or world revolution in 1918. Similarly, far from defeating the Jesuits in the real Church Militant, Pascal found himself face to face with the Bull of Alexander VII which condemned the doctrine of Jansenius. Certainly, the fundamental hope of a Pascal, like that of a Joachim de Flore, a Marx, an

Engels, a Lenin or a Lukàcs, cannot be destroyed by any external difficulty. These thinkers merely discover that values are realised slowly, and that, compared to History or to Eternity, one single human life has scarcely any importance. This is why, in Pascal's view, the individual soul will find its salvation only in eternity, and why, for Marx, Lukàcs or Lenin, humanity will find its salvation only in and through future history. All that the individual man can do is, by clinging to the body and to matter, to save his soul (Pascal) or preserve the dignity of his values (Marx, Lenin and Lukàcs).[1] In 1654 Pascal set out to make truth prevail in the Church and in society. In 1657 the Bull *Unigenitus* forced him to rethink his attitude and to become aware—this time definitively—of the 'anguish of finding oneself between God and the Pope'.

At this stage the problem is still not tragic, for faced with the choice between God and the Pope, the Christian can choose only God. But if this phrase is an adequate description of Jacqueline's attitude (which proves how close she was to her brother, in spite of the fact that she chose to see only one side of the question) Pascal himself was soon to discover that his duty to submit to the Pope is no less absolute than his duty to confess and proclaim the truth. He has really to choose between God and God, and this is why his position is tragic. The difficulties of 1652 now reappear in a more complex and elevated form: how can one bring together two extremes and unite the soul with the body, sincerity with submission to authority, God as the Church Militant and God as the demand for absolute truth? Once again, Pascal is faced with the compromise suggested by his most immediate collaborators, Arnauld and Nicole, who, in fact, want only one thing: an effective means of avoiding the choice of one or the other of these twin extremes.

We do not really know whether Pascal did in fact feel the temptation to accept their attitude. From 1654 to 1657 he was very close to Arnauld both in thought and action, but he nevertheless concluded the *Provinciales* in 1657 by writing the phrase which I have already quoted several times: 'The anguish of finding oneself between God and the Pope.' Four years later, in 1661–62, he no longer had anything at all in common with Arnauld. But what was his attitude between 1657 and 1661? All we have is a number of clues: when talking to Beurrier

---

[1] It was obvious to Hegel and Marx that the mind could not be the sole object of knowledge, but Pascal also knew that 'he who would be an angel becomes a beast' and puts the following words into the mouth of Christ in his *Mystery of Jesus:* 'It is I who cure, and who make the body immortal. Endure the chains of bodily servitude, for it is at this time only from spiritual slavery that I deliver you.' For all three positions, the spiritual greatness which man now enjoys lies in the fact that he seeks a greatness which will be total, both spiritual and corporeal, either in the future or in eternity.

(the priest who received his last confession) he fixed the date of his change of heart and general confession two years before his death, that is to say in the summer of 1660. Even this, however, is only a vague and approximate date, although changes of this kind are not sudden and instantaneous. It was round about January 1660 that the people grouped around Barcos and Pascal began to work at the solution which would combine submission to the Church with a refusal to sign the Formulary. As far as Pascal himself is concerned, however, the philosophical basis of this solution is to be found in the *Pensées*, and it could have grown in his mind at a much earlier date.

One thing is certain, however. Although we cannot date the fragments that we have of the *Pensées*, the texts which we know that Pascal wrote for other people between 1657 and 1661 are incompatible neither with Arnauld's position nor with that of the extremists such as Barcos and the Pascal of 1661–62. But the fact that between writing the *Provinciales* in 1656 and the *Ecrit sur la signature*, Pascal discussed the problems of the Church and of religion only in texts written for himself surely indicates some measure of uncertainty and hesitation on his part. During this period he openly expressed his views only by collaborating in the writing of texts of which everybody[1] approved (*Ecrits sur des curés de Paris, Mandement des grands vicaires*).

In 1661 Jacqueline once again made her influence felt, and in just as direct and one-sided a way as in 1652. She was now just as ready to place truth above submission as she had been to abandon the world and science, and wrote: 'Since bishops show themselves to have the courage of girls, then the time has come for girls to show the courage of bishops.' In 1652 she saw only God, and God was truth; in 1667 she saw only truth, for the truth is God. Barcos was struck with horror and wrote to Mother de Lagny that he 'feared for her salvation if she died in this persuasion'.[2] The Abbess of Port-Royal merely replied that 'we have great grounds for hoping that God will look upon the rightness of her heart, and will not count as a fault what she did through the love of justice and of truth'.[3] And if we are to accept Gilberte's evidence—which is not always very reliable—Pascal asked that 'God should grant us the Grace to die as well as she', in spite of the fact that he himself had submitted to the authority of the Church.

In my view, Jacqueline attained the highest greatness open to her by adopting this uncompromising attitude, and we should be grateful to her for probably having helped her brother to resist temptation

---

[1] Or, more precisely, Barcos and Arnauld. For there was a group that did not agree with the *Mandement* of the Grands Vicaires.

[2] Bibliothèque Municipale de Troyes, MS. 2.207, fol. 58.

[3] Bibliothèque Municipale de Troyes, MS. 2.207, fol. 68.

at a critical moment of his life. It is not that he adopted his sister's attitude, for the author of the *Mystery of Jesus* would never have been able to return to the spiritualist and one-sided views of Jacqueline on the same subject.[1] What did happen, however, is that once again he was reminded by his sister of one of his own fundamental ideas: that at all times and at all places one should stand out for absolute truth. Jacqueline's letter of June 23rd, 1661, seemed to remind him of what he himself had once taught her. Pascal himself would have to go beyond this teaching, but he could not go back upon it. And once again, in my view, it was Jacqueline's influence which led to the crystallisation of a particular attitude which had been slowly evolving since 1657 but which, without her intervention, might have been prevented by his death from reaching its full development.

Jacqueline would probably have been no more able than Arnauld, Nicole or even Barcos to understand and agree with the *Pensées*. Her influence was nevertheless almost decisive in enabling Pascal to leave us the text which we possess today.

I realise that, in this discussion of Jacqueline's influence on her brother, I have not mentioned the problem of what factors determined her own psychological evolution. A depth psychologist, and especially one of the Adlerian school, would not find it difficult to explain Jacqueline's conduct by the conscious desire to go one better than her brother, and to be able once again to speak to him in terms of superior authority. For thanks to her talents as a versifier, Jacqueline had begun by being the pride of the family, but had then been put into the shade by her brother's scientific achievements. Her decision to become a nun, the ease with which she mistook the extent of her wealth, the quarrel with Blaise over her dowry, the letter of December 1st, 1655[2]—and, especially, that of June 23rd, 1661—would all, in the Adlerian view, express basically the same desire. There is probably some truth in this theory, but such an explanation has no possible interest for the historian of ideas. Similar events are happening all the time, and have at the most a purely anecdotal interest. It is because Jacqueline was Jacqueline and Blaise was Blaise that their relationship is important in the history of philosophical ideas, and this importance lies not in its similarity to other experiences but in its uniqueness.

---

[1] Cf. *Œuvres*, Brunschvicg edition, Vol. II, p. 452.

[2] Cf. Brunschvicg edition, Vol. LV, p. 82. The ironical tone of this letter fits in perfectly with a psychological explanation of Jacqueline's behaviour in terms of her intention to teach her brother a lesson. However, since no psychological crisis can be found in the latter's reactions, it remains simply a loose and unattached fact which shows to what extent, when we are dealing with Pascal's relationship with his sister, the essential element remains the clash between two world visions.

V

I should like to conclude by repeating that this chapter is not meant to be a scientific study of Pascal's life, for neither the information nor the essential methodological rules are available. I have merely expressed a few random ideas which, I realise, also present an idealising schematisation of events. What these ideas do is provide the basis for a kind of myth, expressing the collective representation of a man of action, a representation parallel to the rationalist ideal already mentioned of the open-minded and objective scientist. It corresponds to the similar 'myth' which exists about the life and nature of Descartes, Galileo or Lessing, and it is not necessarily completely wrong. What it enables us to do is to bring out, from among all the variety and incoherence which characterise any individual experience, the real essence of Pascal's life, an essence which might be neglected by more down-to-earth biographers.

The slight importance accorded by these biographers to the turning-point of 1657–58 (in the few cases where they even mention it) is a startling example of that failure to understand Pascal which any genuine study of him has to overcome. I hope that these few reflexions will enable scholars to fit both past and future discoveries into a more adequate framework. It may be that this framework will be open to criticism, but it is nevertheless essential to any truly scientific and dialectical investigation which will enrich it and make it more accurate. It may be, of course, that such an investigation will even modify it both in detail and as a whole, but any study of Pascal had to begin by setting out the essential elements which go to make up this framework.

IX

PARADOX AND FRAGMENT

I

MY task is now to show how the concept of tragic thought enables us to see the fragments which make up the *Pensées* as having a coherent unity. I shall not do this by studying each fragment individually, but shall choose a certain number in order to illustrate my general method. The reader will then be able to see for himself whether the other fragments fit into my general pattern or not.

I shall begin by considering Pascal's style as a writer, in spite of the fact that I am not qualified to give expert judgment on questions as important as that of the construction of the Pascalian sentence. (The studies which have already been made of this question, however, show this particular line of study to be an especially fruitful one.[1] However, since form and content are closely linked together in Pascal—as they are in all great writers—I shall have to begin by examining the problem of the paradox and the fragment.

From 1670 to the present day the paradoxical form of the *Pensées* has been a stumbling block to almost all the commentators who have not approached them from a tragic or dialectical point of view. It is thus not surprising that we find scholars attempting to discover the 'real', or at least the 'most valid', meaning of his work by freeing it from what they call 'verbal exaggerations'.[2] This method has two

[1] Cf., for example, Th. Spoerri, *Des Verborgene Pascal* (Hamburg: Fursche-Verlag, 1955. Also *Sur les pensées de derrière la tête*, in *Pascal, l'homme et l'œuvre* (Paris: Editions de Minuit, 1955).

[2] I will quote a number of typical examples of this. In *La Foi selon Pascal*, Vol. I, p. 17, Mademoiselle Russier states: 'It quite often happens that Pascal considers reality not in itself but in the mind of the person thinking it, and nevertheless uses the verb "to be" where "to appear" would be less misleading. "Things are true or false," he says in fragment 99, "according to the way in which one looks at them." When the Jansenists who prepared the Port-Royal edition substituted the verb "to appear" in this context, they did so with the praiseworthy intention of making Pascal's meaning clearer and more accurate. Similarly, it is

defects: it opens the door to the most arbitrary interpretations and involves the presupposition that Pascal was a very bad writer who failed to keep any of the rules which he laid down in this very work.

Let me make myself clear: for the dialectical aesthetic—of which Pascal was one of the main founders—no literary work is valid unless it contains a necessary, organic unity between a coherently expressed

---

"true in one sense (sc. that the birds and the sky prove the existence of God) for some souls to whom God gives this light, but nevertheless this is false as far as most men are concerned" (fr. 244). Here again, it is obvious that this either is or is not true; it cannot be true sometimes and false at other times, except in relation to certain individuals. But this is the only point of view which interests the apologetic writer.'

I will repeat yet again that for tragic thought things are true or false whether or not they are seen in the context of the use made of them in an apologetic argument; and that paradox can be avoided only by going back to rationalism or by introducing the idea of historical development—that is to say by moving from tragic to dialectical thought. As far as fragment 244 (E.26) is concerned, Pascal's text does specifically state that this is true for 'some souls' and 'most men'. And it must be added that for tragic thought this is both true and false.

Monsieur Jean Laporte refuses absolutely to accept the fact that what Pascal actually wrote shows that he held, first, that there is a real justice which man must always seek, secondly, that it is radically impossible for him ever to know this justice and, consequently, that all human laws are equally relative.

Pascal had already shocked Arnauld by maintaining this, and the latter was prepared to go no further than simply to allow Pascal to hold a position which was different from his own, and which was, in his opinion, fundamentally wrong. Monsieur Laporte, on the other hand, insists on attributing Arnauld's position to Pascal. He does this, of course, by talking about Pascal's 'verbal exaggerations' and of the need to 'arrive at a true understanding of his work'. Thus, we see Arnauld writing in the following terms of Pascal's work: 'It is a gross exaggeration, smacking of Calvinism, to maintain as the author of the *Pensées* does, that there is nothing essentially just among men outside Christianity, taking justice in the sense of *quae jus est* and appertaining to acts rather than persons; of that kind of justice, for example, which makes us say that it is just not to kill or not to steal, or that such and such a law is just in society', and this is certainly a valid, if not necessarily justified, criticism of Pascal's position. But Laporte has chosen to comment upon it in the following terms: 'Pascal maintained, as we know, that there "doubtless are natural laws, but that our fine and corrupted reason has corrupted everything else". In fact, if we once free his ideas from the exaggerated style and language in which they are expressed, they are not very different from those of Saint Augustine or of Arnauld. It is enough for corruption not to have so deeply penetrated into reason as still to leave untouched those basic principles of Right by virtue of which a minimum of justice does reign in human societies. And, if we understand Pascal correctly, this is not something which he denies.' Cf. Laporte, *La doctrine de la Grâce chez Arnauld* (Paris: P.U.F., 1922), pp. 148–9.

It is, of course, obvious that if we do not 'free Pascal's ideas from exaggerated language' and do not 'understand him correctly' but, on the contrary, give the words he uses their natural meaning, he does indeed deny that corruption has left anything at all intact (since, as he says, it has corrupted everything) and that there still subsist elements of justice. Perhaps the most extraordinary thing about the whole of Laporte's statement is his reference to fragment 453 (E.405). Whereas

content and an adequate form. A writer who tries to achieve stylistic effects unrelated to his subject matter is necessarily a bad writer. Pascal himself expressed this idea better than anyone when he wrote:

> 'People who produce antitheses by straining the meaning of words are like architects who put in false windows for the sake of symmetry; they are not trying to speak correctly, but to make correct figures' (fr. 27, E.971).

Similarly, in fragment 48 (E.969), he wrote:

> When your attempt to improve a text by removing repetitions merely worsens it, then it is an indication that the repetitions should stand. Only envy would like to change them, for it is blind and cannot know that repetition is not a fault in this context. For there is no universal rule.

False windows are the external forms which do not correspond to real content but do a purely formalistic desire for symmetry. Contrariwise, all considerations of pure form should give way before the demands of content which is 'the indication' that certain repetitions are essential. It would be surprising, to say the least, if Pascal had achieved such lucidity in his ideas on style and then failed to keep his own rules.

In fact, he kept his rules and nowhere pursued paradox systematically and for its own sake. This is clear from what he wrote before 1657, when the content of his work did not demand paradoxical modes of expression. Indeed, his style remained perfectly adequate to the content of his works throughout his life, and never involved exaggerated or far-fetched modes of expression. In fact, in his later work his style is sometimes less paradoxical than the ideas which he is expressing.

In our world, as Pascal sees it, no statement is true unless immediately completed by its opposite, and no action is good without a completely different action which completes and corrects it. It is indeed for this reason that Pascal sees our world as insufficient, as a world without God, a world which crushes man, and which man must necessarily outsoar if he is to remain man.

This is why, in my view, the *Pensées* illustrate the transition from

---

Laporte's argument would lead one to expect a fragment stating the relative validity of human laws, we find Pascal insisting on the inadequacy of every law.

'Men have contrived and extracted from concupiscence admirable rules for administration, morality and justice. But basically they have done no more than cover over the fundamental wickedness of all men while in no way removing it.'

We can thus see, from Pascal's own words, that such laws do not contain a 'rudiment' of authentic justice, unless we admit that such a justice can exist even though it only 'covers over' concupiscence without ever removing it.

rational to dialectical thought. For dialectical thinkers such as Hegel, Engels or Stalin, the whole of reality is a dynamic whole which progresses by the conflict between thesis and antithesis to a synthesis which both integrates and goes beyond them. For Lukàcs, in 1923, this was true only of human reality, and it is difficult to say what exactly Marx's views were on the problem of the dialectic in nature. Pascal resembles these thinkers in disagreeing with rationalism and empiricism and asserting the simultaneous truth of contradictory propositions. He differs from them, however, by the essentially static, tragic, and paradoxical nature of his thought. It is static because, while insisting that only the synthesis of true truth or just justice has any real value, it also denies that man can ever achieve or even begin to draw near such a synthesis. Pascal sees no possibility for man to achieve progress in human time, and his thought remains paradoxical because he looks upon all reality as consisting of a clash between opposites, and a conflict that cannot be transcended in this world. He is a tragic thinker because he sees man as unable either to avoid or to accept this paradox, and yet as being man only in so far as he makes the impossibility of achieving any genuine synthesis into the very centre of his existence. For Pascal, man must remain constantly aware that even the statement 'all truth is paradoxical' is itself a paradox, and that the highest certainty which he can achieve belongs neither to the field of reason nor to that of direct and immediate intuition. He can only be certain about things which are uncertain but practical (as in Kant), and even this certainty is only a postulate, a wager, and a certainty that springs solely from the heart. Nevertheless, if he wants to say anything true about himself, about the world, or even about God, paradoxes are both inevitable and the only form of truth within his reach.

It is for this reason that any criticism of the paradoxical nature of Pascal's thought, any attempt to see it as an accidental or contingent element of his style, or to treat it as mere 'linguistic exaggeration' is also a criticism of his type of faith and his form of Christianity, and an attempt to reduce them to a type of Christianity which was foreign to him and that he rejected. To do this would be to betray the whole essence of the message of the *Pensées*, which any commentator would strive to emphasise rather than diminish.

'Atheists should say things which are perfectly clear,' writes Pascal, and his statement means two things: no one has the right to be an atheist unless he can conceive clear ideas; and if one could do this, then one would be justified in being an atheist. Any attempt to tone down the paradoxical nature of this text and make it more acceptable to Cartesian common sense would also involve toning down the scandal of this world and thus making it more bearable. From the point of view of the *Pensées*, this would lead to a justification of the atheist who renounces Grace, the wager and faith.

The same argument can be used to show that the fragment is an essential and inevitable feature of Pascal's style. Paradox is the only valid form for the expression of a philosophy that holds truth to lie in the meeting and reunion of opposites, and the fragment is the only valid form for a work whose essential message is that man is a paradoxical creature who is both great and small, strong and weak. He is great and strong because he never gives up the demand for pure goodness and truth unmixed with baser matters; he is small and weak because he can never even draw near these values, to say nothing of attaining them.

The category of 'all or nothing', fundamental to tragic thought, prevents man both from giving up the quest for absolute values and from falling into the illusion that this quest might succeed. Thus, if Pascal himself had even for one moment given up looking for the final order in which to present the *Pensées*, or had even for one moment thought that he had found it, or even begun to draw nearer to it, then he would not only have provided the strongest possible argument against his own philosophy but also left behind him an incoherent work unworthy of a great writer. Any attempt to discover the 'true' order of the *Pensées* seems to me to be the anti-Pascalian exercise *par excellence*. It goes against everything which gives the text its coherence, and fails to recognise both its intellectual content and the essence of its literary merit.

A rationalist thinker can have a logical plan, and a work of apologetics can be written in a way most likely to convince the reader. But there can be, for the tragic work, only one valid form: that of the fragment, which expresses a quest for order that has not succeeded and cannot even begin to succeed. If Pascal is a great writer—as he is —it is first of all because he went against the aesthetic values of his sceptical and rationalist contemporaries and was able to find and exploit the two forms of literary expression demanded by his own philosophy. By giving the *Pensées* a paradoxical form, and by leaving them as fragments, he made them into a paradoxical masterpiece, complete by its very lack of completeness.

II

The essential point of this chapter has now been made. It should be added, however, that Pascal was not only immediately successful in finding the literary form most suited to the expression of his ideas, but also that he was *fully aware* of what he had done—something which is extremely rare in literary history. Certain essential notions of dialectical aesthetics were already current in extreme Jansenist circles, although in an incompleted form. Three fragments, in particular, illustrate Pascal's own awareness of the importance of paradox:

> All are more dangerously deceived in that they each follow one truth. Their mistake lies not in following a falsehood, but in not following a different truth (fr. 863, E.455).
>
> If ever there is a time when one should make profession of opposites, it is when one is accused of omitting one of them . . . (fr. 865, E.947).
>
> The faith includes several truths which appear self-contradictory. 'A time to weep and a time to laugh' etc (Eccles. iii. 4) 'Answer . . . answer not'? (Prov. xxvi. 5, 4).
>
> . . . The source of this is in the twin nature of Jesus Christ. As also the two worlds (the creation of a new heaven and a new earth; of a new life and a new death; a twin nature for all things while the same names remain); and finally the twin nature of the righteous (for they are the two worlds and both members and images of Christ Jesus. Thus all names can be correctly applied to them; righteous, yet sinners; dead, yet alive; alive, yet dead; elect, yet reprobate, etc . . .)
>
> There are thus a great number of truths, both of faith and morals, which seem contradictory but which nevertheless hold good within the same admirable order. Each heresy springs from the exclusion of one of these contradictory truths (fr. 862, E.462).

No one could express more clearly the idea that any abolition or reduction of paradox makes faith heretical and truths false.

The problem is equally clear as far as the 'plan' of the *Pensées* is concerned. The central idea of the dialectical aesthetic lies in the correspondence between style and subject matter. Tragic thinkers could not, however, see this in its historical form, which recognises that values are relative and that each finds an aesthetically valid expression when it discovers a particularly suitable form. Tragic thought cannot recognise the existence of relative values, and sees only the choice to be made between absolute values and the widely different but equally invalid forms which error takes.

For Jansenist thinkers, and for Pascal—the boldest and most radical among them—the problem of the relationship between form and content therefore presented itself rather differently. They had to discover which form was most suited to the expression of a content that was wholly true, and which was most suited for fighting against erroneous contents. Pascal and Barcos, however, had similar but not identical ideas about what constituted 'true content'.

The problem of a rational plan seems to have been a fairly familiar one in Jansenist circles, since Barcos, as we have already seen, wrote a letter to Mother Angélique pointing out to her that charity, when it is perfect, needs no other order but that which it gives itself (cf.

197

letter quoted on page 159). For him, disorder was thus the only valid form for a Christian, since a true believer could place no trust in the workings of reason in this world. His statement thus already implicitly contains the idea of an agreement between form and content.

Pascal is, however, much more aware than Barcos of the nature of this relationship. As far as we know, Barcos was certain of the value of revealed truth, and never felt any doubt at all about the existence of God. He can therefore quite unambiguously say 'No' to the world and to everything worldly in man's mind. But Pascal extends uncertainty and paradox to God himself, to the God whom man's heart can feel, but whose existence is both certain and uncertain, presence and absence, hope and risk. In a word, God's existence is a wager, and it therefore follows that Pascal cannot merely refuse the world and reason. A 'Yes' has to be added to Barcos's 'No', and the quest within the world for authentic values put in the place of a direct refusal of the world because of its inadequacy.

Pascal considers Barcos's position to be one-sided, and he says so in a very well-known fragment:

> If there ever is a time when one should make profession of opposites, it is when one is accused of omitting one of them. Thus both Jesuits and Jansenists are wrong in hiding them; but the Jansenists more than the Jesuits, since the latter have better proclaimed them both (fr. 865, E.947).[1]

[1] In addition to its importance on the plane of ideas, this fragment is also important from an historical point of view (Thus the Jesuits, etc., . . .). The preference which Pascal seems to show for the Jesuits is, to put it mildly, a little unexpected from the author of the *Lettres Provinciales*, and needs to be explained. According to Mlle Lewis, it is 'doubtless a question here of grace and free will' (cf. her note on p. 554 of the edition of Pascal's *Pensées et Opuscules* published by La Bonne Compagnie), but I do not find this a very satisfactory explanation: the Jansenists insisted just as much as the Jesuits, if not more, on the all-powerful nature of grace and free will (even to the extent of suggesting the possibility of resisting grace). It would be surprising if it were on this point that Pascal found the Jesuits less unilateral than the Jansenists. Moreover, if this had been the case it would be difficult to explain why he should have written the *Provinciales*, or should never have gone back on what they said.

It seems to me much more probable that Pascal was thinking about another characteristic of the Jesuits, and one on which he always insisted: their readiness to make the concessions and compromises demanded by life in the world. (Both he and the other Jansenists, it should be noted, always looked upon the Jesuits as Christians who more or less keep in mind the duty to prefer God to the world.) The extreme wing of the Jansenist party, however, simply refused the world completely. If, in fact, one looks at the matter rather superficially it would seem that the Jesuits were nearer than the Jansenists to that attitude of 'refusing the world while remaining within the world' which Pascal adopted in the last years of his life. This ceases to be the case, however, if we look at matters closely, for in

This is why Pascal looked upon the disorder which Barcos saw as the only acceptable mode of writing for a Christian as being, on the contrary, the style most suited to the expression of the inadequate and false position of the Sceptics. This is shown by the fact that he expressed the idea of a relationship between the impossibility of finding truth in the world and the absence of a rational order in the plan of a work in one of the *Pensées*:

> Scepticism. I shall here write down my thoughts without order, and even perhaps in deliberate disorder; this is the true order, for it will always characterise what I am talking about by its very disorder. I should be doing my subject too great an honour if I were to treat it in an orderly manner, for I want to show that it is incapable thereof (fr. 373, E.44).

However, tragic thought goes beyond Scepticism, and therefore demands forms of a different type. It sees man as a being who cannot —without falling from his true nature—give up his eternal and eternally unsatisfied quest for order.

> Order. I could easily have composed this book in the following way: taking as my aim to show the vanity of all conditions, begin by showing the vanity of the common life, and then the vanity of lives based on Stoicism or Scepticism. But I should not have been following true order. I have some little idea of what this is, and of how few people follow it. There is no purely human science that observes it. Saint Thomas did not. Mathematics does, but is useless because of its depth (fr. 61, E.47).
>
> The last thing one discovers when writing a book is what ought to have come first (fr. 19, E.8).

This is the clearest possible expression of the dilemma: all human order is inadequate, and yet man must never give up his quest for adequate order. For if the first of these fragments insisted upon the inadequacy of the Thomist and Cartesian methods followed by Pascal's contemporaries the second emphasises that the quest for order must go on. Similarly, if one were to write the work a second time one would once again realise when it was completed that something different should have been placed at the beginning.

'making profession of both' the Jesuits placed themselves not at both extremes but in the centre, at an equal distance from both. They live neither wholly in the world as the unbelievers do, nor entirely in God like the 'solitaries' of Port-Royal. Even less do they demand, as Pascal did, that the two extremes be brought together. Their life in this world is as corrupted by their religious character as their religiosity is by their desire for domination and intrigue. The *Lettres Provinciales* were right: the Jesuits are dangerous, and even doubly so, since by corrupting truth, they have an attitude which can serve as a screen, in the same way as it is used by Pascal in the passage I have just analysed.

We must, however, examine fragment 283 (E.575), which seems to contradict the analysis of Pascal's ideas which I have just put forward.

> Order: replying to the objection that the Scriptures have no order. The heart has its own order; the mind has its own, based upon first principles and the demonstration of truths; and the heart has yet another order. It would be ridiculous to try to prove that one should be loved by setting out for oneself the causes of love.
>
> Jesus Christ and Saint Paul follow the order of charity and not that of the mind; for they wanted to stir men up, not to instruct them.
>
> The same is true of Saint Augustine. His order consists principally of digressions upon each point, which is then related again at the end, in order to keep it present in the reader's mind.

In fact, this fragment really confirms my analysis. Pascal has already told us that 'no human science' can observe true order, and we shall see later that this science is just as incapable of proving the existence of God or the axioms of geometry as of finding the order in which a work of argument should be presented. However, man does have a superior synthesising faculty which enables him to find these three essential realities—the existence of order, the validity of geometrical axioms, the existence of God—which are out of the range of his mind. This is his heart, his capacity for feeling, by which he can at least wager his life on the possibility that such realities do exist. But, in this earthly life, man can never give up being a rational creature, and his reason will always force him to introduce doubt and paradox into the realm where he takes his heart as guide. He will always be looking for a rational justification for the decisions taken by the heart, in spite of the fact that he knows them to be a part of an arbitrary wager. He is certain that God exists, but can never forget that this certainty is a wager; he knows that geometrical axioms are valid, but always needs to remember that they cannot be rationally demonstrated; he knows that order exists, but must remember that 'purely human science' cannot retain it.

These limitations, however, are peculiar to man but do not apply to those who transcend his mortal and fallen nature. God, the Saints and the Elect of God have sure and certain knowledge of His existence and of the number of dimensions of space. It is therefore natural that they should possess true order and that this should be present in the writings which they have left for us. Christ, Saint Paul and Saint Augustine have reached a level unattainable by any mortal man, and certainly beyond the reach of a Blaise Pascal, who, more than anyone else, was aware of his own condition and limitations.

III

This criticism does not, however, apply to the two most important editions of the *Pensées*, that of Brunschvicg and that of Lafuma.[1] These are better than all the others because they are not said to be based on an 'authentic' or 'valid' plan, or even to be nearer in form to the book which Pascal would have 'finally written'. Any edition has to present the *Pensées* in a certain order, and the whole problem lies in trying to decide whether this actual order is also the right one. I have already said that, in my view, the only form suited to the content of the *Pensées* is the fragment, in so far as this is the expression of a quest for a 'right order' that has not been successful. Any edition of the *Pensées* must therefore recognise that the actual order in which they are presented is not to any extent to be regarded as even approaching the 'right one'.

The order in which the *Pensées* are presented does nevertheless affect the reader's understanding of the work, and there does seem to me to be one particular order which is better than the others: the one which begins by insisting upon the paradoxical nature of man (wretchedness and greatness), leads us to the wager, and concludes by the valid but not compulsive reasons which Pascal gives, in his discussion of miracles and of the Bible, for believing in Christianity. Thus, it is much easier to understand the need for the wager when one has seen how man is unable to make any clear or valid statements in any domain whatsoever, and the historical and empirical reasons for believing in Christianity are similarly much more important once one has understood that, for 'practical' reasons of the heart, man needs to bet on the existence of God even when he has no positive proof.[2] This is in fact the best order, though we have no reason at all for thinking that it is the best in any absolute sense. It does, however, provide the best standard for judging the respective merits of the Brunschvicg and Lafuma editions.

For a number of philological arguments which I am not competent

---

[1] Although, like most scholars, I refer to this as the Lafuma edition, the idea of following the actual order of Pascal's manuscript (B.N.F., Fr. 9203) as if he himself had decided on it was adopted first of all by Zacharie Tourneur. Since, however, Lafuma's edition is much more easily accessible, I am following the customary appellation.

[2] This seems to me to be the point of fragment 187 (E.35), in which Pascal says that we must 'begin by showing that religion is not contrary to reason; that it is venerable and worthy of respect (because of its recognition of the paradoxical character of man, L.G.); next show that it deserves our love, and make good people wish it were true (the wager, L.G.)'. That it is 'worthy of veneration because of its true knowledge of man, and worthy of love because it promises true goodness'.

to judge but which I find plausible, Z. Tourneur, P. L. Couchoud and Monsieur Lafuma maintain that the manuscript which we possess of the *Pensées* represents the classification that Pascal himself made at a particular moment of his life. They therefore maintain that this classification is the best, since no one knew better than Pascal himself what order his book was to follow. In fact, this classification also follows the order which I think preferable, since it moves from the paradoxical nature of man to the wager and concludes by the historical proof. But whatever its value may have been in the seventeenth century, it now seems to present itself to the modern reader with all Pascal's own authority. It has consequently led certain scholars to maintain—Monsieur Mesnard and Monsieur Orcibal, for example—that the order which it follows is ideally the best, and fairly close to the one which Pascal himself would have adopted. I have already said that I consider such an idea to be a betrayal of the essential message of the *Pensées*, and it is because the Lafuma edition may mislead readers into thinking that there is an 'ideal' order that I prefer Brunschvicg. By classifying the fragments in thirteen sections (and introducing a certain order by making one come after another), Brunschvicg tried to avoid, as he says, 'any preconceived idea of what Pascal's *Apology for Religion* would have finally been'. He limited himself to 'presenting the fragments in such a way as to enable the reader to understand them . . . but without making them cease to be fragmentary and without suggesting that this classification reveals the secret of the plan which died with Pascal'.[1]

I have only one objection to make to the Brunschvicg classification. It is that he places the wager in Section III, and thus makes it precede certain considerations on the paradoxical nature of man (social life, philosophy, ethics) contained in sections IV, V and VI. The editors who follow the manuscript are, in my view, preferable in that they place the wager at the very centre of the work.

Whatever may be their respective merits, the Brunschvicg and Lafuma editions are certainly better than any one which maintains that it follows the 'right' order. Neither Brunschvicg nor Lafuma, however, is responsible for this particular superiority of their editions. By a final posthumous paradox of this eminently paradoxical text these editors find the best order for reasons of which they are not aware, and they justify this order by arguments that run the risk of hiding or even of compromising its validity.[2]

---

[1] Cf. Brunschvicg edition, p. 269.

[2] In a recent article, 'La Crise des "Pensées" de Pascal', *Le Flambeau*, No. 2, 1955, Monsieur Paul-Louis Couchoud argues in favour of an historical edition of the *Pensées*, which, if it could be achieved, would be extremely useful.

X
MAN AND THE HUMAN CONDITION

I

AS in the work of Kant, the domains of theory and practice, epistemology and ethics are in the *Pensées* both clearly distinguished and exactly parallel. This consequently obliges us to examine what basis these domains have in common, and we must begin by studying what relationship men have with opposite extremities. In other words, by studying the problem of how man is linked with the two infinites.

Most Pascalian scholars, it is true, agree on a certain number of points, as, for example, that Pascal sees man as a 'middle' or 'average' being, neither beast nor angel, and placed at an equal distance from both extremes. However, once this has been agreed, divergencies begin to appear, for the concept of a 'mean' which is 'equidistant from both infinities' is ambiguous: it can be interpreted in two completely different ways, of which the first leads to the tragic vision and the second to the views of Arnauld and even, eventually, to the everyday attitude of common sense.

For scholars such as Jean Laporte—whose views on Arnauld are perfectly valid—there is no essential difference between Pascal's and Arnauld's ideas. Thus, he consistently argues that Port-Royal is a mean, and that as such it stands half-way between the Molinist teaching that man can do everything and the Calvinist doctrine that he can do nothing. Even if this was not the actual doctrine of Port-Royal, it was nevertheless accepted by quite a large number of thinkers, but it is not, in my view, the doctrine set forth in the *Pensées*. I shall need to prove this, and I shall try to do so by studying a number of *pensées* which seem, at first sight, to bear out Laporte's interpretation.

Pascal certainly sees man as an 'average' being, and one who is always destined, whatever he may do, to remain equally far from both opposite extremes. He does not, however, see this as an ideal situation, but as a tragic and an unbearable one. For man could 'naturally' (if this word has any meaning here) find happiness not in the middle but by being at both extremes simultaneously. Since, however, he can in fact approach neither, he is doomed—in spite of his apparent agitation—to remain motionless. But the fact that he does not move in no way implies that he has reached a point of balance. He is in a state of constant tension, where he moves but remains motionless, and where he strives after rest and certainty but never succeeds in finding them.

Nevertheless, there are certain *pensées* (Brunschvicg numbers 34–38 and 69–71, E.984, 987, 985, 386, 988 and 78, 251, 75) which do appear to support the idea that man is actually intended to live in a mean, and to remain equally far from both extremes. It is these which we must now examine.

Two extremes and the mean: when we read too fast or two slowly, we understand nothing at all (fr. 69, E.78).
Too much and too little wine: give him none, and he cannot find truth; give him too much, and the same thing happens (fr. 71, E.75).

Taken out of context, these two fragments doubtless seem to recommend a golden mean, a normal rate of reading, a normal intake of wine, in spite of the fact that they thereby seem to contradict a large number of the other *pensées*.

They can, however, be given another interpretation, one that may at first sight seem far-fetched, but which nevertheless has the immense advantage of fitting them into the rest of Pascal's work and thereby maintaining its coherence. One could in fact take them to mean that both wine and reading speed have the same characteristics for man as the rest of the universe; that they, too, have the contradictory qualities of being both a necessary and a dangerous part of man's understanding, of being both a help and a hindrance to him in his quest for truth.

The first three words of the first of these *pensées* seem to me to indicate that this is the better interpretation. When Pascal writes: 'Two infinites, the mean', it is difficult to see the point of his reference to 'infinites' if all he wants to do is to recommend that we should strike a happy medium. His phrase, however, is both natural and easy to understand if we accept the idea that, for Pascal, any real understanding always demands that two opposite extremes be brought together, and that every tendency towards an infinite in one direction is dangerous because it takes man away from the opposite infinite which he must always try to observe. In order to reach a valid understanding of events we must drink wine and not try to read too slowly;

but when, in the quest for understanding, we seek to pass from error to truth by increasing the amount of wine we drink and the speed at which we read we destroy any good effects which this quest might have by moving away from the other infinite. It is thus our own very condition as men which forces us to remain within the bounds of approximate understanding, which is a mixture of truth and false-hood and which is therefore unacceptable and valueless. As men, we cannot try to achieve the absolute, but, at the same time, we cannot as men remain satisfied with any understanding that does not strive after it.

This interpretation seems to me to be acceptable for two reasons: it guarantees the coherence of the rest of the *Pensées* and also gives the words 'Two infinites . . .' a natural meaning. However, I do not maintain that these two reasons are decisive. Pascal could even have been contradicting himself, and the words 'Two infinites: mean' may have a significance which we cannot even suspect.

My interpretation is nevertheless reinforced by fragment 70 (E.251):

> Nature has placed us so exactly at the very centre of things that we cannot move to one side without upsetting the balance: *Je fesons, zôa trékei*. This leads me to think that there are springs in our heads which are so arranged that we cannot touch a single one of them with-out also touching its opposite (fr. 70, E.251).

The idea fits in excellently with my interpretation. Placed by nature at the very centre of things, in a paradoxical and contradictory situa-tion (explained and illustrated here by the bringing together of the singular and the plural), man is linked to the two opposite scales of the balance in such a way that he can never escape from contradiction by going definitely to one side. Any movement towards one side would instantly strengthen the attraction of the other.

The famous fragment 72 (E.390) on the two infinites seems to me to solve the problem by containing a passage which is very similar to the two *pensées* that I have just quoted:

> Excessive youth and excessive age both obstruct the mind, as do too much and too little learning.

These texts are so similar in wording that they must all obviously be interpreted in the same way, that is to say in the light of the quota-tion from 72 (E.390), whose meaning is made quite clear by the way in which it continues:

> . . . finally, extremes are for us as if they did not exist, and as if we did not exist for them either: they escape us and we them . . .

205

This is our true state; and it is this which makes us incapable either of achieving absolute knowledge or of remaining in complete ignorance.

> We sail over a vast expanse, for ever drifting and uncertain, and driven from one extreme to the other. If we find a point at which to tie up and stay awhile, it shifts and fails us; if we try to follow it, it slips from our grasp and is lost to us for ever. There is nothing fixed and constant for us. This is our natural state and yet the one we find most contrary to our taste and inclination. We long to find a firm footing and a sure foundation on which to build a tower that would reach infinity, but our whole foundations crack and shudder and an abyss opens up before our feet.
> Let us then cease to look for certainty and stability. Our reason is always taken in by the changing nature of appearances, nothing can fix the finite between the two infinites which both set it around and flee from its approach.

If the words 'excessive youth and excessive age obstruct the mind, as do too much and too little learning' mean that 'our state makes us incapable either of achieving absolute knowledge or of remaining in complete ignorance', then it is difficult to maintain that *pensées* 69 and 71 (E.78 and 251) advise us to accept our average 'mean' condition. The verbal similarities between all these texts are too great for such a meaning to be probable.

II

Before actually putting forward my own interpretation of Pascal, I shall begin by discussing those *pensées* which seem to contradict my thesis. The first of these is in fact to be found in the continuation of the text which I have just quoted:

> Once man has clearly understood this, then I hold that he will remain at rest, each person in the state in which nature has placed him. Since the middle state which has fallen to our lot . . . (72, E.390).

This text is already sufficiently disquieting for us to need to ask what it really means. Is Pascal advising man to be satisfied with his condition, to stay at rest and to give up the demand for a union of opposites? I do not think so. A little lower down, the passage clearly indicates that the word 'rest' applies to activities *within this world*, to the illusion that by changing his place in the world—by becoming a great scientist or a king, by adding ten or twenty years to his life— man could alter his condition. For the tragic thinker, everything limited and imperfect is equally valueless. One of the most fundamental of human illusions lies in the belief that there are degrees of

goodness and truth, and not an absolute opposition between goodness and evil or between falsehood and truth. In reality, man has no
reason at all for placing any hope in things bounded by time and
space, since he lives only for Infinity and Eternity.

Pascal continues:

> Since the middle state which has fallen to our lot is always distant
> from extremes, what profit is there for a man in having a slightly
> greater understanding of things? If he does obtain it, then he takes a
> very slightly higher view of them. But he still remains just as far from
> the final end, and our span of years is just as imperceptible in eternity
> even if it does last ten years longer.
>
> Looked at from these two infinites, all finite things are of equal size;
> and I can see no reason for basing our imagination on one rather than
> the other. Merely to compare ourselves to the finite is painful to us.

It is the illusion of sensualists and sceptics[1] to maintain that we can
find in the world of reality values which, although only relative, are
sufficiently valid to make life bearable. The rationalist illusion, however, is a complementary and equally dangerous one. It lies in the
belief that by directing his efforts towards a single infinity, that of *a
priori* truths or absolute first principles, man can attain not only relative but also absolute values, and that he can do so without paying
attention to the opposite infinity.

The rationalist cannot understand paradox, and does not know
that 'the springs in man's mind are so disposed that one cannot be
touched without the opposite being disturbed' (fr. 70, E.251).

Pascal exposes the rationalist's error when he writes:

> Man naturally looks upon himself as much more capable of reach-
> ing the centre of things than of embracing their circumference. The
> visible extent of the world is obviously much larger than we are; but
> since we are obviously much larger than small things, we imagine
> ourselves much more capable of understanding them. Yet, in fact, we
> need just as much ability to reach nothing as to reach everything; in
> both cases, our ability must be infinite, and it appears to me that
> someone who had understood the first principles of things would also
> be able to know the infinite (fr. 72, E.390).

This is why, on this earth, man is doomed to remain motionless,
and can never make any real progress. He can be satisfied only by
absolute values—that is to say, by the infinite—and he cannot move

---

[1] I am certainly prepared to admit that such a position becomes sceptical or
empirical only if carried to extremes, and that it puts itself forward as a moderate
form of rationalism. But as soon as one begins to 'moderate' rationalism one is
already beginning to move towards empiricism and scepticism. Monsieur Laporte
is well known for his sympathetic attitude towards David Hume.

towards one infinite without being immediately held back by the quest for the other. Does this mean that despair is the only authentic form which the human mind can assume, and that we are brought round to admitting that Pascal was either a sceptic or a pessimist? Not at all, for although he considers that the meeting of opposites provides the only real and absolute value, he in no way looks upon this as a Utopian illusion. He himself writes that 'opposites meet and re-unite through the very distance which separates them, and thereby come once again together'. 'But,' he adds, 'in God and in God alone', and it is this insistence which he should never forget.

III

The natural order for any study of the human predicament in Pascal should proceed from the fragment on the two infinites to that of *le divertissement* (distraction, or amusement). However, my aim is not only to expound his ideas but also to criticise any attempt to credit him with a doctrine that in any way accepts the limitations and the in-between nature of man. I must therefore now examine the texts which support this particular interpretation. In the Brunschvicg edition they are to be found in fragments 69–72 (E.78, 251, 75, 390), and also in 34–38 (E.984, 987, 985, 386), in the passages dealing with the difference between the specialist and the 'universal man'.

All the texts express the same idea: that the human ideal is not to be found in the specialist, who has an extremely detailed knowledge of one field—poetry or mathematics, for example—but in the 'universal man', who, equally skilled in all domains, will 'talk about the matter under discussion when he came in', and of whom men will 'not say that he speaks elegantly if it is not a question of elegance of language', but of whom 'they will say that he speaks elegantly when this is the matter at issue'.

Now among the texts which discuss the characteristics of the 'universal man', there is one which does seem to support the idea that Pascal recommended acceptance of the limitations placed upon man and the human condition.

> Since one cannot attain universality by knowing everything about everything, we ought to know a little about everything. For it is much better to know something about everything than everything about something: this kind of universality is the best. If we could have both, then so much the better; but if we have to choose, then let us choose the second. Society is often a good judge in these matters, and society both makes and approves of such a choice (fr. 37, E.386).

We must recognise that, for once, Pascal does not put all worldly activities on exactly the same plane. He clearly prefers the *honnête homme* to the specialist, and praises society for doing the same thing. How does this come about, and how can we reconcile this particular text with the many others in which Pascal says the opposite?

The first explanation that springs to mind is a superficial sociological and historical one. The Pascalian concept of the *honnête homme*, so it might be argued, is merely the one developed in the seventeenth century both in the Court and in the upper regions of the *noblesse de robe*; Pascal's relationship with Méré naturally leads one to think that this idea is one which he took from the courtly circles in which his friend was trying to give it theoretical expression. Thus, Brunschvicg naturally compares these fragments with certain passages from Montaigne, Molière, and Méré, and his comparison is to some extent justified: the terminology used—not only 'universal man' but also '*honnête homme*'—indicates that Pascal himself had linked the two ideas together.

However, in spite of their apparent similarity, there does seem to me to be a considerable difference between the idea of the *honnête homme* current in seventeenth-century Court circles and reflected in the texts quoted by Brunschvicg, and the idea here expressed by Pascal.

For the Court, the *honnête homme* is the man who, amply provided with wit and *savoir-vivre*, has a certain culture and even a certain nobility of attitude, but who is really knowledgeable only in the few domains where the social life in which he takes part demands high skill: war, cards, intrigues and perhaps the art of rhyming madrigals and sonnets. No one, for example, would ever think of expecting an *honnête homme* to know physics or geometry.

All this represents the ideal—one that was still to some extent a living one—of a ruling class endowed with sufficient wealth and leisure to look upon any useful professional activity (apart from that of war) as a sign of inferiority. By its very absence of specialised knowledge, such a class sets itself apart from all those who follow a trade, and who therefore—however much wealth they may acquire—remain of the people. The notion of the *honnête homme* represents an aristocratic ideal, admirably suited to the noble courtier, but which also had a certain influence among the richer members of the middle class, especially those whose wealth enabled them to look upon their functions as offering them not so much the opportunity to exercise their skills or make money as the right to claim a particular rank in society.

This comes out even from the passages quoted by Brunschvicg. In one of them Méré recommends the *honnête homme* to have a good knowledge of military matters, but never to make an excessive display of it; in another, he advises his reader to avoid at all costs being taken for a professional man. Clitandre, in *Les Femmes Savantes*, acknowledges that a woman should have a minimum of general culture: 'I agree,' he says, 'that a woman should know something about everything'. Finally, Montaigne says that our aim in education should be to form 'not a grammarian or a logician but a gentleman.'

All this is quite a long way from Pascal's preoccupations. What he attacks is not a deep and scholarly knowledge in certain domains—on the contrary, he demands such knowledge in every subject—but *one-sided* and narrow specialisation. As he remarks in another fragment: 'Universal men are called neither poets nor geometers, etc; but they are *all these things* (my italics L.G.) and are judges of all others.' Moreover, they 'make no distinction between the calling of poet and that of an embroiderer'.

What in fact Pascal has done is to assimilate the social ideal of the *honnête homme* to the ideal of the universal man demanded by his own philosophy. He has not really borrowed this idea at all, with the result that the human type whom he recommends in fragments 34–38 is much closer to the *Bildungsideal* of Lessing, Kant and Goethe, and to the 'total man' of the classless society in Marxist thought than to the *honnête homme* of the Court of Louis XIV.

The central, dominant category of any dialectical mode of thought —and of any tragic thought, for on this particular point there is no difference between the two—is, as I have already said, the category of Totality, and it is one which applies to all three realms, that of the individual, that of the human community and that of the universe. The essential characteristic of any non-dialectical mode of thought is the conscious or unconscious acceptance of a partial or one-sided view of reality. The central image dominating any dialectical thought is that of the sphere or circle, and from this point of view we must not allow ourselves to be misled by the many dualistic or triadic expressions—two infinites, thesis, anthithesis and synthesis, etc.—that we find in the theoretical writings of dialectical thinkers. The number of places at which a cross-section of reality can be taken is naturally infinite, with the result that any disturbance of the balance which makes up human reality will necessarily bring about an equal and opposite reaction, an antithesis. For tragic thinkers, this original balance is static and taut, and any attempt to break it leads to an un-bearable immobility; for dialectical thinkers, it is dynamic and constantly expanding, and the disturbance is resolved in the synthesis of a higher balance.

The superseding of rationalistic or sceptical individualism by tragic thought led necessarily to the idea of the 'universal man', and Pascal merely saw in the refusing of a 'calling' or 'profession' by people such as Méré the expression by analogy of the ideal of universality which was essential to his own philosophy. Compared to the competent, one-sided and narrow-minded specialists whom he met in the rationalistic bourgeoisie of his time, the *honnête homme* seemed merely the lesser of two evils.

It would be unfortunate if today, after Lessing, Holderlin and Goethe, after Hegel and Marx, we were unable to see the clear distinction between these two human types: on the one hand, we have the *honnête homme*, who, in spite of certain progressive characteristics which continue to keep Molière an up-to-date author, was nevertheless the highest expression of a social group that history was outgrowing; and, on the other, the universal man of Pascal, who was the first sketch of a new ethic that is still awaiting its full realisation. Pascal himself gave a clear expression to this distinction when he wrote the *pensée* already quoted (38, E.386), and insisted on the need for breadth of knowledge rather than for narrow specialisation.

Society, he said, is right to judge as it does, since man must choose either to know something of everything or everything of something. But we must not forget that, for Pascal, choice is the evil *par excellence*; when we wager that God exists, then we refuse this human choice and make hope instead of resignation into the fundamental category of existence.

In fact, however, Pascal recognised in this case that we cannot 'know everything about something' and that we must not merely resign ourselves to 'knowing something about everything' but actually resolve to do so.[1] This is why, seeing the rise of the specialist who was going to dominate the immediate future and who still rules today, Pascal wrote this fragment, which, in spite of its reference to 'society', is much closer to the ideas of Hegel, Goethe or Marx than to the position of Molière or Méré.

IV

Can we then say that the *Pensées* constitute, as a whole, a rigorously coherent system? Do we ever find Pascal temporarily giving up his insistence on the paradoxical character of human reality? In spite of appearances, I do not think so. Barcos's position—which we shall meet again in the first two of Racine's tragedies, *Britannicus* and *Bérénice*—was certainly a coherent one. We shall see, however, that by going beyond it, Pascal found himself in a doctrinal position which was a kind of 'unstable balance', but which, for the sake of its own inner coherence, developed towards a position that could be compared to that of dialectical thought.

---

[1] Goethe, Hegel and Marx were aware of this problem and would certainly have agreed with what Pascal is saying in this fragment, which fits in extremely well with the general pattern of their own positions.

The position of Barcos is, in effect, a dualistic one: on the one hand, there is the evil, paradoxical and contradictory world from which God is absent; and, on the other, there is the clear, certain and unambiguous universe of the divinity. The ethic which he deduces from this is simple and straightforward: evil consists of wanting to live in the world, and goodness of withdrawing into solitude, into the divine universe and, in the final analysis, into death.

Pascal, on the other hand, goes a long way towards transcending this dualism when he extends the paradox from the world and man to God. For Barcos, God exists in absolute certainty; for Pascal, God exists in an uncertain certainty, in a wager. These different attitudes give rise to important consequences: for if Barcos's dualism enables him to withdraw from the world and seek refuge in solitude, Pascal evolved naturally from the idea of the wager to the paradoxical position whereby he lived in the world but at the same time refused it, and led the solitary but active life of his final years. Moreover, his own attitude towards the life which he then led could be nothing but one of simultaneous approval and disapproval, and we shall see that he carried both attitudes into practice. This was the farthest limit to which this position could be carried, since the elevation of paradox to the rank of first principle gives rise to an ideology which cannot in fact be made coherent. In order to remain consistent with paradox itself, we must both accept and refuse it at one and the same time.

In spite of the complete opposition between them, there is a similarity between this position and that of the sceptic, since it has often been said that the statement that we know nothing is itself a statement that we do know something. Pascal's ideas cannot be pushed to their logical conclusion, since to do so would involve refusing and going beyond paradox, and thereby reaching the position of dialectical thought. This means that, in a thinker of Pascal's class, who did not himself arrive at the notion of the Hegelian dialectic, we ought nevertheless to find a point at which, on the plane of his own ideas, the paradox is abandoned without, however, actually being transcended.

This point does in fact exist. It lies not in Pascal's attitude towards God, for we have already seen that, for man, His existence is paradoxical, but in his attitude towards the Christian religion, in so far as this affirms the existence of a paradoxical God. There is, in fact, a point at which Pascal does say 'Yes' without immediately adding an opposite and supplementary 'No', one truth that he does accept without then pursuing a contradictory truth: it happens when he states the correspondence between, on the one hand, the paradoxical nature of man and of the world, and, on the other, the paradoxical nature of Christianity. The statement that the Gospels have understood the nature of man and that they are a certain proof, not only of the existence of God but also of the venerability of the Christian religion, and that, in addition, this religion in no way contradicts reason and the senses is the statement of an absolutely certain truth. Pascal thus states the correspondence between the Christian religion and the nature of man.

There is, however, one more question to be discussed: did Pascal acknowledge the existence of a human *nature*? Yes, and no. Not, this time, paradoxically, but in two different senses of the word. Or, rather, his paradoxical language hides a dogmatic and a non-paradoxical position.

We can, in fact, understand the word 'nature' as indicating a norm, a truth, a way of acting which is linked to the human predicament and which is therefore valid, not absolutely and in itself, but at least for all men at all times and places. We use the word in this sense whenever we talk of *natural* rights and *natural* law.

It is obvious that, throughout the *Pensées*, Pascal denied the existence of any human nature in this meaning of the word. Everything which men take for natural law, for the first principles of reason, etc., is nothing but custom, and consequently varies from place to place. Thus, he writes:

> What are our natural principles except the principles to which we have become accustomed? . . . Different customs will give us different natural principles, as we see from our experience; and if there are some natural principles which cannot be effaced by custom, there are also customs opposed to nature, ineffaceable by nature, or by any second custom. This depends upon disposition (fr. 92, E.240).

> Fathers are afraid that the natural love which their children have for them may fade away. What then is this nature, if it is subject to obliteration? Custom is a second nature which destroys the first. But what is nature? Why is custom not natural? I am very much afraid that this nature itself is merely a first custom, in the very same way that custom is a second nature (fr. 93, E.241).

> Memory and joy are feelings; and even geometrical propositions become feelings, for reason makes feelings natural and natural feelings fade away through reason (fr. 95, E.914).

The word 'nature' has, however, another set of connotations which we should nowadays express more exactly by the term 'essence'. From this point of view, Pascal takes his place in the great line of classical thinkers who, from Descartes through to Kant, Hegel and Marx, have never doubted the existence of a human 'essence' or human 'nature'.

The difference lies in the fact that for Pascal man's 'nature' is

H

nothing more than his 'customs', so that man has no 'nature' in the true sense of the word. This is the meaning of passages such as:

Custom is our nature (fr. 89, E.194).
The nature of man is wholly nature, *omne animal*.
There is nothing that cannot be made natural; and nothing natural which cannot be wiped out (fr. 89, E.161).

There is nothing particularly surprising about this. The idea which Pascal expresses in fragments 89–95 (E.194, 133, 922, 240, 241, 162, 165), is repeated with no modifications and with no complement in Marx and Engels, who both completely transcended paradox by the notion of historical process and change.

However, if Marxist thought can, thanks to this idea of the historical process, say both 'Yes' and 'No' to all human reality without falling into self-contradiction, and if it can also look upon man as a creature who acts and therefore state that he is constantly changing reality—thereby transforming truth into error and error into truth—the same is not true of Pascalian thought. This is completely a-historical, and rejects the idea of movement or progress in history.

Dialectical materialism embodies and comprehends itself as a moment in universal history, and a moment which this history will necessarily transcend and outgrow. If, however—like all classical thought—it states that there is such a thing as human nature, and that this lies in man's ability to go beyond the present situation by acting upon it, then it can avoid any incoherence by giving the notion of progress a relative content which situates every historical period only by its relationship to other past epochs and to the present day. It thus removes the only really difficult problem, that of an 'end of history' as something which, in the present state of our knowledge, we can never grasp. It is this which constitutes one of the main superiorities of Marxist over Hegelian thought, which tried to be Philosophy in an absolute and not merely in a relative sense.[1]

Pascal, on the other hand, cannot make his own position a relative one, in spite of the occasional attempts which he did make and which I shall be discussing shortly. Thus, since by 1658 he had rejected the idea of progress, he judged everything by the absolute standard of 'all or nothing'. He thus put all erroneous positions on exactly the same plane: for him, there are thus only mistakes (in the plural) and truth (in the singular).

It therefore comes about that when he looks at his own theories about the nature of man, of the world and of the divinity he gives up the theory of equal and opposite truths and of thesis and antithesis.

[1] As early as 1920 Lukàcs has already called one of his essays *The Changed Function of Historical Materialism*.

For Pascal, man is a paradoxical being who attains his own true nature only by demanding absolute justice and truth and the union of opposites. He is also however, a being who can find in this world only statements and laws which are equally relative and unsatisfactory. He sees the world as inadequate and closed to any realisation of true values, and finds that only God possesses absolute validity; this God, however, still remains a paradoxical being, who is both present and absent, certain and uncertain. But precisely because of this, Christianity is the true religion because it is the only one to have understood the true nature of man, and because it sets forth its paradoxes of the Incarnation, of an incomprehensible and hidden God, and of original sin. It is the only religion that provides an explanation for these paradoxes and which does not contradict reason. Christianity is venerable, and even true, precisely because it presents itself as being both absurd and obviously true, both certain and uncertain.

Here, however, the paradox is quite apparent: what is both certain and uncertain is God's existence, and the possibility of giving meaning to human life; what is certain is the link between the human predicament and the content of Christianity. In order to maintain its very existence, paradox has to give way before Christianity and before Pascal's own doctrine. For him to have carried this paradox even further, to have made his own position a relative one which stated that it, too, needed the existence of equal and opposite truths would have meant discovering dialectical thought and thus going beyond tragedy and paradox. The social conditions of the seventeenth century were not yet favourable to such an intellectual advance, which was not to be realised until more than a century later.

V

To say that man's character is paradoxical is to imply that his state is unbearable and that he cannot both know himself and live. It is from this incompatibility between activity and awareness that springs the ontological necessity of *le divertissement*.

To live in the world means living in ignorance of the nature of man; to understand this nature means realising that man cannot preserve authentic values except by refusing life in this world, by choosing solitude and, in the last analysis, by choosing death. This conclusion had already been drawn from a much shallower analysis of the human predicament and of the vanity of the world by the nuns and solitaries of Port-Royal.[1] However, these were conclusions that still

[1] The reason why we do not find, in the work of Barços, Hamon or Mother Angélique, so accurate or far-reaching an analysis of the world and of life in this world as we do in Pascal is that these thinkers had rejected the first and given up

implied complete certainty of God's existence and of the possibility of abandoning the world completely and seeking refuge in His arms.

Pascal, as we know, extended paradox to the very existence of God himself, and his conclusions have consequently been assimilated to those of Barcos. During the last years of his life he did indeed hold the same views as Barcos and the other solitaries, and categorically rejected the world and science; he did so, however, not at Saint-Cyran or Port-Royal, but in Paris, in the midst of his own scientific and economic activity. It is in this light that we must examine the well-known *pensées* on *le divertissement* (fr. 138–143, E.277, 269, 275, 76, 270, 272).

As in the case of the texts on the two infinites, it is convenient to concentrate on one particular *pensée* which expresses the core of Pascal's ideas. It is fragment 139 (E.269).

It contains first of all a long passage which, although perhaps better written than anything which Barcos or Mother Angélique could have achieved, nevertheless does not go further than their position. Assuming that they considered such a subject worthy of discussion, they could have reproduced it almost word for word on their own account:

> ... I discovered that all the unhappiness of man stems from one thing, that he cannot remain alone in a room. A man with enough wealth to live at home would not, if he were happy there, set out to journey on the sea or to besiege an enemy stronghold. ...
>
> But when I thought more closely about it, and after having found this cause for all our misfortunes, I tried to discover the reason for it: and I found that there is an overwhelming one, which lies in the natural unhappiness of our weak and mortal condition, which is so full of wretchedness that nothing can console us when we think attentively of it.
>
> If we bring together all the goods which might belong to us in whatever condition we can imagine, we shall find that to be king is the finest position in the world. Yet let us think of it with all the delights with which it can be accompanied. If a king is left without distraction and amusement, and allowed to think and reflect on what he is, this languid enjoyment will never sustain him. He will of necessity fall to thinking of the threats that hang over him, of the rebellions that might arise, and, finally, of death and illnesses, which are both inevitable. So that, left without distraction, he is unhappy, and more so than the least of his subjects, who plays and who amuses himself.

the second, and had therefore no interest in discussing either. One of the main consequences of the difference between the way Barcos and Pascal looked upon the relationship between man and God (absolute certainty in the case of the first, wager in the case of the second) is precisely the realistic and pre-dialectical character of Pascal's work.

It is for this reason that the man who thinks he is pursuing profits or a stag is in fact concerned only with gambling and hunting, and, in these activities, with *divertissement* in the etymological sense of the word. It is a way of closing one's eyes, of turning away from this unbearable condition and avoiding awareness of it.

This hare would not protect us from the sight of death and misfortune, but the actual hunt, which takes our mind off them, does thereby provide a protection.

The advice given to Pyrrhus—that he should take the rest that he pursued with so much effort—was indeed difficult to follow.

Telling a man that he should live quietly and at rest means telling him that he should live happily; it means advising him to take on a completely happy condition, one which he can contemplate at leisure and find in it no cause for dissatisfaction.

It shows a complete misunderstanding of nature.

Thus, men who have a natural awareness of their condition and avoid nothing so much as rest and repose, will do absolutely anything to find difficulties.

The whole passage seems to lead directly to the tragedy of refusal in Racine (Junia and Titus) and to the ethic of the nuns and solitaries of Port-Royal and Saint-Cyran. Then, suddenly, there is an unexpected twist in the argument, and we find two complementary passages of which one—clearly personal in tone—justifies men who live in *divertissement*. It is, moreover—since the letter challenging mathematicians to find a solution to the problem of the cycloid dates from June 1658—one of the few Pascalian passages which we can date at least from a *terminus a quo*.

... It is thus wrong to blame them; their fault lies not in their quest for tumult, if they did but seek it merely as a diversion to their woes; the evil lies in their seeking it as if the possession of the things which they chase after really were going to make them happy, and this is why they can be accused of vanity; so that, in this matter, both those who express blame and those who receive it lack a true understanding of man's nature.

Others sweat in their study to show other scholars that they have solved an algebraic problem which had not before received a solution; and so many others expose themselves to the utmost perils in order to boast afterwards about the stronghold which they have taken—and, in my view, thus act rather stupidly; and, finally, other men exhaust themselves in taking note of all these things, not in order to grow any wiser, but simply to show that they know them. And these, in my view, are the stupidest of the lot, since they know that they are stupid, and one can at least continue to believe of the others that they would be less stupid if they really knew what they were doing.

217

These passages are especially important in Pascal's work, since they complete the fragment on the wager, and show that Pascal was fully aware of having gone beyond the position of Barcos in the direction of dialectical thought. He is in fact more conscious than anyone else that life in this world inevitably involves *divertissement* and inauthentic awareness, but far from drawing from this fact the conclusion of the extreme Jansenists—solitude, and the renunciation of any attempt to argue the truth of religion—Pascal acts quite differently. After having refused the world just as absolutely as they do, and explained why men should avoid all *divertissement*, he nevertheless 'sweats in his study to show other scholars that he has solved an algebraic problem which had not before received a solution' and 'exhausts himself in taking note of all these things'.

Finally, after having consciously adopted this attitude, which is different from that of the solitaries in spite of its apparent similarity, Pascal then goes beyond it once again. He makes it a relative one by telling us that those who act in this manner 'are the stupidest of the lot, since they know that they are stupid'.

Once paradox is carried to this point, it can scarcely still be maintained; it is still true, however, that unless we explain both these two passages and Pascal's activity in the last few years of his life as mere weaknesses or inconsistencies (toothache, for example), it is difficult to find any other link apart from the 'wager' argument which connects them both with the very precise analysis of *le divertissement* and with the rest of this work. Thus, once again, the wager is the central concept to which any analysis of Pascal's work inevitably leads.

VI

Pascal's sketch of the human predicament emerges gradually from all the different ideas in his work—the two infinites, the universal man, the concordance between the teachings of Christianity and the paradoxical nature of man (especially the dogma of original sin), the impossibility of living in the world with one's conscience clear and intact, the refusal of the world while remaining in it—and thereby enables us to begin the study of the general principles governing his epistemology, ethics and aesthetics. Two ideas, however, should especially be retained, since they enable us to situate Pascal's philosophy in the broad historical process which led from the atomism of empirical and rationalistic thought to Hegelian and Marxist dialectic. These are:

First, that man as we know him is a creature torn apart by different tendencies, made up on every plane of antagonistic elements, each of which is both necessary and inadequate: body and mind, good and evil, justice and power, form and content, the geometrical and the intuitive mind, reason and passion, etc. The choice of any one of these antagonistic elements necessarily leads to an error which is all the more dangerous, since, like all errors, it is a partial truth. 'All err,' says Pascal himself in fragment 863 (E.455), 'and all the more dangerously since they each follow one truth. Their fault lies not in pursuing a falsehood, but in not following another truth.'

Secondly, that the essence of man lies in the very fact that he can neither choose one of these antagonistic elements nor accept tension and antagonism. His very nature impels him to strive after a synthesis—pure goodness, absolute truth, real justice, immortality of the body as well as of the mind—on all and every plane. But this ideal synthesis can never be achieved on earth, and can come only from a transcendent being, from God.[1]

Under a different, reified form, these are the fundamental concepts of any dialectical thought: the antagonistic quality of all human reality, and the aspiration to synthesis and totality are what characterise other thinkers who came centuries after Pascal. All that needs to be added is that this antagonism is much more intense in tragic than in dialectical thought, since while in Hegel and Marx the very possibility of a future throws its light back on to the conflict between thesis and antithesis, the situation with which Pascal is confronted is entirely different. The complete absence of any possibility of a historical perspective renders the antagonism correspondingly more acute.

One last remark. For a man such as Pascal, who himself lives through this tragic experience, the analysis of what man can achieve on this earth in the realm of epistemology and aesthetics is of secondary importance compared to the only things which really count: ethics and the aspiration towards the absolute in religion.

[1] Each of these two truths proves in turn the truth of the Christian religion and the dogma of original sin. The fact that man is torn between different tendencies proves his fallen nature, while his longing for an absolute proves that he can remember a state of greatness that came before original sin, and can also conceive the possibility of redemption.

XI
LIVING BEINGS AND SPACE

I

IF, unlike the tragic vision, dialectical thought does recognise that human achievements can have a relative value, it still refuses the logical and geometrical method recommended by Cartesian rationalism. Any increase in knowledge about a particular set of facts depends, for dialectical thought, on the perpetual movement to and fro from the whole to the parts and from the whole back to the parts again; this is why, in this and the following chapters, I shall not be dealing with Pascal's ideas under rigidly defined sections, but shall frequently be going back to what I have already said in order to see it again in a new light.

However, I shall try to observe a certain logical order, and shall therefore go against the spirit of the *Pensées* in following the study of the human condition in Pascal by a consideration of the problems of space and living beings. I shall try to show how, within the framework of his general ideas, Pascal envisaged the possibilities open to man on the plane of knowledge (epistemology), of expression (aesthetics) and action (ethics, life in society), always bearing in mind the fact that all these possibilities are, in his view, empty of all real value.

The need to situate the parts in relation to the whole will lead me to establish the relationship between Pascal's position and those of Descartes and Kant, and also, although less frequently, those of Hegel and Marx. I shall begin by defining more exactly the nature of these comparisons.

The comparison between Pascal and Kant, or between Pascal, Hegel and Marx, is first of all essential to a correct understanding of Pascal's own text, which often does little more than introduce certain ideas whose importance has been revealed by the subsequent development of philosophical thought in general.[1] The comparison with Des-

[1] From the point of view of a positivistic approach to history, the only way to understand a text is by taking into consideration the various factors which were in fact detectable at the time when it was written—the writer's intentions, the

220

cartes, on the other hand, has both its own interest because of the light which it throws on the text and also a secondary interest resulting from certain contingencies of seventeenth-century literature.

In spite of the well-known antagonism between Descartes and Pascal confirmed by a large number of texts—especially on Pascal's side—Jean Laporte has tried to show that the two thinkers put forward very similar if not absolutely identical viewpoints. He has done so with such skill and learning that he has created a 'Laporte school' whose members include, among others, Monsieur J. Mesnard and Mesdemoiselles Jeanne Russier and Geneviève Lewis,[1] and

[1] Monsieur Goldmann here gives a long note referring to the interpretation of Pascal's work in the following studies:

Jean Laporte. *Le Cœur et la Raison selon Pascal* (Paris: Elzévir, 1950).
Jeanne Russier. *La Foi selon Pascal*.
Jean Mesnard. *Pascal. L'Homme et l'Œuvre*.
Geneviève Lewis. *Augustinisme et Cartésianisme à Port-Royal* in *Descartes et le cartésianisme hollandais* (P.U.F., 1951).

In his view, all make the mistake of maintaining that Pascal and Descartes adopted basically the same attitude, especially as far as scientific method is concerned. Monsieur Mesnard, for example, considers (op. cit., pp. 159–61) that, like Descartes, Pascal saw animals as pure automata.

---

influences he underwent and so on. For dialectical thought, on the other hand, the meaning of any human fact depends upon its position and on its different relationships within the context of a whole made up of the past, the present and the future. And since this whole is essentially dynamic, it is the future which contains the most important explicative value (cf., among others, my book *Sciences humaines et Philosophie*).

Marx, who brings in questions of the studies of the humanities most frequently when he is writing about problems in economics, noted in one of his suggested introductions to the *Contribution to the Critique of Political Economy* that:

'Bourgeois society is the most highly developed and differentiated stage in the historical organisation of production. The categories which express its conditions, together with an understanding of its own mode of organisation, enable us to understand the mode of organisation and production relationships of all forms of society that have now disappeared. For bourgeois society has been built up from the elements which they left behind them, and still retains those vestiges which have not yet been transcended, while at the same time those features which had merely been sketched out in earlier societies have now attained their full significance. Human anatomy offers us the key with which to understand the anatomy of the ape. Those features in inferior species which foreshadowed the higher form can be understood only when the higher form is known. The economic organisation of bourgeois society provides us with the key to the understanding of the economics of classical society, but not after the manner of those economists who wipe out all historical differences and see bourgeois society in every form of society which they encounter. We can understand the payment of tribute or of tithes only when we understand the payment of ground rent. But we must not see them all as being the same thing' (translated from the Paris edition, M. Girard, 1928, p. 342).

I find these remarks completely valid as far as the history of literature and of philosophy is concerned.

which puts forward its own interpretation of the French seventeenth century. It is therefore important to produce facts to show the falsity of this approach, certainly in so far as the link between the position set forth in the *Pensées* and the central positions of Cartesianism are concerned. Pascal, in fact, did fully understand Descartes, and then decided to oppose his views with complete awareness of what they implied.

I should also point out that in spite of the many and genuine resemblances between Pascal and Kant, there are also great differences between the two thinkers and that these must always be kept in mind. They are due partly to the general historical circumstances in which the two thinkers developed their ideas, but also to the more immediate problems facing them in the form of the other thinkers whose views they had to combat. Thus, both philosophers agree that action is more important than theoretical knowledge, since both recognise that real knowledge, knowledge of the thing in itself, is, like wholeness, systematic determination, true truth, the meeting of opposites, and the logical demonstration of the truth of geometrical axioms, something which for us can never be anything more than an idea of reason or a wager made by the heart. Where they differ, however, is in the fact that Kant does attribute much higher importance to the purely relative and inadequate achievements which man can attain in the realms of science, aesthetics or ethics. Thus, we find in his work concepts such as the categorical imperative, the importance of science and the greatness of works of art which cannot be paralleled in Pascal.

This is why Kant could construct and develop his own system and pursue the tragic vision into every domain of historical thought, why he could elaborate an epistemology, an ethical and aesthetic system, a theory of living beings and a philosophy of religion, as well as lay the first foundations of a philosophy of history. Pascal, on the other hand, was obsessed with the only thing to which his vision accorded authentic value, and which lay outside the reach of human achievement. He was concerned only with transcendence, and therefore insisted in both his ethics and his epistemology on the inadequacy of human achievements. It was only incidentally and by the way that he dealt with questions of aesthetics and with the philosophical problem of living beings. Similarly, more consistent in his tragic vision than Kant was to be a century later, he made no contribution at all to the philosophy of history.

This difference, like a number of others that we shall come across, can in my view be first of all expressed by the fact that in eighteenth-century Germany Kant expressed the ideology of the most advanced section of the bourgeoisie. This gave his system its great historical significance, and, in spite of himself and in spite of his tragic vision, linked him to the real, present-day and concrete world. Pascal and Jansenism, however, expressed the maximum possible consciousness which the *noblesse de robe* could achieve in seventeenth-century France, and this social group had already been overtaken by history, had no future and was consequently cut off from all forms of effective action. This is why Pascal was much more able than Kant to live out the final consequences of the tragic vision and to concentrate entirely on things transcendent and beyond this world.[1]

There was, however, another factor which helped to accentuate this difference: the different ideological positions which the two thinkers had to attack.

In seventeenth-century France the rising class, the Third Estate, is represented philosophically by the dogmatic rationalism of Descartes.[2] Kant, however, had to confront a bourgeoisie that had already seized power, and which had adopted English empiricism, especially in the form given to it by Hume.

One of the signs of the profound similarity between the two thinkers lies in the fact that Pascal created for himself a partly fictitious sceptical opponent in Montaigne, while Kant stood out against the rationalism of Wolff and Leibnitz. It is still true, however, that while Pascal's most urgent and essential talk lay in proving against the Cartesians that human reason was limited and inadequate, Kant endeavoured to prove against Hume and his followers that there were certain things that human reason could achieve, however relative and inadequate they might be.

I shall myself try, in this chapter, to insist on the similarities between Pascal and Kant, which seems to me to be both deeper and less realised than the genuine differences which do separate them.[3]

---

[1] Similarly, it may be noted that, in Kant and in the German literature and philosophy of the early nineteenth century, the tragic dichotomy lies between thought and action, whereas in the case of Pascal and Racine the split is within the mind itself between reason on the one hand and the passions on the other. In my view, this difference is linked to the fact that the German bourgeoise was torn between its admiration for the French revolution and the objective impossibility of carrying out a similar revolution in Germany, whereas in seventeenth-century France the legal nobility was divided, on the intellectual level, between its attachment and its opposition to the king's authority.

[2] This is why, in spite of its dialectical character, and in spite of its depth and penetration, Pascal's tragic thought was fated—like Jansenism as a whole—to remain a transient phenomenon bearing no permanent fruit. It was Cartesianism that provided the inspiration for the real development of social life and constructive thought in general.

[3] I thought I was the first to have noted the similarity between the two thinkers when I came across the following statement in Antoine Adam's *Histoire de la littérature française aux XVII siècle* (Vol. II, pp. 294–5 (Paris: Domat, 1954):

II

I shall study Pascal's conception of life and the nature of living beings only briefly. There is already an excellent study of the subject,[1] and I shall come back to it in the next chapter. We should, however, note one very curious and suggestive fact: Arnauld and his followers were strongly influenced by Cartesianism, and there were also 'Disciples of Saint Augustine' who adopted the Cartesian view of animals as machines. When we remember with what naïvety, one might almost say with what good faith, the Jansenists either hid or suppressed heretical tendencies within their group (especially in the case of people such as Barcos and Pascal, who were dead and could no longer defend themselves) we need not be surprised to find two witnesses—Marguerite Perrier, a follower of Arnauld, and Baillet[2]—who state that Pascal himself adopted Descartes's views on animals. Although the historian cannot pass over these statements, he must nevertheless treat them with circumspection.

This is especially important when we see the number of scholars who, influenced by Laporte,[3] have accepted these statements without

---

[1] Cf. Georges Desgrippes, *Études sur Pascal* (Paris: Pierre Téqui), Appendice I: 'Les animaux-machines', pp. 103–25.

[2] Cf. Adrien Baillet, *La Vie de Monsieur Descartes*, 2 volumes (Paris, 1661, Vol. I, p. 52.

[3] I must add that Laporte himself was much more prudent. In his view, Pascal 'never made his views wholly clear on this point, where it was, in the last analysis,

---

'One day, in a moment of discouragement, Victor Delbos, the author of *La Philosophie morale de Kant*, remarked that he had found nothing in the German philosopher that was not already in Pascal'.

Monsieur Adam then adds the following remark himself: 'The *Pensées* denied the existence of Natural Law. But Rousseau later did exactly the same thing, and took up precisely the same arguments as Pascal, arriving at the conclusion which Pascal himself could not reach in 1660, but which nevertheless lay there as the natural development of his ideas: the theory of the General Will. The *Pensées* said that the law was just because it was the law. Rousseau says the same thing, as does Kant after him, and we should not be far wrong in saying that the *Pensées* contain the seed of the categorical imperative. The Kantian ethic is based on the idea that the philosophy of the enlightenment, by being a philosophy of unity, compromises any truly moral life and involves a misunderstanding of the essential nature of moral action, which lies in effort and self-sacrifice. This idea, which Rousseau also shares, is one that comes out most clearly from a reading of the *Pensées*. Finally, Pascal does not believe in according pride of place to the intelligence. What else was there for him to put in its place, but the primary importance of ethics, that is to say the fundamental thesis which Rousseau and Kant share with each other?'

The idea of bringing together the views of Pascal and Kant is thus not as novel or unexpected as I had thought when beginning to write this book. It was nevertheless important to make it clearer by a concrete analysis of the general pattern of the two philosophies.

making any serious attempt to check them, in spite of the fact that neither Marguerite Perrier nor Barcos was particularly well qualified to understand Pascal's ideas.

However, when Desgrippes listed the Pascalian texts dealing with animals his results were quite conclusive, in spite of the fact that he had originally been inclined to accept the view of Marguerite Perrier and Barcos. There are, in fact, two fragments of the *Pensées* (341 and 342, E.230 and 209) which explicitly state the obvious fact that animals have neither mind nor language. There is, however, *no text by Pascal which puts forward the thesis that animals are machines*, and no text which even allows us to think that he probably accepted this view without explicitly formulating it. On the contrary, there are a number of texts that use expressions which, interpreted literally, would lead us to infer that he thought precisely the opposite. One may, perhaps, as Desgrippes suggests, believe that Pascal 'considered it sufficient to stick to ordinary language, without making his views clear as to what he thought instinct was' (p. 116). But Desgrippes himself is forced to admit that 'one cannot resist the strong impression that Pascal is not using the language of someone who adopts a mechanistic interpretation of animal behaviour'.

Finally, there is a fragment (340, E.231) which explicitly contrasts the most perfect machine yet made, the calculating machine, with animal's 'endowed with a will'.[1] Since I have followed Desgrippes so far, I will now quote his conclusions:

> The question therefore remains an open one. There are neither sufficient reasons to contest the evidence available, nor a sufficient number of explicit texts in Pascal to call this evidence seriously into doubt. All one can do is raise a certain number of questions, without committing oneself definitely on the question of whether Pascal did or did not believe that animals were machines.

> What is beyond doubt, however, is the fact that Pascal's language varies with the circumstances: sometimes he almost adopts Cartesian terminology, sometimes he speaks in the normal manner about 'instinct'. Surely this is an indication that he was not particularly interested in constructing a system to explain animals as automata? As we have seen in earlier chapters, he was as a Christian apologist much more interested in another type of automatism: that which brings into play the relationship between body and soul, and that makes us spontaneously fall into a belief without our realising that we are doing so. And, in his view, there was no need to have decided on the exact

[1] Cf. *Pensées*, fr. 341 (E.230), 342 (E.209), 340 (E.231).

---

impossible to do anything but hazard a series of conjectures'. Cf. Jean Laporte, *Le Cœur et la raison selon Pascal*, p. 89. This is moreover, also the conclusion that Monsieur Desgrippes finally adopts.

nature of instinct before studying the laws governing these spontaneous functions. We should not forget that Pascal is much more a moralist, and exegetist and a converter of souls than he is a philosopher, and that he made no mystery of his sceptical attitude towards philosophical systems. Surely, after having come to the conclusion that it was useless to try to provide a detailed description of the 'machine' of the universe, he would have found it equally ridiculous to 'construct the machine' of animal organisms?

I need perhaps go no further, and will refer the reader to Desgrippes, whose conclusions are all the more convincing because of his moderation and refusal to state definitely what his analysis nevertheless suggests: that, far from being automata, animals are for Pascal what they were for Kant: a third, intermediary realm of reality, placed between matter, which is controlled by fixed laws, and the human realm, which is governed by the mind.

However, there is one point where I differ from Desgrippes. It is in the interpretation of fragment 79, which he mentions in the last lines of his conclusion. The fragment runs (E.174):

> Descartes.—We must say, approximately, 'This occurs by figure and motion', for that is true. But it is ridiculous to try to say which figures and motions, and try to reconstruct the machine. For it is unnecessary, uncertain and difficult. And even if it were possible, I do not consider the whole of philosophy to be worth an hour of trouble.

Monsieur Desgrippes, giving a traditional interpretation of this fragment, and one which, to my knowledge, has never been seriously questioned, thinks that Pascal is referring solely to the 'machine of the universe'. In my view this is highly doubtful, and I would maintain that it applies to everything in Cartesianism which was part of the 'machine', that is to say both to animals and to the physical universe as a whole. To my knowledge, no one has seriously argued that fragment 79 (E.174) applies only to the physical universe, and that because no one has ever seriously considered the possibility that it might equally well apply to animals. Like the statement by Laporte's disciples that Pascal looked upon animals as machines, this is one of the commonly accepted interpretations which have never been closely examined. In fact, it is based upon slender if not completely non-existent evidence. And although I cannot prove definitely that fragment 79 refers also, or even primarily, to animals, this suggestion does fit in much better with Pascal's general epistemological position than does the traditional view. Moreover, this view makes fragment 79 (E.174) into little more than a commonplace, which could have been expressed by almost any one of the nuns or solitaries in Port-Royal, but which it is difficult to imagine being written down by Pascal.

He expressed his view on geometry in the well-known letter to Fermat in August 1660, and these almost certainly applied to science in general. He remarked then, as we have seen, that he saw geometry as 'the highest exercise of the human mind', but also added that he saw no difference between a first-rate geometer and an artisan (see pp. 50–51).

In spite of appearances, there is a wide gap between the paradoxical statement in this letter and the completely different idea—which contradicts everything Pascal thought or said—that we should be satisfied, as far as science is concerned, with a few general approximations which do not involve detailed research. It is even more important that we should not see Pascal as suggesting that even if truth were accessible we should not make an effort to discern it. If he would not 'take two steps for geometry' it is because geometry does not offer absolutely perfect truths whose first principles can be adequately demonstrated.

If once we admit that in fragment 79 (E.174) the word 'machine' also means 'animal'—and there is no real reason for thinking that this is not the case—then it becomes one of the most remarkable, and, for its time, one of the most modern texts in the history of biological thought. Monsieur Koyré has pointed out to me that it is probably a critique of Cartesianism from an Aristotelian viewpoint. This is probably true, but a view which rejects Aristotelian physics and metaphysics to retain only biological organicism is, in fact, an *avant-garde* position in the seventeenth century. Moreover, this interpretation fits perfectly well into the other texts about animals which Desgrippes analyses, and into a whole collection of texts setting out Pascal's views on epistemology. What is most important, however, is the fact that it brings Pascal's views on the question much closer to those of Kant, and underlines the similarity between the two thinkers on a number of other points, especially on the general scheme of their philosophical positions. This is why my own interpretation seems to me to be preferable to the traditional one, which is not supported by any convincing evidence.

What then happens when we read fragment 79 (E.174) as applying not only to the physical universe but also to animals? What is Pascal saying, and how does his position conflict with that of Descartes? (In order more easily to compare Pascal's position with later, and even twentieth-century, thinkers, I shall substitute the words 'mechanistic interpretation' for the Pascalian 'by figure and movement'; this does not alter the meaning, and enables ùs to compare Pascal's position not only with those of Descartes and Kant but also with that of modern behaviouristic reflexology.)

In my view, he is admitting—as Kant was to do later and as modern

Gestalt psychologists or thinkers such as Goldstein or Merleau-Ponty do—that a living organism is made up of a very large number of mechanical processes, or of 'conditioned reflexes'. It is this way that I should interpret: 'We must say, approximately: "This occurs by figure and motion", for that is true.' However, as Kant himself pointed out, we cannot explain the whole of an organism by mechanistic concepts, and Pascal, like most Gestalt psychologists and dialectical thinkers, is saying exactly the same thing: 'But it is ridiculous to try to say what these are and to reconstruct the machine.' Moreover, Pascal is much more up to date even than Kant, for Kant did no more than note the impossibility of 'reconstructing the machine' while still considering that mechanistic interpretations, although of limited validity, did apply in the same way in biology as in physics. It was the work of the Gestalt psychologists which in fact indicated that conditioned reflexes are transferable, and that one can quite easily take the place of another if it is more suited to the needs of the organism or if the first stops working. Thus, to express the idea in Pascalian terms, one of the advances of Gestalt psychology with respect to Kant's position lies in the realisation that not only is it impossible to 'reconstruct the machine' but also that, even if we can tell 'approximately' that 'it works by figures and motion', it is impossible to say exactly what these are. This is because certain reflexes can take the place of the usual ones if need be, according to the function which they perform in the general pattern of behaviour. Similarly, Pascal also anticipates the critique which Goldstein put forward of reflexology when he said that the attempt to construct the organism on the basis of its acquired reflexes is pointless and unreliable, since we are constantly obliged to introduce more and more new factors, inhibitions, inhibitions of inhibitions and so on—all of which are remarkably similar to the famous epicycles, which had to be made infinitely complicated in order to defend the geocentric against the Copernican hypothesis.

There remains the final proposition: 'That even if this were possible, I do not think that the whole of philosophy is worth an hour's trouble.' This is, I must admit, the most difficult part of the fragment to explain in a satisfactory manner. For reasons that I have already suggested, it cannot be reduced—in this context—to the statement which would be quite normal in the case of Barcos or Singlin, namely that knowledge of physical objects or processes has no importance compared to the truths of faith. (Pascal certainly thought this, but he would not have said so in this way.) What he is more probably saying is that this science is worthless, since it denies its own principles, and has not explained but denied the specific quality of living things by reducing them to inanimate objects. In this interpretation—and the text itself does not really favour any other—Pascal's remark would be accepted by any dialectical thinker, and still conform to the spirit of Kantian philosophy. Thus, although dialectical thought looks upon every being as being in the process of becoming, and tragic thought sees this process as fixed and frozen in a discontinuous hierarchy of qualitative differences (the three orders in Pascal and Kant), both philosophies agree on this: that one can never validly explain the higher by the lower or the future by the past. These factors certainly exercise some influence, which must be studied with great attention, but both from the static scheme of thought of the tragic vision and for Gestalt psychology the essential factor which acts on the environment within the framework of determinism is the particular element which pertains to the order of which the object in question forms part. For dialectical thought this essential factor is the future, and the movement of history.

I will repeat once against that although there is no decisive evidence available to prove the absolute valid<ty of my interpretation of fragment 79 (E.174), any attempt to reject it must be based upon evidence at least equal to that which I have presented here. However that may be, I do think it is important to realise that the tendency to identify Pascal's position on animal consciousness with that of Descartes—which has become almost a commonplace for Pascalian scholars—has no real basis. It results, in fact, from the general ideological tendency to Cartesianise the tragic position of Jansenist extremism, and is an example of the danger involved in assimilating Pascal to any thinker who simply happened to be one of his contemporaries. Pascal is an original thinker in that strongest meaning of the word, and the first place where we should look for the meaning of his work is in what he actually wrote.

III

When one studies Pascal's philosophical writings about the physical structure of the universe (and not his actual work in physics and mathematics, which has already been discussed by specialists and which I am not competent to analyse) it almost seems a commonplace to point out how close he is to the critical philosophy of Kant, until one notices that this commonplace seems to have escaped most historians.

For both thinkers the physical universe—together with everything that can be known on the theoretical plane of reason in Pascal, or of the understanding in Kant—has ceased to present the existence of God as either certain or probable. There is no physical or ontological proof of His existence, and the famous proposition by which Kant summed up his own position—'I have had to abolish knowledge in order to make room for faith'—is also an exact description of the conclusion of the *Pensées*. And in my view one would be wholly justified in saying that there is no essential[1] difference of content between Kant's practical postulates and Pascal's wager.

Monsieur de Gandillac[2] has shown how a classical image, that of the sphere whose centre is everywhere and whose circumference nowhere, originally designated God, either as intelligible or as unintelligible; then later on, how it came to be used by Nicolas da Cusa and Giordano Bruno to mean the world; and how it then became, in Pascal, an image which meant nothing more than the world, together with the impossibility of reaching a genuine understanding of it.

Both Pascal and Kant see the physical universe in a similar way. Both consider that science cannot bring us absolute knowledge either of the parts or of the whole, and yet both retain the idea of such knowledge as part of their philosophy, while still continuing to see it as an impossible demand. Both, moreover, see the world as completely neutral in all matters of faith, and recognise that it offers us neither reasons to believe nor reasons to disbelieve in God. It is perhaps an extrapolation of their original position, but nevertheless a valid one in my view, to say that both Pascal and Kant see the physicist—*qua physicist*—as an agnostic.[3]

I do not intend to set out a formal comparison between the two thinkers, for this can easily be discovered by reading their work. What I shall try to do is briefly consider some aspects of the problem of space, and of the physical universe, that show a certain contrast between their respective positions.

[1] There is nevertheless a difference, and one to which Kant himself would have certainly given the greatest importance. The autonomy of the moral law, on which the postulate of God's existence is based in the critical philosophy, naturally does not exist in the context of the *Pensées*, where Pascal sees the refusal of the world and the wager on God's existence as inseparably linked together.

[2] Cf. Maurice de Gandillac, 'La sphère infinie de Pascal', in the *Revue d'Histoire de la philosophie et d'Histoire générale de la civilisation* (Lille, 1943), No. 33, pp. 32–45; and 'La Cosmologie de Pascal', in *Pascal, L'homme et l'œuvre* (Paris: Editions de Minuit, 1955).

[3] As we shall see in the next chapter, the only way in which it is possible to give a certain appearance of validity to Laporte's analyses is to limit them to the philosophical context within which Descartes and Pascal conceived the rôle of the physicist and the mathematician. Even then, however, we have to isolate this problem from the whole context, which is not only different but also in direct opposition to it.

As far as their work as physicists is concerned—as Monsieur Brunschvicg has very adequately shown—the two thinkers are profoundly different, and as philosophers they are completely opposed to each other. The only valid comparison that might be made between them lies in the rigid distinction which they both make between physics, as a science, and theology.

Everyone knows the famous fragment 206 (E.392): 'The eternal silence of these infinite spaces casts me into dread.' And although one can also quote passages such as the conclusion of fragment 72 (E.390) —which deals with the universe as a sphere whose centre is everywhere and whose circumference nowhere and which says that 'it is the most striking proof of the omnipotence of God that our imagination should lose itself in this thought'—it does seem that fragment 206, in which he insists upon their silent and unknowable quality, is Pascal's last word on the subject of space and the physical universe.

From a certain point of view—doubtless the most important— things are similar in the criticial philosophy of Kant. Space is a form of pure intuition, and tells us nothing about the freedom of the will, the immortality of the soul or the existence of God. On the contrary, by limiting the realm in which our theoretical knowledge is valid to the phenomenal world of experience, it hides the solution of these problems from us.

It is still true, however, that space itself, and other aspects of the physical world, do have another meaning in Kant's critical philo- sophy, and that this does seem to lead in a different and even oppo- site direction. One has only to think, for example, of the famous conclusion to the *Critique of Practical Reason* which brings together the moral law and the starry sky and the chapters in the *Critique of Judgment* devoted to an analysis of the sublime under its two forms, the mathematical and the dynamic,[1] to see the difference between the two thinkers. In all these texts space and the physical world are seen as linking men to the practical idea of God on the aesthetic plane, and, through this, also on the practical plane, in spite of the absolute separation which they introduce on a theoretical level. We must therefore ask what justification there is for bringing together two sys- tems of thought which differ so widely on such important questions.

Although I cannot deal with Kant's thought in detail, it should be noticed that, from its very beginning, it is dominated by the idea of totality. From the publication of the *Monadologia Physica* in 1756, Kant separates space from its physical content precisely because space is a whole that precedes all the parts composing it, while its physical content is made up of autonomous elements which alone explain the constitution of wholes.

This distinction is at the origin of the future separation between the forms of pure intuition—space and time—and the categories of the

[1] The second form, in my view, comes fairly close to the Pascalian image frag- ment 397 (E.218), in so far as, in Kant, we are concerned with a world which could crush me but which, even while doing so, would still remain smaller and weaker than I because of the moral law which lies within me and which will always enable me to resist it.

understanding in the *Critique of Pure Reason*. (Not only can space be infinitely divided, but any limited space can be conceived only against a background of the infinite space from which it has been abstracted.)

If, however, we look at Kant's thought in an earlier stage of its development we can see the idea of totality gradually taking shape. It begins on the moral plane with the idea of the universal community of minds and on the theoretical plane with the idea of the universe, before being increasingly visible as the only possible basis for God's existence. In the meantime, however, this totality, which began by simply being, gradually becomes what it will be in Kant's critical philosophy: a possible totality, in whose reality we must believe and to whose final creation, for reasons which are certain on a practical plane, we must all contribute. The turning-point between the pre-critical and the critical philosophy can be found in a comment in the *Dissertation* of 1770.[1]

Kant's posthumous fragments, which are difficult to date, also contain, like the *Opus Posthumum*, a certain number of passages that bring the notion of space nearer to that of divinity.

The link which, in the pre-critical period, is expressed in the feeling of the sublime, and which links the perception of space to the idea of suprasensible phenomena, thus seems to be a fundamental theme in Kant's thought, which can be followed through from his earliest to his latest texts.

Since the category of Totality is common to both the philosophy of Pascal and to that of Kant, I now have to explain why the latter made space, and even time, into one of the privileged forms of expression of this category while the former did not. The problem is a difficult one, but there are two types of consideration which might help us to solve it.

A. The first concerns the internal structure and coherence of the Kantian system. One of the principal differences between Kant and Pascal lies in the fact that Kant placed the contrast between form and matter at the very centre of his system; that he also, in the *Critique of Practical Reason*, found a relationship between what was formally given in the moral law and the practical postulate of God's existence; and that he might therefore be reasonably expected to look for a relationship between, on the one hand, the formal totality of the universe towards which the categories of the understanding continually tend without ever being able to reach it, and, on the other, the idea of God, which in his system could only be a practical one. There was thus a reason of internal consistency which impelled Kant to-

---

[1] Cf. Kant, *Dissertation of 1770*, German Academy edition, Vol. II, pp. 409–10. Cf. also pp. 70–71 of John Handyside's translation. Open Court Publishing Company, Chicago and London 1928.

wards the quest for a relationship between space, time and God which would be analogous if not similar to the one which he had been able to set up on the practical plane between God's existence and his own.

B. We must also add a second, purely historical factor. In Pascal's day the concept of space which prevailed in science was that of Descartes, while in Kant's day it was that of Newton. We need only recall the famous expression of *Sensorium Dei* to realise all the consequencies of this distinction. Certainly, Kant completely rejected the Newtonian idea of a real space that would reveal the existence and active intervention of God, but he had nevertheless undergone the influence of a whole current of ideas which we can find expressed in the correspondence between Leibnitz and Samuel Clarke. Madame Hélène Metzger[1] has shown how Newtonian physics constituted a turning-point in the history of the relationship between physics and theology by insisting on the existence of gravity, a force which would have been quite inconceivable for a consistently Cartesian thinker, and by conjoining with this the existence of absolute space, and the need for God constantly to govern the universe which fills this space by infusing it with energy.

If Cartesianism seemed to Pascal, and later to any dialectical historian, as basically atheistic, separating God from the physical universe and leaving Him only a very dubious relationship with time, Newtonian physics, on the other hand, was felt by most seventeenth- and eighteenth-century thinkers to mark a return to the union between physics and theology. Kant, by bringing together God and space, was merely repeating the ideas expressed by Clarke, and by the other thinkers studied by Madame Metzger, and doubtless by many other writers of his time, and providing them with a philosophical basis.

Because it is completely uniform, entirely rational and completely devoid of qualities, Cartesian space hides the existence of God. Newtonian space, on the other hand, reaffirms the existence of points which are different from one another, and contains a universe which is held together—until Einstein—by the profoundly irrational link of gravitation; it therefore answers man's quest for reality by the affirmation that God exists. Thus, Pascal and Kant, who both declared that it was impossible to prove the existence of God, but who also declared that it was essential to postulate His existence for practical reasons, and who both agreed on the need to investigate the physical universe in order to discover reasons that pointed at His existence as a probable but not certain fact, both found an analogous practical reason but differed, while they did so, on the problem of

[1] Hélène Metzger, *Attraction Universelle et religion naturelle chez quelques commentateurs anglais de Newton*, 3 vols. (Paris: Hermann, 1938).

space. This was not because of a difference between their philosophical systems, but a result of the fact that each of them was concerned with a different system of physics, and one that was called upon to fulfil a different rôle within the same basic scheme.

I shall conclude by mentioning another philosophically important difference between Pascalian and Cartesian physics, the one which concerns not God but the associated problem of individuality. The two problems are, in fact, undoubtedly linked together, for in an atomistic philosophical system which carries individualism to its logical extremity, and which abolishes both the community and the universe, the individual who can no longer base his existence on any transcendent reality can find justification for it only by becoming a type and losing any specific character.

It is almost a commonplace to recall that in Descartes's physical geometry bodies have only an apparent individual existence, since they are separated by the same symbolic representations within an identical extension. It is much more important, however, to mention that exactly the same concept applies to souls, which are in theory all identical with one another, since their only attribute is thought, and since 'the ability to judge exactly and to distinguish truth from error, which is correctly called common sense or reason, is naturally equal in all men'.

Basically, individuality exists in the Cartesian system only by virtue of the union between the soul and the body, that is to say by an aspect of reality that is completely certain and effective, but which is nevertheless incomprehensible from Descartes's own dualistic starting-point. By contradicting this idea, and by distinguishing matter from empty space, Pascal maintained the individuality even of physical bodies; and we have already seen how he did so even more on the biological and on the human plane.

The discussion in this chapter of Pascal's views on living creatures and on physics has led to the starting-point, on an ontological plane, of the epistemological controversy which I shall analyse later between Descartes's and Pascal's philosophical positions. That of Descartes, continuing a tradition dating back for over a thousand years, recognised only knowledge of general principles, while that of Pascal opened a new chapter in the history of philosophy by establishing, if not the reality and possibility of a scientific and methodological knowledge of individuals, then at least the demand that such knowledge be pursued.

XII

EPISTEMOLOGY

THE student of the *Pensées*, like the student of any philosophical doctrine, comes across innumerable epistemological problems, and these cannot all be studied in one chapter. Here, I shall concentrate on three such problems which I find especially important. They are:

(*a*) The problem of our knowledge of individuals and of the category of totality.
(*b*) Thesis and antithesis, or the problems of opposite truths.
(*c*) Consciousness and 'the machine', the problem of the relationship between thought and action.

I

In his Brussels lecture *Capital and Wage Labour*, Marx put forward an analysis that was to lead to a long philosophical discussion:

Capital consists of raw materials, tools and nourishment of all kinds, which are used to produce new raw materials, new tools etc. These elements are thus creations of labour, products of labour, accumulated labour. Capital is accumulated labour which is used to create new products. This is what the economists say. What is a negro slave? A man belonging to one of the black races. One explanation is as good as another.

A negro is a black man—it is only under certain conditions that he becomes a slave. A loom is a machine used for weaving. It is only under certain conditions that it becomes *capital;* isolated from these conditions, it is as far from being capital as gold, in its natural state, is from being coin of the realm, or sugar the price of sugar.

In his comments on this and similar texts,[1] Georg Lukàcs later brought out the great importance which it has for epistemology. What Marx implies here is an idea expressed for the first time in the

[1] G. von Lukàcs, *Geschischte u. Klassenbewsslein.*

235

realm of the positive sciences, although Hegel had already used it on the plane of philosophical analysis: that there is a dialectical approach to problems which is completely opposed to the one used at the present day in the sciences of physics and chemistry. In these, progress is achieved by using a system of hypotheses to move from the individual and empirical fact to a general law governing all phenomena of the same type. In the historical sciences, on the other hand, we move not from the individual to the general, but from the abstract to the concrete, from the individual part to a relative whole—which is individual in its turn—and from the whole back to the parts again. For the student of history, the meaning of the individual fact depends neither upon its immediate sensible appearance—we must never forget that the empirical fact with which the historian begins is an abstraction—nor on the laws governing it, but on the totality of its relations to the social and cosmic whole of which it forms part.

A car is a car, and it is only in a certain context that, without altering its physical appearance, it ceases to be an article for everyday use and becomes a piece of individual capital. Similarly, when a man buys a pair of shoes and pays for them with a certain sum of money, the meaning of his action and the laws under which it takes place are completely different according to whether he does so in a liberal or a planned economy, in peace or in war. A number of further examples could be given, and I have already mentioned some literary and philosophical ones in the first part of this work. What we must do now is bring out the methodological and, above all, the epistemological consequences which these involve.

They are numerous, but two seem to be particularly important both in their own right and for a study of Pascal.

A. That thought can proceed according to two basically different methods, both of which can be applied to any object. The first of these is especially fruitful in the physical sciences, but generally barren as far as knowledge of man is concerned. (As Marx pointed out in the preface to his *Critique of Political Economy*, it can give only a few formal truths of sociology or economics.) The second, on the other hand, almost always gives good results when applied to the human sciences, but is much less frequently successful in the natural sciences of geology or biology, etc.

The first of these methods goes from the individual to the general, and almost always remains abstract (The 'nature' with which the chemist or physicist is concerned is an abstraction that must be made in order for technical action to be possible, but it remains an abstraction none the less. In reality, there is not an a-temporal law governing the fall of bodies, but simply such and such a stone which falls under particular historical or temporal conditions with which, generally speaking, the physicist is not concerned.) The second method goes from the abstract to the concrete, and this means from the parts to the whole and from the whole back to the parts again. For abstract knowledge of particular facts is made concrete by the study of their relationship with the whole, and the abstract knowledge of relative wholes is made concrete by the study of their internal structure, of the functions of the different parts and of their relationship with one another.[1]

B. When we know the particular sections of the universe which science abstracts for its study, and which, having no real existence, cannot be the subject of our action and knowledge, our knowledge of them remains external. When, however, we are concerned with the concrete reality of historical and social events we approach this internally and not externally; for we ourselves are part of the whole which we are studying, and our knowledge is inevitably influenced by the position which we occupy in the whole.[2] This is why it is absurd for a modern thinker to talk about 'objective' knowledge of history and of society. In this particular field the notion of objectivity can be meaningful only in so far as it indicates a relative degree of objectivity when the knowledge in question is related to other doctrines or forms of knowledge elaborated under equally subjective conditions.[3]

I must add, moreover—and this is where dialectical thought goes beyond any tragic philosophy—that, in the human and social whole to which he belongs, man is not only a spectator but also an actor, and that the expression which he gives to his ideas is not the least

[1] The methodological introduction already quoted from one of Marx's recently published posthumous manuscripts (cf. note 1 to Chapter XI of this study) contains the following passage:
'If there is no production in general, there is no general production. Production is always a particular branch of production—agriculture, stock-breeding, manufacture, etc.—or else it is totality. However, we cannot equate economics with technology. The relationship between the general conditions of production and a certain given social level of the development of the forms of production, and, on the other hand, the particular forms that production takes is to be developed later. Finally, production can never be seen wholly in isolation either, for it is always a certain social body, a social subject, which is active in a greater or smaller totality of one of the branches of production. Neither is this the place to discuss the relationship between scientific description and real movement. Production in general. Particular branches of production' (pp. 7–8). The development of the ideas contained in this particular passage could lead to the expression of one of the most important ideas in the dialectical method. Unfortunately, I do not have room to do this here.

[2] Cf. L. Goldmann, *Sciences humaines et Philosophie.*

[3] In a society in which there remained no essential antagonism between different groups (classes or nations) one might perhaps be able to talk about the possibility of objective knowledge in the humanities, objective knowledge, that is, of the same type which can be obtained nowadays in the physical sciences.

effective form by which he makes his action felt. The problem of trying to discover what theoretical view of social reality attains the highest degree of objectivity is therefore connected not only with man's wider and more exact knowledge of himself and of society but also with the way in which a particular historical group acts on society in order to make its doctrines true. Dialectical thinkers do not say that statements about man and society *are* true or false, but that they *become* true or false, and that this happens as a result of the encounter between man's social activity and certain objective, natural and historical conditions.

These introductory remarks are necessary for an understanding of the Pascalian texts which I shall now study.

It is self-evident that some of these ideas were not accessible to tragic thought. Static, foreign to any idea of 'becoming', dominated by the category of all or nothing, it was never able to reach either the notion of degrees of objectivity or that of a series of human actions which could maintain progress by transforming error into truth and present truth into future error. It is therefore even more important to stress the fact that Pascal's work expresses in a perfectly consistent and conscious manner two ideas which are fundamental to any dialectical epistemology. These are:

(*a*) The fact that any valid knowledge of *individual* realities presupposes a method of research which goes not from the particular to the general but from the part to the whole and contrariwise.

(*b*) That, because man's ontological status is that of an integral part of a whole, and because this whole determines the meaning of the individual beings and phenomena which compose it, any knowledge which he does acquire will never be absolutely valid.

All we need to do in order to realise to what extent Pascal's philosophical position marks the birth of dialectical epistemology is to recall the two passages already mentioned in Chapter I (cf. pp. 5–6 (fr. 72, E.390)).

It is impossible to over-estimate the importance of these two texts. Certainly, what they express is not a programme for moving towards a new dialectical and concrete knowledge of historical and individual realities, but on the contrary, the idea that such knowledge is in fact impossible. Pascal is nevertheless obliged, in order to express this impossibility, to give clear expression to the central idea on which such knowledge should be based, and on which it will in fact be based when Hegel and Marx give it the status of a positive science: the movement from the whole to the parts and back to the whole again.

From Aristotle to Descartes, one assumption seems to have dominated the search for true knowledge: that only general principles can really be known. What Hegel and Marx inaugurate is the idea that individual wholes can be known dialectically. The importance of Pascal and Kant lies not in the fact that they stated such knowledge to be possible, but that they formulated a demand for it, and were implicitly aware of the limitations inseparable from any of the mathematical or physical sciences.

It is difficult to understand Pascal's critique of Descartes unless one first realises that it is concerned less with Descartes's actual physics than with the demand for a knowledge of an absolutely new type. This will include, if not historical realities (of which Pascal was not really thinking), but at least those individual realities which we see as being historical, such as man, justice, the choice between different professions, the thought of particular philosophers and, in the last analysis, organic life itself, for this can be seen as depending upon an analogous principle.

Moreover, in spite of the relatively slight importance which Pascal accords to epistemology when compared to ethics, and especially to religion, fragment 72 (E.390) is not necessarily the only one in which we find the idea of a method peculiar to the knowledge of individual realities and to the category of wholeness.

There are also two fragments, 684 and 19 (E.491 and 8) dealing with the expression of ideas in writing, which I have already discussed in Chapter I, and the very famous fragment dealing with the difference between the geometrical and the intuitive mind.

Brunschvicg had already noted the apparent contradiction between fragments 1 and 2 (E.910 and 909), which both discuss geometry. The first contrasts the geometrical with the intuitive mind, and notes that the latter is concerned with principles that are 'subtle and numerous'; the second, on the other hand, states that geometry 'understands principles in great number', and contrasts the geometer with 'those who study the effects of water, in the study of which few principles are involved'.

Like Brunschvicg, I think that fragment 2 contrasts geometry with physics, while fragment 1 deals with geometry on quite a different plane. In my view, however, this plane is that of knowledge of individuals as opposed to knowledge of general principles. This would enable us to give fragment 1 quite a different meaning from the purely psychological one normally attributed to it, and to link it with fragments 72, 19, 684 and 79 (E.390, 8, 491 and 174). However, since the text is not absolutely unambiguous, this is merely a suggestion.[1]

---

[1] If my interpretation is valid this would lead one to argue that the fragment classed as number 1 in the Brunschvicg edition (E.910) was written fairly early, since the relationship between individuals and general ideas is worked out in much less detail than in the four other fragments which I quote in this passage.

At the risk of repeating what I have already said, I shall come back to fragment 79 (E.174), since it applies not only to the plane of biological reality but also to that of epistemology.

The historian of epistemology immediately comes up against something of a paradox. It is that the two most individualistic philosophical positions, empiricism and rationalism, which both want to base truth and morality on the feelings and reason of the individual, finally lead to conclusions that leave the smallest ontological space to individuals. There is, moreover, the fact that rationalism, in particular (the more radically individualistic of the two, since sensation does at least presuppose a starting-point), leads in both Descartes and Spinoza to the most complete denial of individuality.

The reduction of physics to geometry and of bodies to extension in Cartesian philosophy deprives those bodies, in the last analysis, of all individual existence. Similarly, apart from their union with different bodies, souls can hardly differentiate themselves from one another, since by thinking rightly they are all inevitably led to think the same thing. And, finally, there is no realm of life which is specifically separated and distinct from extension. It follows that individuality can exist in the Cartesian system only through man, through the union of the soul and the body and by the errors and passions to which this gives rise—that is to say, by what subsequent rationalist philosophers found most difficult to accept in the Cartesian world view. (One of the lines of development of Cartesianism is, after all, the idea of 'man as a machine', and the materialism of the eighteenth century.)

The true recognition of the ontological reality of individuals begins with the philosophies that transcend individualism. It is Pascal, for whom the self is hateful, who will make the first step towards a theory of knowledge of individual things, and Hegel and Marx, the theoreticians of the absolute mind and of history as the expression of collective forces, who will provide the definitive version of this theory. Each of these thinkers realises that this mode of knowledge applies first and foremost not to physics but to biology, and, above all, to man.

This does not mean that these thinkers will study man as a purely individual being, for they realise that he exists in a physical body subject to the laws governing matter. When Descartes tries to provide a mechanistic explanation of animal behaviour and human passions, and when a later and more extreme mechanistic theory tries to extend this explanation to the whole of human behaviour, no dialectical thinker will ever deny that this approach is justified up to a certain point. As Pascal himself remarks, 'We must say approximately: "This occurs by figure and motion", for that is true' (fr. 79, E.174). Physics and chemistry are indispensable for the biologist, and both the psychologist and the moral philosopher can profit immensely from a knowledge even of the mechanistic aspects of physiology, such as conditioned reflexes, for example. However, this knowledge is useful only up to a certain point, beyond which it becomes an obstacle and a source of error. Physics and chemistry can, it is true, establish general laws governing inanimate nature, and also certain laws valid for organisms. But Pascal and Kant both knew that mechanistic theories could never even establish general laws capable of explaining the structure of living organisms, since they can put forward only partial and fragmentary explanations. These theories are even less able to explain the nature of the smallest living being or historical fact, which can be approached only through the dialectical method. Faced with the whole of living bodies and with the problem of how to know individualised facts and events localised in space and time, mechanistic explanations come to a complete halt.

Brunschvicg sees fragment 79 as an indication that Pascal, like Socrates before him, turns away from the natural sciences towards moral philosophy. In my view, this fragment is far more the expression of the limitations which Pascal saw as inseparable from the methods of the physical sciences, or of any mode of reasoning which goes from the particular to the general, when such sciences are applied to the study of man, or even—though here with more reservations— to the study of living organisms in general. It is, moreover, a critique which still remains valid today.

This may perhaps explain why Laporte and his school have failed to understand Pascal, since for as long as he was working as a physicist and mathematician, Pascal never for a moment doubted the validity of mathematical reasoning or of any method which moves from the particular to the general.

However wide may be the differences between the scientific activity of Pascal and Descartes—and Brunschvicg and Koyré have analysed these with great clarity—these exist only against the background of a fundamental unity which links both thinkers to each other and to most of the other scientists of their time.

When Descartes and Pascal put forward their theories in physics they are interested not in individual facts but in general laws. Where they differ, however, is in the fact that Descartes pays scarcely any attention to the limitations of the physical sciences, whereas these limitations are, for Pascal, at the very centre of his philosophical reflections. It is this which enables him to have a much clearer perception than Descartes of the limitations of mechanistic physics, and to put forward both the basic principles and the demand for a new type of knowledge. This would be aimed at the study of relative individual wholes, even though, in Pascal's day, it was not possible to lay down the exact programme and genuine possibility of such a study.

Monsieur Laporte is certainly right to insist that Pascal never denied the validity and practical value of mathematics and physics in their own fields of enquiry. However, the *Pensées* are not a treatise on the right method to be employed in physics and mathematics. Pascal was certainly concerned with the problems of this method, and put forward some very important ideas about it. But his concern as a philosopher—which dominates the whole of the *Pensées* and even penetrates into his *Réflexions sur l'esprit géometrique*—is to state the limitations which these and similar sciences cannot escape when they try to deal with man. Pascal expressed these limitations in a manner rather similar to that which we find in Kant, pointing out that they can never establish their own first principles, that they cannot 'construct the machine' or completely explain the phenomenon of life, and, above all, that they cannot arrive at a knowledge of individuals.[1]

Before continuing, I must now deal with another question: was Pascal himself aware of the privileged position that a method which went from the whole to the parts and back to the whole again had over one which went from the particular to the general, in so far as the knowledge of man was concerned?

As a matter of fact, it is impossible to state categorically that he was. It does seem to me, however, that we ought to attribute great epistemological, as well as great biographical, importance to fragment 144 (E.756). This introduces a 'third domain', situated between the 'abstract sciences', and the 'true knowledge which man should have of himself' and which, in Pascal's view, is obviously religion. This domain is the study of man, which is neither an abstract science nor a form of ethical or religious knowledge.

It is not, in my opinion, an unjustified extrapolation to link this study of man to Pascal's other idea of the intuitive mind (*esprit de finesse*), and to the intellectual method described in fragment 72

---

[1] This realisation by Pascal that it is impossible to prove the validity of first principles corresponds to Kant's statement that it is impossible to justify 'the species and the number' of the categories and forms of pure intuition. (Cf. *Critique of Pure Reason*, p. 116 of Vol. III of the Academy edition.) Cf. also Norman Kemp-Smith's translation p. 161, B145–146, Macmillan 1961.

The analogy between the two thinkers is not, of course, a wholly exact one, but it does nevertheless seem to me to be real. I would add that since Kant's principal objective was to combat scepticism, he naturally gave much less importance to this impossibility of justifying the basis of rationalism than did Pascal, whose main philosophical opponent was Cartesianism.

As far as the two other points are concerned, the analogy is completely valid. This can be seen from the study of biological thought in the *Critique of Judgment*, as well as in the idea of integral determination, which can be achieved only in relation to 'reality as a whole'. This is, of course, only an idea of reason and not a concrete intuition, a theme which recurs frequently in the *Critique of Pure Reason* (cf. L. Goldmann, *La Communauté et l'univers chez Kant*).

(E.390), which goes from the whole to the parts and back to the whole again. And, if this is the case, then Pascal went a very long way, as far as he could go in the context of his own historical position and tragic perspective, towards the elaboration of the fundamental principle of the dialectical method.[1]

I have also stated that Pascal's second great merit was to have understood why this new type of thinking, which goes from the whole to the parts and then back to the whole again, and which is directed towards the structure of individual wholes, excludes all definitive and absolutely accurate knowledge. On this particular point, Pascal provides a first sketch of the basis of dialectical thought, and especially of what will later become, in Marx and Engels, the basic principle of the theory of ideologies: the conception of the inevitably partial and limited perspective of any thinker.

However, Pascal does no more than sketch this out, and never reaches the two other fundamental elements which can alone make the theory of ideologies into a source of positive knowledge: the idea of social thought, and that of the unequal but qualitatively measurable value of the different perspectives.

There is nothing particularly surprising about this, since the fundamental category in which Pascalian thought works is that of 'all or nothing'. It therefore follows that once it is recognised that this knowledge cannot be absolutely true in every respect, Pascal is no longer interested in the establishment of mere degrees of objectivity. As far as the elaboration of dialectical epistemology is concerned, Pascal goes no further than the realisation of the need to establish the relationship between the parts and the whole, and of the

[1] This distinction in the abstract sciences between the knowledge which man can attain by himself and the truths vouchsafed to him through revelation is certainly a fairly common one in the seventeenth century. However, no one to my knowledge—apart from Pascal—ever then wondered about the problem of a scientific knowledge of individuals, a knowledge which, in fragment 72 (E.390), is sketched out at a level that is to be found again only in Hegel and Marx. I thus think it probable that Pascal saw the relationship between this method which he had just discovered and that branch of knowledge which, in contrast to the abstract sciences, dialecticians call 'knowledge of the concrete', and which in a certain current of Marxist thought (in Lukàcs, for example) is restricted to knowledge in the humanities and science of man.

It is, in my view, within this context of the relationship between the different types of knowledge and fields of study that we should read the famous fragments on the distinction between the geometrical and the intuitive mind (Brunschvicg 1 and 2, E.910, 909). But this is a very difficult problem, for even in our own day we have not reached a satisfactory answer as far as the study of living organisms and certain branches of psychology are concerned, and it is certain that, in fragments such as these, where he is almost certainly taking his starting-point from a number of ideas by Méré, Pascal is discussing it at a much lower level than in 72 and 79 (E.390 and 174).

243

impossibility of ever doing this in a wholly objective manner. The fact that he did this in the seventeenth century is, however, immensely to his credit.

After this realisation he devoted his life to a task which seemed to him to be much more important: that of criticising sceptical, atomistic and, above all, Cartesian epistemology.

On the epistemological plane, his critique of Cartesianism is developed at the two extremes of totality and first principles—or, to speak Pascal's own language, at the two infinites. We have already examined his statement that rationalism cannot understand either the parts or the whole, and that the mechanistic approach is an inadequate and inaccurate means of trying to understand an individual whole, whether this be an organism or the universe[1] (and, today, we should also add: the social group).

He also adds the third point, that rationalism cannot understand its own first principles, and this is all the more telling, since rationalist and empiricist thinkers have often said that we do not really need to understand individual wholes. They have most frequently been satisfied with establishing the general laws governing reality, which rationalists have considered as certain and empiricists as merely hypothetical. The attitude of these thinkers is, however, different when they come to consider first principles. Both when the rationalist considers the obvious truths of reason and the empiricist the established facts of sensations—or of protocol statements, in the language of the Vienna circle—they do make an explicit claim to be setting out from something true. For Pascal, Hegel and Marx, on the other hand, there is no necessary or definitely established starting-point, since these thinkers consider that when one does not know the whole one cannot know the original elements composing it, and vice versa.[2] The

---

[1] It is, in my view, interesting to note that this problem of the relationship between dialectical thought and the possibility of arriving at an understanding of the physical universe is still far from being solved today. Most dialectical thinkers, Marx, Lenin and Lukàcs, have not even dealt with it, preferring to limit their enquiries to a purely historical domain.

However, there have always been in Marxist thought both mechanistic and idealistic tendencies, and the former show themselves in both the *Anti-Dühring* and the *Dialectic of Nature* of Engels. For it should be noted that Engels, in spite of the complete absence of mechanistic explanations as far as history is concerned, does abandon the dialectical position as soon as he begins to discuss the universe as a whole (cf. *Dialectic of Nature*). There is thus nothing surprising in the fact that Monsieur Pierre Naville, the most mechanistically inclined of contemporary French Marxists and a thinker who extends mechanistic explanations to both psychology and history, should have developed these ideas in a paper read to the Philosophical Congress at Strasbourg in 1952.

[2] There is an interesting parallel here with the difference between Marxism and Existentialism. I once heard a discussion that dealt almost exclusively with this

Pascalian and dialectical critique of rationalism, together with the express reference to Descartes, cannot be expressed more clearly than in the passage which I have already quoted from fragment 72 (E.390):

> But infinity in small things is much less visible. Philosophers have very frequently maintained that they can reach it, but it has been the stumbling block for each one of them. It is this which has given rise to such common titles as *Of the First Principles of Things, Of the Principles of Philosophy*, and the like. And although these may appear less pretentious, they are just as much so in fact as *De omni scibili*, where the writer's pretension stares us in the face.
>
> We naturally think of ourselves as more capable of getting to the centre of things than of embracing their circumference, for the extent of the world is so obviously greater than we are. But since we are larger than little things we think ourselves capable of grasping them. Nevertheless, we need just as much capacity for the Nothing as for the All. In both cases, it must be infinite, and it seems to me that anyone who had grasped the first principles of things could also go on to attain knowledge of the infinite. The one depends on the other, and they lead to each other.

Pascal ends by a new statement of the tragic position: 'These extremes meet and are joined together by force of distance', but, he adds, 'in God and in God alone'.

I still have to deal with yet another point at which Pascal's ideas coincide with those of Kant. The critique of 'first principles' is universally valid, and applies to any type of knowledge. However, it is especially significant when it applies to the formal sciences—of geometry in Pascal, of transcendental analysis in Kant—or to knowledge of content. Neither Pascal nor Kant ever questioned the practical validity either of geometrical first principles or of the categories. They both noted, however, that this validity is theoretically unjustifiable as far as these or those particular principles or categories are concerned.

The fragment on the geometrical mind is wholly dedicated to proving the excellence of geometry. However, Pascal feels constantly obliged, in order to avoid any misunderstanding, to recall at several

---

very point, and in which the Existentialist thinker was prepared to accept most of the main theses of Marxism—philosophy of history, class struggle, etc.—provided that the Cartesian position of *Cogito ergo sum* still remained the basic philosophical starting-point. To which the Marxist replied, quite correctly, that to do so would involve giving up the rest of Marxism—unless, of course, one was prepared to contradict oneself, which is scarcely a possibility that one seriously entertains in a philosophical discussion. In spite of the fact that this discussion took place in 1949, it was exactly the same dispute as the one between Pascal and Descartes.

points that this science is not perfect, since it can never prove its axioms.

But I must, first of all, give the idea of a method which is still more eminent and accomplished, but which men can never reach. For what goes beyond geometry also surpasses us; and yet something must be said about it although it be impossible to practise it.

If it were possible to arrive at this true method which would form demonstrations of the highest excellence, it would consist principally in two things: the first in using no term whose meaning had not already been clearly explained; the second in putting forward no proposition which had not been demonstrated by already known truths. That is to say, in fine, in defining all our terms and in proving all our propositions.

Thus, as we carry our research further and further into the principles that we use, we inevitably arrive at basic words that can admit of no further definition, and at principles which are so clear that no clearer ones can be found to provide any further proof of their validity. From which it appears that men are naturally and permanently unable to treat of any science whatsoever in a wholly perfect order.

But it does not follow from this that we should give up all types of order. For there is one suited to geometry, which is indeed inferior in that it is less convincing, but not because it is less certain (*De l'esprit géométrique. Pensées et Opuscules,* Brunschvicg edition p. 164. Section XV.)

However, this still leaves one question to be solved: how can this order be certain if it is not convincing and if—since it deals only with demonstrations and if these are always based upon unproved first principles—it offers our mind no certainty?

Pascal's reply is in fragment 282 (E.214). The certainty of these formal first principles is not of any theoretical order, but is essentially practical. It comes not from reason, but from the heart:[1]

We know truth not only through our reason but through our hearts; and it is thus that we arrive at a knowledge of first principles. . . . For the knowledge of first principles—as, for example, space, time, movement and number—is as sure as any of those which our reasoning gives us . . .

The heart feels that there are three dimensions in space, and that numbers are infinite . . .

[1] Monsieur Brunschvicg—wrongly in my view—gives a Cartesian type of interpretation to this fragment, saying that 'What Pascal means by the heart is our immediate feeling and intuition of first principles'. It seems to me, on the other hand, that we are much nearer to Kantian reason and the Pascalian wager than to Cartesian intuition.

I must recall, in concluding this section, that Pascal never admitted the possibility of reducing the knowledge of physical bodies to geometry. He therefore never implicitly recognised that the practical certainty of the first principles of geometrical knowledge could be extended to experimental knowledge.

II

An exhaustive study of Pascalian epistemology should, by dealing with the demand that opposite truths be reconciled, analyse the double critique which Pascal bases on this demand: a critique of rationalism, which recognises the existence of first principles and of the obvious truths deduced from these; and a critique of scepticism, which believes that man can do without any final synthesis and which does not feel the scandalous nature of paradox.

In spite of the central position which this critique occupies in Pascal's work—since his ideas were developed in opposition to those of Montaigne and Descartes, in the same way as those of Kant developed by reaction against the views of rationalism in general and of Hume in particular—it will not retain us here. The remarks which I have already made about the *Pensées* will enable the reader to find it quite easily for himself.

What is much more important, in my view, is the relationship between, on the one hand, the idea that no truth is valid unless immediately completed by the statement of the opposite truth and, on the other, Pascal's main contribution to the development of modern scientific and philosophical thought: the first sketch of a theory of the knowledge of relative wholes, or, if one prefers less abstract terms, of individual beings and events. The first idea is, in fact, so important in Pascal's view that he uses it to define both error (fr. 682, E.516, and 685, E.493) and heresy (fr. 9, E.5, and 863, E.455) as the exclusion of one of two truths.

Certainly, unlike Lukàcs, Pascal makes no explicit distinction between the physical and chemical sciences, which are governed by traditional logic, and the human sciences, which are governed by dialectical logic. It is a fact, however, that most of the fragments which state or imply the demand for a union of opposite truths are concerned with either biological or human problems. Moreover, it would be difficult to imagine Pascal demanding such a union for geometrical axioms, or for the general laws of physics. Thus, for him— as, later, for Hegel, Marx and all dialectical thinkers—no statement about an individual reality is true unless immediately completed by its opposite. To use the well-known expression of Engels, the logical scheme of truth is not 'Yes, Yes', and 'No, No', but 'Yes and No'.

Pascal sees the universe not as the vast and perfectly ordered machine described by all mechanistic thinkers from Descartes to Laplace (see his famous remark on the 'little flip' which Descartes's God had to give to set the world into motion (fr. 77, Lafuma 1001) but as a whole made up of equal and opposite forces, whose permanent state of tension makes anything wholly solid and stable impossible. However, he does not see this permanent instability as ever leading to any change or progress,[1] either as far as man or as far as animals are concerned—although, like most of his contemporaries, Pascal was not very interested in the latter.

Among dialectical thinkers of the nineteenth and twentieth centuries, the relationship between the idea of progress through the interaction of antagonistic forces and the idea of wholes seems fairly easy to understand, since the insertion of any partial fact in the dynamic whole of becoming is carried out by the notion of negativity. This is why, in my view, it is so remarkable that the idea of negativity, or antithesis, should have assumed so great an importance in the static and humanly unknowable wholeness contained in Pascal's tragic vision. Scholars, too, frequently reduce Pascal's critique of Cartesianism to the attitude of the Christian who rejects any knowledge of the world in the name of the only really valid knowledge, that of the truths necessary to salvation.[2] In my view, this is a misreading of the *Pensées*. This critique is to be considered, if not in relation to physics and geometry, then at least in relation to the general effort to understand truth, and it should be realised that it is based upon the demand for a precise and rigorous knowledge of concrete individuality. It is on this plane that we can never hope to establish first principles, since the very object with which we are concerned is, in so far as our own faculties can perceive it, contradictory in nature. It therefore follows that any human statement is both

[1] The best way of showing the difference between Pascal's philosophical views before and after 1657 is to compare the *Fragment d'un traité du vide* of 1644, where he openly states his belief in the rationalist idea of a continual increase in human knowledge—'the whole succession of men, throughout the centuries, should be looked upon as the same man continually living and constantly learning'—with the complete denial of any idea of progress in the *Pensées*.

[2] This was Barcos's position, for example, and it is because of this that he did not write on any epistemological subjects. In the *Pensées* Pascal does not give up all interest in Cartesian science. Although regarding it as quite valueless from the point of view of man's salvation, he criticises it on the actual plane of its epistemological value, which is a very different standpoint from that of Barcos. The objection that he did this only because he was writing an apology for religion aimed at the unbeliever does not seem to me to be a valid one either. Barcos and Singlin, for example, did not write apologiae and objected to the very idea of writing them. In their view, the conversion of the unbeliever and the heretic can be decided only by God's will and the intervention of Divine Grace.

valid and invalid at one and the same time, since every starting-point from which thought might set out needs to be completed by its opposite, which it naturally tries to exclude and deny.

I do not intend to follow Pascal in all the actual passages of analysis in which he discusses the opposition of contrary truths, and will limit myself to three points which I consider particularly important.

(1) Even a superficial reading of the *Pensées* shows how difficult it is, in most of the paradoxes which the book contains, to make a clear distinction between theoretical judgments of fact and value judgments on behaviour. This difficulty is certainly not caused by any confusion in Pascal's manner of expressing himself or by the fact that he reduces the paradoxical nature of the world to the domain of behaviour, and of morality and religious faith. There is a much deeper reason, which takes us to the very heart of Pascalian and dialectical epistemology. It lies, in fact, in the rejection by dialectical thought of the respective autonomy of the domains of theory and practice which is one of the principal characteristics of the empiricist, and more particularly of the rationalist position. Dialectical thought not only denies that the theoretical and practical domains are autonomous, but also denies that they should be, while Kant's tragic philosophy feels their autonomy as a limit which it rejects but cannot overcome.[1]

Any attempt to understand either an individual man or any human reality on purely theoretical plane—any *scientism*—is both true and false. It is true in so far as it takes note of certain relationships which do exist between the different observable facts; it is false in so far as it necessarily separates the objective aspect of these facts from their active aspect, from their becoming (that is to say, from the values and tendencies from which this becoming results). It can therefore establish neither the true meaning of the realities which it is trying to know nor the limits placed upon the validity of the truths it is trying to establish. For example, the statement that 'man transcends man', which is fundamental to any tragic or dialectical thought, is one which no purely theoretical study that neglects value judgments could ever establish.

Certainly Kant—who believed the same thing—gave quite a different importance to the theoretical study of human reality, which he provisionally separated from its practical aspect. Pascal, helped in this by the Augustinian tradition of *credo ut intelligam*, immediately rejects any idea of a purely rational understanding of man and the world outside religious faith, and therefore places himself, in certain respects, much farther along the line which leads from rationalist to tragic individualism and hence to dialectical thought.

From Marx onwards there is a renewal of the demand for a re-

[1] Cf. Goldmann, *La Communauté humaine et l'univers chez Kant* (P.U.F., 1948).

establishment of the unity between facts and values, between thought and action, even if the actual quest for this involves a relative separation. This demand is powerfully expressed in the main epistemological texts of Marxist literature, notably the *Theses on Feuerbach* and the book by G. Lukàcs, *History and Class Consciousness*.

Since I have written a book about it,[1] I shall not here insist upon the essential problem of the objectivity attainable in the human sciences. I shall merely note that the category of Totality involves, among other things, the demand for a synthesis between theory and practice, and this in the very name of the demand for true knowledge. By renewing the Augustinian tradition, after the long interruption of Thomistic and Cartesian rationalism, Pascal once again showed himself one of the first thinkers to turn Western thought in a dialectical direction.

(2) I have already discussed fragment 79 (E.174), and will merely point out that it provides an exact expression of the dialectical attitude towards mechanistic explanations of reality. Such explanations are partially true—as Pascal has it, 'We must say, approximately: "This occurs by figure and motion", for that is true'—and partially false, since they must always be completed by the opposite explanation. Thus, as soon as we want to rediscover the concrete whole, to 'complete the machine', we must in the case of the individual re-introduce the idea of instinct, will and emotions, and, in the case of History, the notion of negativity in Marxist and Hegelian thought.

(3) Finally, it seems to me important to stress one of the aspects in which Pascal, perhaps more than any other thinker, represents the turning-point at which empiricist and rationalistic atomism turned in the direction of dialectical thought. It is the appearance, by the side of the two traditional orders of the perceptible and the intelligible, or, more accurately, of the two traditional faculties of feeling and reason, of a third faculty, that of the heart. In Kant and Pascal this faculty is characterised by the demand which it makes for the synthesis of all opposites in general and of these two other faculties in particular, while in Hegel and Marx, on the other hand, it inspires man to achieve this synthesis. It is a faculty which brings together mind and matter as well as theory and practice, and, while Pascal calls it 'the heart' or 'charity', Kant, Hegel and Marx call it reason, thus contrasting it with the understanding, which Cartesian rationalists still insist on calling 'reason'.

This is not an arbitrary identification. The tests are quite unambiguous, and it is common knowledge that for Kant the function of *Vernunft* is to seek the union of opposites, the totality inaccessible to the other two faculties, while in Hegel and Marx its function is actu-

[1] Cf. *Sciences humaines et Philosophie* (P.U.F.).

ally to find this union. All we need do is compare Pascal's two famous remarks that 'God is perceived by the heart, and not by reason' (fr. 278, E.225) and that 'extremes meet and come together through the distance between them, and find each other in God, but in God alone' (fr. 72, E.390), to see just how far the heart fulfils in Pascal exactly the same function as the reason in Kant, Hegel and Marx: that of constantly demanding the synthesis of opposites, the only authentic value that can give meaning both to individual human life and to the whole of historical evolution.

It is perhaps not even necessary to add that although Pascal certainly does not use Hegelian and Marxist vocabulary, developed two centuries later, the actual idea of the *Aufhebung*, of the sublation which keeps the essence of the thing sublated while at the same time opposing it, is quite familiar to him. He did, indeed, express it magnificently in a whole series of fragments which deal with the relationship between reason and emotion, from fragment 277 (E.224) that 'the heart has its reasons which the reason cannot know', to fragment 4 (E.911) that 'true eloquence laughs at eloquence, true morality laughs at morality, and to laugh at philosophy is really to philosophise'.[1]

The position is exactly the same in any dialectical move forward, where the synthesis both is and is not the thesis, since the former is the real meaning of the latter precisely because it has gone beyond and differs fundamentally from it. Innumerable examples of exactly the same thing can be found in the works of Hegel, Marx, Engels and the young Lukàcs.

There is, however, one further point. I have tried, above all, to show how Pascal already definitely achieved something that was to be finally completed in the later development of dialectical thought, and to indicate what he had in common both not only with Kant but also with Hegel, Marx and Lukàcs. Is there not, however, a danger that this might create a certain confusion by bringing widely different philosophical systems too closely together? Am I not myself falling into the very methodological error which Marx himself pointed out?

I do not think so, and that for the following reasons: my book is a

---

[1] In fragment 4 (E.911) the actual word 'heart' does not occur, and Pascal talks about 'le jugement' (judgment) and contrasts it with 'l'esprit' (the intellect) However, it seems obvious to me that it is only the word that has changed and that he is talking about the same faculty, the one which goes beyond the order of matter and the order of the intellect. It seems, moreover, quite obvious to me that 'true eloquence, true morality and true philosophy' are for Pascal precisely the eloquence, the morality and the philosophy of the heart.

I should also like to underline the extent to which these fragments correspond exactly to the dialectical position, as long, of course, as we translate 'reason' and 'intellect' by *Verstand* and not by *Vernunft*.

whole of which the parts cannot be isolated, and I have frequently stressed the wide differences between the tragic attitude of Pascal, on the one hand, and that of dialectical philosophy, on the other. This philosophy considers syntheses to be possible[1] and to be capable of being realised by human action, while for Pascal the tragic essence of the human condition lies precisely in the fact that man's demand for syntheses must remain for ever unsatisfied. Moreover, the category of all or nothing which dominates the whole of the *Pensées* leads Pascal to attribute no importance at all to the possible achievements of the new type of thought which he so brilliantly sketched out in unconscious anticipation of later thinkers.

If, as in fragment 72 (E.390), he puts forward the demand for a type of knowledge that brings out the internal structure of wholes, and if, in fragment 79 (E.174), he states so clearly the limitations of Cartesian mechanism, his aim is never to bring out the real possibility of a new form of knowledge that would deal with individual wholes. His sole aim is to demonstrate the tragic nature of man, and to stress the uselessness and vanity of any knowledge which he might acquire. This, I repeat, is a fundamental difference that I have never tried to ignore. My sole point is that by his understanding of the constituent antagonisms of any human reality, by his demand for syntheses and for a knowledge of individuals, Pascal's vision of reality marks the turning-point in the transition from atomistic rationalism to genuine dialectical thought. It is only by indicating the resemblances between Pascal, on the one hand, and Hegel and Marx, on the other, that one can remain fully aware of the immense gulf which lies between them. However, I am myself writing from a dialectical point of view, in which resemblances and differences are not static entities given once and for all and observable by the historian from the outside, but elements and constituent parts of a dynamic whole of which the historian himself is part and whose laws of development he is trying to understand.

III

I shall conclude this chapter, which could be continued almost indefinitely, by studying what seems to me a particularly important point, and which occurs in the 'argument of the wager' in fragment 233 (E.343). It is Pascal's reply to the person who is already rationally convinced of the truth of Christianity, but who nevertheless replies that he cannot bring himself to believe in it.

[1] The possible is one of the fundamental categories of Marxist thought. Cf. Lukàcs, *Geschichte und Klassenbewusstein*, and Goldmann, *Sciences humaines et Philosophie*.

It is true. But recognise at least your inability to believe, since reason inclines you to do so and yet you cannot. You should therefore set to work not at piling up proofs for the existence of God, but at reducing your passions. You would travel to faith, and yet know not the way; you must be cured of unbelief, and ask for the remedy: learn from those who have been bound like you, and who now stake all that they possess. It is they who know the way which you wish to follow, and who have been cured of the sickness for which you are seeking a cure. Imitate the way in which they began: it is by behaving exactly as they behaved, taking holy water, having masses said, and so on. Naturally even that will make you believe, and will make you stupid.— But that is what I am afraid of.—But why? What have you to lose?

Terrified by the word '*abêtir*' (make stupid) Port-Royal left it out, and other thinkers—Victor Cousin, for example—have often been shocked by the suggestion that man should deliberately stultify his faculties. In reply to Cousin's objection, Brunschvicg puts forward a rather modified interpretation which I find rather questionable: 'Pascal,' he writes 'asks the free thinker to sacrifice his artificial reason, which is, in the last analysis, merely a collection of prejudices . . . *S'abêtir* means, in fact, going back to childhood in order to reach the higher truths which the merely clever cannot know'.[1]

However, the actual words that Pascal uses in no way invite his interlocutor in this imaginary dialogue to 'go back to his childhood', and in this he is completely consistent with his argument. He is trying to convince his listener of the intellectual validity of the wager argument, and it is only after this argument has been accepted—'That is obvious, . . . I agree, I accept'—that Pascal advises him to 'make himself stupid'.

Moreover, the text alone makes it quite clear what Pascal means by this. We must make ourselves stupid in order to 'reduce our passions'. From two points of view therefore, he is suggesting the opposite of a return to childhood. We must keep our highest intellectual qualities —which a child cannot possess—and reduce the passions, which completely dominate the child, whereas an adult can, in a few rare cases, bring them under control.

Initially, at least, a Cartesian explanation seems more plausible than the one put forward by Brunschvicg: we must reduce our passions, take away all obstacles, in order to enable reason to see the full power of the truth. However, this interpretation also falls down if we study it more closely. First of all, even if we leave on one side the disputed text *On the passions of love*, Pascal never considered the passions merely as an obstacle to clarity of thought, and, secondly,

---

[1] Cf. Brunschvicg edition of the *Pensées et Opuscules*, p. 461.

the whole argument of fragment 233 (E.342) is completely opposed to a Cartesian attitude.

For Descartes, we must fight against any obstacles which the passions can put in the way of a clear mind in search of truth. Here, however, it is only after his listener has understood the actual arguments put forward that Pascal sees the danger of the passions and asks him to reduce them by 'making himself stupid', by saying masses, taking holy water.

We need do nothing more than read the last paragraph in Descartes's *Passions of the Soul*, called 'A General Remedy against Passions', to see the wide difference between the two points of view. Descartes sees only one problem, that of the disturbance which the influence of the passions can introduce into the valid workings of the mind, and therefore tells us that

> the most common and easiest remedy against excessive passions is to remember, when we feel our blood moved by them, that everything which now comes before the imagination tends to deceive the soul, making those arguments which support the passions seem much stronger than they are, and those which go against them much weaker. And when those things which passion can persuade us are true can suffer some delay, then we must for the time being suspend our judgment, and think about something else until the passage of time has completely calmed the emotions in the blood. But when passion impels us to things which demand instant execution, then our will should mainly be used to consider and follow all those reasons which can oppose the ones put forward by passion, however much stronger these may appear.[1]

For Pascal, the situation is wholly different, and could be expressed in the following manner:

(*a*) In spite of the passions, the mind has reached a valid conclusion by valid methods; this conclusion is that we must wager that God exists.

(*b*) The passions impel man to act in a manner opposed to his intellectual convictions, since they impel him to wager that nothing exists.

(*c*) To overcome this antagonism, Pascal suggests a particular course of action: observe the outward show of piety. This is inadequate from a purely rational point of view, since such an attitude demands a wholly sincere wager that God exists; but it is also opposed to the desires created by the passions (a life based on free thought, and one foreign to any idea of transcendence).

[1] Descartes, *Traité des Passions*, art. 211.

As always, the situation is paradoxical, but we already know that it is precisely this paradoxical quality which makes the argument valid and enables us to fit it into the whole of the *Pensées*.

The other fragments dealing with the passions support my interpretation.

There are some which refer to the wager, such as 203 (E.345):

> In order that passion may not harm us, let us act as if we had only a week longer to live.

Similarly, fragment 412 (E.253) describes the situation which I have just analysed

> Internal warfare between the reasons and the passions: if there were only reason without the passions . . . If there were only the passions without reason . . . But, having both, man cannot live without war since he cannot be at peace with the one without being at war with the other: thus is he always divided, and opposed to himself.

There are other fragments, as for example, 277 (E.224), which show us the heart, the synthesis of reason and of passion, deciding the meaning of life by the choice which it makes:

> I say that the heart naturally loves the Universal Being and also naturally loves itself, according to the choice which it makes; and that it hardens itself against one or the other, again according to its choice. You have rejected the one and kept the other: is it by reason that you love yourself?

There is, however, not a single fragment which tells us why, without believing in Christianity, we should take holy water and say masses in order to diminish our passions. The reason is that fragment 233 (E.343) is unique in Pascal's work, since it is the only one which deals with what we should do after accepting certain theoretical arguments. It is therefore by using this fragment as our starting-point that we should try to understand the other *pensées*, while they, on the other hand, do not throw much light on the fragment itself.

The interpretation which sees this fragment merely as a piece of good common-sense advice can be dismissed immediately. No one who really understood Pascal would suggest that he was capable of putting such an initially shocking passage at the very centre of his work if he had not a very profound reason for doing so.

All we now have to do is to interpret this passage by itself, in the light of what we already know about Pascal's system.

The question is obviously one of the choice between betting on nothingness and betting on faith. But Pascal does not see the possibility of betting on faith as a mere accident. For him, it is based on a historical reality, on the Fall of Adam and the corruption of the human race.

Man now finds himself, after the Fall, torn between reason and the passions. If he is wholly consistent in following what reason tells him he is led to a realisation of his own inadequacy and to the need to seek God—or, in other words, to the wager. The passions, on the other hand, bind man to himself. In its natural state the heart is a faculty which leads to synthesis, since it does for man what no other faculty can do: it leads him to go beyond contradiction and, at one and the same time, to love both universal being and himself. It leads him to achieve a true selfishness which laughs at selfishness, for it enables him to understand that it is by making a gift of himself that he can really love himself, and by going beyond man that he can really become a man.

This is, in my view, the meaning of fragment 277 (E.224): 'I say that the heart naturally loves the Universal Being, etc.', which I have just quoted. But it is precisely the heart, this synthetic faculty, which has been most deeply marked by the consequences of the Fall. In man's present state it can no longer achieve the synthesis where man loves God and himself at the same time, and therefore finds itself face to face with a tragic and inevitable choice, for it can love only the one or the other 'according to the choice which it makes', as Pascal tells us.

If this analysis is correct, man in his present state has no alternative but to choose between an animal existence, which gives up any attempt to go beyond his condition, and a tragic existence, which gives up the passionate side of his nature, together with the body, and renounces any attempt to achieve anything in this world. This interpretation is supported by a number of fragments that I have already studied and that I shall be analysing further in the course of this book.

In order to appreciate the originality of Pascal's ideas on this point, it is useful to compare them with those of the three main Christian groups with whom he came into contact. The position of each of these groups is conveniently illustrated by one name—Descartes, Arnauld and Barcos.

For Descartes, thought was an autonomous reality, able—if it resisted the passions—to achieve knowledge of the truth. The problem for him was therefore situated entirely on the plane of the intellect and the will: to convert the free thinker one had merely to teach him to think correctly and see how infallible the Cartesian method of reasoning was.

Barcos, on the other hand, is intensely aware of the distance separating intellectual conviction from faith, and he exaggerates this distance to such an extent that there is no longer any possibility of interaction between the two. By its very nature, thought is corrupt and incapable of attaining true knowledge; only faith enables man to think correctly. It is the old Augustinian position of *credo ut intelligam* carried to its logical conclusion. However, from this point of view, the free thinker can never discover truth, and consequently faith, by himself, since he must already have faith before he can know truth. His conversion can therefore only be the result of Divine Grace freely given, Grace to which he can add only prayer. While one can pray for the conversion of the sinner, the free thinker or the infidel, it would be useless and even harmful and contrary to the respect which we owe God to write books defending either faith in general or even Catholicism against Protestantism or the position of Jansenius against the decisions of Rome.

In the last analysis, Arnauld adopts a Thomist position, which becomes increasingly marked towards the end of his life. He admits the existence of a domain where reason is valid and of another which goes beyond it.[1] It is therefore quite normal for him to write apologiae, and approve of other people doing so, as long as these are concerned with defending facts, refuting slander and interpreting texts. He never, however, has the illusion that these will have the slightest effect upon the free thinker unless they are completed or even preceded by Divine Grace.

Pascal's text differs from all three of these positions. Unlike Descartes, he realises that even the most convincing intellectual proof is never sufficient to make us act. Moreover, he recognises something which is quite inconceivable for a rationalist: that intellectual conviction and outward behaviour (his listener admits that the truth is 'obvious' and agrees to take holy water) are not yet in themselves total commitment. They are only the beginning, and the problem is once again one of synthesis.

Unlike Barcos, Pascal thinks it both useful and necessary to discuss things with his interlocutor and to try to convince him. And finally, unlike Arnauld, he recognises the existence of an intermediate level which lies between the intellectual conviction and grace and which can be reached by behaviour. We cannot exaggerate the importance of the words 'naturally, that will make you believe and will make you stupid' for the 'Disciples of Saint Augustine', in whose opinion, since human nature was totally corrupt, God alone could grant the power to take even the first step in prayer and faith.

We know that for Marxist epistemology, awareness and action are closely and intimately associated. They constantly act upon each

[1] When I say that he is a Thomist this word must be given a very general sense, for what he does is to replace, in the domain accessible to reason, the Aristotelian content by a Cartesian one.

other, so that awareness is only real when engaged in action, and action authentic only when it leads to understanding and awareness.

It would be easy to show how, in fragment 233 (E.343), Pascal's ideas coincide with those of Marx in the *Theses on Feuerbach*. However, this would perhaps be going too far, since it would involve assimilating two positions which differ on one important point: Pascal saw this interaction of thought and action only in one particular instance, whereas Marx based a whole theory upon it. But even bearing this reservation in mind, it is still true that fragment 233 foreshadows the *Theses* and that this similarity is a result of the fact that both sets of ideas are based on the same category, that of totality.

For Marx—and for Pascal—thought is never autonomous and cannot by itself discover any truths at all. It is a partial aspect of a total reality, and it is this reality alone which constitutes a genuine whole governed by its own evolutionary laws. This whole I shall call 'human behaviour', for want of a better word to express the joint concept of thought and action. The *Theses on Feuerbach* criticise Feuerbach for having considered not only thought but also perception as autonomous and contemplative. In fact, man is always *homo faber*, and even his most elementary knowledge of the external world comes not from a passive perception but from a perceptive activity. (In his experimental work, Jean Piaget has reached the same conclusions.) There is therefore no such thing as purely intellectual knowledge of truth, since all true knowledge implies activity and is dependent on it. Moreover, Marx and Piaget reached the same conclusions as far as the mechanism of progress in knowledge is concerned, the first in the realm of the social life, the second in that of the psychic life of the individual.

For both these thinkers, the factor which ensures progress is not the intellect alone, for consciousness by itself often has a conservative influence. Progress stems from an active coming to terms with reality, followed after a greater or lesser interval by a realisation of what has happened. Certainly, man does not come to terms with reality by methods that are wholly implicit and devoid of all consciousness. He has an uneasy feeling that the balance between subject and object has been destroyed, and therefore looks for a new mode of activity; he must however, find this mode of activity before he can fully understand what it means. Fragment 233 (E.343) fits very neatly into this kind of process. After having shown his interlocutor how convincing the need to wager on God's existence is on an intellectual plane, and having thus destroyed the false balance between himself and the world on which the unbeliever has previously based his life, Pascal suggests that he should follow this out in action; that he should change his behaviour in order to create the only conditions that will enable him genuinely to assimilate the truth which he has understood, and henceforth to give an authentic meaning to his behaviour.[1]

We must not, however, go too far in interpreting Pascal's text. Nowhere in his work is there even the suggestion of the dialectical mechanism of progress, and, implicitly, of the primacy of behaviour over awareness. The most we can conclude is that as a result of the fundamental importance which he accords to the category of totality, Pascal never shared Descartes's belief in the possibility of a habitual agreement between the judgment and the will. He realised that any truth concerning God and man could be known on both a theoretical and a practical plane only as a result of a synthesis between thought and action. It therefore followed, in his view, that God's existence could not be known directly but only as a result of a wager that was necessary on a practical plane; as long as it is not aided and assisted by the way he behaves, a man's consciousness is not adequate to enable him to discover truth.

Despite these reservations, Pascal's position still marks an extremely advanced stage in the development which leads from rationalist and sceptical individualism to dialectical thought, and this especially in the problems of epistemology, aesthetics, and theories of social life. We must always remember, however, that from my own dialectical point of view, epistemology takes on a far greater importance in Pascal's system than it ever had for Pascal himself. He developed the elements for a theory of the knowledge of individual facts less as a positive doctrine than as a means of critising rationalism and scepticism, of destroying man's illusion that he has real knowledge, and of making room for the only thing which he considered important: faith in God.

[1] Fragment 252 (E.7) is an implicit criticism of the Cartesian position.

XIII

ETHICS AND AESTHETICS

I

AT the risk of repeating myself, I shall begin this chapter by recalling two points.

(a) Even more than epistemology, physics and biology, aesthetics is for Pascal a secondary domain in which he is really very little interested, and which he mentions only incidentally. Ethics, on the other hand, has great importance because of its link with salvation, but does not, in spite of this, constitute an autonomous reality, for man can attain truth and goodness only through faith.[1]

(b) Any study of Pascal's ethics should begin with an analysis of his critique of Stoicism and Epicureanism, a critique which parallels his concern with dogmatism and scepticism on the epistemological plane. I shall not, however, deal with this critique in detail, in order to avoid making this book too long.

L'Abbé Brémond made frequent mention of the 'panhedonism' of Port-Royal. If he meant by this that the 'Disciples of Saint Augustine' agreed in seeing all men, whether Elect or Reprobate, as characterised by this aspiration to happiness and therefore inspired in all their actions by 'delectation', his analysis was correct.

There are, in fact, innumerable quotations to support his point of view. 'All men wish to be happy, and none wishes to be miserable. . . . The only thing on which the soul is naturally determined is the desire to be happy,'[2] writes Arnauld, and on this point Pascal agrees with him completely: 'All men strive to be happy; there are no exceptions' (fr. 425, E.300).

But in man's fallen state, his reason and his passions are in per-

[1] Cf. fragment 425 (E.300), in which Pascal states that: 'Without faith, man cannot know either true goodness or justice.' Here his position differs from that of Kant.

[2] Cf. *De la liberté de l'homme*, from Antoine Arnauld, *Ecrits sur le système de la Grâce générale*, two volumes, 1715, Vol. I, pp. 242–3.

petual and unsurmountable conflict, and neither is capable of making him happy. As Pascal writes in fragment 413 (E.249):

> This internal strife between reason and the passions has brought it about that those who seek peace have divided themselves into two sects, the first trying to renounce passions and become as gods, and the second trying to cast off reason and become as the beasts of the field (Des Barreaux). But neither sect can succeed in its aims: reason still lives on, denouncing the lowness and unjust nature of the passions, and troubling the repose of those who give themselves over to them; while the passions still remain alive in those who strive to give them up.

The quest for happiness, Pascal tells us in another fragment (425, E.300) is:

> . . . the motive of all the actions of all men, even of those who go and hang themselves.
>
> And yet, after so many years, no-one has ever, without faith, reached that state towards which all continually aspire. They are all full of complaints, both princes and subjects, nobles and those of the commonalty, young and old, the strong and the weak, the fool and the wise, the saints and sufferers. In all countries, in all times, in all sorts and conditions of men.
>
> What is it then that this great desire and accompanying inability proclaim to us, but that man possessed, at some former time, a true happiness of which he now has only the mark and the empty shadow; and that he tries in vain to fill up this emptiness with everything that he sees around him, seeking in things absent the help which things present cannot give. But all things are equally unable to give him this help, for this infinite gulf can be filled only by an infinite and unchanging object, that is to say by God himself.

And, again, in another fragment (431, E.394):

> Lift up your eyes to God, say some; look upon Him whom you resemble, and who has created you that you may adore Him. You can make yourselves like unto Him; wisdom will make you His equal, if you will but follow Him.' 'Lift up your heads, for you are free men,' says Epicurus. And the others say, 'Lower your eyes to the earth, miserable worm, and contemplate the beasts whose companion you are.'
>
> What will man then become? Will he be the equal of God, or of the beasts of the field? What a terrifying distance between the two! What then shall we be? Who can fail to see from all this that man is lost, that he has fallen from his proper station, that he is anxiously seeking it, but can no longer find it? And on whom can he call to help him find his way? The greatest men have not been able to do this.

Further examples could be given, but there is little point in labouring to prove a point about which most Pascalian scholars would agree. What is interesting is the similarity between Pascal's attack on stoicism and Epicureanism, as well as on reason and the passions and the ideas expressed by Kant in the *Critique of Practical Reason*. Like Pascal, Kant also sees happiness as an essential part of the supreme good which is alone capable of satisfying man's aspirations. Like Pascal, he also insists that his happiness should be associated with virtue, and sees such an association as possible only in God.[1]

The error of the Stoics and Epicureans lay in thinking that one of these two elements, which in man such as we know him as antagonistic and irreconcilable (virtue and happiness in Kant; reason and the passions in Pascal) could replace the other. As Kant put it:

> The Epicurean said: To be conscious of one's maxims as leading to happiness is virtue. The Stoic said: To be conscious of one's virtue is happiness. To the former, prudence amounted to morality; to the latter, who chose a higher term for virtue, morality alone was true wisdom.

Kant sees both these positions as containing regrettable and dangerous illusions and writes that:

> We cannot but regret that these men . . . unfortunately applied their acuteness to digging up an identity between such extremely heterogeneous concepts as those of happiness and virtue.[2]

For him, virtue and happiness are principles of maxims which are 'wholly different . . . and . . . which limit and mutually exclude each other in the same subject'.

Similarly, the error of all pre-Christian philosophers is, for Kant, to be found in their belief that man could attain supreme goodness by his own natural strength:

> If I now regard Christian morals from their philosophical side, it appears in comparison with the Greek schools as follows: the ideas of the Cynics, Epicureans, Stoics and Christians are, respectively, the simplicity of nature, prudence, wisdom and holiness. In respect to the way they achieve them, the Greek schools differ in that the Cynics found common sense sufficient, while the others found it in the path of science, and thus all held it to lie in the mere use of man's natural powers. Christian ethics, because it formulated its precept as pure and uncompromising (as befits a moral precept), destroyed man's confidence in being wholly adequate to it, at least in this life; but it re-

[1] Cf. fragment 542 (E.726). 'Only the Christian religion makes man both lovable and happy at one and the same time. Unless one is honest, one cannot be both happy and lovable.'

[2] Cf. *Critique of Practical Reason*. This passage is taken from the translation by Lewis Beck (University of Chicago Press, 1949), p. 216, cf. Academy edition, Vol. V, p. 111.

established it by enabling us to hope that, if we act as well as lies within our power, what is not in our power will come to our aid from another source, whether we know in what way or not (loc. çit., pp. 230–231. Note).

After having indicated that Pascal and Kant resemble each other in their critique of these contradictory dogmas, I now have to show that they put forward the same positive reply to the moral problem, especially in the way that they both chose to consider it.

On the surface, it would be difficult to find two positions which seem more different from each other than that of Kant's critical philosophy, which resolutely affirms the autonomy and independence of the moral law, and that of the Augustinians, who, as I shall show, deny this autonomy with equal resolution.[1] There is, however, a striking analogy between the teaching of Port-Royal and the attitude of Kant's critical philosophy, especially in the similarity of their approach to the problem of behaviour, or, more accurately, to that of action. This analogy is also relevant to what seems to me to be the very basis of Kant's vision of the moral law in his critique of knowledge.

Kant defines practical philosophy as the reply to the question: What ought I to do? In my view, this definition is in no way self-evident, but is, on the contrary, peculiar to the different forms of individualistic or tragic thought. I have already, in Chapter III, stated what I consider to be the difference between tragic thought and the doctrines of philosophical individualism, which are either sceptical or dogmatic. Faced with the question What ought I to do?, rationalism and hedonism give an amoral reply—seek pleasure, act according to reason, be courageous, etc. Tragic thought, on the other hand, gives an essentially moral reply: act in accordance with the demand for universality which is independent of any selfish, emotional or purely rational motivation, act in such a way that you can refer your act to eternity.

Each of these three doctrines—rationalism, hedonism, the tragic vision—is basically individualistic, the third even more so than the two others, since it defines man in terms of his absolute but impossible demand for transcendence and for a movement beyond the present situation by means of the wager. Other doctrines, whether that of Augustinian Christianity or that of dialectical materialism, change

[1] Without going so far as to say that either Pascal or Jansenism are wholly Augustinian on this point, I must underline the fact that one of the principal differences between Pascal and Kant lies in Pascal's complete denial of the autonomy of the moral law in respect of faith. It is, however, a difference which exists within the framework of the same tragic vision which is common to both philosophers.

the very position of the problem by inserting the present moment into the concrete totality of eschatological or historical time, and by replacing the question What ought I to do? by the essentially different one of How ought I to live?

The question What ought I to do? admits of either the amoral replies of stoicism or hedonism or the moral reply of tragic thought. The question How ought I to live? in no way admits a specifically moral reply, since it is meaningful only in a perspective which sees life as a relative temporal whole which fits into a larger whole that goes beyond and transcends it. As soon as one has asked the question How ought I to live? seriously and with all its implications, the reply is already implicit: by situating one's life inside an eschatological or historical whole in which it inserts itself by faith.

The essential truth of Augustinianism and of dialectical materialism is that we must believe in order to understand reality and to act in a humanly efficacious manner, and it is for this reason that there is no autonomous and independent Augustinian and Marxist ethic.

Now, since there is not in fact any genuine rationalist, hedonist or affective ethic either, we are forced to the conclusion—initially a surprising one, but quite natural when one thinks seriously about it— that the only perspective which affirms the autonomy and the authentic primacy of ethics is the tragic one, and consequently that there is only one ethic which has genuine foundations and is fully justified as such: the tragic ethic.

Pascal, imbued with Augustinianism and fully aware of all the implications of the demand for totality and for the union of opposites—which, for him, characterises man as man—expressed this idea perfectly in the famous fourth fragment (E.911):

> True morality laughs at morality, that is to say that the morality of judgment laughs at the morality of the intellect.

But for him, as for Kant, the morality of judgment, which transcends the morality of the intellect, can never be anything more than an impossible demand of the heart, an idea of reason and not a human reality governing the behaviour of the individual in his daily life.

We thus find, in the ideas of the 'Friends of Port-Royal', and in Pascal in particular, a predominance accorded to ethics which is rather unexpected in an intellectual movement that thought of itself as Augustinian. Historians have frequently said that the great difference between Jansenist and Calvinist theology on the question of Grace and Predestination lies in the fact that the Calvinists insisted upon habitual grace while the Jansenists were primarily interested— if not in words, then at least in practice—in present grace. This expresses in theological terms the same difference which I have just mentioned as existing on the philosophical plane between the questions What ought I to do? and How ought I to live?, between, on the one hand, the primacy of an a-temporal morality and, on the other, the faith which inserts the act in the concrete totality of biographical, historical or eschatological time.

On this particular point, Pascal certainly had the same attitude as the other 'Friends of Port-Royal'—we only need to read his *Ecrits sur la Grâce* to realise this—so that there is nothing surprising in the fact that he should have at least put forward, if not actually worked out in detail, the basic principles of an ethic which is similar on a number of points to the Kantian idea of the categorical imperative. (Such a view depends, of course, on our not giving the categorical imperative the traditional interpretation that stems from what I have described elsewhere as the neo-Kantian error.)[1] Like Kant, Pascal knows that the true demand made by man, the aspiration which alone gives him human dignity, is for a totality which—in the language of fallen man —would be the reunion of opposites, the coming together of virtue and happiness and of reason and the passions. This would mean, implicitly, that man would go beyond all morality—as in fragment 4 (E.911)—and insert his individual existence into a totality which takes in all time and, in the final analysis, is joined to God. (fr. 473–7, E.687, 684, 690, 689, 313).[2]

Unfortunately, man does not really succeed in going beyond ethics, since Pascal writes that 'we do not possess true goodness' (fr. 385, E.298), so that totality, even on the plane of 'natural and civil communities', is out of reach. His ambition remains therefore merely a demand, and an impossible one at that, for 'the will of man is naturally depraved' (fr. 477, E.313), it has 'become his own will' (fr. 472, E.678), which refers everything not to the whole but to man himself.

The problem thus becomes one of looking for a set of rules that can govern human actions, and at least say what they ought, ideally, to be, in a world which, in so far as it is a social and physical world contained in space, is for both Pascal and Kant a world that hides God.

However, the fact that God is absent from the world shows itself precisely by the absence of any general and wholly unambiguous rule capable of giving meaning to our acts within the world. We cannot separate good from evil or truth from error, for, as Pascal says:

> Everything here on earth is partly true and partly false. But essential truth is not like this, for it is wholly pure and wholly true. The mixture that we find here on earth both dishonours and destroys this truth.

[1] Cf. *La Communauté humaine et l'univers chez Kant* (P.U.F., 1948).
[2] Idem.

Nothing is purely true, so that it follows, if we take truth to be wholly pure, that nothing is true. Men will say that murder is wrong. Agreed, for we do know the difference between good and evil. But what of chastity? This is not wholly good, for otherwise there would be no more world. Marriage? No: continence is better. Not to kill? No, for the resulting lawlessness would be dreadful, and the wicked would kill all the just men. To kill? No, for this destroys nature. We possess truth and goodness only in part, mingled with both evil and wrong (fr. 385, E.298).

Nevertheless, there are two reasons why we must find this 'wholly pure and wholly true' general rule which can guide our behaviour. As long as he is alive, man is 'embarked' and cannot avoid action, so that he cannot, on the plane of action, bear with paradox and the contradiction of opposites in the same way as he can on the plane of thought. Here, every act demands a solution, an urgent and immediate movement beyond the present situation.

We know what Kant's reply was to this problem: we must give up any personal emotional interest for ever, in spite of the fact that we can never really do this and in spite of the fact that our desire for happiness is justified within the framework of the supreme good. Pascal put forward a similar idea when he said:

Self will can never be satisfied, even if it were to secure everything it wanted; but we are satisfied the moment we give it up. Once we lose it, we cannot be dissatisfied; for so long as we have it, we cannot be satisfied (fr. 472, E.678).

Pascal and Kant both put forward a general rule to replace man's own, selfish will, and as long as we do not isolate their texts or read them superficially, but try instead to find out what they really mean and fit them into the doctrine as a whole, and as long as we begin by acknowledging the wide difference of emphasis and general direction between the two, we shall see considerable similarities between them.

Take, for example, the famous categorical imperative: *Act always as if the maxim of your action were to become by your will a general maxim of nature.*

Compare it with fragment 203 (E.345): '*Fascinatio Nugacitatis.* That passion may cause no harm let us act as if there were only a week left to live', and with fragment 204 (E.335): 'If one ought to give a week to life then one might just as well give it a hundred years.'

It seems to me that these two texts both present similar if not analogous reactions to the physical and social world that hides God. The moral problem is in fact closely linked to that of human time, whose function is precisely to determine the nature of the insertion of man into the world. Now Pascal and Kant both mean basically the same thing: both refuse temporality and, implicitly, any insertion of man into the temporal pattern of the world. Both mean: act as if the act you are about to perform were unique, without any link with the real time of human life—where every moment is transition from the past to the future—and with no link except with eternity.

For both Pascal and Kant this is the only rule which, if strictly applied, would enable man to free his actions from emotional motivation; it would also, however, prevent him from inserting it into the world of conflicting and warring egoisms.

But, as I have already pointed out in my book on Kant, this rule is expressed in a tragic form, since both texts involve the words: as if.[1]

A wholly valid and non-tragic demand would be one which inserted the whole of one's life in the living world of divine eternity, and this would be the position of Saint Augustine. In order to preserve the link with eternity—which is possible although not absolutely certain— man must act as if life did not exist, and must 'give' his life, whether it lasts a week or a hundred years, in order to live. In fact, both Pascal and Kant are fully aware that life does exist in time, that a hundred years are more than a week, that acts do have both a past and a future, that they do have consequences in the time that we now see, that egoisms do enter into conflict, that individuals do relate everything to themselves and that acts do lose all contact with eternity. This is why, if in spite of all this man still wants to save his soul, he must go forward from appearances to essences, from the phenomenal to the noumenal, and act 'as if' life did not exist.

Life does not exist. This is a tragic statement even for those who, unlike Barcos and the extreme Jansenists, assumed its full consequences, because they believed that life really was valueless appearance, because they believed that they really would find the realm of essences outside life in this world, and because, if they had expressed their ideas philosophically (this would have been self-contradictory and they did not do it) they would have used a similar expression but without the words: as if.

But Barcos and his group carried their position to its logical conclusions and did not write philosophical or apologetic works. Similarly, at the time of the great persecution of the Jansenists, when faced with the problem of whether or not to hide their material possessions from the temporal powers, they refused to take thought for the morrow and give any consideration at all to the future.

No one has ever doubted the personal disinterestedness of Pascal, for it was never a question of his own personal future but of the future of a group of men and women who were defending either the

[1] Cf. L. Goldmann: *La Communauté humaine et l'univers chez Kant.*

general truth of Catholicism or the particular truth of Augustinianism or Jansenism. Nevertheless, on both occasions he did adopt a
completely different attitude and did take thought for the future.

There is no contradiction in Pascal between fragment 203 (E.345)
and these two decisions, for he was, in this fragment, very probably
considering only the biographical time of an individual human life,
and implicitly rather than explicitly the time of social or political
institutions.

In fact, his work contains only scattered and superficial considerations on the problem of the Church Militant in time, and on its place
in the eschatological plans of God. He would probably have refused to
consider the personal, social or political consequences of an act, while
at the same time continuing to pay attention to the future of the
Church and of the little group of the 'Disciples of Saint Augustine'.

These considerations enable us to make the comparison and
contrast between Pascal and Kant a little clearer. I have already said
that Kant was at the very forefront of bourgeois thought in eighteenth-
century Germany, and gave much more importance to the phenomenal world than did Pascal. The author of the *Pensées*, on the other
hand, carried the tragic vision to its final consequences, and attributed
little or no importance to the social world as an historical whole. Let
me make myself clear: I am not reducing Pascal's position to that of
Barcos, for the latter considered that the world has no real existence
of its own and was simply valueless. For Pascal, on the other hand,
the world did have a fundamental importance, for in so far as God
remains radically hidden it is impossible for man simply to leave the
world of phenomena and seek refuge in that of essences. In Pascal's
view it is only by confronting the world and time that man can assert
his demand for the absolute, and thus proclaim his own humanity.

However, Pascal sees this reality of the world as essentially limited.
The world is only the field of individual action, of the quest for goodness and truth, and nothing more. It is a field in which man must
'try out' his strength but never 'use' it. He does not, unlike Kant, see
it as a domain in which man can hope to achieve certain definite
ambitions—eternal peace, an international world order, scientific
advance, beauty, etc.

It is because Pascal carried tragedy to its logical consequences,
because he sees an unbridgeable gap between man and values, on the
one hand, and man and the world of visible appearances, on the other,
that the 'as if' of fragment 203 has, from certain points of view, a less
poignant and brutal character than it has in Kant's statement of the
categorical imperative. For in Kant this 'as if' suddenly reminds us of
the fact that a whole set of hopes which play an important part in his
philosophy are, in the last resort, quite impossible to achieve.

I have already said that in spite of its importance, this difference concerns less the general structure of the two philosophies than the way in which Kant talks about the phenomenal world and the quantitative position that it occupies in his work. I should, perhaps, recall once again that for dialectical thought there is a point at which a quantitative difference becomes a qualitative one, and that, in this comparison between Kant's and Pascal's moral philosophy, we are very near this point.[1]

I should add in conclusion that if, as we would naturally expect, Pascal sees true happiness as attainable only through man's refusal of the world and of time, and through his concern to relate each one of his actions to God and God alone, there are a certain number of fragments (473–7, E.687, 684, 690, 313, 311) which explicitly indicate the relationship between his idea of God and the category of totality. He thus sketches out—but does nothing more—the road which leads from the tragic vision to dialectical thought.

II

There is, in Pascal's epistemology and ethics, an internal consistency between the different elements which is quite visible within the framework of the system itself. As far as his aesthetics is concerned, however, the link between the different fragments is hard to detect by immanent analysis, and becomes clearly visible only from the standpoint of the later development of dialectical aesthetics.

I have already said that the dialectical aesthetic sees every work of art as the expression, in the specific language of literature, painting, music or sculpture, etc., of a world vision; and that, as we would expect, this vision also expresses itself on numerous other philosophical and theological levels, as well as on that of men's everyday actions and activity. The essential criteria by which the aesthetic of dialectical materialism judges the value of any expression of a world vision are the inner coherence of the work of art and especially the coherence between form and content. It also, however, has another criterion, corresponding on the philosophical plane to that of truth, and which enables a hierarchy of values to be set up between the different aesthetic expressions of world visions. This criterion is what the artistic theories of dialectical materialism call the 'degree of realism', implying by this the richness and complexity of the real social relationships which are reflected in the imaginary world created

[1] In fact, Kant sees the moral law as constituting a valid and autonomous demand, which Pascal does not. What is tragic about it lies in its wholly formal quality and in the fact that it does not effectively govern the real conduct of men.

by the artist or writer. Finally, precisely because the dialectical aesthetic accepts realism as the next most important criterion after coherence, it takes its stand on a classical aesthetic which refuses to admit any formal, autonomous element which is not justified by a particular function, either—as in architecture for example—in the utilisation of the object or in the expression of the reality of a committed, essential man.

Once we take into account the differences already mentioned between the tragic vision and dialectical thought—absence of degrees, absence of any notion of relative values, dichotomic distinction between truth and falsehood, good and evil, value and non-value—we find that Pascal's fragments on aesthetics contain these three basic criteria of coherence, realism and relevance which we have seen to be characteristic of the dialectical aesthetic.

The notion of expression is developed in fragments 32 and 33 (E.931, 932) with a clarity and accuracy that can scarcely be equalled, and which make Pascal the great precursor of modern aesthetics. The only difference between the idea which he puts forward and the principles governing a dialectical theory of expression lies precisely in the dichotomic distinction between models which are true and models which are false, and which are separated from one another by an absolute difference admitting neither degrees nor gradations.

Fragment 134 (E.77), which has so often been discussed and criticised, is, like fragment 11 (E.713) on the theatre, nothing more nor less than a statement of the principles of realism, always remembering that this notion is linked to that of truth as a reflected image, and that Pascal's concept of truth is different from that of a modern follower of dialectical materialism. Once this reservation is accepted, I would maintain that any serious modern writer on aesthetics would be prepared to sign Pascal's condemnation of a certain naturalistic art that modifies reality by giving it a purely negative quality, or of an art which, putting the wrong accent on certain human values, would dehumanise reality. As to fragment 13 (E.934), it develops the idea which we find frequently repeated in any theory of realism, that the author should always know more about his characters than they do themselves. There is also, of course, the remark that passion conscious of itself would 'displease', which is an opinion peculiar to Pascal himself.

Finally, in a number of fragments Pascal puts forward the general rules of the classical aesthetic, rejecting any purely decorative element and demanding perfect unity between form and content. Here again Pascal takes up a position midway between the aesthetic that gives pre-eminence for form (art is the creation of forms beautiful in themselves independent of their context) and the aesthetic which gives pre-

270

eminence to content (art is above all else one of the means of attaining truth). He thus places himself at the very heart of the classical aesthetic, and does so in an explicitly dialectical context which sees aesthetic value in totality, in the coherent synthesis between form and content. Any formal accessory not demanded by the content, and any absence of an element which the content makes necessary, are, like inadequate means of expression themselves, essentially aesthetic faults (fr. 26, 27, 48, E.955, 971, 969).

But the beauty of a work of art, which, in Kant's tragic thought, was the only authentic value which man could attain in life and in the world, had very little importance for the completely and unreservedly tragic attitude of the *Pensées*. The aesthetic ideas which I have just mentioned are there almost by accident, not because Pascal wanted to develop even a fragmentary theory of aesthetics, but because he was interested in the best way of winning over his listener, or because theatre going was an important part of the wordly life whose vanity he was illustrating. It is therefore, in my view, all the more important to show how he put forward, even in these fragmentary passages, a whole series of ideas that are fundamental to what later became the classical aesthetic of dialectical materialism.

271

XIV

SOCIAL LIFE: JUSTICE, POWER AND WEALTH

FOR the Pascal who wrote the *Pensées*, no human law is completely just or completely valid. There is no possible ambiguity about his ideas on this subject, and the first editors of his work—notably Arnauld and Nicole—understood him as denouncing all social life as unjust. It was precisely this that shocked them and led them to modify Pascal's ideas in the version of the *Pensées* that they presented.

The only way to interpret fragments 294, 297 and 385 (E.108, 176 and 298) as anything other than complete denunciations of human justice is to maintain that they are mere 'verbal exaggerations'. I have already pointed out that this is not the correct way to interpret Pascal, and it is indeed impossible to argue that the man who wrote the following lines admitted the slightest possibility of a human law ever being valid and just.

> On what could man base the economy of the world that he wishes to govern? On the whims of each individual? What confusion there would be. On justice? He does not know what this is.
>
> For certainly, if man did know what justice is, he would never have established the maxim which is most generally accepted by all peoples: that each should follow the customs of his own country. The splendour of true justice would have made all peoples bow down before it, and legislators would not have neglected this unchanging justice to follow the fancies and caprices of Persians or Germans. We should see it established in every country and in every century, whereas in fact we see nothing just or unjust that does not change its quality as it changes its climate. Three degrees of latitude upset the whole system of jurisprudence, and truth depends upon a degree of longitude. A few years' possession suffice to change fundamental laws, and law itself has its times and seasons, the entry of Saturn into Leo marking the origin of such and such a crime. Justice is indeed laughable when it is bordered

272

by a river. A truth on this side of the Pyrenees becomes an error when we cross them.

They admit that justice is not to be found in these customs, but that it resides in 'natural laws', which are known in all countries. They would indeed stubbornly maintain this if the unpredictable hand of chance which has distributed human laws had laid down at least one that was universal; but the absurd fact is that human caprice has taken so many different forms that there is no such law. Theft, incest, the murder of children or of parents have all been numbered among virtuous actions. Can there be anything more stupid than the fact that a man should have the right to kill me because he lives on the other side of the water and because his ruler has a quarrel with mine, although I have none with him?

Doubtless there are natural laws; but this fine corrupted reason has corrupted everything else; *Nihil amplius nostrum est; quod nostrum dicimus, artis est. Ex senatus consultis et plebiscitis crimina exercentur. Ut olim vitiis, sic nunc legibus laboramus.*

The result of this confusion is that one man will say that the essence of justice lies in the authority of the legislator, another in the interest of the ruler, another in present customs. The last is most probably true, since if we follow reason alone we find nothing just in itself, for everything changes with time. Equity is based on custom alone, simply because custom is what men accept. This is the 'mystical foundation' of its authority, so that whoever pursues justice to its ultimate source at the same time destroys it. Nothing is so imperfect as the laws that seek to correct our faults, and whoever obeys them because he thinks they are just is obeying his own conception of justice and not the essence of the law. This essence is something wholly turned in upon itself; law, and nothing further. Anyone unaccustomed to the contemplation of the wonders produced by human fancy will, on examining the basis of law, find it so weak and trivial that he will be astonished to see how the mere passing of a hundred years has bestowed so much pomp and reverence upon it. The art of defying and overthrowing states lies in shaking established customs, in going down to their first principles in order to demonstrate how completely they lack authority and justice. Men say that we must 'go back to the original and fundamental laws of the state, which have been overthrown by an unjust custom'. It is an infallible remedy for ruining everything, for if we use this as our standard then nothing will be just. Nevertheless, the people are quite willing to listen to such speeches. As soon as they recognise their yoke they throw if off, with the result that the great take advantage of their action to harm both the people themselves and these curious critics of established customs. This is why the wisest of lawgivers used to say that men must often be duped in their own best interest, and another, who was a skilful politician, maintained that: *cum veritatem qua liberetur ignoret, expedit quod fallatur.* The people should not be made conscious of the usurped nature of authority, for if it was originally introduced without reason, it has nevertheless become reasonable with the passage of time. We must make people look upon it as eternal and authentic, and, unless we want to bring it to a speedy end, we must hide its origin (fr. 294, E.108).

Similarly, in fragment 297 (E.176), Pascal remarks:

Veri juris: we no longer have it: for if we did, we should not base our justice on following the customs of our country.

It is for that reason that, having not been able to find justice, we have found strength etc.

Each thing [he tells us in fragment 385 (E.298)] is partly true and partly false. This mixture dishonours and annuls it. Nothing is wholly true; so that nothing is true, if we take truth to be something complete.

This last fragment goes much further in its critique of natural laws, for Pascal tells us:

Men will say that it is true that murder is wrong; yes, for we do know the difference between right and wrong; but can we say what is right? . . . not to kill? No, for the civil disorders would be terrible, and the wicked would kill all the good people. . . . We have both goodness and truth only in part, each mingled with evil and falsehood (fr. 385, E.298).

Thus, even the few statements which are completely true—as, for example, that murder is wrong—cease to be so once an attempt is made to transform them into positive commandments, rules of behaviour or universal laws.

These long quotations are essential to show the unity of Pascal's ideas. Since men cannot, in this world, achieve either goodness or truth, then they are obviously unable to set up any wholly satisfactory form of social or political organisation. For Pascal, there are absolutely no exceptions to the statement that all activities connected with the world are infected with its vain and fallen nature. Moreover, there is no contradiction between his ideas on epistemology and ethics and his social and political opinions. When he demands complete truth and justice on the epistemological or ethical plane it is precisely because truth and justice have a transcendent quality that brings them inevitably into conflict with the things of this world. Law and politics do not have this transcendent quality, and Pascal would be going against his own tragic philosophy if he were to place any hope in them. A world ruled by the commandments of divine love would achieve perfect justice, and would not need either laws or institutions. It can therefore be considered as automatically in conflict with the inadequate social and political institutions of the imperfect world in which we now live. Here again, of course, Pascal is merely carrying on an old Christian tradition. It is an Augustinian one—but on this particular issue Augustinianism is linked with the eschatological views of the early spiritual masters—and one which, after having been duly secularised and freed from any transcendental associations, will recur at a later period as a central concept of dialectical thought: the disappearance of the state.

Pascal's own political attitude was certainly a highly conservative one, but not as a result of any respect which he had for law or order. His conservatism stems directly from the a-temporal nature of his tragic vision, and from the conclusions which this draws from the impossibility of ever achieving a wholly valid law. The tragic vision maintains that half a loaf is no better than no bread, and therefore rejects any idea of attempting to achieve a social change which, of its very nature, is bound to be unsatisfactory. Any attempt at reform is likely, in Pascal's view, to bring about civil war, and this is 'the worst of all possible evils'.[1]

Here again, we must notice a number of analogies with Kant's position, certainly as far as any attempt to change the political order by force is concerned. I should, however, note that, from 1789 onwards, the Kantian position led to a defence of the victorious revolutionary order in France, and therefore had a concrete meaning which differs from the abstractly analogous position of Pascal.

In his reflexions on the relationship between justice and force, Pascal went much further than the rather commonplace views often attributed to him, and elaborated what is in fact a realistic and penetrating analysis of the social order. It is this which I shall now study in the light of the subsequent development of dialectical thought.

The first thing to note is that Pascal recognised the true basis of any social or historical life: the desire which every man has to be 'esteemed'—or, as later thinkers have it, to be 'recognised'—by his fellows. It is true that as a Jansenist, and consequently as a man for whom solitude was the highest of virtues, Pascal spoke rather ironically of this desire for 'esteem', which he saw as one of the consequences of original sin. This idea does, however, represent an important step on the road from Descartes to Hegel, and it is also noteworthy that, in fragment 404 (E.91), for example, Pascal does

---

[1] It would be interesting to try to find out why civil wars are 'the worst of evils'. Within the framework of Pascal's ideas this would seem to me to be because they would be the worldly distraction par excellence, and exactly the kind of events that would turn men's hopes away from the only domain in which he can seek authentic human values, that of eternity.

However, Pascal also has a personal hostility to civil wars, and this takes us outside the actual system of his thought—there are, after all, many other 'distractions'. This hostility is linked, on the one hand, to the historical situation of the *noblesse de robe* and of the Jansenist group, and, on the other, to his own personal memories of the Fronde and of what followed the revolt of the 'va-nus-pieds' in Normandy.

reveal, in spite of his irony, a certain understanding of the positive aspects and genuine functions of life in society, as well as of its vices and drawbacks.

> We have such an elevated idea of the human soul [he tells us in fragment 400 (E.223)] that we cannot bear to be despised or not to be esteemed by any human soul; and the whole happiness of man lies in that esteem.

It is this which distinguishes man from the beasts, for as he also remarks in fragment 410 (E.96):

> Animals do not admire one another. A horse has no admiration for his companion; it is not that there is no rivalry between them in a race, but this has no results, for when they are in the stable we do not see the slower or less handsome giving up his oats to the other, as men would have their fellows behave towards them. In their case, virtue is satisfied with being its own reward.
>
> The lowest thing about man [he also states in 404 (E.91)] is the quest for glory, yet it is this which is the greatest mark of his excellence; for whatever possessions he may have upon the earth, and no matter what degree of health or comfort he enjoys, he is not happy unless he enjoys the esteem of other men. He has so high an opinion of man's reason that unless whatever advantage he may have on earth is also reflected in the way people think of him he is not happy. This is the finest place in the world, and nothing can turn him from this desire, which is the most ineradicable quality in the heart of man.

Thus, for Pascal, man is essentially a social being, and the need to be esteemed by his fellows is a fundamental part of his nature. This is a first version of the idea of 'recognition' which is developed by Hegel and which provides the basis for dialectical thought by differentiating it from all forms of individualism. For, since man can be satisfied neither by his own mind nor by the gratification of his own sensations, and since he realises his true nature only by striving after an absolute which goes beyond him and presupposes the existence of a community, then the esteem of others, their 'recognition' of him and even the 'glory' which he can derive from them, acquire an essential importance.

But if a community is essential to man it by no means follows that the present social order is either perfect or even good and acceptable. For this order is based upon inequality and the clash of egoisms; as fragments 380 (E.913) and 295 (E.112) make apparent:

> Inequality is necessary among men, it is true. But once this is accepted, then the door is open not only to the most absolute authority but also to the highest tyranny.

Mine, thine. ('This dog is mine,' these poor children said, 'this is my place in the sun.') Here we have the beginning and image of usurpation over all the earth.

We must, however, be careful not to confuse Pascal's critique of society with the innumerable similar ideas that both preceded and followed it before the birth of Marxism. During the whole of the Middle Ages, and especially in certain Christian sects, we find a constant attack on the idea of private property and of the prevailing social or political order. Moreover, it continues after Pascal, throughout the whole of the eighteenth century.

However, both before and after Pascal, this critique remains, among nondialectical thinkers, both abstract and one-sided, and this both in its Utopian and in its revolutionary forms. All would-be reformers see the existing order, with its extremes of wealth and poverty, and its defence of privileges, as something fundamentally evil which needs to be replaced by a new ideal order. The terrestial city must be replaced by the Kingdom of God on earth, a society based on ignorance and superstition by a rational social order in keeping with human nature, and ordinary, empirical law by either natural or divine law. The picture of social reality is clearly divided between black and white.

Like dialectical thought, however, tragic thought has always linked together the 'Yes' and the 'No'. It knows that no reality is ever wholly good or wholly bad, and that it must be seen in relation to the whole of which it forms part, if we are to see not only the good and evil which this society contains but also the extent to which the relationship between the two changes in the course of its historical evolution.

As far as the social order is concerned, dialectical thought has always considered that while inequalities of wealth and power were evils that ought to be abolished, they are nevertheless temporary realities which also, in so far as they contribute to the development of society's productive capacities, possess genuine human value.

Pascal, judging society from the point of view of the ideal community, sees selfishness and the defence of individual interests as the most crying evil, and also sees that these are based upon the existence of private property—'Each self is the enemy and would like to be the tyrant of all others selves' (fr. 455, E.141), 'Mine, Thine . . . usurpation throughout the whole world etc.' For Hegel, on the other hand, the ruse of reason causes history to progress and goodness to be realised precisely through the agency of this egoism and selfishness. Man's egoism is, for him, the devil Mephistopheles who, against his own will, leads Faust up to heaven.

K   277

But if the fact that Hegel and Marx see events in an historical perspective enables them to overcome the opposition between goodness and evil, and between the positive and negative aspects of social institutions, the problem is much more complex for Pascal. He has the same point of departure, but not the same possibility of finding a way out.

Pascal knows that there is no human law or moral commandment capable of achieving true justice or real goodness. All human laws are inadequate, as we see from fragment 293 (E.88).

'Why are you killing me?' 'What, do you not live on the other side of the water? My friend, if you lived on this side, I should be a murderer and it would be unjust to kill you like this; but since you live on the other side of the water, I am a hero and it is just to do what I do.'

The ideal would have been to combine justice and power in order to create laws that were at one and the same time both just and efficacious. Unfortunately, men cannot do this, and are consequently obliged to choose between the two. Moreover, in order to maintain balance and peace in society, they choose power and sacrifice justice:

Equality of goods is no doubt just; but, being unable to force others to obey what is just, men have made it just to obey force; in their inability to fortify justice, they have justified force, so that justice and force might be brought together, and peace—which is the greatest good—preserved (fr. 299, E.171).

Similarly, the two other *pensées* already quoted above (279 and 294) also bring out the same idea.

What dominates society (in the case of Pascal, society in general and for thinkers such as myself, capitalist society based upon individual selfishness) is the conflict between individuals. In Pascal and Kant this assumes the abstract form of the fight of man against man, in Hegel it becomes the struggle between the master and the slave, and in Marx it finally assumes the concrete form of the class struggle. Pascal himself knows perfectly well that if it is power—the 'ropes of necessity'—which 'decide the social struggle', it is also the power relationships within society that give rise to ideologies, the 'ropes of imagination'.

The ties whereby men are made to respect one another are, in general the result of necessity; for since all men wish to rule, but only some and not all are able to, there must be different degrees. Let us imagine to ourselves that we see men bringing a society into being. There is no doubt but that they will fight amongst themselves until the stronger party overcomes the weaker and establishes its rule. But once this has been settled, then those who are masters—not wishing the war to

278

continue—decree that the power which is now in their hands shall be handed on in a manner pleasing to them, some entrusting it to popular election, others to hereditary succession.

It is at that point that imagination begins to play its part, for until then it has been naked power which has carried the day. Now it becomes the imagination which bestows power on a certain party, in France on the nobility, in Switzerland on the commoners etc., and the ties which then accord respect to any one individual are ties of imagination (fr. 304, E.207).

These ideologies acquire a real importance for the rulers of society, whose need for them is all the greater because they do not, in fact, any longer possess genuine power.

The custom of seeing kings accompanied by guards, drums, officers and all other things which bend our machine towards respect and terror enables their face, even when sometimes alone and without these accompaniments, to inspire their subjects with terror and respect. For we do not distinguish in our minds between their person and the followers whom we normally see with them. And the world, not seeing that this effect comes from this particular custom, thinks that it comes from a natural authority, so that they say, 'The character of divinity is written upon his face.' etc. (fr. 308, E.62).

The chancellor is grave and gloriously adorned, for his post is false. Not so the king, who has real force and has no need of the imagination. Judges, doctors etc. have nothing but men's imagination to give them authority (fr. 307, E.177).

In spite of the brief and laconic phrases in which he expresses it, Pascal's critique of the authority of justice and of the social order is of the most radical kind imaginable. We must not, however, allow ourselves to jump to any hasty conclusions: this anarchist who denies that there is any justice at all in society is at the same time one of the most conservative thinkers who ever lived, a man who declares that privilege and social injustice are not only necessary but also valuable in themselves.

The greatest of evils is civil war. If we are determined to reward merit, such wars are unavoidable, for all men will lay claim to merit. A fool who comes into his title by right of birth brings with him lesser and less certain evils (fr. 313, E.184).

It is by the very fact of their reality that these privileges also acquire value. For it is one of the characteristics of any dialectical system of ethics that one should not be satisfied either by mind or reality, but should strive after a union between the two. 'Everything rational is real,' said Hegel, 'and everything that is real is rational', and Pascal's ideal is not pure justice but the union between justice and power.

There are certain aspects of social privileges which actually contribute towards the realisation of values:

> Noble birth is indeed a great advantage, for it puts a man at the age of eighteen into a position where he is honoured and respected as much as a man of fifty who might have acquired merit. It is equivalent to thirty years earned with no trouble (fr. 322, E.193).

> A fine appearance does not imply too great a show of vanity, for it indicates that one has a large number of people working for one; one shows by one's hair that one has a valet and a perfumer, by one's clothes that one has linen or embroidery. Nor is it mere appearance or outward show to have several arms at one's disposition. The more arms one has the stronger one is. And to have a fine appearance indicates one's strength (fr. 316, E.185).

> There are four flunkeys (fr. 318, E.56).[1]

Wealth is here identified with power, with the possibility of using other people's strength, and it is precisely for this reason that Pascal attributes value to it. Clearly, this is the feeling of any rising class for whom wealth still represents a positive factor in the development of the productive forces of society. To be rich means being able to create by using other people's strength. Implicitly, it means being strong oneself.

---

[1] Mephisto expresses the same idea in *Faust* when he says:

> 'Six stallions, say, I can afford,
> Is not their strength my property?
> I tear along, a sporting lord,
> As if their legs belonged to me.'

and the young Marx, commenting on this passage, makes the following remarks:

'What exists for me through the agency of money, what I can pay for, what money can buy, is something which I, the owner of the money, then become. My strength is as great as the strength of money, the qualities of money are my qualities and my strength because I possess the money. What I am and what I can do are in no way predetermined by my individuality. I am ugly, but I can buy myself the most beautiful of women. Thus I cease to be ugly, since the effect of ugliness, its repulsive force, is destroyed by money. In my own individual self I am a cripple, but money can buy me two dozen feet; thus I cease to be a cripple. I am a wicked, dishonest man with neither wit nor conscience, but since money is respected then the person who owns it enjoys respect as well. Money is the sovereign good, so that the person who owns it is good as well. Moreover, money frees me from the need to be honest, since I am naturally presupposed to be honest if I have it. I have no real native wit, but since money is the vital spirit of everything, then its possessor is naturally endowed with wit and to spare. Moreover, the wealthy man can buy witty men, and surely the man who can buy witty men has more wit than they? Since by money, I can do everything that a man's heart can desire, then surely I own all human faculties. For does not money change all weakness and inabilities into their opposites?' (Cf. Karl Marx, *Die Frühschriften* (Stuttgart: Kriner-Verlag, 1953), p. 298; *National Ökonomie und Philosophie*.

SOCIAL LIFE: JUSTICE, POWER AND WEALTH

The dialectical thought of Pascal, like that of Goethe, Hegel or
Marx, sees this as a justifiable attitude, but also points out its limitations by insisting at the same time on the injustice which constitutes
the negative aspect of wealth. Hegel and Marx also point to the
material poverty of the exploited and the spiritual poverty of the
exploiters, and insist upon the fact that private property, like the
wealth of bourgeois society, has only a temporary and historical
usefulness.

But if the historical perspective enables Hegel and Marx to harmonise the two apparently contradictory positions where wealth is
both praised and denounced, and to see it as a necessary but
transitory factor that will eventually be superseded by the progress of
society, Pascal cannot do this. One of the main characteristics of the
tragic vision lies in the absence of any idea of the future. It knows
only the present and eternity, so that the dialectic which becomes
historical in Hegel and Marx must, in Pascal, be concentrated in the
present and become purely structural. What later becomes a succession of historical epochs is still, for Pascal, an ascending scale of
qualitatively different levels of human reality, the thesis, antithesis and
synthesis in the different ways of judging society and the State. (In
the following quotations the words *thesis, antithesis* and *synthesis* are
added by me. The text is Pascal's.)

> *Why things are so*—Continual alternation of *pro* and *con*.
> *Thèsis.* Thus we have shown the vanity of man by seeing how he
> prizes things which are not essential; and all these opinions are
> destroyed.
> *Antithesis.* We have next shown that all these opinions are very
> sound, and that since all these vanities have a very good foundation,
> the common people are not as vain as they are said to be; and thus
> we have destroyed the opinion which destroyed that of the people.
> *Synthesis.* But we must now destroy this latest proposition, and
> show that it is still very true that the people are vain, although its
> opinions are very well founded; for they do not see how these opinions
> are true, and since they see truth where no truth is, their opinions
> are still very false and very badly founded (fr. 328, E.183).

Or, again, we have a double triad.

> *Why things are so.* Gradation.
> *Thesis.* The common people honours those of great birth.
> *Antithesis.* The clever despise them, saying that noble birth is not
> an advantage stemming from personal qualities, but merely the result
> of chance.
> *Synthesis* (and, at the same time, the thesis of the second triad).
> The really intelligent honour them, not for the same reasons as the
> people, but for a deeper, hidden motive.

281

Second antithesis. The devout, who have more zeal than knowledge, despise them, notwithstanding the reason for which the truly intelligent esteem them, since they judge by a new light accorded to them by piety.

Second synthesis. But the perfect Christians honour them by another superior light. So that opinions follow one after another according to the light vouchsafed to men (fr. 337, E.180).

Here again, there is a similarity of approach between Pascal and Kant which exists in spite of the wide differences between them. These differences, in fact, can be explained largely by the different historical circumstances under which they were writing, Kant expressing the attitude of the most progressive section of the German bourgeoisie at the time of the French Revolution, Pascal expressing the world vision of an intermediary social level which does not seem to have been affected by the English revolution, except perhaps indirectly through Hobbes.[1] Where they resemble each other is in the need which they both felt to combine a critical and progressive attitude with one of complete conservatism. Pascal does so by the theories which I have just analysed, and Kant by asserting the need for the individual to accept the views of those in power, an attitude which leads him to defend at one and the same time both the French Revolution and the Prussian monarchy.

The real dialectical solution can, however, only make its appearance when men eventually begin to consider society from the point of view of the future, and thereby make possible the development of a genuine philosophy of history.

---

[1] Fragment 176 (E.203) does mention Cromwell, but in a wholly negative manner. Pascal seems to have been aware only of the danger of civil wars.

XV
THE WAGER.

I

A STUDY of Pascal's view of man, of living beings, of the physical universe, of epistemology, ethics, aesthetics and life in society has revealed the permanence of the same basic concept underlying all his ideas: man is a paradoxical being, who is both great and small, and who is equally incapable both of achieving real values in this world and of giving up the quest for them. He is therefore led to place his hope only in religion, and in the existence of a personal and transcendent deity.

There is, however, one further question to be answered: however great and rewarding Pascal's final position may appear on the level of will and of faith, it stands out by its essential poverty when judged by the standards of scientific and philosophical thought, or by those of human achievement in this world.

If the world offers man only the possibility of achieving relative values it can offer a mind governed by the categories of 'all or nothing' sufficient interest to justify the devotion of only a very small fraction of his thought and action. Indeed, any interest shown in the vanity of a world empty of God can be the sign only of the sin involved in compromising with the fallen state of the Evil One. The extreme Jansenism of Barcos's group carried this attitude to its logical conclusion by abandoning the world and considering that the ideas of virtue and of solitude, of the Christian and of the hermit, were virtually synonymous. But—unlike. Pascal—men such as Barcos, Singlin and even Hamon did not leave behind them an analysis of physical and biological reality, and did not write down their ideas on epistemology, ethics or the social life. If they do mention these subjects it is solely in order to condemn any interest in them, and to remind the Christian that he should devote his life to God and God alone.

How, then, can we explain the fact that Pascal, who shared the

views of these men, should not only have indulged in scientific research between 1657 and 1662, writing papers on mathematics and
setting up the world's first public transport service, but should also
have given us, in the *Pensées*, a detailed and realistic analysis of the
relationship between man and the world, and have actually written
an apology for religion?

This is not only a problem which the historian encounters as he
looks back over the relationship between Pascal and Jansenism. It
was also something which was widely discussed by the 'Disciples of
Saint Augustine', and which deeply affected the different ideological
positions that they adopted. Arnauld, Barcos and Pascal were all
fully aware, when they took up their own particular attitude, both of
what it implied and by what arguments it could be defended. It is
therefore not possible to explain the difference between these three
men by accidental factors such as temperament or education.

I have already mentioned the different attitudes adopted by Barcos
and Pascal and the practical results which these had. While the former
refuses the world completely and withdraws into solitude, the latter
both refuses the world and at the same time remains in it. In my view,
Pascal's attitude stems from the fact that he carries the idea of the
hidden God—or, rather, of the God who hides Himself—to the extreme point where he sees God as preventing man from discovering
not only His will but also His existence. It is precisely because, for
man in his fallen state, the existence of God has become a hope and a
certainty of the heart—that is to say, an uncertain and paradoxical
certainty—that man can no longer find a sure and certain refuge by
simply withdrawing from the world. It is in the world, or at least in
the presence of the world, that man must now express both his rejection of any relative values and his quest for values that shall be
authentic and transcendent. It is because man in his fallen state no
longer sees the existence of God as a pure and simple certainty that
Pascal was both able and compelled to work out a theory of the
world and of earthly, biological and social reality. And it is because
man, in order to be man, cannot in any way accept an inadequate
and relative world that this theory could attain so high a degree of
realism, and one as free from any taint of worldly compromise or
illusion. It is precisely because Pascal both rejected the world and
lived in it, because he combined living in it, refusing it and analysing it,
that his work attained the highest philosophical and scientific level
that a thinker of his time could achieve.

Pascal finds everything in the world inadequate and sees no rest for
man as long as he remains in this life. He also, however, denies that
man can find a certain and non-paradoxical proof of God's existence
and that he can turn away from the world to seek refuge in solitude

284

and eternity. It is this dual attitude which must be explained and understood if we are to have any coherent account of his life and work.

It is the fact that no salvation can be found in an absolutely certain religious faith and in a complete rejection of this world that explains the importance and central position of fragment 233 (E.343), generally known as the argument of the wager. If in fact—as I shall try to show later—the idea of a wager is also at the very heart of the Hegelian and Marxist positions it is also completely at odds with the views adopted by most Christian thinkers both before and after Pascal, for whom such an argument is merely a useful *ad hominem* approach in apologetics. Such thinkers always see the existence of God, and, very often the will of God, as revealed to man in an absolutely convincing manner. They may base their arguments on reason or intuition, but they always reject the idea of risk or paradox in religious faith. This habit has led most Pascalian scholars to put forward an interpretation of the wager which I cannot accept. One does not, they say, wager on the existence of something of which one has certain knowledge. Moreover, they continue, Pascal was a Christian, and was therefore certain of God's existence; he could therefore not have attributed any importance to the argument of the wager in so far as he himself was concerned. Once this syllogism is accepted, the only question to be discussed is whether the wager argument was intended to appeal to a free thinker of the Méré type, whether it was merely a 'stylistic exaggeration' or whether it marked a stage in the development of Pascal's own ideas or a step in the logical development of his argument.[1]

The great objection to each of these interpretations is, in my view, the fact that they set out, either implicitly or explicitly, not from the actual text of fragment 233 (E.343), but from a preconceived idea of faith and Christianity. None of the scholars who have put forward these different views seems, in my opinion, to consider the possibility that his conception of Christianity fails to take into account an

[1] I should perhaps mention, however, the book by H. Petitot. *Pascal. Sa vie religieuse et son Apologie du christianisme* (Paris: Beachesne, 1911), which, without actually arriving at a tragic interpretation of the *Pensées*, nevertheless takes account of the text that I analyse and arrives at the conclusion that 'Pascal himself wagers' (p. 234).

There is also the very good study by Etienne Souriau, *Valeur actuelle de Pascal*, which constitutes Chapter 2 of his book *L'Ombre de Dieu* (Paris: P.U.F., 1955). Monsieur Souriau brings out the fact that the wager is valid only within a certain philosophical context, and writes: 'We must, for the wager to be valid, reply "done" as soon as a proposition is presented for our consideration which seems, under certain conditions, to provide a viable though not infallible link between ourselves and infinity, the first condition being that we accept it' (p. 84).

authentic form of the Christian faith, and one which happens to be that of Pascal.

What I propose to do is to adopt the opposite approach. I shall study the actual text of the fragment in order to try to discover to what extent it justifies a view of Pascal as a man who makes the wager himself, and who therefore, unlike other Christian thinkers, links together the two ideas of wagering and believing. I shall study the place of the wager argument in the *Pensées* as a whole, in the ideology of the 'Friends of Port-Royal' and finally in the history of philosophy.

Once we accept the idea that Pascal really believed what he wrote down, and decide to reject any interpretation based upon 'stylistic exaggeration', the evidence of the text seems decisive. There are two passages in particular that in my view are quite unambiguous. In the first Pascal is replying to the objection put forward by a man who is already intellectually convinced (and who is made to say, in an imaginary dialogue, 'That is obvious') but who says that he cannot bring himself to believe:

> You wish to attain faith, but do not know how to go about it; you want to cure yourself of your unbelief, and you ask for the remedy: *learn from those who have been tied as you are now tied, and who now wager all they have,* for they know the way that you would follow and have been cured of a sickness for which you seek a cure (fr. 233, E.343, L. G.'s italics.)

This phrase 'learn from those who now wager all they have' seems quite decisive. It is Pascal himself who is speaking and who, addressing an interlocutor—whoever he may be—says neither, 'Learn from those who now believe', nor, 'Learn from those who have wagered', but, 'Learn from those who *now wager*', emphasising his use of the present tense by the adverb *now*. If we accept that the author meant what he said—and any serious study of a writer must surely start out from this as a basic presupposition—these lines ought to be enough to refute most of the traditional interpretations which set out to minimise the rôle of the wager in Pascal's own religious faith.

There is another passage in the same fragment which I find equally conclusive. Pascal's interlocutor repeats that he cannot believe, and *probably* (the passage can be interpreted in one of two ways) identifies the word 'wager' with the word 'believe'. Pascal's reply, however, identifies them quite unambiguously:

> Yes, but my hands are tied and my mouth is gagged; I am forced to wager, and am not free; they will not release me, and I am so made that I cannot believe. What then am I to do? That is true. But understand at least that your inability to believe comes from your passions, since reason inclines you to believe and you cannot do so.

One might perhaps interpret Pascal's imaginary interlocutor as saying: 'I am forced to wager either that God exists or that there is nothing at all', and I cannot believe in His existence. In that case, 'believe' and 'wager' are not synonymous. However, since Pascal's interlocutor has already accepted Pascal's argument as 'obvious', there is a second and more probable interpretation: 'I am forced to wager that God exists, and I cannot believe.' Here the words 'wager' and 'belief' become synonymous, and there is no longer any distinction between the wager 'written for the free thinker' and the faith of the Christian who does not need to wager. Moreover, the identification between 'wager' and 'believe' in the rest of the passage containing Pascal's reply seems to me to be quite unambiguous. For we know that, for Pascal, reason does not lead men to believe in the sense required by a Thomistic, Augustinian or Cartesian position. All it does is to lead men to wager that God exists, and nothing more.

This is why, if one gives their full importance to the two passages which I have just quoted and which are normally neglected, it becomes very difficult to deny that the wager occupies a central position in the general scheme of the *Pensées*.

There is, moreover, another text which must be considered by anyone who rejects the idea that the wager argument represents Pascal's own position. It is fragment 234 (E.346), which Brunschvicg felt to be so similar in inspiration that he placed it immediately after the passage on the wager. The text can be divided into two parts. The first—very significantly—tells us that 'religion is not certain', although it is more certain than many other things which influence us and determine our actions. It thus becomes reasonable, and in keeping with the general odds, to commit oneself to a religion which is not absolutely certain.

> If we are to act only on grounds of certainty, we should take no action with regard to religion, for it is not certain. But how many things do we not engage in without being certain, sea voyages or battles! In that case, we should do nothing at all, for nothing is certain. And there is more certainty in religion than in our presupposition that we shall see tomorrow; for it is not certain that we shall see tomorrow, but it is certainly possible that we shall not see it. It is not certain that religion is true, but who can dare to say that it is certainly possible that it is not true? And yet, when men work for tomorrow and for uncertain things, they are acting rightly; for one must work for uncertain things, in accordance with the rules governing the odds.

There is, however, nothing new in this, and critics who interpret the passage on the wager simply as aimed at the free thinker could doubtless interpret fragment 234 (E.346) in exactly the same way, in spite of the fact that Pascal now seems to be speaking generally and not addressing any individual person in particular. It becomes much more difficult, however, to defend this interpretation when we come to the second part of the passage, for it is impossible to see how Pascal intended to 'convert the free thinker' by setting out such a vehement criticism of Saint Augustine. In fact, this would have been most likely to produce exactly the opposite effect.

Moreover, when one remembers the immense respect which all Jansenists, and especially Pascal, had for Saint Augustine—whose authority was for them almost as great as that of the Bible—one is forced to conclude that Pascal would be most unlikely to have introduced such a passage if he had not been dealing with a point that he considers to be exceptionally important. The fragment—which also shows us Pascal's views on Montaigne—must therefore be considered as representing an essential argument in the work which he intended to write.

One should also note that the ideas which this passage expresses do not stand alone. They continue those expressed in a text of which we unfortunately have only a second-hand version transmitted to us in the *Mémoires* of Fontaine, the *Entretien avec Monsieur de Saci*, in which Pascal was already putting forward his view of the Christian position and contrasting it with the one-sided approach of scepticism and dogmatism. He took Montaigne as the representative of the first and Epictetus of the second, and showed how Christianity at one and the same time both denied and transcended both positions.

Fragment 234 (E.346) continues this analysis on a higher, and, I am tempted to say, more dialectical level. Pascal has now come to realise that neither the sceptic nor the dogmatic rationalist adopts a purely one-sided approach, since the sceptic recognises man's need for certainty, and even the dogmatist does not deny that chance and uncertainty play an important rôle in human experience. Both, however, consider that the element which happens to go against their philosophy—the need for certainty, the importance of chance—is an incidental and not an integral part of the human condition. In Pascal's own words, 'they have seen the effect and not the cause'. However, there is in fragment 234 (E.346) a significant change in the thinkers whom Pascal takes as representing the two attitudes. The sceptic is still Montaigne, but the dogmatist has now ceased to be Epictetus and become Saint Augustine.

Saint Augustine saw that men work for things that are uncertain, on the sea and in battles. But he did not see the nature of the odds, which shows that we should do so. Montaigne saw that we are offended at the sight of a mind which cannot think straight, and that custom is all powerful; but he did not see why this should be so. Both these men have seen the effects but have not seen the causes, so that compared to those who have seen the causes they are like those who have only eyes compared to those who also have a mind. For effects are, as it were, sensible to sight, whereas causes can be perceived only by the mind. And although these effects can be seen by the mind, this mind is, compared to the mind which sees the causes, like the bodily senses when compared with the mind.

Pascal thus criticises Saint Augustine very sharply for his failure to recognise both the fundamental rôle played by uncertáinty in man's life, and the 'nature of the odds' which shows that man is compelled to work for what is uncertain.

There is perhaps one objection to this interpretation: is Pascal really talking about the wager that God exists, or is he talking about the thousand and one conscious or implicit wagers in the realm of everyday life? For two reasons, I think that the former interpretation is the correct one. First of all, because Pascal does acknowledge that Saint Augustine recognises the existence of the daily wagers which we make 'on sea, in battle', etc., and, secondly, because fragment 233 (E.343) reveals Pascal's own awareness of the main 'dogmatic' objection to the wager: the statement that reasonable men act only when they are certain and refrain from action whenever they are not. He had already replied to this particular objection of Cartesian dogmatism by the remark: 'You must wager, it is not optional, you are embarked.'

Now what exactly do these words mean? Certainly not that we are obliged to accept such and such a particular wager in our everyday life, on the sea or in battle, for example. This is simply not true, for the choice of each one of these particular wagers is optional, and we can always reject or accept it precisely because we are never 'embarked' in advance. The mistake of dogmatic—or, to be more precise, of Cartesian—rationalism has been to divide man up into small pieces, to consider each act in isolation and then to apply the results of such an analysis to human existence in general.

If, on the other hand, we look upon our life as a whole we shall see that we are in fact 'embarked' by virtue of the very quest for happiness which Pascal considers an essential and inevitable part of the human condition. Our freedom is made up of two things: our ability to make a choice in the many wagers that we come across in everyday life, and our need to wager in the one essential choice offered to us between God, on the one side, and nothingness, on the other.

The 'nature of the odds' which Saint Augustine failed to recognise shows that man has to 'work for uncertain things' only in so far as these odds govern the human condition as such, with man's inevitable quest for happiness and the impossibility of ever establishing this quest on a firm and non-paradoxical basis. A religious hermit who was certain of God's existence could, in the final analysis, deny that man had to work for things that are uncertain.

Thus, the Pascalian texts which identify 'wagering' with 'believing' speak of those who 'now wager' and criticise Saint Augustine for not having seen the 'nature of the odds' which show that man must work for things that are uncertain. They criticise him for having, with respect to this truth, been like 'those who have only eyes' in comparison with those who 'also have a mind'. It is for this reason that these texts do, in my view, resist most of the traditional explanations, and to be serious, if not absolutely decisive arguments in favour of an interpretation which gives the 'wager' a central place in the scheme of Pascal's epistemology.

We now have to study the intrinsic significance of the wager and its place both in the *Pensées* and in the general history of philosophical thought.

II

Fragment 233 (E.343) is presented in the form of a dialogue between Pascal and an interlocutor of whom we know nothing except that he 'does not believe' and even that he is 'so constituted that he cannot believe'. We obviously need to try to identify this man, since he is not only the person whom Pascal addresses in this fragment, but also the reader for whom the whole of the *Pensées* are intended.

The problem is this: does this interlocutor represent a particular type of man—a free thinker, for example—and can we therefore conclude that both fragment 233 and numerous other sections of the *Pensées* are merely part of an apology for Christianity which had no great personal importance for Pascal the believer? Or does this person represent an essential aspect of the human condition, and therefore a potential possibility of Pascal himself?

The same problem can be presented in another, complementary form, in the following question: to what extent are the doctrines of Grace and Predestination accepted by Port-Royal compatible with the very idea of writing an apology for the Christian religion? Scholars have, in fact, often noted the incompatibility between the Jansenist attitude towards Predestination and Pascal's decision to try to bring men to faith by persuading them of the truth of Christianity. They have either criticised him for contradicting his own premises or praised him for having been able to escape from the influence of Jansenism, but they have all nevertheless agreed that the Jansenist doctrine taught that man was completely helpless by himself, so much so that not even prayer could be efficacious unless God intervened by His divine grace.

As Monsieur Gouhier has observed in his unpublished lectures on the *Pensées*, any contradiction in Pascal's work cannot be implicit, since his acquaintances at Port-Royal—especially Barcos and his followers—would certainly have pointed out to him the strong objections which they had to any attempt to bring men to the faith by writing apologiae. Moreover, when one is discussing a thinker of Pascal's status one must accept the idea of a 'contradiction' in his thought only when all other possibilities of explanation have been exhausted.

My own view is that there is no contradiction in Pascal's attitude; if he is criticised for acting in a way which, according to his own view, could not be efficacious in itself, then this criticism is valid only if one considers that Pascal was adopting the moral criterion of efficiency and not, as is more probably the case, that of intention.

Let us remember what Kant said in the *Critique of Practical Reason*:

> The judgment which decides whether a thing does or does not fall within the domain of pure practical reason is completely independent of any comparison with our own physical power; the question lies wholly in discovering whether we are allowed to *will* an action related to the existence of an object should it be supposed that this lies within our power.[1]

There is nothing artificial in the comparison between this text and the views adopted by Pascal. Monsieur Gouhier has pointed out that for Pascal, as for all the 'Disciples of Saint Augustine', man can in no way whatsoever come to know how God chooses His elect. We have absolutely no means of knowing whether a particular individual is either probably or certainly one of the Elect or one of those whom God has rejected. We are therefore compelled—as Monsieur Gouhier has observed—to act without even considering hypotheses of this nature. We have to accept as a general rule a formal imperative which makes no distinction at all between men, and which, it should be noted, is very similar to the Kantian imperative.

What we now have to decide is what universally valid rule of conduct we should adopt towards all men. Pascal himself tells us what this should be in one of his own texts on Grace:

> That all men in this world are compelled, under pain of eternal damnation and of the sin against the Holy Ghost for which there is no forgiveness either in this world or the next, to believe that they belong to the small number of the Elect for whose salvation Christ died; and that they should, moreover, believe the same thing about each man and every man who is now on this earth, however wicked and impious he

[1] *Critique of Practical Reason*, Academy Edition, Vol V, pp. 57–8. My own translation of the French quoted by Monsieur Goldmann. Cf. also Beck's translation, p. 166, which gives a rather different version of this passage.

may be; and that for as long as he still has a moment of life; and that all men should leave the distinction between the Elect and the Reprobate as part of the impenetrable secret of God.[1]

And in a highly significant variant, Pascal adds that:

> All men are compelled to believe, but with a belief mingled with fear and not accompanied by certainty, that they belong to the small number of the Elect whom Jesus Christ wishes to save; and that they should never place any man now alive, however wicked and impious he may be, for as long as he has a moment of life, elsewhere than in the ranks of the Predestined, leaving the distinction between the Elect and the Reprobate as part of the impenetrable secret of God. And that they should therefore do for their fellows everything which can contribute to their salvation.

There is thus no contradiction at all between Pascal's complete acceptance of the Augustinian theories on Grace and Predestination and the fact that he acted as if every man could be saved, doing everything possible to contribute to his salvation (in spite of the fact that, in the final analysis, this depends solely upon the Will of God).

However, these two texts which I have just quoted are not exactly similar, at least at first sight. The first says that: 'All men are compelled . . . to believe that they belong to the small number of the Elect, and to believe the same about every man', and if we interpret this text absolutely literally it does not really clear up the problem of whether or not it is legitimate to write apologies for the Christian faith. For if I act *as if* each man taken individually belonged to the ranks of the Elect, it becomes unnecessary to write apologiae, for I no longer need to contribute to their salvation.

The second variant text has more nuances, for it first of all tells us that the belief that we are saved should be 'mingled with fear' and not 'accompanied by certainty'. Secondly, it gives a negative twist to the formal imperative mentioned by Monsieur Gouhier: 'Never place a man . . . elsewhere than in the number of the Predestined.'

Several lines of fragment 194 (E.11)—also quoted by Monsieur Gouhier—expresses a similar idea:

> Since this religion obliges us always to look upon them, as long as they are in this life, as capable of receiving the Grace that will enlighten them, and to believe that they can in a moment of time be fuller of faith than we are ourselves, and that we, likewise, can fall into the blindness where they are now, we must do for them what we would have them do for us if we were in their state, and call upon them to have pity on themselves, and to take at least a few steps to see if they may not find some light.

[1] Cf. Pascal, *Deux pièces imparfaites sur la Grâce et le concile de Trente* (Paris: Vrin, 1947), p. 31.

Thus the formal imperative which justifies the writing of apologiae is this: that we should act as if every man, taken individually, could, in the moments which he still has to live—whether these be many or few—be either saved or damned, and therefore do everything we can to help him 'to take pity on himself'.

Pascal's own view is certainly that God alone can make our efforts fail or succeed (although, in fragment 233 (E.343) he once, but only once, mentions the possibility of 'believing even naturally'), but this is something which no longer concerns us. In fact, man for us is always a being who can be either damned or saved, and we must act as if, by our action, God is going to assure his salvation.

From the point of view of God there are the Elect who cannot be damned and the Reprobate who cannot be saved. From the point of view of man, on the other hand, the categories of 'Elect' and 'Reprobate' are in each individual case merely permanent possibilities. Man must think of himself as an intermediate being who brings these two categories together, but who has not yet chosen and who never can make a definitive choice in this life. This, in my view, is exactly the idea expressed not only in the numerous fragments which tell us that man is 'neither angel nor beast', that he is 'a thinking reed', but also by the two tripartite divisions which make up the very basis of Pascal's thought. One of these divisions is expressed in a text on Grace (the distinction between the Elect the Reprobate and the Called) and the other in fragments such as the following:

There are only three kinds of person: those who, having found God, seek Him; those who, not having found Him, spend their time seeking Him; and those who live without having found Him and without seeking for Him either. The first are both blessèd and reasonable, the last both mad and unhappy, and the second unhappy but reasonable (fr. 257, E.364).

For Arnauld and Barcos, of course, there are, from God's point of view, only two kinds of people: the Elect and the Reprobate. To be strictly logical, Pascal ought to have adopted the same distinction, and seen that, from God's point of view, those who were called but did not persevere in their calling were simply the Reprobate taken after the moment of their fall. However, in his *Écrits sur la Grâce*, Pascal puts these into a third, intermediate category. This is very significant, for he thereby introduces the human point of view expressed in fragment 257 into the divine perspective: while those who are called but do not persevere simply do not exist in the sight of God, who has complete knowledge of reality, they are from the point of view of man nevertheless an essential aspect of the human condition,

293

for man can 'know nothing of the impenetrable secret of God' on the subject of 'the difference between the Elect and the Reprobate'.

Moreover, even a consistent follower of Barcos could only really, from a human point of view, distinguish 'hermits' from people who continued to live in the world. Pascal, on the other hand, recognises the existence in every man, whether a believer or a free thinker, of a reason by which he can be led to seek God and to understand the nature of the wager. He constantly recalls, however, that God is not manifest, that He is both absent and present, a Hidden God.

The rest of this text concerns the nature of Divine Grace, whose 'impenetrable secret' neither we nor other men can understand in the course of this life.

Both the *Pensées* as a whole and fragment 233 (E.343) in particular are addressed not to any one individual category of men but to Everyman, Pascal himself included. For in Pascal's view Everyman both can and must be brought by his reason to seek for God, but Everyman also inevitably runs the risk of being mistaken or even of giving up this quest. Yet he must never—and this is true of any authentic human quest—give up hope.

The formal imperative mentioned by Monsieur Gouhier should be expressed like this: 'Act towards everyone, whoever he may be, whether the best or the worst of men, as if God were to intend to use your action to bring about his salvation.' The resemblance between this and the second formulation of the categorical imperative in Kant is obvious, for we see the German philosopher writing:

Act in such a way as you treat humanity in your own person, as in the person of any other man, always as an end and never as a means.[1]

Thus, in the two tripartite divisions of Pascal's thought the essentially human category is each time the intermediary one, the only one which, as men, we are able to experience in our present life. Similarly, the two people who take part in the dialogue in fragment 233 (E.343) are, in the last analysis, one and the same person, an indissoluble pair of friends, and this because the one who wagers that nothing exists— although he is not aware of actually making a wager—represents a risk which the man who wagers on God constantly runs but into which he never falls.

One could even go so far as to say that these three types of person go to make up one and the same being, the truly human man. The two extreme categories of the Elect and the Reprobate are, in this respect, the two permanent possibilities between which man must choose. They express, on the plane of the individual, the two possibi-

[1] Cf. Kant, *Foundations of the Metaphysics of Morals*, Academy edition, Vol. IV. p. 429. Cf. Lewis Beck's translation p. 87.

lities represented by the wager, in so far as to fear to wager that Nothing exists is to fear damnation, and to wager that God exists is to hope for salvation. In this life the human condition lies precisely in this intermediate category made up of the union between hope and fear.

We should never forget that, for Pascal, man is a paradoxical being on every level of existence; that he is a union of opposites; and that, for him, to seek God is to find Him, but to find Him is still to seek after Him. A man who rested and ceased to search, who attained a certainty which ceased to be a wager, would be the complete opposite of the man whom Pascal knew and whom he presented in his work.

III

Before trying to place the wager in the history of philosophy, it would perhaps be useful to see how it fits into the general system of Port-Royal.

Léon Cognet has suggested the possibility of a curious similarity between Pascal's ideas and those accepted by others at Port-Royal by publishing a letter by Mother Angélique de Saint-Jean. This, in fact, recalls a number of the views expressed in fragment 233 (E.343):

> It is like a kind of doubt concerning everything connected with Faith and Providence, but a doubt on which I dwell very little. For, out of fear that reasoning might offer a wider entry to temptation, my mind seems to reject it with a certain attitude that is in itself opposed to faith. Thus, I almost find myself saying that even if there were to be something uncertain in what I know to be the truth and in what I believe about the immortality of the soul, the best thing for me to do would still be to follow the path of virtue. The very act of writing down such an idea makes me afraid, for I have never before allowed it to present itself so clearly to my own mind; it is rather something which happens almost without my realising it. But surely there is something lacking in one's faith if one is capable of such thoughts? I have not dared to speak to anyone about them, since I found them so dangerous that I was afraid even to suggest them to anyone to whom I revealed the suffering they caused me.[1]

However, this text seems to me to be rather an indication of the extremes to which a specifically rationalistic and Arnaldian view could lead, rather than a pointer to the tendencies of Port-Royal as a whole. It seems in fact, to put forward two ideas which are basically rationalistic and Stoic in inspiration: that of a doubt that God exists and that of a life given over wholly to virtue. What is peculiar both to Pascal's wager and to Kant's postulate is, however, precisely the

[1] Cf. *La Table Ronde*, December 1954, p. 52.

opposite view. One can only doubt something if one at least entertains the possibility that it can be approximately or certainly known. For Pascal and Kant, however, theoretical reason can know absolutely nothing about the existence or the non-existence of God. It would be equally false and equally indefensible to affirm, deny or even doubt it. since all that theoretical reason can do when faced with urgent problems of this kind, which are completely out of its range, is to subordinate itself to a faculty that is capable of going beyond reason because of the ability which it has of making statements in a domain inaccessible to theory. If such a faculty cannot be found, reason must simply content itself with taking note of the radical insufficiency of the human condition.

Now, according to Pascal and Kant, man does possess the synthesising faculty which enables him to eliminate doubt for non-theoretical reasons, and, on the theological plane, to state even the certainly uncertain existence of God.

I have already stated elsewhere that when, in fragment 233 (E.343) the editors of the Port-Royal edition of the *Pensées* replaced the words 'those who now wager' by 'those who do not now have any doubt', they were not distorting Pascal's ideas. Although it is a serious thing to do, they were merely trying to avoid scandal by substituting a general type of argument for the particular argument used by Pascal. For, if it is true that all those who wager do not necessarily doubt, it is equally true that most of those who do not doubt do not wager either.

One can nevertheless see in what respects this letter by Mother Angélique de Saint-Jean differs from tragic thought and even contradicts it.

This difference becomes even more apparent when we consider the second element, the idea of a life given over entirely to virtue. For Pascal's wager, like Kant's practical postulate, is based on the idea that such a life is quite impossible. In order to be virtuous, men must wager that virtue and happiness can be linked together, for no one can genuinely choose to give up all attempts to be happy. But, for both Pascal and Kant, there is in this life a fundamental contradiction between virtue and happiness.

The idea of basing one's life solely on virtue is basically Stoical, and one which is quite natural to find either in Mother Angélique or in any thinker who had been either directly influenced by Cartesianism or indirectly affected by the semi-Cartesianism of Arnauld. It is, however, completely opposed to any tragic thought, and we know that both Kant and Pascal unequivocally rejected Stoicism in all its forms.

Thus, in my view we should not look to this letter for the deeper analogies between Jansenist thought and the Pascalian wager. We should look rather in a less obvious but equally essential direction: that of the doctrines concerning Grace and Predestination. If, in fact, fragment 233 (E.343) expresses ideas peculiar to Pascal himself, the text on Grace quoted at the beginning of this chapter reflects a position shared by the rest of the movement. This text, moreover, also implies the idea of a wager based upon the same absolute ignorance of objective reality, but an ignorance that bears not on the existence of God but on the salvation of the individual. In general, the Christian knows that there are many damned and few saved. Nevertheless, everyone should believe that he is 'of the small number of the Elect for whose sake Jesus Christ died, and should think the same of the men who live on the earth'. And since this belief should remain 'mingled with fear' and not 'accompanied by certainty', and since this fear and uncertainty stem essentially from man's awareness of the small number of the Elect and of the absence of any theoretical and objective reason for believing that we are included among them, there seems to me to be only one difference between this position and the one expressed in fragment 233: in the text on Grace we are concerned with individual salvation and in fragment 233 with the very existence of God. For Jansenism, in general, God's existence was a certainty and individual salvation a hope. The Pascalian wager extends the idea of hope to the very existence of God, and thereby becomes profoundly different from the views of Arnauld and Barcos. But this is not because Pascal escapes from Jansenism but because, on the contrary, he carries it to its logical conclusions.

I shall conclude this section by quoting a text by Barcos which illustrates the similarity between Jansenist theories on Grace and the Pascalian wager in a peculiarly appropriate manner.

> As to the men who say: 'If I am one of the Reprobate, why should I act virtuously?' I would reply as follows: 'Are you not cruel towards yourself if you destine yourself to the greatest of all evils without knowing whether God has destined you to it? He has not revealed to you His secret counsel as to your salvation or damnation. Why do you expect punishment from His justice rather than forgiveness from His Mercy? Perhaps he will accord you His grace and perhaps He will not. Why therefore do you not have as much hope as fear, instead of falling into despair about a gift which He grants to others who are just as unworthy as you? By your despair, you infallibly lose what you will probably gain if you hope. And, in your doubt as to whether you are one of the Reprobate, you conclude that you should act as if you were damned already, instead of doing what might perhaps save you from damnation. Surely this is as much against the reason which you possess as a wise man as against the faith which you hold as a Christian?' 'But,' he may reply, 'what good will good works do me if

297

I am not predestined to salvation?' My reply to him then is: 'What do you lose by obeying your creator, by loving Him, by doing His will? Or, rather, what will you not gain if you live and persevere in His love? And, even supposing that you are of the Reprobate,—an idea which I mention with horror—can you ever, in any condition, free yourself of the services which you owe to God? Does not a good and blessèd life both on earth and in heaven lie in adoring, loving and following God? Are the sufferings which you undergo by not doing His will in this world any greater than those which you will incur in the next?'[1]

IV

As we have seen, there are a number of points of resemblance between the Pascalian wager and Kant's practical postulate of God's existence, and the two theories occupy a similar place in the work of the two thinkers.

In both cases, we find the same basic presuppositions:

(1) That no legitimate theoretical arguments can be put forward to prove either the existence or the non-existence of God.

(2) That the hope of happiness is an essential and legitimate element of the human condition.

(3) That it is impossible to achieve this happiness under satisfactory conditions in this life (infinite happiness for Pascal, happiness linked with virtue for Kant) and that it is consequently both necessary and legitimate to state, on the theoretical plane but for non-theoretical reasons, that God exists.

In spite of these striking analogies, there are nevertheless genuine differences between the two thinkers. One of these is quite obvious: Pascal compares the limited happiness offered by terrestial things to the unlimited happiness promised by religion in the next life, and presents his argument as a calculation of probabilities based on the comparison between what we will win as against what we will lose. Kant, on the other hand, refuses to make any comparison of this nature, and at no time does he think of comparing the happiness of either a Stoic or an Epicurean life centred about the self with the happiness promised by religion. His ethic is quite autonomous, since he teaches that man should in any case act in such a way as to create a moral nature. However, man can do this only if he assumes that reality is such that he can legitimately hope for happiness.

This difference certainly appears considerable from the point of

[1] Martin de Barcos, *Exposition de la foi de l'Eglise romaine concernant la Grâce et la prédestination* (Cologne: P. Modren, 1760), pp. 275–6.

view of a literal analysis which sees these ideas outside the context of the philosophies of which they form part. However, if one examines the problem of the significance of the argument—that is to say, in dialectical terms, if one goes from the abstract empirical appearance to the concrete essence of the text—then this difference seems much less important.[1]

In fact, the concept of the free thinker and of the calculation of probabilities in Pascal seem to me, like the idea of a nature following universal laws in Kant, to be an accidental element linked to the historical context in which the arguments in question were put forward. When Pascal was writing the *Pensées* the calculation of probabilities and the theory of games of chance were at the centre of men's scientific interests; similarly, the idea of a nature which followed universal and unchanging laws was also fashionable when Kant was writing the *Critique of Practical Reason*. But the proof that the argument based on probability is merely an outward cloak can be found in a passage where Pascal is certainly speaking for himself and which is much closer to Kant's argument:

> Now what harm can come to you if you adopt this course? You will be faithful, honest, humble, grateful, generous, and a sincere and truthful friend. It is true that you will not taste the poisoned fruits of glory and of luxury; but will you not have other pleasures? I tell you that you stand to win in this life; and that at each step which you take upon this road you will see such overwhelming evidence of gain and so complete a nothingness in what you are risking, that you will in the end come to recognise that you have wagered on a certain and infinite thing for which you have in fact given nothing at all (fr. 233, E.343).

These lines are not, of course, exactly similar to Kant's approach, for he makes a distinction between any egotistical pleasure linked to a sensible object and the respect which we owe to the Law. It does seem to me, however, that the distinction between the two kinds of pleasure is implicit in the passage that I have just quoted; moreover, Kant argues exactly as Pascal does that one cannot separate moral action from the hope of happiness without inclining it either towards an attitude of laxity or towards one of excessive enthusiasm.

[1] In a passage of the *Critique of Pure Reason* Kant analyses the relationship between faith and the wager, but without giving any indication whether or not he has Pascal in mind. He considers the wager to be the touchstone of 'doctrinal faith', and the logical conclusion at which reason arrives on a theoretical plane. However, he refuses, in the name of the autonomy and absolute necessity of the moral law, to extend the wager to the practical plane.

In so far as it expresses both the similarity and the difference between the two thinkers, this passage seems to me to present a very great interest and to deserve further study. It can be found on pp. 534–7 of Volume IV of the German Academy edition, and on pp. 648–651, (A824–830. B852–858) of Kemp–Smith's translation.

Thus, both Pascal's admirers and enemies, who have seen the wager either as an argument aimed at beating the free thinker on his own ground or as a cunning manoeuvre destined to enable Pascal to defend the position which best suited him personally, have missed the point of one of the most important texts in the history of philosophy.

We can neglect its personal or apologetic intention and concentrate on the two factors which give it this great importance in the history of philosophy: the first of the two ideas which it expresses—that man must wager—is fundamental to the whole of dialectical thought; the second—that we must lay our bets in favour of the existence of God and the immortality of the soul—is characteristic of the tragic vision of the world.

Thus, both rationalists and empiricists attribute no importance at all to the wager. If the highest value to which man can aspire consists of thinking clearly and obeying reasonable laws, then the achievement of values depends upon man and man alone, and on the strength or weakness of his own mind and reason. The self is at the very centre of rationalistic thought. *Ego Cogito* wrote Descartes, and faced with Fichtean self the external world loses all ontological reality. (Pascal, on the other hand, wrote that: 'The self is hateful.') The very idea of help coming to man from outside himself would be contradictory to any rationalistic ethic, for it is precisely in so far as they need external help that the thought and will of an individual are inadequate and fail to come up to the ideal.

Similarly, if it is merely a question of yielding to the invitations of the senses the situation is, in spite of its apparent difference, in reality analogous to the one I have just described. For here likewise the individual is sufficient unto himself. He can work out the advantages and disadvantages of a particular way of behaving, and has no need of any outside help or of any wager.

In the case of dialectical thought, on the other hand, the situation is completely different. The supreme value now lies in an objective and external ideal which man must bring into being, but whose creation no longer depends solely on the thought and will of the individual: infinite happiness for Pascal, the union of virtue and happiness in the Supreme Good for Kant, liberty for Hegel, the classless society for Marx.

Certainly, these different forms of the Sovereign Good are not independent of individual action, for this can help man to reach and achieve them. But the question of whether or not he succeeds goes beyond the individual and depends upon a number of other factors that can either help or hinder his efforts. Consequently, the efficiency or objective meaning of any individual action escapes its author and depends upon factors which, if not foreign to him, at least lie outside himself.

Thus, with Pascal, three elements essential to any action make their way into philosophy, and consequently into the whole of human existence: the elements of risk, of the danger of failure and of the hope of success. However great the will power or intelligence of any individual may be, it is impossible to understand the human condition in its concrete reality without taking these three elements into account.

This explains why, once practical philosophy is no longer centred around an ideal of individual wisdom but comes to deal primarily with external reality, man's life takes on the aspect of a wager on the success of his own action and, consequently, on the existence of a force which transcends the individual. This force must accompany or contribute to the efforts which the individual makes, so that his life becomes a wager that God, Humanity or the Proletariat exists and will triumph.

Thus, the idea of a wager not only occupies a central position in Jansenist thought (wager on individual salvation) or in Pascal's ideas (wager that God exists) or in Kant's philosophy (wager on the practical postulate that God exists and that the soul is immortal). It is also at the very heart of dialectical and materialistic thought under the form of the wager that, in the alternative facing humanity of a choice between socialism and barbarity, socialism will triumph. We also find it expressed quite openly in the most important literary work that expresses the dialectical vision: Goethe's *Faust*.

One could almost analyse the relationship between the tragic and dialectical visions by comparing the wagers of Pascal and Faust in order to bring out their similarities and differences.

Thus, in both Pascal and Goethe the problem presents itself on two levels, that of the divine mind, which in his complete ignorance of the designs of Providence is entirely unknown to man, and that of the human mind.

Similarly, what escapes the individual, what God alone can know, is whether a particular man is damned or saved. On the other hand, on the plane of the individual mind life presents itself both for Goethe and for Pascal as a wager based on the fact that, unless he is to lose his soul, man can never be satisfied with a good that is purely finite.

The differences, which are at least as great as the similarities, lie in the different rôle attributed to the Devil. For if in Pascal and Kant goodness remains the opposite of evil (while, and herein lies the essence of tragedy, remaining inseparable from it) in Goethe, as in Hegel and Marx, evil becomes the only path that leads to goodness.

God can save Faust only by handing him over to Mephistopheles

301

PASCAL

for the whole of his earthly life. Divine Grace thus becomes, as Grace,
a wager which God (who, of course, knows that He will win) makes
against the Devil, and the human wager—while still remaining a
wager—becomes a pact with the Devil.

We can thus see the whole importance and meaning of the Pascalian wager. Far from merely stating that it is reasonable to chance the
certain and finite goods of this world against the possibility of gaining
a happiness which is doubly infinite both in intensity and duration
(this being merely the external aspect of the argument, aimed at
allowing the interlocutor to become conscious of the human condition even on the plane farthest removed from faith), this wager states
that the finite goods of this world have no value at all, and that the
only human life which has real meaning is that of a reasonable being
who seeks God. (And this whether or not he is happy or miserable
because he does or does not find Him, which is nevertheless something that he cannot discover until after his death.) The only life
which has any real meaning is that of the being who places all his
goods on the wager that God exists and that He will help him and
who shows this by devoting his life to realising a value—that of
infinite happiness—which does not depend upon his own strength
and of whose final creation he has no certain proof.

From Hegel and Marx onwards, both the finite goods and even
the evil of terrestial life—Goethe's Devil—will receive a meaning
inside the framework of faith and of hope in the future.

But however important these differences may be, the idea that man
is 'embarked' and that he must wager becomes, after Pascal, the
central idea in any philosophical system which recognises that man is
not a self-sufficient and isolated monad but a partial element inside a
whole which transcends him and to which he is linked by his
aspirations, his actions and his faith. It is the central idea of any concept which realises that man can never achieve any authentic values
by his own efforts, and that he always needs some supra-individual
help on whose existence he must wager, for he can life and act only
in the hope of a final success in which he must believe.

Risk, possibility of failure, hope of success and the synthesis of
these three in the form of a faith which is a wager are the essential
constituent elements in the human condition. It is certainly not the
least of Pascal's titles to glory that he was the first man to bring them
explicitly into the history of philosophical thought.

I will add in conclusion that these elements are only another aspect
of the two tripartite divisions (those who are called, the Elect and the
Reprobate; the men who seek God, the men who do not seek Him
and the men who find Him) whose importance in Pascal's thought I
have already emphasised.

302

XVI
THE CHRISTIAN RELIGION

THE two concepts of generalised paradox and of a refusal of the world from within the world have enabled us to understand both Pascal's behaviour in the last five years of his life and the place of the wager in the philosophical system of the *Pensées*.

I shall not here concern myself with the numerous fragments that deal with the positive proofs which Pascal found for the truth of the Christian religion. The ideas of the fulfilment of prophecies, of the genuine nature of miracles, of the continuity of the Christian tradition, of the style of the Gospels are still very important for any complete understanding of Pascal's work, but are no longer of any great relevance today. The problem which these texts set for the historian is not peculiar to the study of Pascal, but concerns all forms of tragic and dialectical thought (Kant, Hegel, Marx, Lukàcs, etc.): that of discovering to what extent someone who has, independently of any theoretical considerations, made an act of faith in the present or future existence of certain values can also, without being inconsistent, make the effort to discover the largest possible number of arguments which, though not finally decisive, do nevertheless contribute towards proving the validity of this faith on theoretical grounds. And, moreover, of discovering whether the act of faith demands such an effort, once it is accepted that both the present existence and the future creation of such values cannot in fact be proved in any absolutely certain manner on the theoretical plane.

There is, in fact, very little difference between the argument that Pascal obviously did not 'wager' himself, since he several times mentions the proofs of the Christian religion, and the criticism that Marx 'contradicts himself' when he says that socialism will inevitably be produced by the movement of history while at the same time urging men to fight in order to bring it into being. Both criticisms stem from a complete failure, on the part of the rationalist or empiricist thinkers who radically distinguish fact from value judgments, to understand the dialectical nature of human reality.

303

In fact, the action of wagering the whole of one's fortune or possessions on the present or future existence of certain values means committing oneself to do everything possible to bring them into being. One can do this in order to strengthen one's faith, just as long, naturally, as one does not spoil the true nature of this faith by giving up the demand for absolute truth and as long as one rejects any conscious or half-conscious illusions on this subject. And the quest for probable, though not absolutely definitive, reasons in favour of the future creation of certain values forms an integral part of that commitment of one's whole life to a cause which truly constitutes the wager.

I must add that once the wager is seen as legitimate (since no theoretical argument can ever definitively prove its absurdity) and once it has been seen to be necessary (for practical reasons, for reasons of the heart), then it can no longer be shaken by any purely theoretical difficulty. As Pascal himself remarks in fragment 224 (E.353): 'How I hate these stupidities, not believing in the Eucharist etc. If the Gospel is true, if Jesus Christ is God, what difficulty is there in this particular point of faith?'

Thus, the wager based on the impossibility of conceiving the existence of any finally decisive and compelling argument for or against the present or future existence of values gives central importance to all the probable arguments in favour of this present or future existence and deprives any probable arguments against any of practical importance.

Once this point has been cleared up, however, another difficulty arises. My sketch of Pascal's vision of reality has shown why it leads inevitably to the wager that God exists. But we still have to ask why this God should be the Christian God rather than the God of the deists or that of any other religious group.

From a purely psychological point of view, it would naturally be very difficult to say exactly what influence the fact that Pascal lived in seventeenth-century France had on his thought. However, I do not think that this is the really important point, since Pascal was too rigorous and exact a thinker to accept the ideology of the society in which he lived in a purely passive manner. On the contrary, he is very mistrustful of this ideology, especially since he himself had far too great a realisation of both the power and the falsity of custom ever to be taken in on such an important point.

Thus, the Christianity of the society in which he lived was important for him merely for its suggestive value, for the way in which it led him to give particular attention to a solution that he would not, however, have accepted if he had not found it valid in itself and if it had not been demanded by the internal consistency of his ideas.

He tells us all this himself, and we can accept everything he says with complete confidence:

> Whatever may be said, it must be admitted that there is something amazing about the Christian religion: 'That is because you were born in it', they may say. Far from it: I harden myself against it for that very reason, in case this prejudice leads me into error; but although I was born in it, I still continue to find it marvellous (fr. 615, E.429).

Pascal thus found in Christianity a collection of specific facts which give it the unique position of being able to satisfy all man's needs and which therefore make it true.

It is, of course, possible that in order to reach this result he had to modify somewhat the Christianity of his country and of his own particular environment. It is also possible that by the very fact of doing this he also discovered a Christianity that was more authentic and closer to that of its Founder than the Christianity of his time. I shall not venture to give judgment upon this point, since only a specialist in the general history of religions could hope to be competent in such matters. I shall instead concentrate on one problem: What place did Christianity occupy in Pascal's thought as a whole? In studying it, I shall be obliged to present separately a number of related arguments which, in fact, present the same truth seen from a number of different angles.

For Pascal, Christianity is true because, being made up of a number of paradoxical and apparently absurd statements, it is the only religion which explains the paradoxical and apparently incomprehensible nature of the human condition.[1]

> Original sin is foolishness in the sight of men, but it is not presented as anything else. You therefore have no grounds for reproaching me with the irrationality of this doctrine, since I put it forward as devoid of reason. But this folly is wiser than all the wisdom of man, *sapientius est hominibus*. For without it how could we ever say what man is? His whole state depends on this one imperceptible point. And how could he have become aware of it by reason, since it is something which goes against reason and that his own reason, far from inventing it by its own methods, recoils when presented with it? (fr. 445, E.323).

The reasons that make Christianity true are not the rational and positive proofs that can be used to support it, such as the existence of prophecies, miracles, figurative statements, continuity of tradition and so on. What makes it true is, on the contrary, the paradoxical and apparently unreasonable nature of its teaching.

---

[1] Cf. fragment 588 (E.469), in which Pascal insists that Christianity is both 'wise and foolish'.

This religion, although so great in holy, pure and irreproachable miracles; in martyrs; in established kings (David); Isaiah, prince of the blood; and so great in knowledge nevertheless rejects all this and says that it stands neither by wisdom nor signs but by the Cross and folly.

For those who have deserved your belief by these signs and wisdom, and who have proved their character to you, declare that nothing contained in any of this can change us and make us capable of knowing and loving God save only the virtue of the Folly of the Cross, without wisdom or signs; and that without this virtue the signs avail nothing. Thus our religion is folly in respect of the efficient cause, and wise when we consider the wisdom which leads up to it (fr. 587, E.568).

It would be wrong to think that man could be satisfied with a religion that showed him only the greatness of God—or which even gave first place to this greatness—or which promised him sensible happiness. To think this would be the false and one-sided illusion of the rationalists or Epicureans. Man, who is 'neither beast nor angel', would not know what to do with a wholly 'angelic' religion or with one that promised him merely crude and sensual pleasures:

> The God of the Christians is not simply the God who is author of geometrical truths or of the order of the elements; this is the view of the pagans and Epicureans. He is not solely a God who exercises His Providence over the lives and fortunes of men, in order to bestow long life upon those who worship him; for this is the view of the Jews (fr. 556, E.17).

Similarly, the many who think that Christianity insists on the greatness of God are completely and absolutely wrong about its true nature:

> They take it upon themselves to blaspheme against the Christian religion because they have an inadequate knowledge of it. They imagine that it consists solely of worshipping a God who is looked upon as great, powerful and eternal, and this is in fact deism, which is almost as far removed from Christianity as atheism, its complete opposite (fr. 556, E.17).

In reality, Christianity is true because it asks us to believe in the existence of a paradoxical and contradictory God, and one whose nature corresponds exactly to everything which we know about man's nature and his hopes: a God who became man, a God who was crucified, and a God who is a mediator:

> All those who seek God apart from Jesus Christ, confining themselves to nature where they find no light to satisfy them and where they manage to know God and serve Him without a mediator, are led to fall into atheism or deism, which are two beliefs which the Christian religion detests almost equally.

This is why I shall not here undertake to prove by natural reasons either the existence of God or the doctrine of the Trinity, or the immortality of the soul, or anything at all of that kind; not only because I should not feel that I had enough strength to find arguments in nature likely to convince a hardened atheist, but also because such knowledge, separated from Christ Jesus, is useless and sterile. Though a man were to be convinced that numerical proportions are eternal and immaterial truths that depend on a first truth in which they have their being, and which is called God, I should not consider that he had made much progress in his path towards salvation. . . .

If the world existed to reveal God to man, His divinity would everywhere shine forth in an absolutely incontestable manner; but as it exists only through and for Jesus Christ, to reveal to men both their corruption and their redemption, everything stands out as overwhelming proof of these two truths (fr. 556, E.17).

Thus, Christianity, the religion of the God who was made man, of the God who was crucified and who is a mediator, is the only religion whose teaching can have an authentic meaning for a paradoxical being such as man, who is both great and small, strong and weak, an angel and a beast. For such a being, any true and significant message must be paradoxical, so that only Christianity, by the paradoxical nature of each of its dogmas, can explain the contradictory and paradoxical character of human reality.[1]

But this is only a stage in Pascal's argument. If we want another, equally important aspect of Christianity we shall find it in the fact that it is the only religion which enables man to achieve his true aspirations: the union of opposites, the immortality of the body as well as that of the soul, and their reunion in the incarnation.

Man would have no use for a religion that promised him merely physical or merely spiritual happiness. For, even if there is no possible link between him and God or between him and Jesus Christ the righteous, his faith in the paradoxical God who was crucified and who became sin, delivers him as of now from the chains of spiritual slavery; spiritual greatness can thus be neither promise nor hope. It is what faith gives the unbeliever from this very moment; or, as fragment 233 puts it, what 'he gains in this life' and which is precisely characterised—from the human point of view—by its inadequacy.

Thus, what Christ offers in eternity to Pascal and to the believer is the complement to their spiritual liberty and greatness, and what these need to become wholly authentic: bodily immortality, the true healing which gives immortality not only to the soul but also to the body.

[1] Cf. fragment 862 (E.455), where Pascal quotes Ecclesiastes iii. 1–8 to insist upon the dual nature of the Christian teaching.

Christianity is thus the only true religion, from among all the other religions upon earth, because it is the only religion which means anything when placed by the side of the authentic needs and aspirations of a man who is conscious of his condition, his possibilities and his limitations, of the man who 'goes beyond man' because he is truly human. It is the only religion which explains the paradoxical and double nature of man and of the world, the only one which promises the creation of authentic values, and of the totality which is a re-union of opposites. And, finally, to resume and synthesise all these reasons, Christianity is the only religion which not only fully and consistently recognises the ambiguous and contradictory nature of all reality but which also makes this characteristic into an element of God's plan for this earth. For it transforms ambiguity into paradox, and makes human life cease to be an absurd adventure and become instead a valid and necessary stage in the only path leading to good-. ness and truth.

One could certainly show today that the historical wager on the future existence of the human community (in socialism) also possesses all these qualities; that, like Pascal's Christianity, it is incarnation, the joining up of opposites, and the fitting of ambiguity into a pattern which makes it clear and meaningful.

But Pascal lived in France in the seventeenth century. For him, there was therefore no question of a historical dialect. Indeed, tragic vision knows only one perspective: the wager on the existence of a God who is a synthesis of opposites, and who makes the ambiguous existence of man into a meaningful paradox. This wager assumes the existence of a religion which is not only wisdom but wisdom precisely because of its folly, which is not only clear and obvious but clear because of its very obscurity and true because it is contradictory. Pascal would have had every justification for saying to himself that even the most knowledgable and critical mind would not, in the seventeenth century, have been able to find such a religion anywhere except in Christianity.

Subsequently Hegel, and especially Marx and Lukàcs, have been able to substitute for the wager on the paradoxical and mediatory God of Christianity the wager on a historical future and on the human community. In doing so, however, they have not given up the main demands of tragic thought, that is to say a doctrine which explains the paradoxical nature of human reality, and a hope in the eventual creation of values which endows this contradiction with meaning and which transforms ambiguity into a necessary element of a significant whole. In my opinion this is one of the best indications which we have of the existence, not only of a continuity in what I would call 'classical thought' from Greek times to our own day but also of a more particular continuity in modern classical thought, within whose framework the tragic vision of Pascal and Kant constitutes an essential stage in the movement which goes beyond sceptical or dogmatic rationalism towards the birth and elaboration of dialectical philosophy.

PART FOUR

Racine

XVII

TRAGIC VISION IN RACINE'S THEATRE

I HAVE now completed the study of the tragic vision in the *Pensées*, and it would be as well, before venturing into the entirely new field of purely literary works, if I were to define further the aims and limitations of this book.

What, in fact, can this concept of a 'world vision' contribute to the study of literature as such? While it obviously cannot replace either textual analysis, general aesthetic appreciation or historical research, it does nevertheless seem to me that it can contribute greatly to our understanding of literature. The sociological and historical method which uses the idea of 'world vision' is, of course, still in its infancy, and it would be unfair to ask it to produce results comparable to those achieved by methods which have been in use for a very long time. I shall try to show what it can offer by using it to study texts as well known as the nine plays written by Racine between the performance of *Andromaque* in 1667 and that of *Athalie* in 1691.

Before doing so, however, I should perhaps briefly explain my method, while at the same time pointing out that any reader interested will find it more fully expressed in my other works.

For me, literature, art, philosophy and, to a great extent, the practice of a religion are essentially languages, means whereby man communicates with other beings, and who may be either his contemporaries, his future readers, God, or purely imaginary readers. However, these languages constitute only a small and limited group chosen from among the many other forms of communication and expression open to man. One of the first questions that we must therefore ask is this: what is the characteristic peculiar to such languages? Although this is obviously to be found first and foremost in their actual form, it must be added that one cannot express just anything at all in the language of art, literature or philosophy.

313

These 'languages' are reserved for the expression and communication of certain particular contents. My initial hypothesis, which can be justified only by examples of concrete analysis, is that these contents are in fact *world visions*.

If this is true, then there are a number of important consequences to be drawn as far as the study of a literary work is concerned. No one would deny that such a work is the expression of the ideas or intuitions of the individual who created it. One could thus, in theory, discover how an author wrote his books and what they mean by studying his personality. Unfortunately, as I have already said, the nature of our present scientific knowledge of psychology is such that we cannot study an individual in an exact and rigorously scientific manner. Moreover, the literary historian has to deal with a man who has been dead for a long time, and about whom any incidental information which he may obtain—in addition to the author's actual works—will also be drawn from people long since dead.

Thus, even the most careful and painstaking of historians can reach only a very approximate reconstruction of the author he is studying. Certainly, there are occasions when an exceptional psychological flair, an accidental inspiration or simply a lucky chance may enable him to seize certain factors in the personality of an author which are genuinely important for an understanding of his work. But even in this exceptional case it would be very difficult to find a precise criterion that would enable us to separate genuinely valid analyses from those which are merely clever or suggestive.

We can, of course, always turn from the difficulties of a biographical and psychological study and concentrate on a phenomenological study of the work itself. This, moreover, has the advantage of having, in the actual text, a criterion which enables us to reject purely arbitrary hypotheses.

It is, however, important to note that, thanks to the added precision given to the notion of world vision by the methods of historical study, we do have, in addition to the actual text, a conceptual instrument of research that allows us to approach literary works in a new way and greatly helps us in understanding their structure and meaning. One reservation, however, should be made: this method of approaching a work through the world vision that it expresses is valid only for the great works of the past. I must now defend this reservation.

A world vision is, in fact, the conceptual extrapolation in the most coherent possible manner of the real, emotional, intellectual and even motory tendencies of the members of a group. It is a coherent pattern of problems and replies which is expressed, on the literary plane, by the creation through words of a concrete universe of beings

314

and things. My hypothesis is that the aesthetic fact consists of two levels of necessary correspondence:

(1) the correspondence between the world vision as an experienced reality and the universe created by the writer; and

(2) the correspondence between this universe and the specifically literary devices—style, images, syntax, etc.—used by the writer to express it.

Now, if my hypothesis is correct, all valid literary works have an inner coherence and express a world vision; most other writings, whether published or not, are incapable—precisely because of their lack of such coherence—of expressing either a true universe or of finding a rigorous and unified literary genre.

Every text is, doubtless, the expression of one aspect of an individual psychological life, but, as I have already said, it is not possible to analyse any individual in a thoroughly scientific manner. Only the exceptional individual, who identifies himself to a very great extent with certain fundamental tendencies of the social life of his time— and who, on one of the many planes of expression open to man, achieves a coherent awareness of what, among the other members of his group, remains vague and confused, and contradicted by innumerable other tendencies—only such a man, only the creator of a valid work, can be understood by the sociological historian. And the reason for this is that if the sociologist can extrapolate the maximum possible consciousness of a group until this consciousness reaches its highest limit of coherence it is precisely this coherent vision which constitutes the content of the work and thereby the first necessary condition—though by no means always an adequate one—for the existence of either artistic or literary aesthetic values.

This comes down to saying that the mass of texts which have only an average or an inferior value are, at the same time, difficult to analyse by the sociological historian or the aesthetician; and this precisely because they are the expression of particularly complex average individuals who are, above all, not very typical representative members of their group.

My second restriction, that this method can be applied only to works of the past, is a statement of fact and not of principle. Obviously, it is not impossible to bring out the main tendencies which characterise modern society, to extrapolate the world visions which correspond to them and to look for literary, artistic or philosophical works which express them adequately. This is, however, an extremely complex task, but one which, as far as the works of the past are concerned, society carries out for itself.

For if the social factors which determine the success of a book immediately after its publication, during the author's lifetime and for a few years after his death, are both highly numerous and largely accidental (fashion, advertisement, social situation of the author, influence of certain highly placed individuals, such as Louis XIV, for example), these all eventually disappear, and leave only one factor. This continues to act more or less indefinitely, although it can and does vary very greatly in intensity: it is the fact that, in certain works of the past, men rediscover what they themselves think and feel in a confused and obscure manner today. That is to say, in the case of literary works, that they find characters and relationships which together express their own aspirations with a greater degree of awareness and coherence than they themselves have so far attained. If my hypothesis is correct it is precisely this criterion of literary value that can be legitimately approached by a historico-sociological analysis.

What, however, is the contribution which the historico-sociological method can make to the study of literary works? After what I have said, the answer seems fairly clear: it can, by first of all bringing out the different world visions that prevailed at a particular time, throw light upon both the content and the meaning of the literary works that were then being written. The task of what one might call a 'sociological aesthetic' would then be to bring out the relationship between one of the world visions and the universe of characters and things created in a particular work. That of the more literary aesthetic would be to bring out the relationship between this universe and the specifically literary devises used by the writer to express it.

Obviously, these analyses would be complementary, although in the course of this book I am myself almost always using the first of these two aesthetic levels, that of the relationship between a world vision and the universe created by a writer. I shall only treat the second level, that of the relationship between this universe and the literary devices used to express it, in a fairly superficial manner.

The fundamental ideas characterising the tragic vision which I have brought out in this first part of this book enable us to consider the problem of time in Racinian tragedy, and thus, implicitly, the problem of the three unities. In fact, this rule seems to have been adopted in France as early as the sixteenth century by theoreticians such as Scaliger and Jean de la Taille, but for many writers—Corneille is the most famous—these rules still seemed far too restrictive. For Racine, on the other hand, they became an inner necessity of his work. This is a frequent phenomenon in the history of art and one whose workings we must one day try to understand: the instrument by which the world vision is expressed is in being before either the vision itself or the writers who could be capable of making a real use of it. However this may have happened, Racine does seem to have found, in the rule of the three unities, an instrument that was peculiarly adapted to his own theatrical style. What in fact happens is that the action of all his tragedies from *Andromaque* to *Phèdre*, takes place in a single instant: that one moment when man becomes fully tragic by refusing the world and life. One line in particular is spoken by all Racine's tragic heroes, a line which tells us when the relationship between the hero and the object which he still loves in the world is established 'for the last time'. And, indeed, we find Andromache going to see her son 'for the last time' (IV, 1), Junia, in *Britannicus*, expressing the fear that she may be talking to Britannicus 'for the last time' (V, 1), Titus, in *Bérénice*, saying that he is going to see the woman he loves 'for the last time' (II, 2), Berenice herself saying farewell to him 'for the last time' (V, 7) and Phaedra coming to look upon the sun, her ancestor, 'for the last time' (I, 3).

The whole of the rest of the tragedy, certainly in so far as the plays which go from *Andromaque* to *Bérénice* are concerned, is merely an exposition of the situation, and an exposition which is not of essential importance to the play. As Lukàcs remarks, once the curtain goes up on a tragedy, the future has always been present from the first moment of eternity. The die is cast, and there is no possibility of any reconciliation between man and the world.

The constituent elements of Racine's plays never vary, at least in the three genuine tragedies that he wrote: they are always God, the World and Man. It is true that the world is represented by several different characters, from Orestes, Hermione and Pyrrhus to Hippolytus, Theseus and Oenone, but what all these characters have in common is the only really important quality in a genuinely tragic perspective: they all lack authenticity, awareness and human value.

As for God, he is a Hidden God—*Deus Absconditus*—and it is for this reason that it is legitimate to say that all Racine's plays, from *Andromaque* to *Phèdre*, are profoundly Jansenistic, and this in spite of the fact that Racine had quarrelled with Port-Royal, whose members did not approve of the theatre, even when—and perhaps especially when—the plays expressed the vision of Port-Royal itself. I should also add that the reason why the Gods in Racine's tragedies are still those of classical antiquity is that, as a Christian, Racine could no longer—or could not yet—represent the Christian and Jansenist God on the stage. The same element of contemporary convention also applies to the fact that, with the exception of Titus, all his tragic characters are women. Once again, the seventeenth century would not have accepted that such overwhelming passion could form so essential a part of the humanity of a man. However, these are incidental considerations which in no way affect the essential characteristic of each of his plays. The Sun in *Phèdre* is in reality the same tragic God as the Hidden God of Pascal, in the same way as Andromache, Junia, Berenice and Phaedra are concrete incarnations of those who are 'called' and whose recognition constitutes, in Pascal's *Écrit sur la Grâce*, one of the essential criteria for distinguishing the Jansenists from the Calvinists. Or, to take another example, they are the 'righteous in whom Grace is lacking' mentioned in the first of the five propositions condemned by the Church.

Setting out from the central theme of the tragic vision, the radical opposition between, on the one hand, a world of beings lacking in authentic awareness and human greatness and, on the other, the tragic characters whose greatness lies precisely in the fact that they refuse this world and this life, two types of tragedy become possible: those with and those without peripeteia and recognition. The second type is again divided into two sections, that in which the world and that in which the hero is at the centre of the action.

The tragedy 'in which there is neither peripeteia nor recognition' is the one where the hero knows from the very beginning that there is no possible way in which he can fit in with a world that is empty of awareness, and against which he sets up, without the slightest hesitation of illusion, the greatness of his own refusal. *Andromaque* comes close to this type of tragedy, while *Britannicus* realises it in the first of the two forms—that in which the world is at the centre—and *Bérénice* in the second—that in which the hero is at the centre.

The other type of tragedy is the one where the hero's recognition of his fate is preceded by a fall because the tragic character still thinks, at the beginning of the play, that he can live without compromise and impose his own desires on the world. The play ends inevitably with his recognition that this was an illusion. I shall approach *Bajazet* and *Mithridate* as examples of Racine's attempt to realise a tragedy of this type; I shall study *Iphigénie* as an example of how Racine came near to it and shall interpret *Phèdre* as an example of how he finally succeeded.

I shall now study Racine's plays in their chronological order, which for once (although this is by no means always the case) is also the order of their inner logic.

A. THE TRAGEDIES OF REFUSAL

I. *Andromaque*

Before studying the play itself, I must say something about Racine's prefaces. For the sociologist, they are, of course, texts of a completely different nature from his plays. The plays represent a world of beings, objects and relationships which must be analysed from the point of view of their structure and meaning; the prefaces, on the other hand, merely express the writer's own ideas and his attitude towards his work. And although they are extremely interesting and cannot in any way be ignored, there is no real reason why what they say should be absolutely correct, or why Racine should have understood the meaning and objective structure of his own works. There is nothing absurd about the idea of a writer or poet who does not understand the objective meaning of his work. Conceptual thought and literary creation are two completely different intellectual activities, which can, of course, be combined in one person, but which by no means are necessarily found together.[1] However, even when this does not happen, the theoretical writings of an author are very important for any study of his work, for even though they may not bring out his objective meaning, they do nevertheless reflect many of the problems which he had to face while he was actually writing. However, in this case we must read them not in order to discover reliable theoretical information, but particular symptoms. We must not only understand them, but also interpret them in the light of the completed work. In doing so, we shall take account of Racine the individual only in so far as he is the author of aesthetically valid plays, for the rest of his personality remains foreign to this type of investigation.

We should note that, adopting Aristotle's opinion, Racine maintains in the preface to both *Andromaque* and *Phèdre* that tragic characters, that is to say 'those whose misfortune constitutes the tragic catastrophe' are 'neither wholly good nor wholly evil'. It is a formula which did apply to many Greek tragedies, and which is still partially applicable to *Andromaque*; it is not, however, a valid description either of Junia or Titus, both of whom are wholly good, or of Phaedra, whose only real characteristic is that she is 'wholly good and wholly evil at one and the same time'. From the point of view of Racinian tragedy, the expression 'neither wholly good nor wholly evil' also applies to the majority of the inhabitants of this world; and it is this qualitative distinction between tragic man and the man who lives in this world, a distinction peculiar to modern tragedy, which differentiates it from the tragedy of classical Greece. As far as dramatic technique is concerned, this difference can be seen in the fact that the chorus is as indispensable to a classical tragedy as it is inconceivable in a play by Racine. I shall come back to this point when I discuss *Britannicus*, and it goes without saying that I reserve judgment on the problem of *Esther* and *Athalie*.

---

[1] In a letter to the abbé Le Vasseur, Racine himself points out that this difference exists when he writes that: 'Poets are like hypocrites in this, that they always defend what they do, but are never left in peace by their own conscience.' Letter dating from 1659 or 1660. Cf. *Œuvres*, Mesnard edition, Vol. VI, p. 372.

In his views on his own characters, Racine contradicts himself in the two prefaces which he wrote for *Andromaque*. Thus, in 1668 he justifies his presentation of Pyrrhus as a violent man by the argument that 'violence was a natural part of his character' and that he, Racine, does not want to alter the character of his classical heroes. However, in 1676 he says that he has 'respected the idea that we have of that Princess' by making Andromache faithful to Hector. We can conclude from this that he followed the laws of his own universe by expanding the moral grandeur of Andromache in order to emphasise the radical difference between her and Pyrrhus.

In this play only two characters are really present: the world and Andromache. There is, however, one other character who is both absent and present at one and the same time, the God whose two irreconcilable faces are incarnated by Hector and Astyanax, and by the contradictory and therefore impossible demands which they both make.

It is obvious that Hector already foreshadows the God of *Britannicus* and *Phèdre*, but without, however, coinciding with him completely. For *Andromaque* is still a drama, in spite of its great closeness to tragedy.

The world is represented by three psychologically different characters, for Racine creates beings who are alive and vividly individualised, but who are nevertheless morally identical by their absence of awareness and human greatness. Thus, the differences between Pyrrhus, on the one hand, and Orestes and Hermione, on the other, exists only for the spectator who adopts an attitude of psychological analysis which is external to the work. What characterises tragedy and provides its real perspective is a primacy accorded to ethics, and to an ethical system which does not admit degrees of difference. People either have authentic awareness or else they lack it completely, in exactly the same way as Pascal's God is both present and absent, unreachable and even unapproachable through any spirituality or any paths of gradualness or degree.

The basic pattern of the play is that of any Racinian tragedy. Andromache is faced with a choice between two alternatives— faithfulness to Hector, life for Astyanax—which are both equally essential for her moral and human universe. This is why her final choice can only be death, for only death can save both of these antagonistic but, at the same time, inseparable values.

Yet in spite of the fact that she is the only human character in the play, Andromache is not the central one. She is on the periphery of the real centre of the play, which is the world. Or, in more concrete terms, the world made up of the wild animals inhabiting a universe of love and passion.

It would, however, be wrong to draw a rigorous distinction between the passion which characterises Pyrrhus, Orestes and Hermione, and which is lacking in both greatness and self-awareness, from the other domains of life. Throughout the play, the background of war, barbarism, the murder of the vanquished and the ruins of Troy, all show us that people who are wild animals in the realm of passion are also egotists who, devoid of any genuine ethical norm, thereby fall only too easily into savagery in all life's other domains.[1] This can be seen particularly clearly in the speech where Andromache recalls the horrors of the sack of Troy, the killing of a whole people in a single, interminable night and the figure of Pyrrhus, covered with blood, his eyes gleaming in the light of the burning palaces, cutting a path for himself over her brothers' dead bodies and urging on to further slaughter; where she reminds her *confidente*, Céphise, of the screams of the conquerors and of those choked with flame or put to the edge of the sword; where she asks her to try to imagine with what horror she, her mistress Andromache, saw such horror—and then to understand how Pyrrhus must now appear before her[2] (Act III, Scene 8, ll. 997–1006).

The world of Orestes, Hermione and Pyrrhus is already that of *Britannicus*, the play in which Nero is under the power of the same amoral and unreflecting love that we find in these three characters from *Andromaque*. We find the same world in all Racine's plays, each of which differs from its fellows, from this point of view, solely by emphasising a different aspect of it.

It thus becomes an easy and almost an obvious task to analyse the speeches and actions of the characters. Both Orestes and Pyrrhus are confronted with an alternative, but neither of them has a single reaction worthy of a man who has attained authentic awareness. Although to do so would still be inadequate within the Racinian universe, they cannot even openly and deliberately choose one of the two alternatives confronting them. They go constantly from one extreme to the other, impelled not by their own decisions but by external events, and they most frequently contradict both their own statements and their own desires. Ostensibly, Orestes has come to demand Astyanax, the son of Hector whom the Greeks still fear as a possible avenger of his country's defeat; in reality, this mission is merely an unimportant pretext, a lie; the only thing that really

[1] It is not a valid objection to this argument to point out that these were normal customs for the Greeks and that our own moral judgments are therefore anachronistic. In the first place the play was written in the seventeenth century, and in the second place these judgments are expressed within the play itself, and therefore do not need to be brought in from the outside.

[2] Cf. also what Pyrrhus says in Act I, Scene 2, l. 209. 'Everything was just at that time'—i.e. at the moment of the sacking of Troy. All references to the text of Racine's plays are to the *Grands Ecrivains de France* edition (Hachette, 1929).

matters to him is his love for Hermione, and he tells us so in the very first scene, when he confides to Pylades both his intention to take Hermione away with him and his readiness to sacrifice his official mission to his private desires (Act I, Scene 1, ll. 93–4 and 100).

We are also told, in the same scene, that Pyrrhus is characterised by the complete absence of any conscious and controlling norm, and that he is quite capable of 'marrying where he hates and killing where he loves' (l. 122). The same thing is true of Hermione, whom Pylades describes as 'constantly ready to leave yet still remaining' (l. 131). Similarly, the dialogue between Pyrrhus and Orestes is also introduced in exactly the same way, with Pylades advising Orestes to 'ask insistently for everything in order to obtain nothing' (Act I, Scene 1, l. 140).

Thus, with Hermione, Orestes and Pyrrhus we are in the world of mere words and of false awareness. Words never mean what they say, and, instead of being the means whereby the speaker expresses his inner and authentic essence, they become merely instruments that he uses to deceive others and to deceive himself. This is the false and savage world of inessentiality, the world of the difference between essences and appearances.

But in Scene 4, Andromache appears and the atmosphere changes. Her arrival takes us into the world of absolute truths, the world without compromises of the tragic hero. Pyrrhus derives no advantage from the fact of being her master, the man on whom her own life and that of her son depend, for when he greets her with the hope that, for once, she has come in search of him, her reply is clear and unequivocal, uninfluenced by all the dangers he is facing. 'I was going', she tells him, 'to the place where my son is kept. Since I am allowed only once a day to see all that remains to me of Hector and of Troy, I was going to weep with him'. (Act I, Scene 4, ll. 260–4).

The clash between the two characters could not be more complete, and what follows is quite foreseeable from the very beginning. Pyrrhus—the world—tells her of Orestes's mission, the dangers which it involves for Astyanax, and offers her the possibility of a compromise. He will refuse to hand over Astyanax, but—and in the world of Pyrrhus there is always a 'but'—on one condition: that she should look 'less severely' upon the man who 'defends her son's life at the cost of danger to his own' (ll. 290–4). His initial refusal to Orestes was, for all its appearance of finality, merely a ruse intended to influence Andromache. He now asks for his reward, and it is at this point that the play, which had begun as a tragedy, starts to become a drama. Andromache's reply, although possessing at first sight the absolute veracity which characterises the tragic hero, already contains the seed of her future 'sin' or 'tragic error'. She confronts

Pyrrhus with the demands of human greatness and of human morality when she asks him if it is really his intention to defy the enmity of a hundred different peoples solely in order to defend a child, and to give back a son to his mother without demanding that his mother marry him in return. This, indeed, she suggests would be a task worthy of Achilles' son (Act I, Scene 4, ll. 296–300).

Andromache really does believe everything which she says here, and is expressing her own values and her own very essence. This is how she would act if she were in the same position as Pyrrhus. But she neither has nor can have any illusions about the possibility of making him understand what she is saying since the world of absolute truth is one which he cannot even begin to understand. Nevertheless, she pretends to be really talking to him and to be in complete good faith. There is thus, in this speech of hers to Pyrrhus, an element of irony or trickery about her words, for she is talking to a wild animal as if she were speaking to a man.

For the truly tragic character, this is indeed a 'moral error', or a 'fall from grace', but it remains extremely slight, even in the projected marriage with Pyrrhus later in the play. Andromache foreshadows Phaedra, but only in so far as she herself is not taken in by the illusion of being able to live in the world and be reconciled with it. What she is trying to gain by deceiving Pyrrhus are merely the conditions that would make her refusal of the world not merely morally great but also effective. What she wants to do is triumph materially over the world at the very moment she is crushed by it.

This is why Andromache does not finally enter into the tragic universe to which she comes so very close. The difference is certainly a very small one, but it does exist. And in the world of tragedy the slightest difference weighs as heavily as the greatest. There is not, and there cannot be, any progressive scale of values between appearances and essences or between truth and treachery.

We have, moreover, an indication that Racine himself was aware of these problems: it is the differences between the way the first tragedy ended in the 1668 edition and the ending given to it in all the editions after 1673.

The world of a literary work is a single coherent whole. If *Andromaque* were to remain a tragedy Racine would be obliged to treat Andromache, from the fourth scene of the first act, as a tragic heroine who ends as Phaedra does by recognising her error. Racine was still a long way from such a maturity, and, even if he did consider this way of presenting Andromache, we have no evidence to prove it. What he did do, however, was become aware that a tragic ending to such a situation would destroy the coherence of the rest of the work, and draw logical conclusions from this realisation. In the first, 1668, version he inserted a scene in which Hermione liberated the captive Andromache. Nevertheless, he also probably felt the inconsistency that this introduced between the irreconcilable conflict of the first three acts and the final reconciliation which it would thereby bring about between Andromache and Hermione.

This is why he modified his text and replaced this ending by the version which we now have. Although this is not tragic, it does maintain, if not the opposition between Andromache and the world, then at least the difference between her and the three other characters who represent the world in this play.

I will resume my argument: Andromache is tragic in so far as she refuses the alternatives, and confronts the world with her voluntary refusal of life and her freely accepted choice of death. She ceases to be tragic, however, when she decides to accept marriage with Pyrrhus and then kill herself, thus trying to transform her moral victory into a material victory which will live on after her. The play is thus a tragedy which, in the last two acts, suddenly becomes a drama. This is possibly the reason why Racine decided to treat the same theme for a second time in a purely and exclusively tragic perspective in *Britannicus*.

I will now continue the analysis of the text at the point at which I broke off. Naturally, Pyrrhus does not understand what Andromache is saying, and this is quite natural. He sees only that she is refusing his offer and therefore concludes that he has no further reason to protect Astyanax. He even says that this is 'just'—by the standards of this world, of course—when he proclaims that in his 'righteous indignation' he will use the son to revenge himself or the scorn shown by the mother (Act I, Scene 4, ll. 396–71).

As far as Andromache is concerned, she now rediscovers her own universe. Her reply is quite clear, and she accepts the fact that her son's death will follow naturally from the impossibility of any compromise (l. 372).

But Pyrrhus, who judges Andromache according to the laws of his own world (and he is not entirely wrong to do so), asks her to go and see Astyanax again, hoping that this will induce her to change her mind.

Act II marks the appearance of Hermione, the third character who constitutes the world. Like Pyrrhus and Orestes, she lacks real awareness and human greatness and I shall show this by analysing two aspects of her personality.

She is afraid of the truth, and would like to be deceived in order to be able to deceive herself. Indeed, in the very first scene in which we see her she is telling her *confidente* Cleone that she is 'afraid to know herself in her present state', and asking Cleone to 'believe nothing of what she sees at the present moment'; to 'believe that her love is dead, to proclaim her victory', and 'if possible, to make her believe it also' (Act II, Scene 1, ll. 428–32).

The greatness of tragic man lies in his clear and unambiguous awareness of his own condition. Those characters who represent the world, on the other hand, lack greatness precisely because they refuse to become completely aware of their situation, and are afraid to discover the definitive and inexorable nature of the position in which they are placed.

Hermione is also characterised by her desire to run away from reality, and the theme is a particularly important one, since it recurs in *Phèdre*, in the character of Hippolytus. For example, when Cleone proposes in the first scene of Act II that Hermione should reply to Pyrrhus's neglect of her by departing with Orestes, she immediately accepts—at least in principle—but only to hesitate again at the idea that Pyrrhus might come back to her. What in fact she does is to remain, but without becoming fully aware of the danger and of facing up to it. It is, indeed, precisely because she does not understand the real situation and because she allows herself to be deceived by the illusion to which her love for Pyrrhus gives rise that she in fact decides to stay.

We find this same lack of awareness and human greatness in Orestes, Pyrrhus and Hermione through the play.

Orestes gives his own description of himself as a person who always does the opposite of what he means to do when he tells Hermione, in the second scene of Act II, that his destiny is 'constantly to return to adore her, while at the time swearing that he will never come back again' (l. 484) and in Act II, Scene 5 we find exactly the same failure on the part of Pyrrhus to understand the universe in which Andromache lives. Similarly, in Act III, Scene 1 we find the same illusions occurring in Orestes, and the same refusal to accord any importance to the diplomatic mission which he had nevertheless accepted, when he tells Pylades that Hermione will still enjoy his misfortune, however much the Greeks may triumph over the death of Astyanax (l. 766).

We also find Hermione lying in the same way to Orestes, and making him think that she might love him, and still keeping the same illusions about the feeling which Pyrrhus has for her (Act III, Scene 3). She shows her cowardice, when she thinks that she has triumphed over Andromache (Act III, Scene 4); and the unchanging attitude of Pyrrhus towards Andromache reaches its highest point when, in Act III, Scene 7, he offers her in its most abolute form the alternative that the world represents for Andromache: either live or die, either live or reign, save Astyanax and save yourself at the same time (l. 960).

Cephise even finds a Pascalian-like phrase to describe Andromache's situation when, discussing the choice before her, she tells her that 'too much virtue would lead you to act as a criminal' (Act III, Scene 8, l. 982).

Andromache turns for advice to the supreme authority, to the absent being who judges everything but never replies: finally, she decides to visit Hector's tomb in order to discover what his will might be (Act III, Scene 8, l. 1048).

But the play is not a tragedy, and unlike the God of tragedy, Hector does not remain a silent and passive spectator. He intervenes in the action, as Racine indicates quite clearly when he makes Cephise tell Andromache, in the very first line of Act IV, Scene 1, that her 'miraculous' decision to marry Pyrrhus has been inspired by Hector (l. 1049).

Neither is Andromache a genuine tragic heroine. The decision which she takes on Hector's tomb is certainly a great and courageous one, since it will enable her to sacrifice herself in order to save Astyanax's life while at the same time remaining faithful to her husband. There is almost nothing in common between her sacrifice and the self-centred behaviour of Pyrrhus, Orestes and Hermione, but there is nevertheless a common element, and it is this, however slight it may be, which is sufficient to eliminate true tragedy from the play. Andromache will indulge in trickery in order to transform her death into a material victory over the world.

Her decision to do this, which is the decisive turning-point in the play, is announced in two lines, the first of which prepares us for it, while the second expresses it completely, with all the consequences that it involves. We appear, indeed, to be entering into the universe of tragedy when she tells Cephise that she will go to the temple where the wedding is to be held, but that before this he is going to see her son 'for the last time'. She then explains the solution she has found, the trick which will enable her, by killing herself immediately after becoming Pyrrhus's wife, to do her duty towards 'Pyrrhus, my son, my husband and myself' (l. 1096).

This second line would be wholly tragic if, among the people to whom she owes something, there were not Pyrrhus, a being of this world. This distance which separates her from Pyrrhus still exists, and will even continue to do so until the very end of the play; it has, however, become smaller than it was, and is contradicted by the link between her and Pyrrhus that will continue to exist after her own death.

The whole of this distance and drawing together, of this conflict and link, is expressed in a single line. Giving her instructions to Cephise on what is to be done after her death, Andromache tells her that she agrees 'if it is necessary' that her name should sometimes be mentioned to her son (l. 1118).

'If it is necessary' represents the distance, the inner opposition which Andromache feels for any contact with Pyrrhus; her 'agreement' expresses the rest. For Andromache can kill herself, not because, like Junia, Berenice and Phaedra, she has refused the world, but because, on the contrary, she is counting on the loyalty which Pyrrhus will continue to show to her after her death. In fact, she could just as well continue to live in the world, and it is even her duty to do so, since there is nothing at all in Pyrrhus's character to justify the hope which she places in him. He would be just as capable of avenging himself by handing Astyanax over to the Greeks in a fit of anger at the way Andromache has deceived him. Andromache has used trickery, and this is why she might now be tricked herself. In spite of all her moral greatness, she does, in a way, come to fit into the world. This is probably the real reason why, in order not to contradict the general atmosphere of the play, Racine makes Pyrrhus die and Andromache live on. It also explains why he maintains Andromache's moral and material greatness intact by making Pyrrhus, Hermione and Oreste either die or plunge into madness. On the material plane, Andromache's victory is certain. The last two lines of the play tell us that the only reason why Orestes is still alive is that he has gone mad. In Andromache's world—and Pylades's words at the end of the play, telling us that Andromache is now reigning as queen and observing an absolute fidelity to the memory of Pyrrhus, indicate that it is this world which has quite simply taken over from that of Pyrrhus—there can no longer be any place for a living Pyrrhus or for Hermione; neither could there be any place for an Orestes who was still capable of acting with the same ferocious absence of awareness that characterised him when, theoretically at least, he was still sane.

Was Racine himself aware that this is what happened in his play? Would he have accepted the analysis that I have just given of it? Did he, in his own life, quite simply accept the moral laws which govern the lives of Junia, Berenice and Phaedra? In fact, we simply do not know. The problem is one which only scholars, and psychologists who accept the idea of retrospective analysis, can hope to discuss. The probability is, however, that he would have rejected it. Nicole and Mother Agnès de Sainte-Thècle were even more justified than they realised in attacking Racine for writing for the theatre. For, in composing his tragedies, Racine—fortunately for posterity—was not only going against the moral principles of Jansenism but was also contradicting his own ideas. He was presenting the world with a universe where true greatness could be found only in a refusal of the world. A psychologist might perhaps conclude that, in order to write these tragedies, Racine would in fact have been obliged to know and understand Andromache, Junia, Berenice and Phaedra, but without identifying himself with their moral universe; that, in other words, he would need to have been a member of Port-Royal but to have now left it behind him. These questions are not relevant to my purpose, and I am not competent to decide them. My only reason for raising this problem is to insist upon the fact that, in order to create a coherent universe of beings and things, the writer does not need to have a conceptual knowledge of this universe, and, above all, does not need to accept it himself. Literary history is full of examples of writers whose ideas completely contradicted the meaning and structure of their work (Balzac and Goethe, for example). We must therefore conclude that the analysis of a work of art and the study of its author's ideas belong to two different domains. These, it is true, can be treated as complementary, and facts from one can be used to throw light upon facts from the other, but we must not expect our results always and necessarily to agree when we do this.

This is why the analysis which I am putting forward in this book does not claim to make any statements at all about the moral and religious views of Racine himself. It is merely an analysis of the universe of his plays, a universe which is one of the most rigorously coherent to be found in world literature.

II. *Britannicus*

Britannicus is the first of the three genuine tragedies in Racine's work. The other two are *Bérénice* and *Phèdre*, and each corresponds to one of the three ways in which a modern tragic conflict can be realised. For if a tragedy with neither peripeteia nor recognition can be written in one of two ways—by making either the world or the hero into the central character—a tragedy with peripeteia and recognition offers only one possibility: here, the world and the hero are inextricably mingled together throughout the whole of the action.

Britannicus follows the same basic pattern as *Andromaque*, being a tragedy without peripeteia or recognition with the world as central character. This time, however, there is a radical conflict which leads to absolute tragedy. Two characters occupy the stage: in the centre is the world, made up of wild beasts—Nero and Agrippina—of criminals—Narcissus—of people who do not want to see and understand reality, who try desperately to settle everything by half-conscious illusions—Burrhus—and of people who, like Britannicus, are pure and passive victims with no moral or intellectual strength. On the periphery is Junia, the tragic character, standing out against the world and rejecting the very idea of the slightest compromise.

Finally, there is the third character of any tragedy, someone who is absent and present but who is yet more real than all the others: God.

The first two lines contain a hint to the producer as to the time in which the tragedy takes place. Such hints are very rare, and are always important in Racine's plays.

Albina, Agrippina's *confidente*, discovers her mistress waiting, at dawn, in front of the emperor's door. The fact that Nero is not yet awake makes it clear that we are confronted not merely with the moment at which the curtain actually rises, but with the non-temporal instant in which the whole action of the play takes place; the moment when 'the monster is born'. As the preface explicitly states, *Britannicus* is the drama of the 'monster coming to birth' in Nero, and the action takes place at the very moment when the true Nero, who was hidden and sleeping under the man who appeared to be Nero, suddenly wakes up.

This awakening, moreover, takes place as a result of one particular event. As we discover, this is the only really important event in the tragic universe, the event which has led the wild beast to throw off his mask: the meeting between Nero and Junia. Agrippina is the only person to have seen all the implications of Nero's sudden action in having Junia abducted, and it is this which has brought her to wait outside his door for the moment when Nero will awake. A skilful politician, with an immense experience of men and events, Agrippina has long since understood the truth that Nero has hidden from everyone else. However, she has always seen this problem as a practical and not an ethical one. She has been concerned not with judging Nero or rejecting him in the name of certain ethical standards, but of maintaining her relationship towards him. Now, however, the instincts which she has as a political animal have told her that the abduction of Junia has transformed the long-standing threat to her position into an immediate one. The day is rising on a new situation, and we are confronted with the fundamental problem of this tragedy: Nero and Junia, the world and man, have met and have entered into conflict with each other.

The second scene introduced Burrhus, the virtuous politician who cannot—or, rather, who will not—understand anything about reality. He defends Nero's actions in the name of a political wisdom that does not really inspire them, and wants to believe that Nero is still virtuous because of the extreme convenience that this would present both for the external world and for the world of his own values. These, however, have only one defect: they are unreal.

The last lines of the scene barely enable us to understand that he has been defending Nero's actions simply because it is Nero who has committed them, and that, if his advice had been asked, he would have disapproved of what the emperor has done. This is the burden of his excuse to Agrippina, when she accuses him of barring her way to Nero's door, and which is essentially an attempt to deny all responsibility for what is happening.

From the very moment that he comes on to the stage, Britannicus reveals his weakness. Throughout the play, he will allow himself to be tricked and deceived by Nero and by Nero's spy Narcissus. He is someone who is crushed by the world, but who—to paraphrase Pascal's famous remark—never realises this, while the world, on the other hand, knows perfectly well what is happening. It is, in this respect, particularly significant to remark that right until the very moment of his death he sticks quite scrupulously to his promise to believe only what Narcissus tells him (ll. 341–2).

There is nothing to be said from a moral point of view about the values, or rather the absence of values, which characterises Nero, Agrippina and Narcissus. Finally, it is not until the second Act that we see Junia, since Racine brings all the people who represent the world on to the stage before he allows the tragic character to appear.

As soon as Junia comes on to the stage, we see the opposition between her and Nero,[1] for Racine carefully indicates the change in her expression when she finds herself confronted with the Emperor and not with Octavia, whom she had been looking for (Act II, Scene 3). The very first words that she says—'I cannot hide' (l. 529) define her whole character, (l. 530) and later in the same scene she naïvely confesses her love for Britannicus, pointing out to Nero as she does so that she has never lived at the Court and is consequently unused to disguising her feelings (l. 639).

The dialogue that follows in Scene 6, between Junia and Britannicus, is one of Racine's masterpieces. The God of tragedy, hidden behind the world, has his constant enemy in the Devil, the monster hidden behind walls, and who, like God, watches over Junia's actions, words and very glances. Britannicus, so very easily taken in by all the worldly characters who trick and deceive him, is suspicious as soon as he is in the presence of someone who is completely sincere and authentic, and mistrusts Junia when she does everything within her power to make him understand the real situation and make him realise that their every word and gesture are being noted down by Narcissus.

Racine needs only half a line at the beginning of the next scene to bring out the unresolvable conflict and opposition between Junia and Nero, for the moment he begins to speak to her she replies with the simplest of 'No's' (l. 744).

[1] It may be noted that Andromache comes on stage in an exactly similar manner, is greeted by Pyrrhus with the hope she is going to see him and replies that she is on her way to see her son (Act I, Scene 4, ll. 259–64).

From then onwards, the play follows its course. In the great scene between Nero and Britannicus the latter finally seems to behave like a man and stand up to Nero. But Junia, who almost always sees things as they really are, feels that Britannicus is not strong enough to fight successfully against Nero, and suggests, in order to avoid her lover's murder, that she should leave the world and seek refuge with the Gods. And, in my view, it is because Junia is here looking upon the idea of becoming one of the Vestal Virgins as a means of attaining both for herself and Britannicus some kind of temporal salvation —an escape from Nero—that she describes the flight from the world that such a decision would involve as an act likely to 'be importunate to the Gods' (Act III, Scene 8, l. 1078).

After the magnificent scene depicting the meeting between the two wild animals, Nero and Agrippina (Act IV, Scene 3), we are ready for the decisive moment of the play.

Nero has decided to have Britannicus poisoned, and therefore summons him to his presence under the pretence of holding a banquet to celebrate their reconciliation. Britannicus does not call Nero's sincerity into doubt for a single moment, but Junia is not taken in by it. As we see in the first scene of Act V, he rejects all her attempts to warn him of the danger, and the contrast between the two lovers is here most marked. Junia has been at the Court only since that morning, but she has already understood the way of the world. Britannicus, who has lived there for years, is just as easily taken in as he was at the beginning. In response to Junia's insistence on the universality of the deceit which surrounds them, he repeats that Nero is sincere, and that he, Britannicus, is certain of it because Narcissus has described the Emperor's remorse to him. He rejects her suggestion that Narcissus may be a traitor, and can only offer, in reply to Junia's suggestion that she may be speaking to him 'for the last time', a list of all the external signs of Nero's sincerity. He is ready to believe anybody at all except Junia, and in spite of all her efforts, he goes off happy and contented to the banquet where he will be murdered.

If Britannicus were the central character of the play, and if what happens to him were its real subject, then the action would end with his death. We can see that there were critics in Racine's day who thought that this was the case, since he took the trouble of replying to them in both the prefaces which he wrote for the play. 'They say that all this is unnecessary,' he remarks in his preface to the original edition of 1670, 'that the play ends with the description of Britannicus's death and that we should therefore not listen to the rest. People nevertheless do listen to it, and pay it just as much attention as they do to the rest of the tragedy.'

331

As usual, the reason that Racine gives when writing as a theoretician is inadequate, but his instinct as a poet is infallible. For in the play itself Britannicus is only one of a number of people who represent the world; his death is simply an episode whose only real importance is to bring about the final *dénouement*.

The real subject of *Britannicus* is the conflict between Junia and the world, and the play can end only when this conflict has been resolved. This is why Racine, who had himself quite willingly changed the first version of the ending of *Andromaque*, never accepted, and probably never seriously considered, the possibility of changing a scene which was not only extremely important and organically linked to the rest of the play but which also constituted the real ending of the tragedy.

However, this does not solve all the problems connected with the end of the play. Even when we accept the fact that Junia is the principal character, and that the play can therefore end only when her destiny has been decided, the fact remains that she does not meet the same fate as the three other Racinian heroes, Titus, Berenice and Phaedra, who are crushed by a universe which does not know that it is destroying them. Junia, in fact, finds refuge as one of the Vestal Virgins. How, in the universe of the play, can we justify this ending, and what meaning should we attribute to it?

Racine himself felt the need to explain this ending.

I make her become one of the Vestal Virgins [he wrote in his second preface to the play in 1676] in spite of the fact that, according to Aulus Gellus, only maidens of between six and ten years of age were received amongst them. But the people have taken Junia under their protection. And it is my view that, bearing in mind her birth, virtue and misfortune, they could ignore the age limit laid down by the laws, in the same way as they had allowed so many great men who deserved this privilege to become Consul outside the legal age limit.

Critics have not always accepted Racine's arguments, and Sainte-Beuve commented: 'What does this ending mean? As if the people could protect anyone against Nero and allow Junia to become one of the Vestal Virgins under its protection'. Clearly, both Racine and Sainte-Beuve agree on one point: that Junia's entry into the Vestals is a distortion of historical truth. But the only really important question is whether it is also a distortion of the aesthetic truth of the play, and whether it destroys the coherence of the universe which this play constitutes. Does Junia's entry into the ranks of the Vestal Virgins contradict the general meaning of tragedy in the same way as did Andromache's physical survival? The difference surely is that Andromache lives on in the world of men, while Junia lives on in the world of the Gods. Andromache's fate is completely foreign to everything else which happens in the play, whereas Junia's is presupposed and implied as a possible continuation of the action throughout *Britannicus*. Pascal's wager, which like Kant's practical postulate, states that for human reasons (reasons of the heart, practical reasons) an absent God does exist, and that we may meet Him at any moment in life, lies at the very heart of the tragic character. The tragic character lives for God and rejects the world because he knows that, at any moment, God may speak and thus enable him to go beyond tragedy. Most of Racine's plays point forward to further plays that he will write later: *Andromaque* to *Britannicus*, *Britannicus*, *Mithridate* and *Iphigénie* to *Phèdre*, and Junia's fate foreshadows the events in *Esther* and *Athalie*.

This happens not only because of the existence of a divine universe but also for another reason that is equally important.

For so long as a God remains hidden and silent, the tragic character is completely alone, since no dialogue can ever be established between him and the characters who constitute the world; but he will transcend this loneliness as soon as God's word echoes through the world. In the play Junia could never really talk to either Britannicus or Nero. She finds, however—like Esther in the midst of the Children of Israel, like Joash surrounded by the Levites—that when she enters into the temple of God, a whole people will come to protect her, killing Narcissus and expulsing Nero. In the Universe of God there is no place for the wild beasts of this world.

Now this problem of the absolute solitude of the tragic character under the gaze of the hidden God, and his solidarity with a whole people when this God is present, is not only the philosophical expression of the problem of the human community and of the universe; it also raises an aesthetic question in the problem of the chorus.

A very great number of modern tragic poets have been preoccupied with this problem of how to introduce or transpose into their plays the chorus of classical Greek tragedy.[1] They have all failed, for the problem is an insoluble one. Greek tragedies were performed in a

---

[1] Cf. Racine's own remarks in his preface to *Esther:* 'I realised that, working according to the plan which had been given me, I was as it were carrying out a project which I had often entertained: that of linking together, in the manner of the Greek poets, the chorus and its chants with the action of the play, thus using to sing the praises of the true God that part of the chorus which the Pagans had employed to sing of their false ones.'

One might also note the remark of Mme de Caylus, in her *Souvenirs*, to the effect that 'the choruses which Racine, in imitation of the Greeks, had always intended to put on the stage, found their natural place in *Esther*, and he was delighted to have this opportunity of bringing them to the attention of his public and to create a liking for them'.

world where the community was still real and close, where the chorus expressed the pity and terror of this community at the sight of one of its members who, similar in essence to all the others, had called down upon himself the anger of the Gods.

Racinian tragedy takes place in a world where the human community has become so distant that it no longer exists even as a memory.

The complete and absolute loneliness of the tragic man, and the impossibility for him to enter really into contact with the world, constitute the whole subject matter of this type of tragedy. In Western Europe, from the sixteenth and seventeenth centuries onwards, society was increasingly composed of doorless and windowless monads. If a real tragedy were to take place on the first floor of a house no one on the ground floor would even notice it. An unbridgeable gulf now separates the tragic hero from the rest of the world. How, in such a situation, can the emotion of the chorus be organically linked to the life of the hero? The problem is an insoluble one, and we need only think of the failure of Schiller in *The Betrothed of Messina* to realise the extent of this difficulty, which all great tragic writers of modern times must necessarily encounter.

Racine himself never seems to have felt the slightest hesitation on this point. His tragedies have no place for a chorus surrounding the tragic characters, since the presence of a chorus—that is to say, the presence of a community—presupposes the existence of God, the end of loneliness and a movement beyond tragedy. This is why God and the people are strictly concomitant (I am tempted to say strictly identical) in Racinian tragedy. And, from this point of view, the people are capable of everything, and Junia's withdrawal from the world into the ranks of the Vestal Virgins is perfectly in keeping with the rest of the tragedy. It is not only the logical and necessary ending of *Britannicus*, but the first indication of the final movement beyond tragedy in the two last plays, *Esther* and *Athalie*.

One last problem still has to be considered: if the presence of God and of the people constitutes a movement beyond tragedy, can we still give the name of 'tragedy' to a play where the principal character is protected by the people and seeks refuge in the temple of the God's? Is *Britannicus* still a tragedy, or it is already a sacred drama? I think it is a tragedy, for God's universe does not yet replace on stage, as it does in *Esther* and *Athalie*, the world of Nero and Agrippina, it is there somewhere behind stage, hidden like the Jansenist God and yet always present as a hope and possibility of refuge. On the actual stage we see only the fierce and barbarous world of wild beasts, the world of politics and love, and the world which, in its encounter with Junia, comes into conflict with the human being who resists and rejects it because this being has gone beyond man and is living in the sight of God.

After his attempt to do so in *Andromaque*, Racine finally succeeded, in *Britannicus*, in writing a really strict tragedy, one where there is neither peripeteia nor recognition, and where the central character is the world. As in the rest of his work, he never looks back, but turns instead towards a new type of tragic play. It is to this new quest that we come in *Bérénice*.

III. *Bérénice*

Although *Andromaque* is a drama that comes near to tragedy and *Britannicus* a genuine tragedy, both nevertheless permit a certain amount of psychological analysis. This is because the central element in these two plays is not the tragic hero—Junia or Andromache—but the whole set of individual characters who constitute the world. Although these are all similar from an ethical point of view, and especially in the context of tragic ethical values, they nevertheless all have a separate psychological reality. This is why a psychological analysis, that would inevitably leave on one side the objective meaning of the play—the conflict between the hero and the world, and, more particularly, the very essence of the hero's nature—would nevertheless be more likely than a purely ethical approach to reveal the psychic structure of the 'worldly' characters in the play and the relationship which they have one with another. This is merely an expression on the aesthetic plane of the same reality that expresses itself philosophically by the fact that one finds more details about the physical structure of the external world and the psychological and physiological structure of men in the writing of Descartes and the Cartesians than in those of Barcos. This reality is nothing but the essential structure of the tragic vision, a structure which Kant characterised as 'the primacy of practical reason'. We must always, when judging things in a tragic perspective, remember what Pascal said: 'The knowledge of external reality will not console me for my ignorance in matters of good and evil, when I am in a time of affliction; but the knowledge of good and evil will always console me for my ignorance of physical things' (fr. 67, E.60).

Although it would be difficult, we can imagine a study of *Andromaque* and *Britannicus* that combined the psychological analysis of characters such as Orestes, Hermione, Pyrrhus, Nero and Agrippina with the ethical analysis of the two plays as a whole, and especially of the characters of Andromache and Junia. It would still be necessary, however, constantly to subordinate psychological to ethical analysis.

With *Bérénice*, the situation is wholly different. Here, psychological analysis has no importance, since there is nothing for it to deal with. Antiochus weighs far too lightly in the play, and any characters who might resemble Nero, Pyrrhus and Agrippina remain in the wings and do not even come on to the stage. This is why the psychological analysis which could help us in earlier plays has very little relevance to what happens in *Bérénice*.

This also explains why critics in general, who traditionally adopt psychological methods, have made even more mistakes about the meaning and structure of *Bérénice* than about any other play by Racine.[1]

Before studying the actual play, I should like to insist upon three important characteristics which result from its general structure. *Bérénice* is a tragedy without peripeteia or recognition, and a play where the tragic hero is the central character. Moreover, it is a play written from the point of view of this character. It is, one might say, Britannicus seen from the standpoint of Junia.

This enables us to understand why, in this tragedy, the world scarcely appears, and, far from having the intensity and richness of intuitive presence that it has in the other plays, is present only in the rather pale figure of Antiochus. One might perhaps begin to explain this by the fact that the world has moved away from the centre of the play to the periphery. But this explanation, although a genuine and valid one, is not sufficient. For one can find a deeper and much more absolute reason: for tragic man, conscious of the unbridgeable gulf between him and the world, the world ceases to exist as a concrete and sensible whole; it retains only an abstract and general existence, that of an unconscious material force which tragic man despises and with which he refuses to bargain and compromise.

This is so much the case that at no point in the play do Titus and Berenice even listen to Antiochus, the only character belonging to the world whom Racine puts on the stage, and still less understand and accept him.

It also explains why *Bérénice* differs from almost all other tragedies in world literature in having not one but two tragic heroes. For one of the most important features of tragedies without peripeteia and recognition is the absence of any dialogue between the hero and the

---

[1] I do not, of course, mean that we should try to base the understanding of literary works on our own values, or on any principle which is of a purely general nature and which remains external to the work itself. We can understand great literary or philosophical works only by reconstructing their own inner coherence. The pride of place accorded to practical reason is one of the principal elements of this coherence as far as any works dominated by the tragic vision are concerned. The plays of Corneille, on the other hand, require a much greater attention to the psychological analysis of the individual characters.

world. Or more exactly, as Lukàcs puts it, the existence merely of a 'solitary dialogue'—of the dialogue between man and the hidden and silent God of tragedy. Now it is difficult to imagine any play lasting for five acts without any real dialogue. In the tragedies where the world was the central character Racine could keep the action going with the dialogues between different characters who belonged to the world, between Pyrrhus and Orestes, Orestes and Hermione, Nero and Britannicus. When the world no longer has any concrete and sensible reality this solution is no longer possible. In order to avoid a play which would consist solely of a series of 'solitary dialogues' with a silent God, Racine found the best and perhaps the only solution available: he represented the tragic universe by two characters who, while remaining quite alone, since they are irredeemably separated from each other, nevertheless do constitute a moral community, belong to the same universe and therefore can and must speak together.

A third problem is that of the ending of the play. We are accustomed to seeing a tragedy end either with the death of the hero or with his entry into God's universe. These are the only possible endings for a tragic play, and we find neither of them in *Bérénice*. Critics have not failed to notice this and to say that, strictly speaking, *Bérénice* is not a tragedy. Théophile Gautier wrote that it was 'a dramatic elegy in which flow tears but no blood',[1] and the majority of critics have adopted his opinion. Racine had, however, replied to him in advance, remarking in his preface that: 'It is by no means necessary that there should be blood and death in a tragedy; it is sufficient for the action to be heroic, for the passions to be aroused, and for everything to be imbued with that majestic sorrow which makes up the whole pleasure of tragedy.' As usual, Racine's preface simply shows us that he saw where the problem existed and consciously chose his own solution to it. For if the very success of *Bérénice* shows that he was right and Gautier wrong, that there is no need of 'blood and death' in a tragedy, that there can be a tragedy without either the death of the hero or his entry into a divine world, it does not tell us why this should necessarily have been the case with *Bérénice*. It does not tell us why Racine chose to write such a tragedy.

It is easier to see the problem in its proper light once we recognise the fact that the play is written from the point of view of the two tragic characters of Titus and Berenice. From this point of view, both death and the entry into a divine universe are impossible, for they would introduce incoherent elements into the structure of the play. An entry into the divine universe which takes place afar off and not

[1] Théophile Gautier, *L'Art dramatique en France depuis vingt-cinq ans* (Paris: Hetzel, 1859), Vol. III, p. 155.

on the stage itself would transform the tragedy into a sacred drama. *Bérénice* would then turn, in the midst of its action, in the direction of wholly different plays such as *Esther* and *Athalie*. As to the death of the main characters, this is equally impossible both for Titus and for Berenice, since, as has often been said, we can see and know the death of other people but never our own. This is the only event which closely affects us but of which we can never be conscious ourselves. To present the deaths of Titus and Berenice on the stage would involve a sudden and unexpected change of perspective, and Racine was far too strict a writer to destroy the unity of his play in such an incoherent manner.

Having thus explained the structural changes demanded by this new perspective—that is to say, the disappearance of the world, the fact that there are two tragic characters, and the absence of 'blood and death'—we can now begin the schematic analysis of the actual text. Of the three characters in the play only one—or, rather, only the two tragic characters—occupy the stage. The two other, the world (in this play, the Court) and God (in this play, Rome and its people), remain for most of the time hidden in the wings. The Court is only just represented on the stage by the character of Antiochus, who is there solely to emphasise the difference between his standards and those of the tragic heroes. Besides, he is one of the more innocuous of the animals which make up the world, being neither a raging wild beast like Agrippina or Nero nor a self-centred victim of his own passions like Orestes and Hermione. He is of the same family as Britannicus and Hippolytus, someone whose feeble and mediocre 'virtue' always ends up by being crushed. This is why (recalling that Britannicus is loved by Junia and Hippolytus by Phaedra) he can at least appear in the universe of tragic characters.

Only two themes make up the action of the play: the relationship between Titus and Berenice and the relationship between Titus and the People of Rome, who are always present and absent at one and the same time.

The two tragic characters are not, of course, absolutely identical with each other. (A writer like Racine does not create abstract patterns, but living and highly individualised characters). Since Titus is from the very beginning of the play conscious of what the situation is, and since he knows that there can be no compromise, he is, like Junia, the tragic character for whom there is neither peripeteia nor recognition. Berenice, on the other hand, already forms part of the line which leads from Andromache to Eriphile and Phaedra. Wholly absorbed in her love, she has not yet, at the moment when the curtain rises, understood the tragic dilemma created by the obstacles to it. That Titus has now become Emperor represents for her the possi-

338

bility for her love to triumph over the difficulties that the external
world might represent; she does not even suspect that the difficulties
which exist in Titus's own mind are even there. The subject of
Bérénice consists of the dialogue between Titus, who is already a
tragic character when the curtain rises, and Berenice, who becomes
tragic only with the ending of the play. What the play describes, in
fact, is the entry of Berenice into the universe of tragedy.

The curtain rises, as in all Racine's tragedies, on the presence of the
world. Antiochus, King of Comagene and in love with Berenice,
Queen of Palestine, is explaining to his confidant Arsace the nature
of the place in which they are now standing. It is one of the few 'stage
directions' that we have in Racine, and it is to be noted that these
directions always incarnate the subject-matter of the play in time and
space. This, says Antiochus, is the room where the Emperor Titus
comes to meditate alone; here, too, the Emperor speaks in secret to
the Queen of the love which he has for her, since it lies between their
two apartments (ll. 3–10). We are thus between the place where
authority reigns and that where love holds sway.

The lines which immediately follow tell us about the relationship
between Antiochus and Berenice, with the former asking his confidant to request a secret meeting with the Queen, whom he 'fears he is
importuning'. Arsace, who sees from these words something of what
the real situation is while at the same time misunderstanding its true
causes, is surprised at what Antiochus says. Surely, he asks, the fact
that Berenice hopes to become the wife of Titus does not put so
great a distance between her and his master (ll. 15–16).

These few lines express in miniature the very essence of the play:
the need to choose between love and authority, and the unbridgeable
distance which lies between Berenice and Antiochus. The theme is
thus announced before the arrival of the real hero, and the rest of the
action follows with an absolute and inevitable necessity.

The next two scenes show us Antiochus exactly as he will remain
to the very end of the play: hesitant, undecided, afraid of his own
decisions, always acted upon rather than acting himself, falling into
despair every time he foresees the possibility of a marriage between
Titus and Berenice, springing into renewed hope when he sees the
obstacles separating the two lovers, and never understanding the fact
that, whether they marry or not, the distance between him and them
is such that he will never be able to overcome it.

Arsace brings him news about Berenice, telling him that she is
surrounded by this Court, which is foreign to her (and which
will never appear on stage because it has no reality for Titus and
Berenice), and that she is seeking to escape from it (ll. 67–8).

As for Antiochus, feeling that the declaration of love which he is about to make is quite absurd, he decides—as Hippolytus does in *Phèdre*—that he will leave as soon as he has made it. But even this departure is not an independent and irrevocable decision, since Antiochus always depends upon some other person's decision and never on his own. As he makes quite clear in his conversation with Arsace in Act I, Scene 3, he will wait to see whether or not Titus is going to defy the opinion of Rome and marry Berenice before deciding whether or not to leave Rome himself.

When Berenice actually comes on to the stage she is still an ordinary woman, who thinks that she can enter into contact with Antiochus when she speaks to him and hopes to marry Titus. The first of these two illusions disappears at the end of the scene, and the second at the end of the play. For the moment, she has fled from the courtiers—in order, as she herself puts it, 'to escape from the boring speeches of so many friends, and find someone who will speak to me with complete sincerity' (Act I, Scene 4, ll. 135-8).

Antiochus, learning that she hopes to marry Titus, tells her that he is going to leave. When she asks him why, he decides to speak to her, foresees that he will fail and even speaks the most tragic line in Racine's theatre, a line which, although full of truth, remains on the periphery of the actual play. 'At least remember,' he tells her, 'that it is your laws which I am obeying, and that you are hearing my voice for the last time' (Act I, Scene 4, ll. 185-6).

He has scarcely finished speaking before Berenice becomes aware of the abyss which separates him from her, an abyss which Antiochus had sensed earlier but which he had refused to recognise. The distance is so great that what Antiochus says does not even make Berenice angry, and in no way destroys her kindly feelings towards him. It simply surprises her. What comes from the world can never touch her, but is destined always to remain foreign and surprising. Moreover, what Antiochus says to her has so little reality in her eyes that she will immediately forget it. She will, she tells Antiochus, forget the declaration of love which he has made to her on the very day of her marriage with Titus; she is even sorry that he has to say farewell, in spite of the offence which such a declaration causes her, so great is the friendship that she feels for him. Later on, in the next scene, she tells her confidante Phenice that, far from retaining Antiochus, she realises that she ought to forget his very existence (l. 290).

I should like to emphasise, before going any farther, how everything which Berenice and Antiochus say is true, even though in a completely different sense from the one which they themselves give to their words. The day of which Berenice speaks is indeed going to link her fate with that of the Emperor, but not in the sense which she gives to these words, that of joining them together by marriage. The bond between them will be the far nobler and greater one of deliberate sacrifice which they will share together. By giving up their love, the thing dearest to both of them and the true bond between them, they are joined together in another, higher way. It is equally true that Berenice has listened to Antiochus 'for the last time', since their common sacrifice has raised Titus and Berenice to a universe where any nearness or proximity with Antiochus or people of his kind is quite unbearable.

Titus does not appear until the second act. He is the tragic character who is fully aware of reality, of its problems and demands, and of the impossibility of reconciling them. His love for Berenice is absolute, and will remain so until the end of the play. His life will lose all meaning and reality if they have to separate. But, on the other hand, his position as Roman Emperor is equally essential to his existence, and it makes its own inexorable demands. Placed in such a manner between his duty as Emperor and his desires as a lover, unable to live with one if he sacrifices the other, he has only one choice: he must either give up life itself by committing physical suicide or he must commit moral suicide in a reign that will be nothing more than 'an endless exile'.

The pattern of the play is that of *Le Cid* and of most of Corneille's plays. Titus sacrifices love to 'duty' or, in another word, to 'glory'. But while Corneille would have seen his decision a triumph and as a material victory for man, Racine sees it as a moral triumph accompanied by a material defeat, by the sacrifice of his own person and of his life. Titus, like all tragic heroes, is both strong and weak, great and small—a reed, but a thinking reed.

Nevertheless, in spite of the fact that he becomes conscious of this only later, his sacrifice is meaningful only if it enables him to avoid committing the sin of giving up one of the two antagonistic elements which are indispensable to the values of his universe. His separation, the 'long exile' of his reign, is meaningful only if Berenice joins him in his sacrifice, and if, by sacrificing themselves together, their community remains unbroken. If this does not happen, suicide will enable him to avoid both the sin against Berenice and the sin against Rome.

For the moment, however, Berenice does not even suspect that this problem exists, and still hopes to be able to marry Titus.

The Emperor, having already taken his decision, is alone, but compassed about with invisible forces: the world, the Court, with which he could nevertheless come to terms but which he rejects; and, later on, Rome, with its institutions, its people and its Gods. He cannot really enter into contact with Rome, but the city nevertheless exists somewhere, hidden and silent, watching over each of his actions with the same implacable vigilance as the Hidden God of all tragedies. This contrast between the Court, which he knows can easily be won over to whatever he may choose, and the People of Rome, to whom he attributes a kind of divine stability of moral judgment, is brought out particularly well in the scene between Titus and Paulinus in Act II, Scene 2, where Titus is equally aware that he has no means of entering into contact with this God. He himself cannot overcome the barriers of fear and flattery that tradition sets up against him, and he asks his confidant, Paulinus, to interpret the wishes of the people of Rome to him.

The latter's reply, however, reveals the inexorable nature of Rome's verdict: by an unchangeable law, he tells Titus, none of its Emperors may marry a foreigner.

Confronted with this verdict, Titus once again becomes aware of the essential importance which his love for Berenice has in his life, and speaks three times of the intense ardour possessing him. Yet the demands which Rome makes cannot be refused. If Titus is not to betray either Berenice or Rome there is only one thing to be done: both Titus and Berenice must, together, accept a renunciation which will be for both of them a renunciation of life itself. Titus decides to do this, saying farewell to Berenice for the last time and handing her over to the care of Antiochus.

But Berenice arrives, still suspecting nothing, tells him of her love and of her disquiet, and Titus comes to realise how difficult the task he has set himself really is. Overwhelmed at the thought, he leaves Berenice and tells Antiochus to let her know his decision, instructing him to assure her at the same time that the love he bears for her will never change in the future (Act III, Scene 1, ll. 750–5).

I shall not bore my reader by discussing the perpetual oscillations and inability to decide of Antiochus, who lives solely in the hope of a compromise solution, telling Arsace of the delight which he will receive from seeing Berenice (Act III, Scene 2).

It is hardly necessary to say that a message of the kind which Titus is sending to Berenice cannot be transmitted through the agency of an Antiochus, especially since Berenice has now lost any illusion as to the possibility of indulging in a genuine dialogue with him. Titus will have to meet her himself. But the news of the separation demanded by her lover, and the fact that he has asked Antiochus to tell her of it, have caused Berenice to give way. She is the weaker of the two, and allows herself to be invaded by disorder, this supreme non-value of the tragic universe. This can be seen in lines 973–4 of Act IV, Scene 2, where she refuses to allow Phenice to disguise the traces of the extreme emotion which she has undergone. Titus, she tells her confidante, will 'see the fruits of his actions', and the Emperor is then compelled once again to confront the most difficult moment of his life. And he has to do so not only in full and complete awareness of what he is sacrificing but also with the knowledge that he is sacrificing it to a God of whose verdict he can never be absolutely sure, and who has never spoken to him in a clear and unambiguous manner. As he says in his long monologue in Act IV, Scene 4 (ll. 988–1040), it is really his own decision that is making him destroy what he loves most, since Rome has given no sign of what she herself really wants.

Yet he soon recovers control over his thoughts. Rome, he realises, has already judged Berenice by banishing the kings whom she has always continued to hate, while he, Titus, has so far done nothing to make his reign as Emperor a memorable one. It would be, he realises, the act of a coward to give up the Empire and follow Berenice into exile in order to become her lover (ll. 1024–5).

But it is at this very moment that Berenice appears, and she still judges the situation with the straightforward common sense of someone who has not yet reached the level of tragic awareness. She reproaches Titus with the fact that, while he previously resisted the whole world when this world was against them and he loved her, he is now prepared to give her up when he is Emperor and has supreme power to decide his own fate (Act IV, Scene 5, ll. 1085–6).

Titus tries to make her understand that by separating himself from her he is also cutting himself off from life, and that no purely external reasons could ever have made him willingly accept such a sacrifice. His duty, however, is not to live but to rule, and it is this which compels him to accept the separation from her (ll. 1100–2).

Berenice, however, cannot yet imagine this idea of separation, and insists on the suffering which they will undergo in the endless months and years when they will no longer see each other (ll. 1110–14).

Berenice, still hoping that some solution is possible, suggests a compromise whereby she will stay in Rome without becoming his wife; and when Titus tries to make her understand the degradation that would await them in a life which had once accepted the idea of compromise, Berenice does not understand him and announces her intention of killing herself.

Titus then almost hesitates as he confronts his own failure to make Berenice understand the issues involved, but at the same time as Antiochus calls upon him to help Berenice, who is about to commit suicide, he hears the voice of Rome, of the Roman people and of the Roman Gods, reminding him of the demands that they have to make. He gives thanks to the Gods (ll. 1242–4) at having saved him from the error into which he was about to fall, and the end of the play is near. Berenice has decided to kill herself, but Titus tears the letter which she has written to him away from her and prevents her from going out. A stage direction tells us that Berenice is at the height of despair and confusion and that she 'allows herself to sink into a chair' (Act V, Scene 5).

Having failed to make himself understood and to link the fate of Berenice with his own, Titus, who cannot sacrifice either Berenice or Rome, still rejects any idea of compromise. He chooses the only solution by which he can satisfy both the demands of his people and those of love, and decides to kill himself at the same time as Berenice commits suicide. As he explains to her in Act V, Scene 6 (ll. 1411–22), this is the only way in which he can avoid so many contradictions, and it is, moreover, the noblest thing that he can do.

However, faced with the grandeur of soul shown by Titus, Berenice likewise discovers her own true nature. A second stage direction tells us that we have arrived at the decisive moment in the play. 'Berenice rises' (Act V, Scene 7, l. 1468). She has finally understood the meaning of the decision which Titus has taken, and joins herself freely and deliberately to his fate. She recognises her error in having doubted Titus's love for her, and agrees to follow his command and see him no more (Act V, Scene 7, ll. 1491–5).

After she has reminded Antiochus of the gulf which still separates him from her, and asked him to depart, the play ends with the decisive words which she speaks to Titus: 'For the last time, Farewell', and with Antiochus's despairing 'Alas' (ll. 1502–3).

The curtain falls and the play is over. Titus and Berenice, united by the common sacrifice which they have made of their lives, will never see each other again.

It is worth repeating that Racine's dramatic work represents a constant progression without a single backward glance. He never goes back to the type of play that he has already written, but constantly seeks out new problems and new ways of writing. *Andromaque*, *Britannicus* and *Bérénice* together make up one particular cycle, that made up of tragedies without peripeteia and recognition. This contrasts both with plays that have peripeteia and recognition, *Bajazet*, *Mithridate*, *Iphigénie* and *Phèdre*, and with sacred dramas such as *Esther* and *Athalie*.

It would need much more detailed research than I can present in this book to show that Racine is, in world literature, the creator of this type of tragic hero. There is, however, one thing that does, in my view, seem probable: if he was influenced by any outside event this was less the reading of any work of either Christian or pagan inspiration than the exceptional human reality which he encountered when he was a young man, and that at a time when it was in all its strength and richness: Port-Royal des Champs and the first generation Jansenists.

The attitude of Berenice and Titus towards the world, and more particularly towards the Court, is the theatrical transposition of the attitude of Saint-Cyran, Antoine Lemaître, Singlin, Sylvestre de Saci and the first solitaries towards the Court and towards the social, political and even ecclesiastical society of their time.

The 'long exile' of Titus, like the temple of the Vestal Virgins, is the refuge hidden behind the world, and the translation into sensible and pagan language of the real Christian and spiritual lives which Racine beheld as a schoolboy at Port-Royal and which profoundly influenced his way of thinking and feeling.

Certainly those solitaries who did have a knowledge of Racine's plays did not recognise themselves in his characters. They were too Christian to accept the idea that their qualities might be shown under different costumes. What, for them, was there in common between Christ and the Roman Gods, between the Vestal Virgins and the holy daughters of Port-Royal? When Arnauld finally does admire a play by Racine it is *Esther*, his first Christian but also his least Jansenist work.

The fact remains that Pascal's *Pensées* and Racine's tragedies, works that 'horrified' Port-Royal, constitute its greatest achievement. Far more than the lives of the solitaries, it is they which justify it in the eyes of posterity. This is yet another sign that we should never confuse what men want to do and what they think they are doing with what they actually achieve.

B. THE DRAMAS OF THIS WORLD

IV. *Bajazet*

With *Bajazet*, Racine's work enters a new phase, and there is as much difference between this play and *Bérénice* as between *Alexandre* and *Andromaque* or *Phèdre* and *Athalie*. After the plays which deal with refusal and with tragic greatness, *Bajazet* is the first which represents an effort to achieve compromise and retain life. There are, certainly, a number of features reminiscent of earlier tragedies, but they tend to disappear after *Mithridate*, and even in *Bajazet* the new perspective from which Racine is writing gives them an entirely different meaning.

Thus, as we come to study the plays which Racine wrote after *Bajazet*, we have to consider a number of methodological problems. First of all, should we include in a book devoted to a study of tragedy an examination of three plays—*Bajazet*, *Mithridate* and *Iphigénie*—which are not tragedies? I think we should, for the meaning of any particular work can really be seen only against the wider background of the pattern formed by its author's other books and of its whole historical context. This is why, although I am interested primarily in *Britannicus, Bérénice* and *Phèdre*, I think it not only useful but also essential to study the three plays which Racine wrote between *Bérénice* and *Phèdre*. Any attempt to isolate the three tragedies from Racine's work as a whole may distort their meaning.

There is, however, another problem: *Andromaque, Britannicus* and *Phèdre* make up a homogeneous group of plays defined by the refusal of the world and of life. But when we are dealing with the four later plays we can approach them in two different but equally valid and complementary ways. We can group *Bajazet, Mithridate, Iphigénie* and *Phèdre* together as plays where the hero tries to live in the world; on the other hand, the first three can be seen as historical dramas and the fourth as a return to tragedy. The first approach sees *Bajazet, Mithridate* and *Iphigénie* as unconscious efforts on Racine's part to do what he finally managed to achieve in *Phèdre*; the second looks upon each play as having its own coherence and meaning.

Now although it is certain that *Phèdre* does constitute a synthesis of elements that were latent and isolated in the other three plays, it would be totally misleading to concentrate all our attention upon it. Nothing, in fact, is more dangerous for the literary historian or critic than the tendency to drag certain elements from their context in order to give them an individual and often arbitrary meaning. It is already a dangerous practice in philosophy or theology, and it is fatal to literary criticism. In philosophy and theology the total work of a writer is, much more than any one of his individual books, an organic whole which has its own meaning. This compels us to interpret each book in the light of the author's work as a whole, and especially in the light of what he was to write in subsequent volumes. The situation is completely different, however, when we are dealing with an imaginary creation, and with an intuitive universe made up of individual beings and individual relationships—in other words, when we are dealing with works of art or works of literature.

Here, each text or painting is—in so far as it is aesthetically valid—an organic whole; indeed, it is probably even more an organic whole than the rest of the writer's or painter's work of which it forms part. This is why I shall here consider *Bajazet, Mithridate* and *Iphigénie* as, primarily, texts which are autonomous and self-sufficient, each having its own coherence and meaning. It is only later on that I shall try to show how, as he wrote them, Racine gradually developed elements which he later integrated into his last tragedy.

I should also like to define more exactly what I mean by an historical play—a term that I find highly applicable to *Mithridate* and partially applicable to *Bajazet* and *Iphigénie*. In French the word history is used in two different ways which must be carefully distinguished in any philosophical discourse.[1] Thus, we can refer to any past event which affected political or social life as an historical event, and in this sense, history is the knowledge of the past as past, without any conscious and deliberate reference to the present or the future of individuals in society. This kind of historical knowledge claims to be 'objective', and, in certain important aspects, resembles the knowledge of the external world provided by physics, chemistry and biology.

Everyone knows, however, that when we talk about thinkers such as Saint Augustine, Joachim de Flore, Hegel or Marx, we say that they worked out a philosophy of history, and we realise that it would be impossible to talk in the same way of a philosophy of chemistry or physics. Here the word 'history' is used differently, for, on the one hand, it refers to future events (and, indeed, these thinkers are interested in the past only in so far as it bears upon the future) and, on the other hand, the central problem of this type of philosophical thought is not future events as external and knowable, but future events in so far as they concern the values, life and behaviour of past, present or future individuals.

If we take the word 'historical' in its first sense *Andromaque*, *Britannicus*, *Bérénice* and *Phèdre* are all to a certain extent 'historical' plays. The central problem in each case is, admittedly, an individual one, but we see in the background a number of decisive events for the life of the people as a whole: the Trojan war, Nero's reign, the Roman state, the succession to the throne of Athens.

If, however, the word is given the meaning which it has in this book, that which it has when we speak of a philosophy of history, then these plays are, like all tragedies, wholly a-historical. For, on the one hand, the tragic universe is characterised by a complete absence of any personal or collective future (since the relationship between the individual and the world is unchanging, the future of the community can have no meaning), and, on the other, there is no positive relationship between the problems governing the hero's mind and the reality of collective life. The life of the collectivity is, like everything which belongs to this world, simply one of the obstacles with which tragic man comes into conflict and which will lead him to reject life and the world as a whole.

As far as *Bajazet*, *Mithridate* and *Iphigénie* are concerned, however, these do have a certain 'historical' significance even in the second sense of the word. In all three there is either a real future (*Mithridate*, *Iphigénie*) or a possible future (*Bajazet*) and, similarly, the future of

[1] German has two terms, *Historisch* and *Geschichtlich*, which correspond to some extent to the distinction which I am trying to make. Thus, one can say, *Historische Schule* and *Geschichtsphilosophie*.

the community has a decisive importance for the solution of the hero's individual problems. These problems, in fact, are closely associated with his fate—the fall of Acomat and life or death for Bajazet, the war against the Romans and the love of Xiphares and Monime, the Trojan war and life or death for Iphigenia. The only difference between the plays, from this point of view, lies in the fact that individual life still retains most importance in *Bajazet* and *Iphigénie*, while in *Mithridate*, the only really historical play in the narrower sense of the word, the fusion between the individual and the collectivity is so complete that there is almost no individual hero. Mithridates, Xiphares and Monime are all almost equally important, and the true hero of the play is the group that they constitute, in spite of the conflicts between them, in their common struggle against Rome.

Coming now to an analysis of *Bajazet*, I shall begin by noting that although the play has its own meaning and unity, it is still a transition between a tragedy such as *Bérénice* and an historical play like *Mithridate*, exactly as, later on, *Iphigénie* will be a transition between *Mithridate* and *Phèdre*.

Bajazet does contain—and this is its weakness—certain elements which are absolutely analogous to the three earlier tragedies: the situation, and the demands, of the tragic ethic. In *Britannicus* and *Bérénice* the hero has to choose between compromise and death, and Bajazet likewise knows that the only truly human and genuinely valid attitude would be a rejection of compromise and the deliberate acceptance of death. There the resemblances end, however, and differences appear which completely change the meaning of the whole, For, unlike Junia or Titus, Bajazet does not act in accordance with the demands of his own conscience. Under Atalide's influence he tries to deceive Roxana, and to manoeuvre in order to stay alive. Far from refusing the world, he accepts compromise.

This is not, however, the only change, and it is not true to say that *Bajazet* has the same background and the same characters with merely a dramatic hero who tries to come to terms with the world in order to stay alive replacing a tragic hero who rejects the world in the name of an absolute of moral purity. For the Triad of God–Man–the World, which we have seen to be the essence of the tragic universe, constitutes a coherent whole, in which a change in any one of the three elements must inevitably produce changes in the two others if incoherence and aesthetic failure are to be avoided.

Thus, the silent and hidden God of tragedy, who was absent because he never gave the hero any advice on how to live and how to achieve his values, was nevertheless always present in the universe of the play through the very consciousness of the hero, present under the form of the hero's demand for a totality and purity unobtainable in this life. As soon, however, as this hero reduces the demands of his own conscience by acting against these values or coming to terms with the world, this presence disappears. The Gods can then find dramatic reality only as external and providential Gods, as in *Iphigénie*, or as the incarnation of justice and order, as in *Bajazet*. Or, a third possibility, the fusion between the hero and the world in a truly historical drama may abolish all transcendence by identifying God with social life, as in *Mithridate*. This explains why the hidden and tragic Gods of *Britannicus* and *Bérénice* become the dramatic Gods of justice and vengeance in *Bajazet*.

But, in this Triad God–Man–the World it is perhaps the third element which undergoes the deepest change in *Bajazet*. In the three earlier tragedies there was an infinite and qualitative difference between the world and the hero. Faced with the absolute purity of tragic man, for whom there are no relative values, the world which did not satisfy his ethical demands became a purely negative reality. Everything which happened in the world was, by definition, lacking in value, moral significance or any reality at all. The hero saw it as merely a collection of unbridgeable obstacles, as an occasion to make his own values explicit, but nothing more.

This situation inevitably changes as soon as the hero tries to reconcile himself with the world and live in it. His increased closeness to the world necessarily affects the structure of the play's universe. As the human level of the hero sinks, the moral level of the world rises, and the qualitative difference is replaced by a difference of degree. If the hero is no longer wholly good, then the world is no longer wholly evil, and they finally completely coalesce in *Mithridate*. This is why the static and meaningless world of *Andromaque*, *Britannicus*, *Bérénice* and *Phèdre* is replaced by the dynamic world which progresses towards the realisation of the good—or, rather, to what constitutes the good in this particular play. This does not mean that the world necessarily realises the good through its own internal processes. There is simply a change of direction and interest within the play. Roxana, Acomat and Atalide engage in action against Amurat; Mithridates, Xiphares and Monime fight against the Romans, the main characters in *Iphigénie* want the Greeks to defeat the Trojans.

Evil certainly still exists in the world, but it is no longer the single constituent element. It remains behind stage (Amurat), in a subordinate position (Pharnace), or completely absent (as in *Iphigénie*). In *Bajazet* this evil is in absolute conflict with the good, with the gods of order and of justice. Like them, it is hidden behind stage, not as a passive and absent spectator, but as an active force, intervening from outside in the universe of the play. And in this conflict between good

349

and evil we see all the characters, Bajazet himself, on the one hand, Acomat, Roxana and Atalide, on the other, taking up an intermediary attitude between one or other of these extremes.

Sometimes the world even seems morally superior to the hero. For if Bajazet is guilty before the Gods and before himself for the lie which he accepts in order to remain alive, Roxana and Amurat, for all their selfishness, lack of generosity and lack of values transcending any individual concerns, are equally in conflict with evil and on the side of goodness—as long, of course, as it suits their passions and interest. They are at least superior to Bajazet in their frankness and truthfulness.

I need hardly say that I am not judging what happens in the play from any external standpoint[1] and am not saying that Racine judged the characters in *Bajazet* in this way in 1671. I am merely talking about the meaning of their behaviour within the context of the universe created by the play.

I can now explain the structural lines of the universe in which the action takes place: a hero who, because he tries to keep alive by lies and compromise, is not wholly good; a world which is not wholly evil and whose general development is even in the direction of the good; and, finally, Gods who are the only representatives of justice and order and who will therefore punish both Bajazet himself as well as the world. This is the framework in which the action of *Bajazet* takes place. The action in the play has less *moral* tension than in Racine's earlier work, and can therefore be treated more succinctly especially since I am not here primarily interested in a psychological analysis of the characters or a socio-political analysis of the situations.

As usual, the first lines sum up the main theme of the play and indicate where the action is taking place. Acomat and Osmin have chosen to ignore the threatening barriers of a world which lives under threats and terror, and are meeting in a place which to visit previously would have meant death. Events which will be described later have shaken the foundations of this world, and for all their danger the barriers defining it have become less rigid. The opening exchanges between Acomat, the *grand visir*, and his *confident* Osmin explain to us that the reason why they can both penetrate into the Harem is that Roxana, who is in love with Bajazet, and Acomat, who has himself been inspired by jealousy of the king to seize power during his absence, are preparing a palace revolution in order to replace the

---

[1] From our present point of view, for example, it matters little whether Troy falls or not. In *Andromaque*, however, the fall of Troy constitutes a negative reality, but in *Iphigénie* a positive one. Similarly, Pyrrhus and Roxana seem very like each other; in the two plays in which they figure, however, each has a different value.

wicked Amurat by the virtuous Bajazet. As we see from lines 6–7, the passage of time is a reality in this play, so that there is a qualitative difference between yesterday and today.[1]

Acomat's authority, however, is not very firmly established as yet, and the Janissaries are hesitant and mistrustful, still dreaming nostalgically of the time when the Vizir himself commanded them. The sultan is facing a battle whose outcome will decide the army's loyalty, and consequently the stability of his reign (ll. 44–8 and 49–60).

Roxana, who is in love with Bajazet, has decided to associate herself with Acomat, but neither she nor Bajazet wholly trusts him. They fear, with some justification, that once he is in power he will betray them. This is why both want to insure themselves against treachery, Acomat by marrying Atalide, a princess of royal blood, and Roxana by becoming Bajazet's wife. Such guarantees are in fact necessary, since although Bajazet feels guilty at what he is doing, he is trying to obtain power by making promises that he does not intend to keep. The situation is completely different from what it was in the earlier tragedies, where the hero was on one side and the world on the other; here we see Bajazet and the world allied together in a struggle against Amurat, the very incarnation of evil, and each trying to satisfy his own needs and desires by betraying other people. Throughout the play there is an inextricable tangle of good and evil, selfishness and virtuous sentiments. Once the action has begun, deceit dominates what happens until the middle of the fourth act, and causes the plot to hesitate between drama and *marivaudage*.

All the characters are half guilty and half virtuous. When Roxana follows goodness she does so to satisfy her own selfish passions; but when she abandons Bajazet she does so partly for moral reasons, in order to punish the man who has betrayed her. She is one of the people through whose agency divine justice works, and she knows and foresees that it is her own doom that she will bring about by punishing Bajazet (Act I, Scene 3, ll. 320–5).

Acomat, the skilful politician who thinks only of his own interests, nevertheless consistently defends goodness against evil throughout the play.

Atalide, the person with whom Bajazet is in fact in love, never has

[1] In tragedy, on the other hand, which always takes place outside time, the past is constantly present and the future has long since been decided. Here, in what is a drama, the present is different from the past.

Later on, we shall discover more about the event which has thus allowed these barriers to be transgressed. I mention it here, in spite of its relative lack of importance in the play, because it is the first use of a theme that Racine comes back to in both *Mithridate* and *Phèdre*: that of the false rumour of the king's death (cf. *Bajazet*, ll. 145–52).

the courage to perform any action wholeheartedly, and always does the opposite of what she sets out to do.

Bajazet himself, worthy in his intentions but guilty in his acts, remains ambiguous in his very crime, since he does not act but merely allows misunderstandings to accumulate.

Nothing, in such a universe, is inevitable, and everything is necessarily accidental. Bajazet's stratagem might well have succeeded, and we should then have had a comedy similar to those later written by Marivaux (Roxana being pardoned and reconciled with the two lovers). Racine, however, chose to write a drama, and perhaps did so because he felt that this was the best way of keeping the unity of the play, threatened in its dramatic world by the existence of certain elements surviving from earlier tragedies (Bajazet's uneasy conscience, the Gods demanding absolute purity, etc.). Moreover, he was enabled by the final denouement to strengthen this unity by insisting upon the menace of Amurat on a terrestial plane and that of the Gods on a transcendent plane.[1]

But if he had emphasised them even further he would have destroyed the unity of the play by stressing a necessary and inevitable element in a world where everything else is accidental. This is why he brings about the ending of the play in a deliberately accidental manner: by causing Atalide to faint and Bajazet's letter to her to be discovered. Such an accident would be inconceivable in tragedy, but is a necessary accident in the framework of a drama. It thus indicates more successfully than any detailed analysis of plot could have done how great the distance is between *Bajazet* and the three other plays which preceded it.

Once an accident has tipped the scales between comedy and drama, all that needs to be produced is an ending which ensures everyone's death or disappearance. Bajazet and Roxana are killed, Acomat seeks refuge on the ships that are about to take to sea, and before Atalide kills herself she has time to indicate that her death is the expression of a transcendent justice which manifests itself in spite of all obstacles and confusion. In the very last scene in the play (Act V Scene 12, ll. 1740–6) she appeals to the 'heroes who were all to have lived again in Bajazet' to come, with the mother who entrusted Bajazet to her, in order to exact the vengeance now owed to them.

I shall mention briefly in the appendix to this study some of the external historical factors which may have influenced Racine in this transition from tragedy to drama. For the moment, I should merely like to mention a problem which, because it concerns aesthetics and

[1] There are a large number of passages in the play that recall this double threat —cf. II, 5; I, 2; I, 3; I, 4; II, 1.

individual psychology, does not really come into the framework of this study.

Among the plays which Racine wrote between *Andromaque* and *Athalie*, *Bajazet* has always seemed to me to be one of the least successful and the least important. The main reason for this is probably the fact that it contains tragic elements but nevertheless remains essentially a drama. This disparity, however, itself needs to be explained, and it seems to me to result from the impression which the play gives of being much more a well-written exercise by a highly skilful technician than a work intensely lived and experienced by its author. Perhaps it is this distance between Racine's own subjective awareness and the subject matter of his play which explains the incoherence of the universe which he created? Perhaps Racine writes less well when he moves away from tragedy?

If this is so, then a study of *Bajazet* could throw light upon the important and difficult problem of the relationship between general historical conditions and individual artistic temperament in the creation of literary works. However, anything concerned with individual psychology seems to be far too vague to justify any definite statements being made, and I prefer to leave this problem to scholars and critics more competent than myself.

V. *Mithridate and Iphigénie*

(i)

Like *Bajazet*, these two plays are not really tragedies, and do not really come within the framework of this book. This is especially true of *Mithridate*, which, in intention at least, appears as an attempt to go beyond tragedy, and to do so on the most radical and immanent plane available, that of history.

The problem of historical drama is a complex one, and I can hope to deal with it only superficially. Indeed, anything which I say about *Mithridate* will be aimed solely at helping us to understand the meaning, situation and especially the genesis of *Phèdre*.

In the strongest and strictest sense of the word, *Mithridate* is perhaps the only historical play that Racine tried to write. Indeed, it is perhaps the only historical play in the whole of French literature, a curious fact when we consider the work of Shakespeare, Goethe, Schiller, Kleist, Büchner, etc. It is the only play where man is shown to have a possibility open to him, in and through history, of overcoming all his real but temporal and essentially soluble personal conflicts. In this respect, of course, it is vastly different both from Racine's earlier tragedies and from *Phèdre*, for what provides the ontological basis of the earlier tragedies is precisely the unchangeable and unsurmountable conflict which they describe.

But if Junia and Titus, the heroes of tragedies of refusal, of tragedies without peripeteia and recognition, did not even consider the possibility of living a valid life in this world, and if it was assumed from the very moment the curtain went up that man and the world could not be reconciled, there is nevertheless an element common to both *Mithridate* and *Iphigénie* in the fact that both plays do consider the possibility of a valid life in this world. Indeed, this problem·is at the very centre of the two plays, even though the replies given in them are completely different and even contradictory.

Britannicus and *Bérénice* were tragedies of refusal, but *Phèdre* will be the tragedy of someone who tries to live authentically in the world, the tragedy of error, crime and recognition. This is why, on the path which led Racine from *Bérénice* to *Phèdre*, *Bajazet*, *Iphigénie* and *Mithridate*, and especially the latter, are useful and probably necessary stages.

The relationship between *Mithridate* and *Phèdre* shows itself on the most superficial level, that is to say in the anecdote which provides the subject matter for the play. The wife, or fiancée, of the absent king, is in love with his son, and the rumour of the king's death renders the declaration of love possible and creates the illusion that the lovers can live innocently in the world. The king's return, however, transforms this declaration into an involuntary crime.[1]

This is the theme both of *Mithridate* and of *Phèdre*, and it is by no means certain that this similarity is the result of a deliberate and conscious choice. It is possible, although we have no evidence for this, that when he came back to tragedy Racine more or less consciously repeated the theme of *Mithridate* in order to correct the error of perspective, the illusion which had given birth to the play he had written in 1673.

There is, however, an even deeper relationship between the two plays. *Mithridate*, I feel, is the expression of a hope, of a reality which Racine himself experienced, and which certainly helped him to conceive and write *Phèdre*.

The problem of the psychic and biographical conditions governing literary creation is a complex and difficult one, and I shall approach it with some considerable hesitation. However, even though it is

---

[1] I mentioned the first appearance of this theme in *Bajazet*, but while it there remained in the background, it becomes the centre of the plot in *Mithridate* and *Phèdre*. The reason for this is that the subject matter of *Bajazet* is compromise with the world, whereas the theme of the other two plays is the possibility of living in the world without compromise. *Bajazet* begins at the very point where *Phèdre* leaves off.

possible for a writer to have conceived *Phèdre* without having in any way experienced any of the emotions described in the play, the creation of such a work would certainly have been made easier for him if he had lived through an attempt to reconcile opposites in this world and had been obliged to abandon the hope of doing so as illusory.

This is not really the place to repeat my discussion of whether or not the hope born of the Peace of Clement IX in 1669, and the disillusion which began to be manifest round about 1675, did provide the psychic background that helped Racine to conceive *Phèdre*. Even when we consider only Racine's literary work, however, it does seem that the fact of having conceived, and written, in 1672–73, a play of historical hope (whatever may be the individual or psychic background expressed in this play) is a useful or perhaps a necessary condition for conceiving a play dealing with the destruction of this hope, the tragedy of illusion and recognition.[1]

In short, the position of *Mithridate* between two tragedies— *Bérénice* and *Phèdre*—or, more exactly, between *Bajazet*, with its reminiscences of the tragedy of refusal, and *Iphigénie*, which foreshadows the new tragedy, represents the culminating point in Racine's work, the highest expression of immanent hope in this world, the only play (if we leave out *Alexandre*) which celebrates the glory of the state and the king.[2]

There is, however, the same symmetrical difference between the

---

[1] This problem is similar to the one raised by the famous controversy over the question of whether or not Pascal ever did go through a genuinely 'worldly' period and whether he did write the *Discours sur les Passions de l'amour*. Did Pascal really hope, at some period in his life, that he could live in the world without making any concessions at all? Did he write the *Discours*?.From our point of view today the answer to these questions depends, of course, upon what criteria we adopt in our historical and philological researches. In my view, however, it is nevertheless certain that even if the *Pensées* do not necessarily compel us to answer 'Yes' to the first question it is in any case very much easier to imagine them being written by a man who had had a genuine and personal experience of the world, both in its real presence and in its fundamental vanity.

[2] The study of the royal personage in Racinian tragedy is a typical example of the importance for literary criticism of a conceptual instrument enabling us to go beyond the immediately available and abstract fact in order to show its relationship to the whole and its concrete essence. For there are, in Racine, two types of royal characters, each of which has a completely different meaning from the other. On the one hand, we have Andromache, Junia, Titus, Berenice, Eriphile and Phaedra, who are regal by their human greatness, by the distance which separates them from the world, and by our inability to imagine them ever reconciled with the world—or even, in the case of the first three, ever achieving a genuine dialogue with it. On the other hand, we have Pyrrhus, Nero, Agrippina, Antiochus, Mithridates and Theseus, all of whom are kings of this world and who do nothing but exercise their royal power with all its radically evil and inadequate qualities.

hint at historical optimism in *Mithridate* and the individualistic optimism of Corneille's plays as between even the roughest sketch of dialectical thought and rationalism. Cornelian optimism is still pre-tragic, while the optimism hinted at in *Mithridate* is one which has gone through and beyond tragedy, a post-tragic optimism. In one case we see the optimism of glory, in the other the optimism of hope. One is centred round the present, the other round the future—a fact, which explains why, in spite of the differences between *Britannicus*, *Bérénice*, *Mithridate* and *Phèdre*, the Racinian hero never considers the problem of sacrificing passion to reason, but only that of saving the whole man by bringing together the opposing forces of individual passion, reason and social duty.[1]

Having thus sketched the links between *Mithridate* and *Phèdre*, we now have to ask why the first of these two plays is aesthetically inferior to the second. Why is there such a discrepancy between what Racine intended and what he achieved?

This problem must be dealt with on two levels: that of the internal aesthetic coherence of the plays; and that of Racine's own individual psychology.

We must first of all show why the different characters in *Mithridate* and their relationship with one another do not make up a coherent universe, and why Racine allowed this to be so.

There is, in fact, in *Mithridate* a violent contradiction between Racine's aims and his achievements, between the story (in the sense of the anecdote or theme) and the psychology of the characters.

Racine was certainly a very great writer and was aware of the numerous demands of the historical play, notably the need for that fusion between the hero, the world and the Gods which distinguishes it from tragedy, where these elements are in opposition.

In place of the triad, hero, world, Gods, we find in *Mithridate* three heroes of equal importance: Mithridates himself, Monime and Xiphares, who are not in opposition with one another but who make up, together, the world of the play. As for the Gods, they are absorbed in immanence, and made superfluous by the presence of the hero in the world, so that their function is fulfilled by history. We merely learn incidentally that the Gods are linked to the presence of the community, and that it will be difficult for Mithridates's soldiers to

---

[1] This is why it is possible to go back to tragedy from the historical play or the sacred drama, as Racine did when writing *Phèdre*. Goethe feared such a return during the whole of his life, in actual reality when he made the acquaintance of Holderlin or Kleist, in his work when he talks about it to Schiller. It would, in contrast, be difficult to imagine an evolution which led from these literary forms to the drama of Corneille, which, from the point of view of the tragic vision, is something which has definitely been transcended and outgrown.

defeat the enemy in Rome itself, where the city will be protected by its Gods. This is the point of the question that the traitor Pharnace asks of his brother Xiphares in Act III, Scene 1 (ll. 889–90) and shows how, for everyone in the play, there is no question of the Gods being above and beyond human activity.

The main reason, however, why I find this play unsatisfying is that the historical task which should be the prime motive force, which should replace the Gods, reconcile Xiphares and Mithridates, transform the latter from a wild beast into a man and, for the first time in Racine's theatre, conclude the play by opening up a perspective of future progress, in reality exists neither in the minds of the characters nor in the general pattern of the play. Thus, there are two themes—the historical one of the fight against the Romans, the individual one of Monime's love—which are inadequately linked together. The first dominates the structure of the play which Racine set out to write, but it is the second that is more important in the finished work. This is not a purely personal interpretation, for the actual opening of the play clearly indicates that we are in the presence of an historical situation. The curtain goes up on what is apparently a purely political situation: Mithridates is reported dead, Rome is triumphant and the king's two sons, Xiphares and Pharnace, are in bitter conflict with each other, the first showing his loyalty to his father by hating Rome, the second ready to turn traitor (Act I, Scene 1, ll. 1–2, 25–8). In reality, however, the facts are quite different. What separates Xiphares and Pharnace is not their attitude towards the Romans, but their love for Monime, officially betrothed to Mithridates and already possessing the title of queen (ll. 29–30 and 36).

Later on, when Xiphares explains why he hates the Romans, we see that it is not because of his political attitude but because of what might well be called a Cornelian cult of honour. He is inspired not by an ideological hatred which has its immediate and authentic reasons in patriotism or a desire to fight against the oppressor, but purely by feelings of personal glory. He wants to redeem the insult which his mother, through feelings of jealousy for Monime, had earlier inflicted on Mithridates. He had, in fact, as he tells us, loved Monime long before Mithridates (l. 46), but gave up any feelings of jealousy that he might otherwise have had towards his father in order to make amends for his mother's crime. It is, he explains in lines 61–71, because of his mother's attempted betrayal of Mithridates to the Romans that he had been such a ferocious enemy of those whom his father has always hated.

Basically, his choice is between two purely individual elements of his personality: his love for Monime, and his desire to redeem the guilt cast upon him by his mother. Later on, in Act V, Scene 5, he tells Pharnace it is his mother's crime which makes his choice different from that of his brother, and that will cause him to act as he does. He sees history merely as an external and implicitly accidental means of satisfying this personal concern with his own honour.

In the actual text of the play, Monime only once associates herself with the fight against the Romans. Her choice lies between loving Xiphares and fulfilling her duty towards Mithridates. Thus, even when she rejects Pharnace because of the hostility that she feels towards the Romans who killed her father, her attitude is ambiguous. In spite of her statement that it is her duty not to break faith with her father, it is difficult to tell from her refusal of Pharnace in Act III, Scene 3, lines 270–5, whether this is merely a pretext to reject a man whom she does not love, or whether she really does feel a hostility towards Rome which perhaps also influenced her in her fidelity towards Mithridates and love for Xiphares.

It is, however, surprising to note that although Monime speaks least of all of her historical task, this is nevertheless very closely linked to her personal problems: the man she loves is the enemy of the Romans, and the man whose love she rejects is their ally.

There are certain characteristics in Monime which are repeated in Racine's later plays, and fully developed in the character of Phaedra.

There is first of all her paradoxical situation, that she is, as she says. 'a queen in name, but still held captive, and now a widow who has never had a husband' (ll. 136–7). She is, as she later says, 'a crowned slave' (l. 255).

The situation of Xiphares has a similar paradoxicality, in that it is Mithridates himself who orders him to stay with Monime while she wishes him to leave her (Act II, Scene 6, ll. 719–20), who, as he says himself, is cast into an abyss of despair at the very moment when he attains the height of glory and happiness (ll. 712–33), and who is 'both loved and banished' (l. 749).

It is important to note, however, that in all these passages Xiphares passively endures his paradoxical situation, but does not assume it; it is for this reason that there is nothing in common between him and a tragic character.

There is also another feature which Monime shares with Junia, Berenice and Phaedra: almost until the very end the play presents itself as the moment when she lives authentically for the first and last time. Indeed, as we see in lines 676–7, she declares her love to Xiphares 'for the first and the last time'; in Act IV, Scene 1, she feels she can 'breathe for the first time' (l. 1174) at the news of the reconciliation between Mithridates and Xiphares; and, in Act IV, Scene 4 (l. 1315), she is summoned by Mithridates 'for the last time' to fulfil her promise towards him.

She is, indeed, herself aware of how unique a moment this is in her life, and declares in Act V, Scene 2 (ll. 1519–22), that she is at last 'mistress of her own fate'.

Mithridates himself is like Pyrrhus or Nero, except for the fact that he has an historical mission—that of fighting against the Romans—which finally gives him a positive value on the human plane. As both a private and a public citizen, both lover and king at the same time, Mithridates would be the complete man but for the fact that the duality between man and the world which is abolished in the play did not recur—and that almost without any organic synthesis—inside his own character. This duality does not lie in the contrast between his struggle against the Romans and his jealous, authoritarian and completely unethical love for Monime, since both these two features can be justified by considerations of realistic psychology and by Racine's intentions in the play. What does matter is that the two elements are quite autonomous and do not influence each other in any way. Naturally, Mithridates never thinks of reaching an understanding with the Romans that will enable him to devote his time to Monime. But, contrariwise, he never—except at the very end of the play—accepts the love between Xiphares and Monime as a factor which might help him in his struggle against the Romans.

Racine was aware of this problem, and inserted Act IV, Scene 5, in order to show that Mithridates did consider it. There, in a long monologue, the king considers the possibility of having his son killed in order to avenge the affront which his love for Monime offers to his personal honour. However, the folly and madness of such a course of action take only a moment to become obvious to him, as he considers how great a blow it will be to sacrifice a son of whom Rome is already afraid and whom he needs in his present isolation. It is then that he first considers the final solution, which he will attain only at the moment of death, of surrendering Monime to Xiphares and thus binding his son to himself in an even stronger tie of loyalty and friendship (ll. 1392–1402).

The drawback is that this scene is introduced very artificially, since the ideas he expresses have never previously influenced his conduct towards Monime, and do not really do so in the rest of the play. One has the impression that, in his character, the two planes lie side by side but are never linked organically together.

This is why, when they are eventually brought together in the very last act, both Monime's words to Mithridates on his duty to liberty and history and Mithridates's reply, with the disappearance in the face of death of any private feelings or jealousy, can, like the vision of the future on which he closes and Xiphares's final promise to avenge his father's death, be justified psychologically but are only very loosely connected with the actions that preceded them (cf. ll. 1675–95).

Racine himself was sufficiently aware of this to remove, after the first edition, the linés in which Xiphares was urged to join the Parthians in the struggle which was eventually to lead to the defeat of Crassus,[1] and, unlike the changes which he made in *Andromaque*, this alteration in no way affects the ending of the play. This remains intact, with all the elements that originally constituted it—the transformation of Mithridates, his vision of the future, and the continuation of the struggle by Xiphares and Monime, now united in their love.

All that Racine did by removing these lines was to attenuate and render less visible a lack of unity which, without changing the whole of the play, he could not entirely eliminate.

(ii)

The structure of *Iphigénie* also becomes clearer if we look at the position of this play in Racine's work, between *Mithridate* and *Phèdre*.

We have seen that through *Bajazet* and *Mithridate* Racine gradually leaves tragedy behind him and moves towards dramas situated in the world. We have also seen how, in both plays, he was held back from doing this completely by the survival of tragic elements from which he could not entirely free himself and which were incompatible with these dramas. And we have also seen how these tragic elements either destroy the coherence of *Bajazet* and *Mithridate* or prevent Racine from fully achieving it.

In the case of *Iphigénie* the situation is more complex because it is both similar to *Bajazet* and *Mithridate* and different from them. It is similar in that the co-existence of a providential universe which leaves no place for tragedy with a tragic universe which leaves no place for providence destroys the unity of the play; it is different in the very fact that we can, when speaking of *Iphigénie*, talk about a providential universe and a tragic universe, which would have been quite impossible in the case of *Bajazet* or *Mithridate*.

In both these two plays there was a perpetual interpenetration of tragic and dramatic elements, with the result that the aesthetic level, both of the play itself and of each individual element, was weakened and made lower. This is not at all the case with *Iphigénie*, however, since this play is made up of two completely coherent and perfectly homogeneous universes, between which there is only the thinnest of external links: on the one hand, we have the providential universe of Agamemnon, Iphigeneia, Clytemnestra and Ulysses, and, on the other, the tragic universe of Eriphile.

[1] Cf. Edition of 1673. Variant quoted on p. 99 of the III volume in the *Grands Ecrivains de France* edition of Racine's work (Hachette, 1929).

Each of these two universes attains, by its very homogeneity, an aesthetic level far higher than that reached by any fragment of the two other plays; however, *Iphigénie* as a whole nevertheless lacks—precisely because of this duality—the unity which can alone make a work of art absolutely valid. This is why, in spite of the undoubted beauty not only of certain scenes and certain lines but also of each of the two unities just mentioned when taken individually, *Iphigénie* does not quite reach the level of Racine's four completely coherent plays: *Britannicus, Bérénice, Phèdre* and *Athalie*.

There are two characters who move in and between the two universes of *Iphigénie*: Achilles—since Eriphile loves him—and the Gods who condemn Eriphile and save Iphigeneia. It is in the reality or irreality of the links between the two universes that the problem of the play's aesthetic value lies.

In both cases, however, there is an illusion, for Achilles in no way really belongs to the universe of Eriphile. Eriphile certainly loves him, but this love creates no bond between the two characters, and she is never able to declare her feelings. Achilles, on the other hand, is quite indifferent towards Eriphile, and has for her only the feelings which he would have for anyone belonging to the same world as himself. His generosity and polite benevolence are in fact characteristic of the anonymity of personal relationships in certain types of society. Moreover, in spite of her love, Eriphile never manages to have any effect at all on Achilles's life or to intervene in the events of the providential universe which he inhabits. Her only attempt to do this has no influence on anything except her own fate.

Similarly—and again, appearances notwithstanding—the Gods who save Iphigeneia from the deceitful illusion of men are completely different from the Gods who condemn Eriphile, and the only common factor which they have between them is simply the name of 'Gods'. This is shown not only in the fact that they act differently—the same beings can in fact act in a contradictory manner—but also by the fact that there is not even a mention of this contradiction in the play, let alone an attempt to justify or explain it.

Racine could have used the basic situation of the play in order to give some reality to the conflict between the two universes. This would have led him towards a tragedy of the type exemplified in *Phèdre* or, possibly, towards a Shakespearian type. The important thing, however, is that he did not do this, and that there is no real dramatic link—either internal or external—between the two completely different universes. The only way in which they can be said to co-exist is by the presence of the inhabitants of one universe as silent and helpless spectators of the events which take place in the other. This is not an adequate relationship to give unity to a play.

This absence of links is, moreover, visible in the actual dramatic construction. Eriphile appears neither in the first nor in the fifth act, and the long narrative of Ulysses which ends the play is delivered from the point of view of someone who is merely a spectator.

Out of the thirteen scenes making up the three acts in which she appears, Eriphile is alone with her confidante Doris in four of them; in six she is either a completely silent witness (Act II, Scenes 2 and 6; Act IV, Scene 10) or an almost silent one, expressing surprise in single lines in Act II, Scene 4 and Act III, Scene 4 and in a short speech of six lines in Act II, Scene 7. It thus follows that only three times in the play (Act II, Scenes 3 and 5 and Act III, Scene 4) are there even the apparent beginnings of a dialogue between Eriphile and the characters inhabiting the providential universe.

Now in the first of these three scenes (Act II, Scene 3) all Eriphile does in fact is to express the radical difference between her situation in the world and that of Iphigeneia, while another (Act III, Scene 4) contains Achilles's promise to liberate Eriphile at Iphigeneia's request. Now this attempt on Racine's part to link the two universes together not only has no meaning or importance in the play as a whole but is also introduced under the form of a 'dialogue of the deaf' and of a complete misunderstanding between the people taking part in it. Moreover, this misunderstanding is not merely—as was the case in the earlier tragedies—the result of one of those 'solitary dialogues' brought about by the existence of two completely different moral and human levels at which two people were seeking but could never find each other. Achilles and Iphigeneia form a completely self-sufficient couple, who promise freedom to Eriphile as a result of the need which they seem to feel to share the happiness which they themselves have acquired with the whole world. They want to be generous in a kind of abstract and general way, and are convinced that a slave, as a slave, must long for liberty. Eriphile accepts this liberty in order to be able to go away and not to feel despair in the presence of the happiness of Achilles and Eriphile. There is another scene (Act II, Scene 5) in which Racine has tried to establish a dialogue between Eriphile and Iphigeneia, but it costs him a good deal to do it: he is not only forced to introduce an almost irrelevant incident but he also has to distort Eriphile's own character, by making this wholly tragic person perform a petty comedy of deceit. Indeed, Racine himself later finds this scene so artificial and irrelevant that he cannot bring Iphigeneia to recall the wholly justified jealousy which she felt for Eriphile—not believing for a moment the latter's protestations that she does not love Achilles—and at no time refers to it again in the course of the play.

Why, then, in the face of the two wholly different universes, did Racine not abandon the character of Eriphile, or at least exclude her from the dramatic treatment of a theme in which her presence is wholly unexpected? There are two possible replies: Racine himself gave us the first when he wrote in the preface that without the 'fortunate character of Eriphile' he would never have been able to undertake to write this tragedy. 'How could I have besmirched the stage with the horrible murder of a person of the virtue and charms necessary to Iphigeneia? And, moreover, how could I have ended my tragedy by the intervention of a Goddess or a machine, and by a metamorphosis which might have found some credence in Euripides's time, but which would strike us as too absurd and too unbelievable?' However, this merely means (a) that Racine could not accept the sacrifice of someone who was, like Iphigeneia, wholly innocent; and (b) that he was quite pleased to be able to avoid a 'Goddess or machine' which, nevertheless, given the support of tradition, were just believable, and which he will have no hesitation in bringing in to *Phèdre*. What in fact excluded both the sacrifice of Iphigeneia and her rescue by a 'machine' was not 'probability' (*vraisemblance*) but the actual play that he intended to write, the providential drama of Iphigeneia. But why, in spite of all the aesthetic difficulties of his subject—which he did not wholly overcome—did Racine insist on writing a play on the theme of Iphigeneia?

At this level—the only really interesting one—such a question, which would appear insoluble and even absurd to the traditional literary historian, is one that can be answered only by reference to Racine's own psychological experience. There does seem to me to be a certain relationship between the state of mind in which he wrote *Iphigénie* and the political situation in 1673–74. The Peace of Clement IX had been in existence since 1669, and there was a feeling of national unity which had accompanied the war against Holland. This war, however, had dragged on longer than expected, Racine felt suspicious of the compromise reached in 1669, and, living at the Court, could doubtless feel, by countless little signs which are now quite invisible to us, that the Jansenists were about to be persecuted yet again. These facts suggest that there is a relationship, complex but nevertheless generally comprehensible, between the duality in Racine's mind and the duality which shows itself in the play. It may be that this duality between a tragic and a providential universe which is an aesthetic weakness of the play was the most adequate expression which Racine could find for his feelings at the time when he wrote it. Talent and even genius are not enough to give valid aesthetic expression to simply any state of mind; this must manifest itself in a coherent universe which is a necessary—but not always an adequate—condition for the aesthetic validity of any work of art.

We can now determine the place which *Iphigénie* occupies in

Racine's work, in relation both to *Mithridate* and to *Phèdre*. At least in intention, *Mithridate* expressed the high-water mark of Racine's hopes that certain values could be incarnated in history; aesthetically, however, the expression of these hopes is hindered by the persistence of individualist categories peculiar to tragedy. *Iphigénie* represents at one and the same time a move forward in these hopes (but in a providential rather than an immanent form) and a return to tragedy. This time, however, it is a tragedy with peripeteia and recognition, of the type which will find its full expression and development in Racine's work with *Phèdre*.

Compared to the universe of *Mithridate*, the providential universe of *Iphigénie* is much more coherent and homogeneous. This is obvious from the contrast between the lack of reality which characterises the fight against Rome in the first play and the central position occupied by the war against Troy in the second, where it in fact governs the actions and behaviour of the characters. There are, however, two ways in which tragedy and the Jansenist vision can be transcended—the historical drama in which the Gods are immanent in the world and the sacred drama in which they intervene from outside. It is the second of these possibilities that will be fully realised by Racine in *Esther* and *Athalie*, and it is the second which is more visible in *Iphigénie*. In their relationship to mankind, the Gods show themselves to be fully present and full of help.

But there exists, as a limiting factor by the side of this providential universe, the tragic universe of Eriphile. This, with the one exception of the scene already mentioned (Act II, Scene 5), is to a very large extent a foreshadowing of the tragedy with peripeteia and recognition that Racine will soon write in *Phèdre*.[1]

Thus, during the actual period in which Racine's plays expressed the possibility of hope in this world—from *Bajazet* to *Iphigénie*—there is the gradual development of the elements which go to make up *Phèdre*. *Bajazet* offered the illusion of a possible life in this world, *Mithridate* offered the situation, and *Iphigénie* the character. All that was needed to crystallise this whole in the poet's imagination, and create the masterpiece of *Phèdre*, was a conjunction of external circumstances.

In this analysis of the two universes in *Iphigénie* the theme of this book naturally leads me to give more attention to the tragic than to the providential. Both, however, have one feature in common: they can be studied in relation to the Greek theatre, and particularly in relation to Sophocles. *Andromaque*, *Britannicus* and *Bérénice* had been, as examples of tragedy in the theatre, profoundly original

[1] The similarity between Eriphile and Phaedra has already been noticed by Karl Vossler in his *Jean Racine* (Ed. Buhl, 1948).

creations by Racine. Without these three plays, the Aristotelian concept of a tragedy without peripeteia and recognition would still have a purely theoretical interest for the aesthetician, who would be incapable of finding any concrete content which corresponded to it. In *Bajazet* and *Mithridate* Racine had written dramas of a type that would be developed later in modern literature. But it was only with *Iphigénie* and *Phèdre* that he dealt with situations comparable to those that we find in Greek tragedy. Similarly, in *Esther* and *Athalie*, he rediscovered the other element which is essential to this type of tragedy: the chorus. And, as I have already remarked, union between the tragic character and the chorus is precisely what is most inaccessible to the modern writer.

The world of Sophocles' plays is one where the Gods are deceitful, and in which men can live only in illusion, and where knowledge leads directly to blindness and death.

Initially, this seems to be the world depicted in *Iphigénie*, but the play later presents a universe opposed in every point to that of Sophocles. In *Iphigénie* the Gods are providential and intervene in the life of man, but they do so after the manner of the Christian God— in order to help human beings and bring what they are doing to a happy ending. Men are blind, even as they are blind in the Christian concept of the 'fallen state of man', but their blindness consists of a lack of confidence in Divine Providence, in their misinterpreting the oracles which promise them protection and in their desire to make themselves equal to God or independent of Him, rebelling and fighting among themselves instead of joining together in submission and in love for the Gods.

The play begins with two 'stage directions' which indicate both the time at which the play takes place and the situation of the tragic character: these are the two lines at the beginning and end of the first scene, the first of which announces the very beginning of dawn, while the second speaks of its 'striking and illuminating us' (ll. 5 and 158).

Apart from the central word 'strikes' this is the definition of the time, in which the play takes place, both for Agamemnon, Iphigeneia, etc., as for Eriphile. But while, for the former, the day which at first seems to strike them is protective, the conclusion shows that the person to whom this exact definition of the 'time' of any tragedy with peripeteia and recognition rigorously applies is Eriphile.

The whole of this first scene is a fairly accurate reproduction of the situation in Sophoclean tragedy. The peculiarity of Racine's play is that, while the Sophoclean hero is generally tragic without knowing it, Iphigeneia, who is not really but only apparently in a tragic situation, nevertheless has a complete awareness of it. And, although this awareness is in its way as false as that of the Sophoclean hero, it is an accurate analysis of the tragic hero.

I have already said that men, represented in Sophocles by the chorus, can live only because they are blinded by illusion; the hero, on the other hand, must abandon life because, either through his own or through the Gods' decision, he is condemned to discover the truth: that human greatness and the protection of the Gods, happiness and knowledge, are incompatible. This analysis recurs from the very beginning of *Iphigénie*, modified only by the consciousness which Agamemnon seems to have of his greatness and his situation. This consciousness is brought out by the fact that, at the very beginning of the play, it is Agamemnon himself who begins the action by waking up his servant Arcas and announces his misfortune by envying the state of one who, 'free of the yoke under which a King is bound', lives in the obscure state where the Gods have hidden him' (ll. 1–14).

Thinking that he has understood the threatening meaning of the divine oracle which demands the sacrifice of Iphigeneia, Agamemnon has decided to disobey the Gods, swearing even on their very altars that he will not be obedient to their wishes (ll. 63–8).

But he remains aware of the limits of his strength. Far from thinking, like Achilles, that he can be the equal of the Gods and take their place, he appears as a tragic character torn between his duty as a father and his duty as a citizen and a king, obliged as such to accept the authority of the City's Gods. As he tells Arcas, he knows that as soon as his daughter arrives in Aulis, Calchas will overcome any private protestations of grief, will make the Gods themselves speak and ensure that only the voice of religion, 'in anger against us', will be listened to by 'the timid Greeks' (ll. 134–8). It is for this reason, he continues, that he is sending Arcas with the message to Clytemnestra to delay Iphigeneia's arrival, and he charges his servant to keep the utmost secrecy in order that his daughter may never know to what peril she was exposed (ll. 145–8). And the scene ends with the line (158) which reminds us of the dangers which life and knowledge represent for the tragic hero.

In the following scene Achilles' blindness carries him to the point where he holds himself equal to the Gods, affirming that although the Gods may be the supreme rulers over our lives, our personal honour rests in our own hands. We should, he tells Agamemnon, seek only to make ourselves immortal like the Gods themselves, without worrying about the orders that they may give. 'Let fate do what it will,' he declares; 'Let us run to where courage offers us a destiny as great as theirs' (ll. 257–63).

We then see Ulysses, preoccupied solely by the laws of war and of the city, demanding absolute submission at any price to the cruelty of the Gods; Clytemnestra, a mother, trying above all else to defend her daughter against the sentence of the Gods; and, finally, Iphigeneia herself, completely pure, free of any spirit of rebellion, accepting both her father's decisions and her condemnation by the Gods.

The idea of the cruel and revengeful Gods of classical tragedy dominates the whole play, as we see Agamemnon accusing the Heavens of 'breaking all the devices of his vain prudence' in order to ensure their revenge (ll. 361–2), declaring that he 'surrenders, and allows the Gods to weigh heavily on the innocent' (l. 390), announcing the 'stately sacrifice' being prepared by Calchas (l. 570) hoping that, before it is accomplished, he may be able to 'move their injustice to mercy' (l. 572) and complaining that the Gods, while imposing so severe a law upon him, should have also left him with 'a father's heart' (Act IV, Scene 5, l. 1322).

We even see the hubris of Achilles feeling himself the equal of the Gods, and affirming that 'as long as he lives' it is useless for the Gods to order the death of Iphigeneia (Act III, Scene 7, ll. 1083–5).

But in the end the Gods show themselves not as revengeful but as merciful, as just and providential Gods who in many ways resemble the God of Christianity. The very character of Iphigeneia, and her complete absence of any hubris, in fact foreshadowed this development from the very beginning.

'How could I have besmirched the stage with the horrible murder of a person of the virtue and charms necessary to Iphigeneia,' wrote Racine in his preface, thus indicating the anti-tragic and, in the last analysis, basically Christian character of his play.

The spectator gradually realises that the whole situation has been transformed. The whole of the first scene—the sleeping camp, the oracle, Agamemnon the king stricken by the Gods, separated from the rest of mankind by the fact that he has woken up while they are still sleeping, the hero 'illuminated by this feeble day', but who, in spite of his weakness, 'condemns the Gods' and tries to resist them, who soon feels that 'the rising day' strikes and enlightens him— seemed to announce the kind of situation usually found in Greek tragedy. It was, however, an illusion. The Gods are not cruel but providential, and Agamemnon is not a tragic hero who watches while others sleep, but a man who belongs to the same world as Achilles, Clytemnestra, Ulysses and the sleeping camp. The heroine whose awareness places her above the blindness of men is the innocent Iphigeneia; blindness is rebellion, and truth lies in submitting to the will of the Gods. Christian truth has taken the place of apparent tragedy, and the classical city has been taken over, from inside, by the City of God.

But by the side of the City of God, and in opposition to it, impotent in its desire to do harm but proud and self-sufficient, there rises the tragic city of man, the world of Eriphile. In Racine's world Eriphile and Phaedra are the two characters who come nearest to the hero of early classical Greek tragedy. Eriphile is radically alone, modern in that she is in conflict with the community of other people, determined to discover a truth that will cause her death, eager for purity, even when she sins, and capable, at the supreme moment, of transforming her condemnation by the Gods into voluntarily accepted suicide. She is thus separated by an unbridgeable gulf from all those who, reduced as they do so to the rank of marionnettes, live in the providential universe of the Gods. From the moment she comes on stage, she defines her own character as she tells her confidente Doris that they must 'withdraw' in order to put 'both her joy and my sadness at liberty to express themselves', and leave Iphigeneia to the pleasure of reunion with her father and lover (Act II, Scene 1, ll. 395–9). She is condemned, she says, to die without discovering who she is (ll. 426–30).

Paradoxically, she loves in the person of Achilles the man who is persecuting her, who has murdered her family and been the barbarous destroyer of Lesbos, but she can do nothing but refuse anything which Achilles and Iphigeneia can offer her. The meaning of her whole life lies in the quest for the identity of those parents whom her 'mad love' dishonours. Between her fidelity to her past, to her city and her love for Achilles, there is no possible compromise, and she would have a duty to die even if the oracle had not condemned her. Again in the very first scene, she tells Doris that a 'rapid death' ought to hide her shame in the tomb, and that she has already caused too much dishonour to the parents she is still seeking (ll. 525–8).

However, in contrast to the tragedies with neither peripeteia nor recognition there is a 'story' of Eriphile as there is a 'story' in *Phèdre*. It is the story of an illusion, the illusion that life might be possible, that the Gods might tolerate an existence which would destroy the whole order of the universe, and which might enable the tragic character to bring together the two impossibly contradictory sides of his life; that, in spite of the barbarous and unchanging order which accepts life only partially, in so far as it gives up the demand for totality, there might nevertheless be some chance of bringing together the Divine will and guilty passion, purity and sin, virtue and happiness.

What Eriphile attacks in Iphigeneia is not only the latter's happiness but also the legitimate nature of this happiness, its general recognition and consecration by the whole providential universe in which she lives. It is the fact that Iphigeneia can give up any attempt to reach a synthesis, and can find happiness in virtue itself—a virtue which, unlike that of Phaedra, is an authentic reality because it forms part of the Christianised universe of Providence. It is this which gives rise to her outburst in Act II, Scene 8, when she complains to the Gods of having to suffer both from the happiness and from the insults of her proud rival Iphigeneia (ll. 756-9).

She is perhaps even more envious of the general acceptance of Iphigeneia's happiness than she is of her marriage with Achilles, and it is this which explains the envy which she feels for Iphigeneia at the very moment that her rival seems about to be put to death. She replies, in explanation to her astonished confidente, that she has never said anything more truthful. For, she continues, the apparent imminence of Iphigeneia's sacrifice has brought with it an increase in her glory and in the concern which Achilles shows for the fate of the person he loves (Act IV, Scene 1, ll. 1085-94).

She is too perspicacious in her hostility to believe that the Gods could or would condemn someone who is so generally accepted by the community, and points out to Doris, in the same scene, that she will soon see that the Gods have ordered the oracle to announce Iphigeneia's death solely in order to increase her glory and Eriphile's own discomfiture. She explains to Doris how, in spite of the fact that the altar is all ready for the sacrificial victim, the victim's name has not yet been announced; this is clearly, she realises, a sign that Agamemnon is still hesitating, and is unable to withstand the combined onslaught of Clytemnestra's fury, Iphigeneia's tears, the despair of his whole family and Achilles' wrath; in the presence of such obstacles to her death, she says that Iphigeneia will be saved and that all the preparations will have served only to make her more beautiful in Achilles' eyes. In her clear perception of reality, Eriphile sees that it is, in reality, herself alone who is condemned to misfortune (ll. 1113-25).

This is why her illusory hope can spring only from the apparent if not real weaknesses in Iphigeneia's world. It is not surprising that she is so attentive and perspicacious in seeing such faults, and is able to tell Doris what she has noticed: that Iphigeneia is not being told the truth, that people are hiding from Achilles, that Agamemnon is groaning in anguish. It is these signs that she is quickest to perceive, that lead her to hope that fate may still take her side in her hatred against Iphigeneia and able her not to weep alone or die without achieving her revenge (Act II, Scene 8, ll. 760-6).

Similarly, it is not surprising that she finally falls into the illusion of a possible alliance between herself and the Gods, an alliance that would enable her to achieve, in this world, the most contradictory demands: the death of Iphigeneia, her rival in her love for Achilles, and the satisfaction of her fidelity to her ancestors and the community from which she sprang, a fidelity which demands that the destruction of Lesbos by Achilles be avenged. It is this which leads her, in Act IV, Scene 1, to entertain the project of revealing all the plots that are being made against the Gods, by whom she is seeking to be recognised, and thus bringing about the complete ruin of all the ambitions of the Greeks. If only, she thinks, she could cause civil war to break out in the midst of the army on its way to Troy, make Achilles fight against Agamemnon and thus make a happy sacrifice to her own fatherland of the whole Grecian camp. It is this ambition which brings her, at the end of this scene, to depart to consult the Gods and see what furies they will authorise in order to prevent this 'odious marriage' (ll. 1133–44).

However, all this is an illusion, and there is no possible community between Eriphile and the world or between a living Eriphile and the Gods. The Gods that are providential for Iphigeneia are jealous and angry towards Eriphile, and their oracle, which seemed to promise hope, finally leads to her death. It is Calchas who puts an end to her illusion by revealing to Eriphile at one and the same time her royal birth, her sin and the sentence which lies upon her.

As he does this, however, he finally consecrates the abyss between the two universes, for Eriphile now knows that she comes from elsewhere, from another world, and that there can be nothing in common between her and the world of providence in which Iphigeneia lives. When Calchas tries to come near her in order to fulfil his sacred mission she speaks the words that perhaps contain the whole key of the play. She tells him to hold back, assuring him that the blood of the heroes from which he has now told her she descends is quite able to flow without being shed by his 'profane hands' (Act V, Scene 6, ll. 1771–4).

Both the providential Gods, their oracle and their priest are merely profane things in the universe of Eriphile. The slightest contact with them, indeed their very approach, are enough to destroy the purity and royal quality of the tragic character.

Eriphile, who knows the truth that the Gods hide from the marionnettes ruled by Providence, is now too great and pure to be punished or condemned by the providential Gods. The play ends when she discovers herself and the values which she represents.

As she leaves a universe in which she thought she could live, the order of this world is restored. Her freely accepted death removes the monstrous and rebellious being which had, previously, hindered the smooth working of the world of providence. This world can now resume its course, and her death is described as being accompanied by a roll of thunder by which the Gods signify their pleasure, the 'happy' quivering of the air in the newly returned wind, and the reply to the winds by the sea (ll. 1776–80).

I should, however, point out that by concentrating on Eriphile I have given her a much larger place than she has in Racine's play. Moreover, the idea of a struggle between the normal order of the world and the disturbance introduced by a tragic character, while entirely valid for Phaedra, is only partially true for Eriphile. For although both women disturb the cosmic order, the purity of the sun and the rule of the winds, only Phaedra succeeds in penetrating into the universe of people such as Theseus and Hippolytus. Eriphile remains constantly outside the world of Achilles and Iphigeneia, and, conversely, neither the Gods of Agamemnon and Achilles nor the men whom they protect can have any effect on her. She kills herself in order to avoid the sacrifice which would make her part of a universe that she despises. The word *profane* which she uses when speaking to Calchas points to the abyss separating the two worlds. The sacrificial killing of Eriphile would have made *Iphigénie* into a wholly Christian play, dealing with the victory of good over evil and of God over the Devil; her penetration into the providential universe of Iphigeneia would have made it into a tragedy with peripeteia and recognition, and in either case the play would have achieved its unity. What Racine gave us, however, is a play that expresses the co-existence of two entirely different worlds between which there is no communication whatsoever: the universe of Providence, where the Gods direct the destinies of the marionettes who have no understanding of what is happening; and, afar off, in a dark and threatening background, the world of the hidden and absent God, the world of passion and purity, the world of paradox, of the heavy and sacred action of tragedy: a world which is the universe of man and the universe of tragedy.

C. TRAGEDIES WITH PERIPETEIA AND RECOGNITION

VI. *Phèdre*

I was going to discuss the problem of the link between Racine's plays and the life of the Jansenist group and the political events of the seventeenth century in an appendix. However, the fact that the final paragraph of the preface to *Phèdre* raises the question of the relationship between this tragedy and the 'Friends of Port-Royal' leads naturally to a discussion of it here.[1]

[1] Cf. Racine's remarks in his preface. 'However, I do not yet dare affirm that this play is the best of my tragedies. I leave time and my readers to decide as to its true worth. What I can state with certainty, however, is that I have written none in which more insistence is placed on virtue. The slightest faults are severely punished, and the mere thought of crime is regarded with as much horror as crime

The prefaces of his six earlier plays already raise a certain number of problems, for there is a curious lack of relationship between what Racine says in his prefaces and the final impression given by the plays. He always avoids explicitly mentioning in the preface any aspect of the play that might have shocked his audience. In fact, at the very basis, both of Racine's literary work and of its success in the world, there is a characteristic duality.

A Jansenist who was consistent in his views would not have written plays, and a man who was wholly at home and integrated in the world would not have written tragedies. Racine must therefore have been half-way between the two extremes, in a situation which either mingled them together or reached a synthesis between the two, to have written the plays that he did.

Moreover, in addition to a brilliant psychological analysis of life in this world, with its passions, weaknesses and thirst for power, Racine's tragedies also represent a whole universe which is ruled by moral laws wholly foreign to those accepted by his audience and even in violent opposition to them. The real Jansenists never went to the theatre, and it is improbable that those members of the *noblesse de robe* who sympathised with Jansenism formed a very large section of the theatre-going public. This is why, although we find it natural that 'the Court and the Town' should have recognised themselves in Molière and Corneille, it is much more difficult to understand how they also assured the success of Racine's tragedies. This is a problem that deserves a thorough sociological study.

Seventeenth-century theatre-goers certainly saw a fairly accurate description of themselves in Hermione, Orestes, Pyrrhus, Nero, Britannicus, Agrippina, Antiochus, etc.; but these characters are condemned and reduced to nothing in the universe of the plays in which they appear by heroes such as Andromache, Junia, Berenice and Titus.

It is difficult to believe that Racine, who was closely acquainted both with the ethical attitude and daily life of the 'solitaries' and nuns of Port-Royal, was not also aware of the 'subversive' aspect of his

---

itself. Weaknesses due to love are here regarded as real weaknesses. The passions are presented to the spectator's eyes only in order to show him all the disorder to which they give rise; and vice is everywhere painted with those colours which cause its deformity to be both known and detested. This is indeed the true goal which every man who works for the public should set himself, and this is what the first tragic poets had in view in everything they undertook. Their theatre was a school in which there was no less teaching of virtue than in the schools of the philosophers. . . . If authors were to think as much of instructing the public as of entertaining it, and follow in this the true aim of tragedy, this would perhaps be a way of reconciling with tragedy a number of persons famous for both their piety and doctrine, who would then doubtless judge it more favourably.'

plays. It is, however, not possible to maintain that he consciously and deliberately introduced this aspect in an almost Machiavelian manner, especially as we have no document to prove it. It is not, in fact, very important whether Racine was himself fully aware of the difference between the ethical attitude implicit in his plays and the general views of his public or whether, accepting with his conscious mind the moral views of 'the Court and the Town', he subconsciously created a universe that completely contradicted these views.

The truth probably lies between these two extremes, in an intermediate zone with which both writers and psychologists are quite familiar: a subconscious attitude which is flattered and encouraged by the external or psychological advantages of certain situations.

However that may be, it is certain that the tragic and Jansenist quality of his plays, which was an aesthetic and perhaps a moral necessity for Racine himself, was precisely the feature which he could not allow to become obvious to his public if his success as a playwright was to continue. We need only think of the immense distance between, on the one hand, characters such as Pyrrhus, Nero, Agrippina and Theseus and, on the other, the generally accepted image of royalty in general and of Louis XIV in particular to realise how true this is.

It is also easy to understand why Racine did not publish his *Short History of Port-Royal* in his life-time and why his prefaces, in spite of the general truths which they contain about the composition and structure of his plays, are not only frequently inaccurate but also never go beyond the commonly accepted view of tragedy in seventeenth-century France. And this without reference to whether or not these rules are implicitly or consciously observed.

Compared to the prefaces of the earlier plays, the final paragraph to the preface to *Phèdre*, written not primarily for 'the public' but for Racine himself, and reinforced by the speech by Theseus which concludes the play, is nevertheless an exception.

It is not that Racine has abandoned all caution. When he suggests that *Phèdre* is the best of his plays—a view fully confirmed by posterity—he does so with a certain hesitation, saying that he 'does not yet dare to affirm'. Similarly, when he addresses the Jansenists who accept Arnauld's views (and in 1677 this simply means the Jansenists) and underlines the fact that the play is essentially moral—a remark which is valid for *Phèdre* as it is for any tragedy—he is talking about a morality which is not tragic but dramatic.

Many critics have noted the dissonance between, on the one hand, the preface and Theseus's last speech and, on the other, the rest of the play. Thierry Maulnier, for example, has argued that the poet's subconscious mind and creative inspiration carried him much farther than he consciously wanted to go, and that it was the horror which he felt at the sight of the tumultuous and elemental passions which he had released that explains his withdrawal from the theatre into a conventional and pious middle-class life. This is an attractive but not a wholly convincing explanation. The principal difficulty in accepting it lies in the fact that Racine's prefaces were written after his plays, and that they are not only more prudent but also incapable of telling us much about his initial intentions and state of mind when he began to compose them.

As far as the earlier prefaces are concerned, it is by no means certain that Racine, who refrained from publishing the *Short History of Port-Royal* in his life-time, and who, even in his private correspondence, used somewhat veiled terms when he treated controversial matters, was blind to the real meaning of his plays. It is therefore difficult to accept Thierry Maulnier's view that Racine saw what he really meant only in the case of *Phèdre*. It is equally possible that he was aware of what *Britannicus* and *Bérénice* meant, that he wanted to write them as they are, but that he refrained from giving his enemies ammunition against himself by openly stating their real significance.

Whether or not Racine was himself aware of the dichotomy between his plays and their prefaces, my explanation is certainly not valid for the last passage in the preface to *Phèdre* (and, in the play itself, for the last lines spoken by Theseus). The real question is this: why did Racine, after carefully avoiding any mention of Jansenism in relation to his other plays, suddenly refer to 'persons famous by their piety and doctrine' in his preface to *Phèdre*? Thierry Maulnier's suggestion does not really fit the facts: for if Racine had suddenly been overtaken by his intentions, and if he had intended to become reconciled with Port-Royal by writing the play of the virtuous Hippolytus and the wicked Phaedra, and had realised only later on that what he had really written was the play of the greatness of Phaedra and the mediocrity of Hippolytus, then why did he say that *Phèdre* could be a starting-point for a reconciliation with Port-Royal?

My own tentative explanation is very different, since I look upon all Racine's tragedies as closely linked to the problems of Jansenism and to the teachings and experiences of the 'Friends of Port-Royal'. But if *Andromaque*, *Britannicus* and *Bérénice* were a transposition on to a literary plane of the experience of the 'solitaries' at the time of tragic Jansenism before 1669 (or, at any rate, of this doctrine and experience as seen through the idealising mind of someone who had long since left Port-Royal), and if the similarity between the ideas in these plays and the position of the persecuted group was a reason for avoiding any mention of Jansenism in the prefaces; and if the next three plays—*Mithridate*, *Bajazet* and *Iphigénie*—expressed a quality of attitude towards a Jansenism which had agreed to enter into the world with the Peace of Clement IX, then *Phèdre* marks the return of a single and consistent attitude, but this time on a totally different plane. With *Phèdre* Racine gives up writing from the point of view of the tragic Jansenism which rejected the world. Instead, he transposes on to a literary plane the real experience of the Jansenist group between 1669 and 1675. The uneasy conscience of Lancelot's pupil becomes the mind of the defending counsel for Port-Royal.

The renewal of persecution after 1669 confirmed the doubt which Racine had felt about the validity of Arnauld's attempt at compromise, and which we have seen expressed in *Bajazet*, *Mithridate* and *Iphigénie*, where Racine both approved and felt hesitant at one and the same time. *Phèdre* is first and foremost the literary transposition of an experience which has already taken place: the tragedy of error and illusion. However, the same revival of persecution also brought Racine closer to Arnauld's position. For if, as I have already said, Arnauld's and Nicole's position is essentially a dramatic one, the drama of compromise which lasted from 1669 to 1675 now becomes the drama of a struggle, in the world, for what is right, just and pure. After having first of all identified himself, in his work, with the tragic position of Barcos, and after having followed, with a number of reservations, the dramatic compromise of the Peace of Clement IX, and after having made out the tragic balance sheet for this compromise in *Phèdre*, Racine now adopts a new attitude. After the renewal of persecution he identifies himself, in *Esther*, *Athalie* and the *Short History*, with the drama of Arnaldian Jansenism.

The two passages under discussion, the paragraph that concludes the preface and the lines which end the play should in my view be seen as part of this evolution, which continued until Racine's death.

Whatever may be the value of my hypothesis, it does at any rate seem difficult, if not impossible, to reconcile the two dramatic passages with the tragic text of the play as a whole. Scientific accuracy obliges me to state that, when he was finishing his play, Racine thought he was writing a drama. From my point of view it is the tragedy, objectively speaking, that he actually wrote which I am going to analyse.

The statement that *Phèdre* is—among other things—a mediatised transposition of the illusion that they could still live in the world and reach agreement with the civil and religious authorities which the 'Friends of Port-Royal' experienced from 1669 to 1675 is an unprovable hypothesis, and is presented as such. But whether it is true or false, it gives us the key to the structure of *Phèdre*: the play is the story of the illusion which the tragic hero undergoes that he can still live in the world and impose his own laws upon it, without choosing or abandoning anything.

If, however, Racine gave up the Jansenist vision in order to write *Phèdre*, and transposed only the experience of the 'Friends of Port-Royal', he did nevertheless succeed in rediscovering the other great literary tradition which he had always tried to follow: that of the Greek tragedy with peripeteia and recognition, the tragedy of human illusion and of the discovery of truth. There are, of course, wide differences between *Phèdre* and *Oedipus Rex* or *Antigone*, and, first and foremost, the absence of a chorus. But there is also an essential similarity, in that all three plays deal with an error, with a guilty and fatal action, and this is a similarity which cannot be neglected by the historian. The fact remains, however, that if Racine rediscovered Greek tragedy when writing *Phèdre* he did so from the starting-point of Jansenist tragedy, of a tragedy without peripeteia and recognition. The play, therefore retains a number of the characteristics of this type of tragedy: the world is full of vanity and empty of all moral worth, God is a silent spectator and the hero is completely alone. But Phaedra, the central character, is entirely different from Junia or Titus. While they were rigorously aware of the impossibility of accepting life, she wants to live and has the illusion that this is possible. Critics have said that Phaedra was a Christian to whom Grace has been refused. I do not find this an accurate definition. When Grace is refused or withdrawn the Christian gives up seeking God and lives in the world with no scruples and no further demands. If it is absolutely necessary to use theological terms Phaedra is much more the incarnation of the character around whom the great battle between the Jansenists and the ecclesiastical authorities took place: the 'man summoned by God' whom we find in the *Pensées*, who was a prefiguration of Goethe's *Faust*,[1] the character whom the Jansenists most frequently denied existed in their theology, but whom we find explicitly in the *Pensées*: the righteous man fallen into sin.

Phèdre represents, in Racine's work, the tragedy of the hope that men can live in the world without concessions, hopes or compromises, and the tragedy of the recognition that this hope is doomed to disillusion.

If we try to place Racine's plays in relation to the three ideological positions discussed in this book we find the following pattern. *Andromaque*, and especially *Britannicus* and *Bérénice*, are a fairly close

[1] In order to show what there is in common between Phaedra and Faustus—by the side of the many differences which lie between them—it is enough to quote the lines which define each of the characters at the beginning of the play. Phaedra is 'The daughter of Minos and of Pasiphae', while Faust is one who 'hankers after heaven's loftiest orbs' and 'demands from earth the choicest joy and art'.

reflection of the extremist Jansenism of Barcos; the three dramas, *Bajazet*, *Mithridate* and *Iphigénie*, are a reflection—incorporating all the reservations that this would involve for an extermist attitude—of the attempt which Arnauld made to live in the world and to reach a compromise with the powers that be; *Phèdre*, on the other hand, raises the whole problem of why the attempt to live in this world is inevitably a failure, and is thus nearer than any other of Racine's plays to the vision of the *Pensées*.

This means that the key to *Phèdre*—and to the *Pensées* as well—lies in the statement of the human value of the paradox, a value which concerns the realm of ethics in Racine's tragedy, and both the realm of ethics and that of the general theory of knowledge in the *Pensées*.

Discussing tragedy, Lukàcs makes the following statement:

> The problem of the possibility of tragedy is the problem of the relationship between being and essence. It is the problem of trying to discover whether everything which exists does so simply because it is. Are there not levels and degrees in being? Is being a universal property of things, or is it a value judgment that we make of them, a judgment that separates and distinguishes them from one another? ... Medieval philosophy expressed this idea with perfect clarity when it spoke of the *ens perfectissimum* also being the *ens realissimum;* the more perfect a being is, the more it exists; the more closely it corresponds to its idea, the more it exists.[1]

This is one of the constituent laws of the tragic universe: existence, value and reality are synonymous. One creates the other, and the paradox which lies in a refusal of choice and a demand for total truth is, by that very fact, both value and reality; in the language of the theatre, this is expressed by stage presence.

It has often been rightly said that, on the stage, the character of Phaedra completely overshadows the other characters and deprives them of all value. This is true, but we still need to show how and why this happens, and what is the basis for it in the structural laws of the play's universe.

My contention is that this devaluation of the other characters in the play belongs to the practical realm and to that of morality; that it is based not upon the ethical standards of the world, but upon those implicit in the tragic universe, in which the category of Totality constitutes the supreme value. Thus, there are in the play itself three characters who represent three kinds of reality and value: the Gods—the Sun and Venus—who are silent spectators and on whose level Phaedra's moral conscience is situated; then comes Phaedra's actual behaviour, which from the standpoint of her moral universe is vice

---

[1] Cf. G. von Lukàcs, *L'Ame et les Formes*, pp. 335-6.

and error; and then there is the world—Hippolytus, Theseus, Aricia, Oenone—which, by the side of Phaedra, has no reality or value, except in so far as it provides the occasion for her error and return to truth.

There is nothing surprising in this dual rôle of the Gods in the fact that we see them both as the Sun and as Venus. One might say that the Gods of the tragedies of refusal were also potentially double —in the case of *Andromaque* they were actually incarnated in the two characters of Hector and Astyanax, since the tragedy is not wholly rigorous—in exactly the same way as the refusal of the world by Barcos also potentially contained the paradox of Pascal. That is to say that tragic refusal springs from the fact that man cannot live in the world except by virtue of a choice between two extremes which are both equally necessary and equally opposed to each other. Each of them presents itself with the same absolute and unavoidable demand that is incarnated in the idea of a Hidden but Watching God.

When the solitaries of Port-Royal and the heroes of Racine's tragedies rejected the world the two opposing Gods took on the same single form, both leading to the same demand and the same action: the refusal of a world in which it is impossible to perform one's duty without falling into sin. If the dual nature of their contradictory demands does not show itself in the plays it is because neither Junia nor Titus envisages for one moment the possibility of living in the world; it is, as I have already said, because the tragedy is outside time and because the tragic character is a person who is fully aware of the moral impossibility of compromise. However, once the idea of an authentic life in this world appears, we see the appearance of two characters incarnating this silent and watching God. This may happen either because the play is not rigorously tragic or because it is a tragedy with peripeteia and recognition. Astyanax prevents Andromache from living while remaining faithful to Hector, and Hector prevents her from living and saving Astyanax. Similarly, the Sun prevents Phaedra from living in a forgetfulness of her personal reputation and Venus prevents her from living and forgetting her passion. But the Gods are silent and passive spectators who never give the hero any help or advice as to how to reconcile their contradictory demands. He has to choose between illusion—inseparable from error—and death.

Hippolytus, Theseus, Aricia and Oenone are people who do not exist in the tragedy because they are satisfied with relative values. They do not even know that in the tragic universe existence involves a demand for totality and a life made up either of paradox or of refusal.

Between the two extremes of the Gods and of Nothingness, Phaedra alone is human. She lives in a demand for totality which is

378

all the more Utopian in that this totality is made up of a union of values which, in the everyday, empirical world, are completely contradictory. What she wants, and what she thinks she can achieve, is the union between passion and personal reputation, between absolute purity and forbidden love, between truth and life.

In the actual world, however, which she believes to be pure and real, she meets only ordinary, average men, who are terrified by her monstrous demands. Hippolytus, first of all, has only one reaction throughout the whole play: he wants to run away. He says so in the very first line, announcing his intention to go off and look for his father, and the spectator, like Theramenes, can still look upon this as a courageous action inspired by filial piety. Soon, however, Hippolytus tells us his real motives: he is, indeed, performing his duty in going to seek his father, but he is also 'fleeing from a place that he dares no longer see' (Act I, Scene 1, ll. 27–8).

What, however, is he running away from? The text is ambiguous, for Hippolytus gives two different, contradictory replies, of which—as the rest of the play will show—only the first is the correct one. The second contains a mistake, something which is, however, quite natural in the case of Hippolytus, for like all those who live in this world, he never achieves a clear awareness of his own nature and situation.

When Theramenes asks him why he is leaving 'this pleasant place' which he has always preferred to Athens, Hippolytus first of all replies that he simply does not know. This is not only the absolute truth but also the very key to his character and to the rôle which he plays in the tragedy. Racine's genius is truly admirable here, for he goes beyond the psychological truth to the essential truth which lies behind it, making Hippolytus say what he does not yet think and what he does not himself clearly know as yet.

What he is really afraid of, what he is really running away from, is Phaedra, who disturbs the traditional, convenient and established order of things, by combining in herself the most contradictory elements: heaven and hell, justice and sin. This is the truth which he reveals in the famous lines lamenting that 'all has changed', since the heavens sent to Athens 'the daughter of Minos and of Pasiphae' (ll. 36–7).[1]

[1] Much has been written on this line, whose beauty has always seemed more obvious than its actual meaning. However, I do not find it difficult to understand. Written—in spite of the fact that it mentions only Greek gods—for a Christian public, it is an exact definition of the tragic hero, the paradoxical character who brings together in himself not only heaven and hell but what is sinful in heaven and just in hell.

It should be added that, on a purely formal level, the bringing together of the closed block formed by the name of Minos with the open series of 'a' and 'e' in

Immediately, however, as Theramenes begins to expound the rational motives which Hippolytus has for being afraid of Phaedra—she is his stepmother, etc., and a potential political rival—the latter corrects his mistakes, and declares that the person he is really fleeing from is 'the young Aricia' (l. 50).

Everything in this line is false. In the play Phaedra's enmity does not even exist, her moment of jealousy will not be without consequence and Hippolytus will flee, not from Aricia as he now maintains, but, as he said initially, from Phaedra. Yet if Hippolytus had understood and brought out one of the essential aspects of the play from the very first scene this would have contradicted its essential and constituent theme. This is not only Phaedra's illusion but also the complete inadequacy of the world when faced with her demands. Such an understanding on the part of Hippolytus would have contradicted the laws of the tragic universe, according to which knowledge is the main privilege and the distinctive characteristic of the tragic character himself.

The same concern for the structural unity of the play seems to be at the basis of Racine's creation of Aricia. If Hippolytus had, in the play, met only Phaedra it would have been difficult to distinguish his flight from the straightforward refusal of life, for he would have been similar to the heroes of the tragedies without peripeteia and recognition, and to the solitaries of Port-Royal. His love for Aricia eliminates any ambiguity. What he is fleeing is not the world, which he accepts and even pursues, but the paradoxical creature who disturbs the order of this world by striving after a unification of opposites.

Hippolytus, throughout the first scene, continues to play-act both to himself and to other people, rejects Theramenes's suggestion that he is really in love with Aricia and repeats that his intention is to go and seek his father (l. 138).

But Theramenes, who is—in the play—the messenger of truth, but of a truth that remains superficial and incomplete, asks him if he is not going to see Phaedra before he leaves. As long as it is merely a question of words and not of actions, Hippolytus is quite prepared to face reality, and is actually telling Theramenes to inform her of his departure when Phaedra herself appears (ll. 140–1).

This, of course, is mere talk, and the moment Phaedra actually arrives, he resumes his true nature and decides to leave immediately, pretending that his face would be 'odious' to her (ll. 151–2).

He is never prepared to go out and face reality and danger. It is

---

Pasiphae achieves once again, at a third level, this same paradoxical bringing together of opposites.

not he who goes to meet Phaedra, but she who comes to look for him. And when she finally meets him his reaction is just the same. When, in Act II, Scene 3, Theramanes arrives to tell him that she is about to arrive, he does everything he can to avoid her, both before her arrival and when she is actually there (ll. 561–70 and 576).

However, Phaedra eventually arrives and eventually declares her love to him. His immediate reaction is again one of flight, and we can see his whole character in what he tells Theramanes after his discovery: 'Let us flee' (l. 716).

From Act III onwards reality becomes more complex for Hippolytus, for it includes Theseus as well as Phaedra. However, his reactions undergo no change, as we see from the fact that he greets his father with the request that, 'trembling', he should be allowed to 'leave the place inhabited by your wife' (ll. 923–6).

Moreover, when he begins to become aware of the dangers threatening him, he shows a naïve—we might almost say a simple-minded—trust in the justice of the established order of things. In spite of all the threats implicit in his father's speech in Act III, Scene 5, he dismisses his forebodings with the reflection that 'innocence has nothing to fear', and remains convinced that it will be enough to look 'elsewhere' for the means of preparing his father to greet the news of his love for Aricia.

His reaction is similar when he learns that Oenone has accused him of trying to seduce Phaedra, for he declares that he is unable to speak and justify himself (Act IV, Scene 2, ll. 1076–80).

And, again, when Aricia urges him to try to justify himself in Theseus's eyes he refuses to do so on the grounds that 'the Gods are just' and have his interests at heart (ll. 1351–2).

The very last scene in which he appears (Act V, Scene 1) ends, appropriately enough from this point of view, with Aricia again urging him to run away (l. 1407).

Three other characters in the play, Oenone, Theseus and Aricia, make up the world. Theseus calls for little comment. He is an agèd Britannicus, possessed of power instead of having to endure its effects. It is the tyrant's victim who has become tyrant in his turn. Like Britannicus, Theseus accepts all the lies told to him as truths and all the truths as lies. He is the character who, in the strictest sense of the word, lives in error. He is the most imperfect character and therefore, implicitly in the laws of the tragic world, the most unreal. Like most of the characters representing the world, he wants to be deceived, and accepts the final truth only with the greatest reluctance. When Phaedra tries to stop his fury against Hippolytus and make him rescind his fatal curse he merely invites her to urge him on to greater cruelty and brutality by repeating her description of Hippolytus's crimes 'in all their blackness' (Act IV, Scene 4, ll. 1180–4).

In the final scene, when Phaedra's arrival gives him an intimation of the truth, he rejects it and refuses to make any attempt to discover the truth. He agrees, he says, that Hippolytus, now dead, should be considered as criminal, 'since Phaedra accuses him'. He has, he continues, already too many causes for tears without seeking for additional knowledge which might make his grief even more bitter (Act V, Scene 7, ll. 1595–1604).

His very last words, at the end of the tragedy, are highly significant from this point of view. For one moment it seemed as if Phaedra's confession and death had shown Theseus the truth, and that he had caught a glimpse of the richness, greatness and validity of the tragic world. His speech shows that this is far from being the case. The abyss which he saw for a moment opening up under his feet did nothing but strengthen him in his own nature. He saw only one thing: that Phaedra's action did not conform to the laws of his world. The best thing to do, he thinks, would be to forget it, but since this seems impossible, he must restore the accustomed order which has been temporarily endangered. A few prayers over Hippolytus's grave, his replacement by Aricia and the memory of Phaedra will soon become little more than an unpleasant but harmless legend.

The last words of Phaedra might perhaps have allowed a certain vagueness and misunderstanding to exist. In trying to live in the world—and this was her illusion—she had tried to raise it to her own level in order to achieve a dialogue with it. Until the very end she had spoken to a Hippolytus who was wholly good and wholly courageous, and she is now leaving this world in order to enable the cosmic and social order ('the heavens and my husband') to resume its course. Theseus's final remark, however, shows us what this order really is by coming immediately after the tragic lines of Phaedra, and thereby appearing essentially comic. After the disappearance of the hero, who had, for a moment, opened our eyes to all the immense wealth of reality, we have another glimpse of ordinary life, which we consequently see as a world of farce and comedy. Aesthetically, this world has no place in a tragic play, since the hero has emptied it of all reality. It is a dying world, one that will probably go on living for centuries, but which is nevertheless already a corpse. And in tragedy, the most living of all theatrical forms, the one whose threshold is highest, corpses do not exist.

By the side of Hippolytus and Theseus there is Aricia, who is more real than the two men for the simple reason that she does not come into direct contact with Phaedra. Such an encounter would, indeed, have brought out all her weakness. Compared to Theseus and

Hippolytus, whom the text indicates as fairly negative characters, Aricia might seem almost a zero, a completely neutral character who did not even exist. But, either consciously or unconsciously, Racine seems to have maintained the unity of his work entirely by a series of contrasts. This is the main reason why he wrote the lines in which, at the most threatening moment in the tragedy, when the destiny of Hippolytus and Phaedra lies in the balance, Aricia starts to talk about marriage. This corresponds exactly to the last speech of Theseus. Compared to the tragic character, the world becomes, both in its most serious and most banal aspects, merely farce or comedy.

Thierry Maulnier has correctly noted that this passage makes Aricia into a little convent girl. But the real reason for this lies in the fact that, compared to Phaedra, the world can consist only of either wild beasts or of little convent girls. Aricia would still have been one even if she had not asked Hippolytus to marry her, and is made to do so in the text solely to make her own character completely explicit and thereby avoid any possibility of misunderstanding.

But in reality neither Hippolytus, who is constantly running away, nor Theseus, who is constantly mistaken, nor Aricia, who is a model of virtue, has any real existence for Phaedra. And yet *Phèdre* is the play that deals with the illusion of being able to live in the world, and thereby contains a real dialogue between the hero and the world instead of the solitary dialogues which we find in the Jansenist tragedies. And, for Phaedra, the world evidently consists of an idealised Hippolytus and Theseus—but also contains, first and foremost, the character of Oenone. This can, in fact, be seen in the very construction of the play: in addition to the scene in which she declares her love to Hippolytus, and of the three scenes in which she speaks to Theseus, Phaedra is on stage twice completely by herself but eight times with Oenone.

After having studied the world in so far as it manifests itself in characters who are peripheral to Phaedra herself, we now have to analyse the very core of the play: the dialogue, on the one hand, with the silent Gods, and, on the other, with Oenone.

After the initial scene between Hippolytus and Theramanes the play begins with a situation that is almost identical to those in the tragedies without peripeteia and recognition: Phaedra, who is aware of the incompatibility between her demands and the order of the world, has decided to leave this world and die. The scene takes place in the sun, but since the sun is a God, and one of Phaedra's own ancestors, we can say that it takes place within the sight of God. This is the world, the place in which beings live, and to leave the stage is to leave life and the world behind one.

Thus, Phaedra comes on to the stage only reluctantly, half dragged on by Oenone, and her first words are a complaint that she can go no farther, that her strength is leaving her, and that she cannot stand the sight of the day (Act I, Scene 3, ll. 153–6).

The first of the 'stage directions'—always important in Racine—comes very soon after Phaedra's return to the world and expresses her crisis and disorder in a material form. In the fifth line of the scene, Racine indicates that she sits down. After this the pseudo-dialogue continues, and immediately illustrates the structure of the tragic universe. For if Oenone speaks to Phaedra the latter never replies to her. The apparent replies of Phaedra are in fact the most radically solitary of all the dialogues between a tragic hero and the silent Gods of tragedy. The ornaments in which Oenone has decked her in order to bring her back into the world themselves form part of it and seem strange and painful to her (ll. 156–61). The only person whom she addresses directly is the sun, her ancestor, declaring that she has come to look upon him 'for the last time' (ll. 169–73), but this speech is followed almost immediately, after three lines spoken by Oenone but completely ignored by Phaedra, by an appeal to the Gods to allow her 'sit in the forest's shade and watch the dust raised by a hunter's chariot' (ll. 176–9).

It is almost by force that Oenone, glimpsing the allusion in what Thierry Maulnier calls an 'incantation', and which I, following Lukàcs, prefer to call a 'solitary dialogue', and, realising that her mistress is talking about Hippolytus, penetrates into Phaedra's universe. The reaction of the latter is one of horror that she should have allowed her desires so to escape from her conscious control (ll. 179–84), but Oenone has already grasped that there is a crack in the wall separating her from Phaedra. It is this which leads her to pile up the arguments capable of bringing Phaedra back to the world, but it is by chance, at the end of a twenty-line speech, that she pronounces the name of Hippolytus. This then provokes a second reaction of horror from Phaedra (l. 208), which Oenone completely fails to understand.

In this dialogue, in which every line is a masterpiece that should be studied in detail, we follow the complete lack of understanding between the two women. Oenone, still believing in Phaedra's hostility towards Hippolytus, insists on the political reasons for which Phaedra should stay alive, and points out what harm her death would cause to her son's hope of one day claiming the throne of Athens. It is for this reason that she urges Phaedra to live (ll. 210–16), but Phaedra does not give way and speaks of how she has 'already too long pursued the guilty course of her life' (l. 217).

Oenone completely fails to understand the meaning of the word 'guilty'. For her, a crime is an action performed in time and space, something essentially visible. It is here that the real dialogue begins, for Phaedra explains to her the nature of the wholly different demands of the tragic ethic. It is, she affirms, her heart which is guilty—not her hands, for with Heaven's help she has kept them guiltless (ll. 221–2).

Oenone persists in her attempt to find out what is the horrible project which causes such terror to Phaedra's heart; but her mistress still hesitates to tell her. She knows that the real crime and error lie in the dialogue with the world; and, for the moment, she still has the greatness and refusal which characterise Titus and Berenice. She will, she repeats, die rather than make so 'fatal a confession' (ll. 225–7).

Oenone, however, still insists, and threatens to kill herself. Phaedra, on the point of surrender, now clearly explains to her what consequences she foresees if she continues to follow the slope down which she feels she is being dragged. A confession will, she says, merely increase her guilt when she eventually does die (ll. 241–2).

But Oenone has far too much 'common sense' to believe in Phaedra's 'exaggerations',[1] and therefore continues to encourage Phaedra to confess. Phaedra finally gives way—thinking that she will do so only for the moment needed for the confession, and that she will then be able to fulfil her resolve to leave the world—and accepts—if only for a moment—to bring Oenone into contact with tragic reality. It is a solemn moment, and is therefore indicated by another 'stage direction' as she calls upon Oenone to stand (l. 246).

For it is standing that one greets the approach of the universe of tragedy.

But, on the brink of revealing her desires and demands to Oenone, Phaedra once again recoils. The first attempt at a dialogue with Oenone—the world—has gone to the point where Phaedra has decided to break off her solitary dialogue with the Gods in order to confide in her nurse, to the point where she calls upon Oenone to stand. Yet at the very moment when she is about to do this Phaedra recoils and resumes her dialogue with the silent Gods. She appeals to the Heavens to guide her in what she is to say to Oenone (l. 248), and then, in three couplets interspersed by appeals from Oenone to forget the Gods, she calls successively upon Venus (ll. 449–50), the memory of her sister Ariadne and again upon Venus to accomplish her intention of making Phaedra die 'the last and the most miserable of her race' (ll. 253–254 and 256–7).

But the die is cast, Phaedra will finally speak to Oenone, she will confess her love for Hippolytus, but not for the real Hippolytus, who

---

[1] It is impossible not to be reminded here of the two versions of *Faust* written by Lessing and Valéry, where in the first play the hero does not believe in the Devil and where, in the second, he can see neither his usefulness nor his danger.

is going away and who loves Aricia, but for another, imaginary Hippolytus, a being pure and without weakness, capable of inspiring a fatal and criminal weakness. It is a passion which Phaedra certainly condemns, but of which she is also proud—as long, that is, as she can resist it by refusing life and leaving the world. She does not, she tells Oenone, have any feelings of repentance for having now admitted her crime; she had done everything possible to combat her love for Hippolytus, and has now drawn back from death only because of her pity for Oenone's grief; now, moreover, she calls upon Oenone to respect her approaching death and no longer refuse to help her in finding a refuge out of this world (ll. 307–14).

But Oenone's appeal to Phaedra not to abandon life completely is accompanied by a series of apparent transformations in the external world. Panope announces that Theseus is dead, Phaedra's passion consequently seems to become legitimate, and Oenone immediately seizes upon the opportunity to convince Phaedra that 'her love becomes an ordinary love' (l. 350). She also insists upon Phaedra's duty to protect her son, whose interests coincide with those of her passion. All occasions conspire together, and the world—we could equally well say the Devil—succeeds in persuading Phaedra. Illusion, accompanied by error—the supreme fault in the universe of tragedy—has now begun.

Thierry Maulnier has correctly insisted upon the profoundly paradoxical nature of Phaedra's hope that she will be able to win over Hippolytus. For what she loves in him are precisely those qualities that make him unable to love anybody—Phaedra herself included: his purity and apparent dissimilarity to Theseus and the world.

But Hippolytus is quite incapable of understanding Phaedra's passion. He sees it as the triumph of desire in its most ordinary and carnal sense, a desire against which he immediately erects the barrier of his laws—of his own laws and of his own Gods.

To begin with, he refuses to believe that Theseus is dead, and that laws protected by the Gods can be destroyed. Neptune, he replies, cannot have failed to hear any appeal for help that Theseus may have made to him (Act II, Scene 5, ll. 621–2).

Phaedra speaks a different kind of language, for she has accepted to live in the world because she believes that it is real, that values are carried to extremes, and that the fate of men, like her own destiny, is stronger than the will of the Gods. It is useless, she tells Hippolytus, to hope that Theseus will be able to escape the lot of all men (ll. 623–5)—but then, she suddenly continues, he is not really dead, since he is now alive before her very eyes in the person of his son. The only difference is that, in Hippolytus, he becomes pure and idealised, the husband whom she can, in real life, love without any sin against

386

her passion or against her personal reputation. She catches a glimpse of valid love involving no crime and no renunciation.

But Hippolytus, who is acquainted above all with the laws of his world, understands nothing which Phaedra tells him, except her desire for something which, since the laws forbid it, must be monstrous. This is why his first and immediate reproach to her is that she is forgetting that Theseus is his father and her husband (ll. 663–4).

But this is something which Phaedra has never forgotten, and, rightly indignant at his failure to understand her, she replies that the care she has for her own reputation has never allowed her to forget it (ll. 665–6).

In fact, she has not for one moment fallen into this 'forgetfulness of her glory' with which Hippolytus reproaches her. Indeed, it is this which constitutes her tragic paradox, and which remains incomprehensible to characters such as Theseus and Hippolytus, who live in this world.

This is why the misunderstanding then becomes even deeper, with what one might almost call a Cartesian[1] logic. Hippolytus, who first of all thought that Phaedra had forgotten the law in declaring her love for him, now considers that he has misinterpreted her. He is ashamed for having thought that she loved him, and once again wishes to run away (Act II, Scene 5, ll. 667–9).

In actual fact, however, he was both right and wrong on both occasions. For although Phaedra does love him, she condemns herself for this, and does so in the name of a quest for purity which—in the world—she cannot express except by her love for Hippolytus. It is this which she explains to him in her long speech of self-accusation and self-justification (ll. 670–90), which ends with her snatching Hippolytus's sword with which to kill herself.

No one can live with all these contradictions, and she once again sees that there is no possible solution except in death. But this is precisely something which the world cannot and does not understand. Oenone suggests a solution with which we are now quite familiar when she implores Phaedra to run away and 'escape certain shame' (ll. 112–13).

Phaedra, however, cannot run away, and the 'stage direction' implicit in Theramanes' question—'Is it Phaedra fleeing, or, rather, being dragged away?' (l. 715) removes all possible ambiguity on this point.

The being who is left in a state of terror by this encounter between two universes is not Phaedra but Hippolytus, whom Theramanes similarly describes as 'speechless and stricken with pallor' (l. 717). And, since Phaedra herself does not run away, Hippolytus must do so himself. He reveals this in his first words to Theramanes after

[1] 'Too much clarity darkens,' wrote Pascal in criticism of Descartes.

Phaedra has departed (l. 719), but the news then arrives that Phaedra's son has been elected king of Athens. Hippolytus's only reaction is to criticise the injustice of the Gods in regarding Phaedra's 'virtue' in this manner (ll. 726–7), and for not having conformed to his own simple-minded conception of the nature of providential action.

Act III shows us how Phaedra and Oenone react after the meeting between Hippolytus and Phaedra in Act II. Phaedra's illusion that she can still live in the world has now come to an end, and a new 'stage direction' tells us that the only reason why Phaedra has not killed herself is that Oenone, to whom she still remains closely linked, wrenched the sword out of her hands (Act III, Scene 1, ll. 747–8).

But Oenone, the incarnation of common sense, and consequently of compromise, suggests that since Hippolytus rejects her love, Phaedra should devote herself to something else—to ruling over Athens, for example. This is, in fact, the most reasonable solution: in order to remain alive, we must give up trying to get what we cannot have, and busy ourselves with things within our reach. We must either choose Minos (power) or Pasiphae (passion). The idea of trying to achieve totality by a union of opposites is completely foreign to Oenone, as it is to Hippolytus, and she instinctively finds the same solution as Hippolytus, to whose universe she belongs. Phaedra, she urges, should flee from Hippolytus and occupy herself with 'nobler cares' (ll. 753–6), and when Phaedra tries to avoid giving a definite answer she insists again on the necessity for flight (l. 763).

Phaedra's reply, however, is in accordance with the universe in which she lives, for she insists that she cannot leave Hippolytus (l. 765).

For the rest of the play, the rôles are reversed. Phaedra's love for Hippolytus, which she had tried to destroy by killing herself in order to protect her reputation ('*gloire*') has now shown itself to be impossible. Oenone had, initially, tried to use common sense—which never understands human greatness—in order to persuade Phaedra that her love could be satisfied. She now uses the same common-sense argument to make her mistress abandon this love, but Phaedra refuses. Her love compels her to go to extremes, and she consequently does everything possible in order to secure Hippolytus for herself. This is the lowest point which she reaches in her illusions and in her struggle to reconcile life and purity. Thus, almost as soon as Oenone has left her, Phaedra resumes her solitary dialogue with the Gods. Asking Venus whether she has not now triumphed enough in the abyss of shame to which Phaedra has now descended, she implores her to cast a spell over Hippolytus. Here, she says, is someone who has always defied Venus and refused to pay homage to her; he is a victim more worthy of her attentions (Act III, Scene 2, ll. 813–24).

But her failure cannot be overcome, and the world which had once seemed about to open up and admit the tragic character into its bounds now closes its ranks. Theseus returns, and the laws resume their unshakeable unity, bringing together Thesus, Oenone and Hippolytus in the same community.

Oenone, naturally, sees only one solution: life is the main value, and one must therefore fit oneself into this reviving universe, play the game according to the rules and accuse Hippolytus. This is precisely the course of action which no longer has any meaning for Phaedra. She was prepared, in order to attain Totality, to fall to the lowest possible level, but she sees any attempt to use compromise merely in order to live on in the partial world of relative values as equally absurd and unworthy.

It is in the course of this discussion that Oenone asks Phaedra how she now looks upon Hippolytus. Phaedra's reply is outstanding by its rigour, and reveals, by antiphrasis, just how much of the Jansenist world vision Phaedra has still retained. The argument conducted by the Jansenists about the theological concept of the 'righteous sinner' ('*juste pécheur*') is well known to scholars. Phaedra expresses her views by two lines which follow almost immediately one after the other, being separated only by what Oenone has to say. She sees Hippolytus, she replies, 'as a monster horrifying to my sight', and exclaims, in reply to Oenone's suggestion, the horror at the idea that she should 'oppress and blacken innocence' (Act III, Scene 3, ll. 886–94).

If the expression 'righteous sinner' is the definition, in theological terms, of tragic man, then this person can look upon the ordinary everyday man as his exact opposite: the innocent monster. This is exactly how Phaedra sees Hippolytus.

Oenone suggests that she herself should accuse Hippolytus, and needs only Phaedra's silence in order to be able to do so. The latter, however, wholly given over to her passion and to the hope of living in the world, lost in the whirlwind of illusion into which she has allowed herself to be dragged by Oenone, gives way to her servant.

But her surrender lasts only for a moment, for she immediately recovers awareness of what she has done and goes on to reveal Theseus the truth. It is then, however, that she receives the really mortal blow and learns that Hippolytus loves Aricia. This discovery is all the more terrible in that it affects Phaedra in two or even three ways; it arouses her jealousy as a woman in love, it offends the desire for purity which characterises her as a tragic heroine and it destroys the illusion that she had discovered a being with whom she could live in the world.

She learns not only that Hippolytus loves Aricia and that she,

389

Phaedra, therefore has a rival but also that the Hippolytus, who she had thought of as being hostile to the world, is in reality part of it, and therefore differs in no way from Theseus, Aricia or Oenone (Act IV, Scene 6, ll. 1220–3). And, perhaps the most terrible thing for her, Phaedra discovers that the love between Hippolytus and Aricia is approved by the order of the world, and by the Gods which protect its laws (l. 1238).

After the initial fury of her jealousy Phaedra understands her fault and her illusion. Life—which is possible for Hippolytus and Aricia in that they receive the approval of the Gods—is, in her eyes, the supreme error and the supreme crime. She had been right at the very beginning when, determined to leave the sun and the earth behind, she could still have saved her purity. While other people live under the eye of the Gods who protect them, Phaedra can live only under the eye of another God: one who judges her, and to whom forgiveness is a completely alien concept. It is this which explains her terrified vision (Act IV, Scene 6, ll. 1273–84) of a world in which there is no place to hide from the judgment pursuing her. Jupiter, king of all the Gods, is, like the all-seeing sun, numbered among her ancestors; and, if she goes down into the eternal night of hell, there will the Gods be also, for Minos, her father, is judge of all the dead, and will tremble with horror at the sight of his daughter and of all her crimes.

This is the end both of her illusion and of her error. Oenone once again tries to talk of compromise, but Phaedra, who has now recovered the clear awareness of her own condition that characterised her at the beginning of the play, who knows the truth and who can no longer be drawn into error, rejects her completely. She has now broken off all contact with the world, whether under the form of Theseus, Hippolytus or Oenone, and tells Oenone so quite unequivocally. It is Oenone, she says, who is responsible for what has happened, she who has prevented Phaedra from dying, made her meet Hippolytus, and now perhaps brought about his death by the false accusations she has made. And, in her final curse on Oenone, she includes all those whose 'cowardly skills' nourish the weakness of feeble princes (ll. 306–25).

There is no better illustration of the abyss which separates the tragic hero from the world than Oenone's reply to this speech. She finds nothing to reproach herself with, and can only appeal to the Gods to bear witness to the injustice done to her (ll. 1327–8).[1]

Phaedra then disappears from the stage until the very end of the play. What we see are merely the disorder and fateful reactions of a

[1] Hippolytus has a similar reaction on learning that Phaedra's son has been chosen king of Athens, for he ironically asks the gods if this is a reward for her virtue (ll. 723–4).

world completely defeated by a tragic being, and which is still suffering the final consequences of this being's once having been in it. She will return only at the end, standing upright, having already taken poison, coming in order to re-establish the truth and inform Theseus that her presence, which both disturbed the order of the world and obstructed the clear light of the sun, has now come to an end (Act V Scene 7, ll. 1635–43). She is, she says, already dying, killed by a poison brought to Athens by Medea, and can see only through a cloud both the 'heavens and my husband, insulted by my presence'. Now, however, she declares in her closing words that as death takes the light from her eyes it will give back its purity to the day.

Her presence is an insult to Theseus, but it is her presence before the world and before Theseus that would be an insult and an outrage to the sun. Now that Phaedra is separated from the world, from Hippolytus, Theseus and Oenone, by an unbridgeable gulf, her fault has been transcended. The time of tragedy has been abolished, for it was not linear but circular. This can be seen in the fact that the very last words that she pronounces, promising that the day will now recover its purity (l. 1643), correspond exactly to her first words on coming on to the stage in Act I: 'Sun, I have come to look upon you for the last time' (l. 172).

The sun, an impassible and silent God, will continue to shine upon a world which has too little reality to be perceived in the light of its beams. No one neither knows or ever will know whether Phaedra has rejoined Minos and Phaeton, her true companions. Now that she has gone the world resumes its course, its trivial and inessential communities resume their form and the memory of disaster falls into the pattern of everyday life. Even enmities disappear before the recollection of the monstrous being who made those who were most hostile to one another in the world realise how closely they are linked together by a similarity that goes deeper than any hatred. However, when at the very end of the play Theseus once again speaks forth and states that the order of the world has been restored, actors are sometimes reluctant to perform this part of the play. It seems to them to constitute too rapid a transition from tragedy to what, taken by itself, would be drama, but which, through its proximity to the tragic universe, becomes almost farcical comedy.

This part of the play is still necessary, however, in order to remind the universe that, for God—who sees the essence of things—the real corpse is not off-stage, with the body of Phaedra. It is there, standing before them, in the presence of the king who is going to reign and govern the State.

391

D. THE SACRED DRAMAS
VII. *Esther and Athalie*

The two plays that Racine published after the long silence which followed the production of *Phèdre* are not really within the province of this study. They are, in fact, not tragedies, but plays in which the Gods manifest themselves in a clear and ambiguous manner. They are sacred dramas.

I shall therefore treat them only briefly, in order to underline the formal consequences of this movement beyond tragedy.

The first point to be made is that, in spite of the obvious transposition which they contain of certain episodes in the history of Port-Royal and of its 'friends',[1] and even of Racine's own memories, these plays no longer correspond, in their totality, either to the extremist forms of Jansenist thought before the 'Peace of Clement IX' or to the real experiences of the 'Friends of Port-Royal'.

The vision which they express is, in fact, at the opposite pole to that of tragic Jansenism, since they replace the silent and hidden God of tragedy by a universe in which He triumphs and manifests Himself in the world. Similarly, they do not express the actual history of Port-Royal, which never in fact did triumph over its enemies in this world.

In so far as these two plays are linked to the Jansenist movement, they express the ideology of the 'moderate' followers of Arnauld, who preached the defence of goodness and piety in this world. Even here, however, *Athalie* carries this ideology to its extreme conclusions, and goes much farther in criticising the King's power than either Nicole or Arnauld. One might, in fact, even go so far as to compare the attitude implied in the play to the one adopted by Jacqueline Pascal.[2]

These two plays—like the twelve-year silence which followed *Phèdre*—thus present the historian with a problem to which he cannot, at the moment, find a satisfactory solution. What did lead Racine to return into private life, and what then inspired him to write the two plays where God triumphs, in the world, over the forces of evil?

[1] I am, on this particular point, entirely in agreement with the objections put forward by Jean Pommier (*Aspects de Racine* (Nizet, 1954), pp. 221–2) against the book by Jean Orcibal *La Genèse d'Esther et d'Athalie* (Vrin, 1950), which maintains that *Esther* is to be seen in the context of the *Filles de l'Enfance* at Toulouse and *Athalie* in that of a projected restoration of James II to the English throne.

[2] The moderate and generally 'middle of the road' positions of Arnauld and Nicole could have been—and were—made more radical in two directions: either by refusing to compromise in the struggle for the defence of truth (the attitude of Jacqueline Pascal, or Le Roy); or by refusing the world and withdrawing into solitude (Barcos).

The demands of his post as royal historiographer, emphasised by Monsieur Pommier, seem to me, like Madame de Maintenon's wish to organise plays at Saint-Cyr, to be merely external occasions. Any really valid reply to this question should enable us to discover why Racine accepted—or even requested—to be royal historiographer, and why, from among all the requests made to him, he chose to grant those that led him to write *Esther* and *Athalie*.

Monsieur Pommier is quite right to criticise the explanation put forward by Monsieur Charlier and Monsieur Orcibal by pointing out that *Athalie* tells the story of an internal uprising and not of a foreign intervention. It is, however, tempting to see the revolution of 1688, the overthrow of James II and his replacement by William of Orange as a series of events which enabled Racine to believe in the possibility of overthrowing the government from inside the country There is, however, little reliable information to suggest how the theory of Charlier and Orcibal might be modified to meet Monsieur Pommier's objection.

I myself feel equally critical of any attempt to link *Esther* to the enmity between Madame de Maintenon and Louvois. Mordecai and Esther are representatives of the Will of God, and Racine's plays contain too exact a vision of God for us to be able to accept the suggestion that he now saw Madame de Maintenon and Colbert as His servants.

The most convincing explanation of this evolution in Racine's theatre seems to me to lie in the parallel evolution of Jansenist thought. After the Peace of Clement IX, and the renewal of persecution after 1679, the influence of Arnauld began to deprive Janseism of its tragic character and to transform it into a demand, in this world, for a theocracy which obeyed the commands of God and of the Church.

We must remember that although Arnauld appeared, until 1669, as the theoretician of the more moderate faction—especially compared to Mother Angélique, Barcos, Pascal and Singlin—his rôle in 1689 was very different. He was, now that Nicole had given up the struggle, the sole survivor of the earlier Jansenists and the leader of a strong opposition to any misuse of royal power.

The similarity between Arnauld and the characters of Mordecai in *Esther* and Jehoiada in *Athalie* has often been stressed, and, in my view, correctly. Moreover, we must remember that if Port-Royal had categorically rejected Racine's first tragedies Arnauld almost went so far as to express approval for the sacred dramas (especially of *Esther*, it is true, which was much less radical than *Athalie*).

However, the two plays cannot be placed on exactly the same plane, from a literary and dramatic point of view. *Esther* certainly contains a number of very beautiful lines, but the play is constructed in a schematic and conventional manner. It is, indeed, tempting to look upon it as the first attempt to represent the victory of God in the world, an experiment which was to be carried to perfection only in *Athalie*.

It would be difficult to think of characters who are more conventional than Ahasuerus and Haman. The picture of the good king taken in by the wicked minister, of Haman inspired in all his political actions by feelings of jealousy and puerile vanity, is indeed highly stereotyped, and is made acceptable only by Racine's poetry. The only people who really come to life are Esther, Mordecai and the young children of Israel, and these are probably inspired by Racine's own memories as a young man at Port-Royal.

The universe of *Athalie*, on the other hand, is completely different, and here again there is no lack of transpositions of the different experiences of Port-Royal. In addition to the similarity which I have already mentioned between Jehoiada and Arnauld, there is the parallel between the scene in which Jehoash describes his education in the temple and Racine's own childhood memories of his life as a pupil at Port-Royal.

There are also lines such as the following, in which there seems to be an almost direct reference to contemporary events. When, for example, Athaliah confides in Abner that she tolerates what the priests say about her, and that they have therefore some reason to be thankful to her kindness (Act II, Scene 5, ll. 594–8), or when the chorus of the children of Israel complain of how the wicked rise up against them, coming to insult the Lord even in His temple (Act II, Scene 9, ll. 810–15), the reference to the atmosphere of the late seventeenth century in France seems very clear.

But the great difference between *Esther* and *Athalie* lies in the structure of the world, in the portrait drawn of the kings and of the royal court. While *Esther* seemed to have lost the implacable realism of Racinian tragedy—replaced by the stereotyped picture of a good king betrayed by a vain and jealous minister—*Athalie* repeats, without any concessions, the theme of the absolute inadequacy and radically evil nature of the world. It is not only Athaliah herself who is wholly evil and lacking in all moral value but also Joash, God's instrument and the lawful king. Joash remains pure only for so long as he is the pupil of the levites and has not yet become king. We are expressly told, however, that his triumph empties him of all human value. Similarly, the Court is described in a manner that none of the radical Jansenists of the first generation could have criticised. It is, says Salomith in the chorus in Act III, Scene 8 (ll. 1119–204), a place where there is no law but force and violence, where honours and positions go to those whose obedience is most servile and lowly, and where no one can be found to speak out in the cause of oppressed innocence.[1]

And yet, in spite of all this, the play tells the victory of God over a world which is wholly evil, and which will remain so until the coming of the Messiah. As is so often the case in Racine, the first line sums up both the character who pronounces it and the play as a whole, for it is Abner, Athaliah's general, who tells Jehoiada that he has 'come into the temple in order to worship the eternal Lord'. The two spheres, that of God and that of the world, have become so radically different that no compromise is possible between them. Jehoiada says as much in lines which are probably also addressed to the 'Friends of Port-Royal' in the world and implicitly to Racine himself. There, speaking in the Lord's name, he reproves Abner with offering a multitude of sacrifices and vain oblations which, unaccompanied by true repentance, are nothing but an abomination in His sight. He calls upon Abner, instead, to 'wipe out the crimes' from the midst of His people and to offer these victims as sacrifice (ll. 84–91).

And yet God himself will intervene in the affairs of this radically evil world in order to punish the wicked and assure the correct ending to the eschatological drama.

One might even go so far as to say that the God of *Athalie* still retains a number of Jansenistic features. He is God such as the 'Friends of Port-Royal' imagined him to be, not in his present form, but as he will be on the day of His coming, when He will descend to punish the ungodly—a day, or rather a moment, which may come at any time, and which we should always expect as a perpetually possible miracle. He is the God whose ways as well as whose ends are pure, the God who shows himself even now by unending miracles.

The reader accustomed to Jansenist texts can hardly fail to recognise the accents of Jehoiada reproving Abner with failing to see the innumerable miracles and proofs of God's power with which he is constantly surrounded (ll. 104–10), or reproving Josabeth with forgetting that God also fights on the side of the righteous (Act I, Scene 2, ll. 226–34), protecting the innocents, casting down the mighty and already showing evidence of his power in the downfall of Joram, Ahab and Jezabel.

And yet, as I have already said, this present victory of God and the existence of the chorus of young Israelites seems to be at the farthest possible remove from Jansenist thought. It is true that the Jansenists bore the possibility of their victory constantly in mind and

[1] Cf. also the lines in which Mathan explains what means he had to use in order to succeed at court, insisting on how he constantly flattered those in power and 'sowed flowers for them along the edge of precipices' (ll. 931–8).

lived in daily expectation of it. But there is nevertheless an immense gap between this expectation of divine intervention, even in the immediate future, and the idea of this intervention taking place here and now. This is yet another example of a fact that I have several times had occasion to mention in this book: that a particular element assumes its true meaning only when it is integrated into the whole of which it forms part, so that similar or even identical elements can have a totally different meaning according to the particular whole into which they are integrated.

I should like, in passing, to stress the fact that Athaliah's defeat is described in profoundly realistic terms. All the historians and sociologists who have studied revolutions have emphasised the way in which a ruling class passes through an intellectual and ideological crisis shortly before it is overthrown, so that a political defeat is almost always preceded by an ideological one. Nothing is more realistic—on a symbolic level, of course—than the disarray of Athaliah and Mathan,[1] and the attraction which their adversaries—Jehoiada and the Temple—exercise over them.

From the point of the formal structure of the play, this depiction of the direct intervention of God was to involve two major changes: the introduction of the chorus, and the abolition of the unities of time and place.

As far as the first of these two changes is concerned, I have already stated the structural reasons which inevitably lead a modern tragedy, even when, as in the case of *Phèdre*, it is close to Greek tragedies, to dispense with the chorus. Greek tragedy told the story of a man who left the community at the very moment that he recognised truth, whereas Racinian tragedy tells us the story of a man who is inevitably alone from the very beginning.

The community can reappear only when tragedy has been transcended, that is to say at the very moment when the hero finds himself in the universe of a present and victorious God. It is for this reason that we did catch a glimpse of the chorus at the end of *Britannicus*, when the people took Junia under their protection, killed Narcissus and prevented Nero from entering into the temple.

There is nothing surprising in the fact that we find the chorus actually on stage in the two sacred dramas. In *Esther*, where all we can do is admire the way Divine Providence intervenes in and through the world, the chorus plays only a passive rôle; but in *Athalie*, where Divine Providence intervenes against the world, and where the chorus is itself the instrument which Providence uses, then the rôle which it plays is an active one.

[1] Cf. the way in which, in Act III, Scene 5, ll. 1041–3, Nabal has to act as a guide to Mathan.

The direct intervention of God in the action of the play also results in the disappearance of the unities of time and place. Although these unities were generally accepted by seventeenth-century theoreticians, they were also an internal necessity for Racinian tragedy, where the action takes place either in the a-temporal moment of refusal and conversion (*Britannicus, Bérénice*) or in a time which is circular and goes back to the original moment of departure (as in *Phèdre*).

In the sacred dramas, however, this reason no longer applies. We therefore see Racine deliberately give up the unity of place in *Esther*, the play where God intervenes in and through the world, and where each of the three acts has a different setting. In *Athalie*, moreover, where God intervenes in an eschatological manner, we are no longer in the presence of any form of human time but of eternity itself. It is for this reason that, in Act II, Jehoiada is made to describe his vision, in the course of which he clearly foresees the future until the very moment of the coming of the Messiah.

With *Athalie*, Racine's theatre ends on an optimistic note of confidence and of hope, but of a hope in God and eternity which in no way involves any concession or compromise on the plane of earthly reality. It is for this reason that I am not wholly convinced that the note which Monsieur Maugis puts at the end of the Larousse edition—'The play ends on an impression of peace and serenity'—does not show a very serious misunderstanding of the work.[1] What we in fact hear in the last lines which Racine wrote for the theatre is, on the contrary, the voice of the exterminating angel, the threat uttered against king and Court, and the hope that the promise made to the persecuted will be fulfilled.[2]

---

[1] Cf. Larousse edition, p. 98, note 4.

[2] Cf. the very last lines in the play, in which Jehoiada draws from the death of Athaliah the moral that 'Kings have a severe judge placed above them in Heaven, innocence has an avenger and the orphans a father'.

APPENDICES

A. Biographical Problems.

B. Main Events in the Life of Blaise Pascal.

C. Notes on Some of the Main Characters Closely Connected with the Jansenist Movement in France.

D. Notes on Some of the Main Events in the History of Jansenism and of Port-Royal.

E. A Note on the Historical Terms Used in Chapter VI.

A. Biographical Problems

SINCE I have frequently repeated in this book that problems concerning biography and the psychic mechanism of literary creation seem to me to be far too complex for any serious scientific study to be made, I should perhaps now conclude my study of the tragic vision in Racine's theatre.

However, the mere comparison between the facts of Racine's life and the analysis of the plays that I have just put forward suggests a hypothesis which, without being absolutely certain, nevertheless indicates the direction which future research should take.

In a very interesting article Monsieur Orcibal[1] has shown how until he was nineteen or even twenty, Racine was educated either at Port-Royal itself or in places deeply imbued with the Jansenist spirit (*collèges* at Beauvais, Harcourt, etc.) This provides quite a natural explanation of the importance which Port-Royal has for his work and for the rest of his life.

However, Monsieur Orcibal concluded his article by writing that 'the influence of so many strong and vigorous personalities inevitably made the young Racine either into a saint or a rebel.'

In fact, my own view is that he became neither one nor the other, but something much more complex—a renegade with a guilty conscience.

Anyone who is even slightly acquainted with the Jansenist literature written between 1638 and 1661, and especially with the texts coming from the more extreme representatives of the movement, knows how extraordinary an importance is attributed to something which seems, for the Jansenists, to have been the sin above all others: that of attempting to obtain an ecclesiastical living—or even of accepting one—without an absolutely certain and unshakeable sense of vocation. During this period Port-Royal sheltered a very large number of priests who had abandoned their livings because of the uncertainty which they felt about the authenticity of their vocation. Some of these priests—Guillebert, Maignart, Hillerin—were admired by the Jansenists precisely because they had given up their livings for this reason.

[1] Cf. Jean Orcibal, 'La Jeunesse de Racine', *La Revue d'Histoire littéraire*, 1951, No. 1.

Yet almost the first thing that Racine did when he had escaped from the immediate environment of Jansenism in 1661 was to go to Uzès in the hope of using his uncle Sconin's credit to secure a living. This was not so much a blameworthy action as the sin above all others and, in all probability, much less an open revolt against Jansenist ideology than a 'betrayal' within the framework of this ideology itself.

It is, in fact, fairly reasonable to assume that Racine's teachers at Port-Royal had laid much more stress on the difficulties involved in resisting the temptations of this world than on the obstacles encountered by someone trying to make his way in it. Small, persecuted groups always tend to stress how heroic it is to resist the powers that be, and to emphasise the merit involved in rejecting the high price which the persecutors are prepared to pay for any betrayal of the true cause. In Racine's case this probably led him to think that livings were much easier to come by than they were in reality. One of the first things that he discovered on his arrival at Uzès was therefore that the 'world' was a much more complex place than his teachers had led him to believe. He did not, in fact, obtain the living that he had hoped for.

It is therefore not too difficult to imagine the state of mind of the young poet, who, after having betrayed the ideology which had not only been his own until very recently but still remained that of his teachers and of his family, then discovered that betrayal did not pay. He was therefore vulnerable to all the moral and practical reproaches of those whom he had most admired in his youth. The most natural reaction to such a situation was a set of ambivalent feelings towards both Port-Royal and towards 'the world'.

In the meantime, however, Racine had to pretend not to mind, and, since he had now entered 'the world,' to try to find another way of living there in as pleasant a manner as possible. Unable to secure a living in the Church, Racine turned to literature and wrote plays. 1664 saw the performance of La Thébaide and 1665 that of Alexandre—both completely foreign to any Jansenist vision of the universe.

I have just said that his feelings towards Port-Royal were probably ambivalent. It is in any case certain that, while he was having these profane plays performed, he was sufficiently concerned with the reaction of the Jansenist group to feel that the passage in the Visionnaires which attacked Desmarets for having previously written plays and thus been a 'public poisoner' was meant to apply to him. His reaction to this is well known. His first letter to Port-Royal is a virulent attack which might, however, appear less unusual if we bear in mind the fact that, at the very moment when Racine left the Jan-

senist group, Nicole's and Arnauld's authority was much less universally recognised than it later became.[1]

However that may be—and Racine made a point of saying this in
his second letter—he was not an enemy of the Jansenists, but rather,
he maintained, one of their best friends. Moreover, this second letter
was never published, thanks probably to the intervention of his
former teacher Lancelot.

This polemic does, nevertheless, seem to have made him more
aware of the problems involved in his relationship with the world
and with Port-Royal. It is probably this fact which enabled him to
make the great literary discovery from which Racinian tragedy was
later to be born.

The solitaries and nuns of Port-Royal looked upon life as a play
performed in the sight of God. Until Racine, the French theatre had
consisted of plays performed before men. All Racine needed to do
was form a synthesis of these two concepts, writing for the human
stage the play to be performed in the sight of God and adding to the
normal human spectators the silent and hidden spectator who caused
the spectators to fall away to nothingness as he takes their place.
Racinian tragedy is then born.

It was in 1666 that Racine published his 'Letters to the author of
imaginary heresies' and to 'this author's defenders', and it was between 1667 and 1670 that his first tragedies without peripeteia and
recognition, his first tragedies of refusal—*Andromaque*, *Britannicus*
and *Bérénice*—were performed. It was also probably during the same
period that he composed the satirical poems against those who accepted to sign the Formulary, since one of the ways in which he tried
to compensate for his betrayal of Port-Royal's ideology was by
literary creation.

Psychologically, Racine had found a balance which is fairly frequent in literary history: that of a writer who uses literature to express the values which he has not achieved in life, values which he has
even betrayed and which he can—precisely for this reason—now
realise completely and with a high degree of coherence in the fictitious
and imaginary universe that he has created.

However, at the very moment when he had achieved this balance
an event took place which shook him to the very core: the Peace of
Clement IX put a temporary end to the conflict between the Jansenists and the Pope.

Port-Royal was now doing officially and as a body what Racine
himself had done privately and with a guilty conscience in 1661: it
was accepting a compromise with the world and with the powers

[1] Cf. L. Goldmann: *Correspondance de Martin de Barcos*. P.U.F. 1955.

that be. As far as Racine himself was concerned, this event had two main consequences: his own betrayal became rather less serious, and included only relatively minor questions, such as his activity as a dramatist or his various amorous liaisons; on the other hand, however, he now began to feel uneasy not only about his own compromise with the world but also about the compromise which the whole of Port-Royal had now accepted. From this there sprang the duality which I have tried to bring out in the three 'dramas of life in the world' which he wrote after the tragedies of refusal.

Nevertheless, from *Bajazet* to *Iphigénie*, these dramas are more and more linked with contemporary events. From the establishment's point of view, the Peace of Clement IX was only an element in the general movement towards internal unity[1] aimed at facilitating the war against Holland. This began in 1672, and the military superiority of the French seemed to indicate that it would be a short and successful expedition. In reality, the fierce resistance put up by Holland under William of Orange transformed it into a long and difficult war which did not end until 1678. We consequently see Racine produce, in 1672, the play of the hero who tries to succeed in the world without using compromise and lies—*Bajazet*—then, in 1673, the historical play in which all contradictions are overcome thanks to a historical mission—*Mithridate*—and, in 1674, the play of a war which the Gods prolong, which encounters serious obstacles, but which nevertheless finally ends in victory—*Iphigénie*.

By 1675 however, France was empoverished by war, and revolts had broken out in Britanny and Guienne.[2]

The repression which followed the revolts brought with it a general

[1] Even an anti-monarchical pamphlet such as the *Plaintes des Protestants cruellement opprimés dans le Royaume de France* (Cologne 1686) admits that persecutions grew less severe after 1669. After having mentioned the various efforts made to prevent emigration, the text continues: 'But these precautions had little effect, and it proved better to deceive the people by performing occasional actions that gave us some hope of better times or which at least hid from us the plans which may have been drawn up. It was with this in mind that, in the Declaration of 1669, the king was made to rescind a number of violent edicts already issued against us in his Council. This had its effect, although the most enlightened amongst us recognised that this slight relaxation stemmed from no good principle, and was in fact followed later by the putting into effect of these same edicts. Nevertheless, most people did think that we would be treated moderately and that our total extermination was not being planned'. (pp. 48–49).

[2] 'Several years passed during which the calm enjoyed by Paris seemed to have spread to the provinces, and if there were any movements of discontent these were of little moment. It was not until 1675 that two new uprisings, and these the most formidable of the whole reign, took place'. (P. Clément, *Histoire de Colbert*, Paris 1874, vol. II, p. 254.). P. Clément is moreover, to my knowledge at least, one of the few historians writing in French to have made a detailed study of forty pages to peasant uprisings during the reign of Louis XIV.

change of policy, which soon affected the Jansenists: the Peace of Clement IX was at an end.

The reservations which Racine had felt earlier now showed themselves to have been justified. He had been proved right and Port-Royal wrong. The hope of living in the world without making any essential concessions was an illusion, and the situation was just as it had been. Between 1675 and 1677 Racine composed *Phèdre*, which transposes this failure on to a literary plane.

Nevertheless, this end of an illusion brought with it the disappearance of Racine's guilty feelings about Port-Royal, and the consequent disappearance both of the literature of refusal and of any literature at all. Racine returned to literature only with *Esther* and *Athalie*, when Jansenism, now under the influence of Arnauld, had replaced the theme of refusal by that of the victory of religion in this world, and when the revolution of 1688 had shown that the powers that be were not necessarily eternal.

All this is obviously hypothetical, but in my view is no more extraordinary or improbable than most of the theories that have been put forward about Racine. It has, in addition, the advantage of taking into account a number of correlations that have remained unnoticed until recently, as well as giving due weight to the exceptional importance which Port-Royal always has for Racine.

Even if this particular hypothesis turned out to be mistaken, the relationship on which it is based between Racine's works and the life and ideas of the 'Friends of Port-Royal' did nevertheless exist, whether Racine was aware of it or not.

This is why the internal analysis of Racine's theatre sketched out in the earlier pages of this book seems to me to be independent of any biographical hypothesis.

B. Main Events in the Life of Blaise Pascal

1623. Birth at Clermont of Blaise Pascal, only son and second child of Étienne Pascal, *Président à la Cour des Aides* at Clermont, and of Antoinette Bégon. Étienne Pascal, a keen mathematician and amateur scientist, himself undertook the education of his children.

1625. Birth of Jacqueline Pascal.

1626. Death of Pascal's mother.

1631. Étienne Pascal moves to Paris, taking his three children with him. (His elder daughter Gilberte, born 1620, was later to write, under her married name of Gilbert Périer, a *Life of Pascal* which was originally intended to be used as a preface for the edition of the *Pensées* prepared by Port-Royal in 1670). There, he associated with some of the leading scientists of his day, and in 1635 was a foundation member of the Académie of Father Mersenne. The system of education which he adopted for his children insisted on the prime importance of languages, and he therefore forbad any early teaching of mathematics. However, according to Madame Périer, Pascal was filled with such curiosity for this branch of knowledge that, at the age of twelve, he was discovered working on his own at the proof of Euclid's thirty-second proposition.

1638. Jacqueline Pascal is presented at Court and recognised as a gifted poetess for her verses celebrating the pregnancy of the Queen, Anne of Austria. (Cf. pp. 187 and 190.)

Étienne Pascal takes part in a demonstration directed against the Government's failure to pay interest on money invested in the Hôtel-de-Ville in Paris, and is compelled to leave the capital for Auvergne in order to avoid being sent to the Bastille. (Cf. p. 130 and p. 131 n.)

1639. As a result of a plea made by Jacqueline to Cardinal Richelieu, Étienne Pascal is forgiven for his part in the riots of 1638, and is sent to Rouen with a King's Commission setting him up as an inspector and collector of taxes (tailles).

1640. Violent protests against the Government and against tax collectôrs in Rouen are fiercely put down by the Chancellor Séguier, assisted by Étienne Pascal. (Cf. p. 275 n.)

Pascal's first work, a short, preliminary *Essay on Conic Sections*, is published in Paris.

1642. In order to help his father in his work as a tax officer, Pascal begins to elaborate a calculating machine (*machine arithmétique*), and completes the first model in 1645. However, full permission to develop the machine was not granted until 1649, and it appeared in its definitive form only in 1652. Eight models are still in existence. Pascal is said to have thought of his calculating machine as a potential commercial proposition, and was hindered in developing it only by the lack of skilled artisans.

1646. Étienne Pascal is compelled to spend a long time in bed after having dislocated his hip. He is looked after by the brothers Deschamp, who bring into his household some of the religious fervour already being disseminated by the works of Saint-Cyran and by the publication, in 1643, of Antoine Arnauld's *De la Fréquente Communion*. All the members of the Pascal family come under the influence of this new seriousness in religion, and some of Pascal's biographers refer to this as his 'first conversion'. (Cf. Chapter VIII, pp. 169–171 and passim.)

Later in the same year, Pascal and his father repeat at Rouen the experiment first conducted by Toricelli, and which consisted of inverting a tube of mercury, closed at the top end, into an open container, and noting that not all of the mercury flowed out of the tube. The traditional physics of Pascal's day argued that this was because nature had a 'horror of the void' and that it was this which prevented all the mercury from flowing down. Pascal mistrusted these explanations, and published, in October 1647, his *Expériences nouvelles touchant le vide*, in which he criticised the traditional view. This brought him into controversy with Father Noël, a Jesuit priest, and led him to conduct his famous experiment at the Puy-de-Dôme on September 19th, 1648. He described this experiment in his *Récit de la grande expérience de l'équilibre des liqueurs* in October of the same year, where he pointed out that, since the mercury came farther down the tube at the top of the Puy-de-Dôme than it did at the bottom, it was scarcely reasonable to argue that Nature's 'horror of the void' decreased whenever one went up a hill. These experiments involved Pascal in further controversy and are referred to on pp. 25, 27, and 179.

1647. Pascal goes to live in Paris and keeps house with his sister Jacqueline. He meets Descartes, whom he may have consulted about his poor state of health. The two men tended, however, to disagree widely on a number of subjects.

1648. Pascal writes, in Latin, the complete treatise on Conic Sections which he had announced in 1640, and which may perhaps have been later used by Leibnitz. The manuscript of this has been lost.

Étienne Pascal returns to Paris, where he finds his children in close contact with the convent of Port-Royal, which, since the appointment as director in 1634 of the Abbé de Saint-Cyran, has become the centre of the Jansenist movement. Jacqueline is already expressing the desire to take her vows and enter the convent, but is dissuaded from doing so by her father and brother.

1651. Death of Étienne Pascal. Jacqueline hands over her share of her father's property to Blaise, who undertakes to pay her an annuity of some 1,200 *livres*. However, as Monsieur Goldmann points out in a long note to Chapter VIII (cf. p. 185), Blaise did derive a certain financial profit from this arrangement, and there also remained some 20,000 *livres* which had still not been divided out between Gilberte, Blaise and Jacqueline. Blaise objected to Jacqueline's intention of handing over her share of this money to the convent of Port-Royal, where she took her vows of novice in May 1652, and seems to have given up his objection only after Mother Angélique had agreed, in June 1653, to take Jacqueline without a dowry of any kind. He is said to have considered this as a form of 'moral blackmail', and to have borne a grudge against Port-Royal for several years afterwards.

According to Madame Périer, 1652 marked the beginning of the 'worldly period' of Pascal's life, characterised by his continued interest in science (he sent a model of his calculating machine to Queen Christina of Sweden in June 1652, wrote further descriptions of his experiments with barometric pressure and pursued his mathematical researches), and by his association with men such as Méré and Mitton who were closely connected with the 'free thinking' Court circles of the time. This period, however, did not last very long.

1654. In September Pascal withdraws from the world in disgust, and goes to see Jacqueline in order to ask her advice.

From ten thirty to twelve thirty on the evening of November 23rd, Pascal has a mystical-type experience during which he feels, with the intensity of fire, the truth of 'the God of

Abraham, the God of Isaac, not the God of the philosophers and scientists'. He keeps his own description of the experience, a parchment later called *Le Mémorial*, sewn into his doublet until the end of his life.

1655. In January Pascal withdraws, temporarily, to Port-Royal des Champs. He holds his famous *Entretien avec Monsieur de Saci sur Epictète et sur Montaigne* (cf. p. 288), in which he criticises both thinkers for the incomplete nature of their ideas, accusing Montaigne of disparaging human reason and Epictetus of exaggerating its power.

1656. Antoine Arnauld's defence of Jansenius is condemned by the Sorbonne. Pascal is persuaded to take part in the subsequent controversy, and begins to prepare, with the help of Arnauld, Nicole and other theologians, the first of his *Lettres Provinciales*. This appears in January 1656, and is followed by seventeen further letters, the last of them dated March 24th, 1657. They are placed on the Index on September 6th, 1657. The miracle whereby his niece, Marguerite Périer, was cured on March 24th, 1656, of a fistula on her eye by being touched by a Holy Thorn had earlier been seen by Pascal as a sign encouraging him to pursue his struggle against the Jesuits. The arrival in France in March 1657 of the Bull of Alexander VII condemning Jansenius leads Pascal to suggest, in a phrase quoted several times by Monsieur Goldmann (cf. pp. 84, 171 and 188), and found in a draft for what was to be the nineteenth of the *Lettres Provinciales*, that he was torn between obeying God and obeying the Pope. It is at this moment in his life, and in response to this situation, that in Monsieur Goldmann's view Pascal begins to move away from the implicit rationalism of the *Lettres Provinciales* and to develop the tragic philosophy of the *Pensées*.

1657. From December of this year to July 1658 Pascal continues the struggle against the casuists begun in the *Provinciales*, and succeeds in securing the condemnation of Father Pirot's *Apologie pour les Casuistes*. He begins to write the *Pensées*.

1658. In June Pascal issues a challenge to all the scientists and mathematicians of his day to solve the problem of the Roulette, to which he himself has already found the answer. According to Madame Périer, Pascal turned his attention to the problem of the Roulette solely in order to forget his tooth-ache. Monsieur Goldmann rejects this account of events (cf. p. 54) and argues instead that when Pascal was thus simultaneously denouncing the vanity of science and yet indulging in scientific research himself, he was illustrating the paradox and the simultaneous

'Yes' and 'No' of the tragic vision. During the last four years of his life Pascal's health grew steadily worse, and he also led an increasingly austere life, devoting much of his time, energy and money to caring for the poor.

1661. On February 1st the *Assemblée du Clergé* insists that every person in holy orders shall sign the *Formulaire* of March 1657 condemning the five heretical propositions said to be found in Jansenius's *Augustinus* (1640). In June, however, Arnauld succeeds in maintaining the distinction between whether the propositions are actually in the *Augustinus* (question de fait) and whether they are heretical (question de droit). However, this distinction, set forth in the *Mandement des Grands Vicaires*, is itself annulled in the following month. Jacqueline Pascal, deeply affected by what she sees as a tendency to laxity in moral and theological matters, insists in a letter to Blaise that no one ought to sign the *Formulaire*. Exhausted by the struggle, she dies on October 4th. Pascal himself maintains, in a text known as the *Ecrit sur la Signature,* and probably written as late as November 1661, that no one ought to sign such a condemnation of Jansenius. However, when he received the last rites from Father Beurrier on July 4th, 1662, he stated in his confession that he had wholly accepted the Pope's authority since August 1st, 1660. Monsieur Goldmann again explains this contradiction (cf. p. 189) by referring to the paradoxical attitude of the tragic vision.

1662. In January, Pascal organises the first omnibus service, the *carrosses à cinq sols*, set up in Paris on March 18th. This was one of the last actions of his life, for he died on August 19th of the same year. Once again, different explanations have been put forward for the fact that he indulged in commercial activity at a time when he was arguing, in the *Pensées*, that the Christian should give up all worldly concerns, and *The Hidden God* again finds this attitude typical of the tragic vision.

C. Notes on Some of the Main Characters Closely Connected with the Jansenist Movement in France

AGNÈS, MOTHER. Full name; Jeanne-Catherine-Agnès de Saint-Paul (1594–1671). Sister of Le Grand Arnauld (q.v.) and of Mother Angélique (q.v.) Abbess of Port-Royal from 1636 to 1642.

ANGÉLIQUE, MOTHER. Full name: Jacqueline-Marie-Angélique de Sainte-Madeleine (1591–1661). Sister of Mother Agnès. Abbess of the Cistercian convent of Port-Royal from 1602 to 1636 and from 1642 to 1661. In 1608 she began the reforms which were later to lead Port-Royal to become the centre of the Jansenist movement. For Monsieur Goldmann, she was one of those most strongly influenced by the views of Barcos.

ARNAULD, ANTOINE. 1612–94. Known as Le Grand Arnauld. Twentieth son of Antoine Arnauld, and the leading theologian of the 'moderate' or 'middle of the road' Jansenism. In 1643 he published *De La Fréquente Communion*, in which he insisted that atonement for sins could be obtained only by sincere repentance, and not by frequent attendance at Mass. In 1656 the Sorbonne condemned his *Seconde Lettre à un duc et pair*, attacking a priest who had refused communion to a friend of the Jansenists, and thus began the controversy which led Pascal to write the *Lettres Provinciales*. In 1662 he published the *Logique de Port-Royal*, and remained until the end of his life a firm supporter of Descartes. Monsieur Jean Laporte, whose views on Port-Royal are frequently criticised by Monsieur Goldmann, calls him 'the most authentic and complete representative of the ideas which gave life to Port-Royal'.

BARCOS, MARTIN DE. 1600–78. Nephew of Antoine Arnauld and also secretary to Jean-Ambroise Duvergier de Hauranne, Abbé de Saint-Cyran, (q. v.). He succeeded Duvergier in 1643, and carried on an active correspondence with the other members of the Jansenist group. Monsieur Goldmann, who published this correspondence in 1955, sees him as the person whose ideas lay at the source of the 'world vision' which found its expression in Jansenism. His influence on the Jansenist movement remained important until 1661, and was especially concerned with two main issues: his hostility to any participation of the Christian in the affairs of this world, and his conviction that the Christian should, at one and the same time, be prepared to acknowledge the authority of his superiors and to proclaim the truth. His position on the first point expressed, for Monsieur Goldmann, the essence of Jansenism, and the reason for which the powers that be were so remorseless in their persecution of the movement. The views on the second question are also important in that they constituted the starting-point for the attitude expressed in the *Pensées*. After the death of Mother Angélique in 1661, of Pascal in 1662 and of Singlin in 1664, Barcos's influence declined, and his final break with Port-Royal in 1669, when he condemned the acceptance of the 'Peace of Clement IX', marked in Monsieur Goldmann's view the end of 'the period of tragic theology, thought and literature in France'.

NICOLE, PIERRE. 1625–95. One of the leading theologians at Port-Royal, a close friend and collaborator with Antoine Arnauld. He was probably the person who invented the famous *distinction de droit et de fait* (the five propositions are heretical, but they are not in the *Augustinus*) which enabled certain Jansenists to sign the *Formulary* of March 1657. Much of what he wrote was aimed at minimising the differences between the Jansenists and their opponents, but his attack on novelists and playwrights in *les Visionnaires* (1666) led to the quarrel between Racine and Port-Royal.

PAVILLON, NICOLAS. 1597–1677. Bishop of Alet and member of the extremist group of the Jansenist movement. One of the leaders in the opposition to the signature of the *Formulary*.

SINGLIN, ANTOINE. 1607–64. Son of a wine merchant. In 1637 he entered Port-Royal and later became Pascal's 'Directeur de conscience'. He was a close friend of Barcos, and, like him, was prepared to sign the *Formulary*.

SAINT-CYRAN, ABBÉ DE. 1581–1643. Full name: Jean Duvergier de Hauranne. Director, from 1634, of Port-Royal and responsible for introducing the ideas of his friend Jansenius, with whom he had studied theology at Bayonne from 1611 to 1616. From 1638 until his death he was held in prison by Richelieu (cf. pp. 114–5).

D. Notes on Some of the Main Events in the History of Jansenism and of Port-Royal

1581. Birth of Jean Du Vergier de Hauranne, subsequently Abbé de Saint-Cyran and, from 1634, director of the convent of Port-Royal.

1585. Birth of Cornelius Jansen, subsequently Bishop of Ypres from 1636 until his death in 1638.

1594. Antoine Arnauld, a well-known lawyer, pleads a famous case against the Jesuits. He was the father of twenty children, a number of whom, including his youngest son Antoine (*le Grand Arnauld*) and three of his daughters, were central figures in the history of Port-Royal.

1608. Jacqueline Arnauld, installed as abbess of Port-Royal in 1602 at the age of eleven, begins her reform of the monastery. She is generally known as Mother Angélique de Sainte-Madeleine.

1619. Jansen, deeply influenced by his reading of St. Augustine, begins to develop the distinction between sufficient and efficacious Grace which is fundamental to Jansenism. The first is the Grace which Adam had before the Fall and which enabled him to act freely, while the second is the redemptive Grace of Christ against which man, after the Fall, is powerless. The Jansenists later accused the Jesuits of wrongly attributing sufficient Grace to fallen man.

1620. Meeting between Saint-Cyran and Robert Arnauld d'Andilly, elder brother of *le Grand Arnauld*, and, in the words of Nigel Abercrombie, 'a courtier with every prospect of advancement before him'. In 1621 Arnauld d'Andilly arranged for Saint-Cyran to meet his sister, Mother Angélique, on whom, however, he seems to have had little direct influence until 1633, when he came to the defence of her sister, Mother Agnès, when one of the latter's theological pamphlets was attacked by the Archbishop of Sens.

1634. Mother Angélique invites Saint-Cyran to become Director of the Convent of Port-Royal, which in 1625 had moved from the Vallée de la Chevreuse to Paris. By this time, however, Saint-Cyran was already beginning to seem suspect to the authorities. In 1635 Jansen published a pamphlet entitled *Mars Gallicus* which was a violent attack on Richelieu's policy of alliance with the Protestants in the Thirty Years War, and Saint-Cyran was known to be closely associated with him. In the same year Saint-Cyran also offended Richelieu by showing his hostility to the annulment which the Cardinal had arranged of the marriage between Gaston d'Orléans and Marguerite de Lorraine.

1637. In August Antoine Le Maitre, a brilliant lawyer and a nephew of Mother Angélique, withdraws from public life and places himself under the direction of Saint-Cyran. On December 15th he publicly announces his decision to live in penance and retreat, and withdraws to the buildings formerly occupied by the Nuns of Port-Royal in the Vallée de la Chevreuse. There he becomes the first of the 'solitaires', and is later joined by a number of other men, including the grammarian Lancelot and the priest Singlin, as well as by two of his brothers. The number of solitaries seems to have varied, however, since Antoine Adam states that there were only four in 1643, but twelve in 1646 after the publication of Antoine Arnauld's *De la Fréquente Communion*. However, such was the concern caused by the action of Le Maitre that Saint-Cyran was, in the words of Louis Cognet, 'accused of depriving the State, by his excessive theology, of its most gifted subjects', and he was arrested on Richelieu's order on May 2nd, 1638, remaining in prison until his death in 1643.

1640. Posthumous publication, in September, of *Cornelii Jansenii Episcopi Iprensis Augustinus*, a long commentary of some 1300 pages on the work of St. Augustine. By August 1st, 1641, the *Augustinus* was condemned by the Inquisition, but certain French theologians welcomed it with enthusiasm. However, in 1649 Nicolas Cornet demanded, in the Sorbonne, the condemnation of seven propositions which he said the book contained. These were later reduced to five, which were considered by Bossuet to be 'the soul of the *Augustinus*'. These were condemned by Innocent X in the Bull *Cum Occasione* on May 31st, 1653. Combined reference to Cognet, (op. cit., p. 50) and to Hasting's *Encyclopaedia of Religion and Ethics*, gives the following version of them: (1) There are commandments which good men cannot obey, however hard they may try. These men also lack the Grace by which they would be able to follow these commandments. (2) In the state of fallen nature, internal Grace is never resisted. (3) To make actions in the state of Fallen Grace meritorious or otherwise, it is not requisite that they

414

should be free from internal necessity but only from external constraint. (4) The semi-Pelagians admitted the necessity of an internal anticipatory Grace for each action, even for the beginning of faith, and were heretical in wishing to maintain that man's will could either resist or obey this Grace. (5) It is a semi-Pelagian error to say that Christ died or that He shed His blood for all men, with no exceptions.

The Jansenists adopted two main lines of defence. One of these consisted of saying that to condemn these propositions amounted to a condemnation of St. Augustine; the other consisted of agreeing that these propositions were heretical, but denying that they were actually in the *Augustinus*.

1643. August. Publication of Antoine Arnauld's *De la Fréquente Communion*, a work which originated in the quarrel as to whether a woman could take communion in the morning and go to a ball in the evening. Arnauld argued in favour of a careful and rigorous spiritual preparation for the act of taking communion—so careful and rigorous, in fact, that *The Catholic Encyclopaedia* suggests that 'his book would have been more correctly entitled *Against Frequent Communion*'. The book had considerable success and went into a large number of editions. Its publication marked the beginning of the proselitysing and polemical aspect of French Jansenism.

1648. A number of nuns return from the monastery in Paris to the older buildings of Port-Royal des Champs, where they found the *Petites Ecoles de Port-Royal des Champs*. It was there that Racine received his early education from 1655 to 1658.

1655. On January 15th an Assembly of fifteen Bishops draws up a Formulary to be signed by all people in Holy Orders, and declaring that the condemnation of the *Augustinus* was at one and the same fully justified and yet not applicable to the true doctrine of St. Augustine.

On February 1st the confessor of the Duc de Liancourt, Picoté, refused to grant the Duke absolution until he agreed to break off all association with the Jansenists. Antoine Arnauld protested violently against this decision, in his *Seconde Lettre à un duc et pair*, dated July 10th, 1655, and it was on his invitation that Pascal decided to write the *Lettres Provinciales*, the first of which is dated January 23rd, 1656.

1656. On October 16th Alexander VII reaffirmed in the Bull *Ad Sacram* that the five propositions are in the *Augustinus*, and that they stand condemned in the sense given to them by Jansenius. Louis XIV had to hold a *lit de justice* in order to compel the *Parlement de Paris* to register this Bull on November 29th,

1657. Arnauld then began to insist on the distinction between right and fact (the Pope is quite right to condemn these propositions; however, they are not in the *Augustinus*), but the Jansenists were divided on what attitude they should adopt. Barcos, who held that it was the priest's duty both to obey his superiors and to proclaim the truth, disagreed with Arnauld's polemical insistence on the grounds that it was uncharitable and that God's Providence would in any case make the truth prevail, and he was joined in this attitude by Singlin. Nicole supported Arnauld, and his readiness to abandon the more strictly Augustinian position is said to have encouraged the Thomistic tendencies visible in much of Arnauld's later thought. The extremists at Port-Royal, however, including Angélique de Saint-Jean, Mother Angélique's niece, and Jacqueline Pascal, argued that the position of Rome was fundamentally wrong and that the duty of the Christian was to fight for the truth and purity of the true doctrine.

1661. Inspired by the vigorous attitude of Louis XIV, the *Assemblée du Clergé* once again demanded the signature of the Formulary, and the lodgers and postulants were expelled from Port-Royal by the police. On June 22nd the Nuns signed the Formulary, but with a clause expressly setting out the distinction between right and fact, and repeated this action on November 22nd. The quarrel dragged on until, in April 1664, the new Archbishop of Paris, Péréfixe, took up office. On August 21st and 26th he visited Port-Royal, and had twelve nuns, including Angélique de Saint-Jean and Mother Agnès, removed by the police. In July 1665 the nuns who still refused to sign were removed to Port-Royal des Champs, where they were kept under police supervision.

1667. Alexander VII dies in January and is succeeded, in June, by Clement IX, a man of a more peaceful disposition who wished to avoid the schism that was threatening as the result of the sympathy shown for the Jansenist party by a number of French bishops. Louis XIV was also preparing for the war against Holland, and wished to avoid any further internal dispute. Consequently, a compromise was worked out whereby the four bishops who had objected to the Bull *Regiminis apostolici* in 1665 would nevertheless sign it, provided that 'secret' conventions recognised the *distinction de droit et de fait*. This led to the *Peace of the Church*, or *Peace of Clement IX*, which is normally dated from February 18th, 1669, to May 16th, 1679. According to Louis Cognet, this marks the end of 'religious Jansenism properly so-called'.

416

1679. May 16th, Harlay de Champvallon, the new Archbishop of Paris, expels everyone except the nuns themselves from Port-Royal des Champs, and forbids the monastery to receive any more novices.

1709. Louis XIV gives the order for the last remaining Nuns to be expelled from Port-Royal des Champs, and in 1711 orders the destruction of the buildings.

1713. On September 8th Pope Clement XI signs the Bull *Unigenitus Dei Filius*, which, in condemning 101 propositions taken from the *Réflexions Morales sur le Nouveau Testament* published in 1671 and again in 1699 by Pasquier Quesnel, marked the final defeat of the Jansenists. According to Fénelon, French public opinion credited the Bull with condemning St. Augustine, St. Paul and even Christ himself, but the intention had been to make out a kind of 'brief definition' of the Jansenist position in order to condemn it more succinctly. In the course of the eighteenth century Jansenism became generally associated in the public mind with criticism of Royal authority, and also with the mystical phenomenon of 'speaking with tongues'.

Note. This account of Jansenism and Port-Royal is intended solely as a list of references for readers of *The Hidden God*, and no claim is made either for its originality or its comprehensiveness. The main authorities consulted were:

Antoine Adam. *Histoire de la Littérature Française au XVII Siècle* Vol. II, Domat 1957.

Paul Bénichou. *Morales du Grand Siècle*. Gallimard 1947.

Nigel Abercrombie. *The Origins of Jansenism*. OUP 1936.

Louis Cognet. *Le Jansénisme*. P.U.F. 1961.

Hasting's *Encyclopaedia of Religion and Ethics*, *The Catholic Encyclopaedia*, and *The Oxford Companion to French Literature*.

It is perhaps interesting to note that other scholars emphasise a slightly different aspect of the relationship between the Jansenist movement and the conflicts between the different social groups in seventeenth-century France. Paul Bénichou, for example, speaks of 'the resistance put up by the leaders of the bourgeoisie against the spirit of absolute government', and explains the long duration of the movement by reference to 'the awareness which the bourgeoisie had of its own importance' (op. cit., p. 127). Similarly, Antoine Adam sees Jansenism as a form of bourgeois protest against the position of moral privilege accorded to the aristocracy by the Jesuits, and writes that this explains how Jansenism became 'if not a political party, then at least an attitude of revolt on the part of the enlightened bourgeoisie against the combined forces of absolute monarchy and the Society of Jesus' (op. cit., p. 257). In his short introductory study, first published in 1961, Louis Cognet comes fairly close to repeating some of Monsieur Goldmann's ideas when he writes (p. 48) that 'Under Louis XIV, the struggle against Jansenism and Port-Royal becomes a fundamental aim of the central government, while, at the same time, the traditional centres of opposition to royal absolutism—the legal nobility, the *Parlements*—tend fairly naturally to gravitate towards Jansenism—even more so since it is at this very moment that the development of the system of *commis* is depriving the legal nobility of its *raison d'être*.'

On a slightly different plane, that of the interpretation of Pascal's relationship with Jansenism, Antoine Adam goes so far as to write (p. 209) that it would be 'scarcely a paradox to maintain that there was only one really consistent Jansenist, and that was Pascal'.

E. A Note on the Historical Terms Used in Chapter VI

IN order to avoid any possible confusion stemming from the attempt to translate French historical terms where no English equivalent exists, I have not tried to translate the terminology used in this and other chapters. The basic distinction is between the *officiers*, or office-holders, who purchased and owned their legal charges and were allowed to transmit them to their heirs, and the *commissaires*, who held a royal commission to perform a particular function, and who could therefore be removed from office at the King's pleasure. Monsieur Goldmann argues that the decision to create *Intendants* to govern the different Provinces, and thereby to deprive the *officiers* of their social functions, was an important factor in turning many of the legal nobility towards Jansenism. The *officiers* were still economically dependent upon the King, and therefore could not rebel against him politically, and were consequently tempted, especially after the failure of the Fronde in 1648 and 1653, simply to withdraw from the world.

In seventeenth-century France the holders of certain legal offices were also granted patents of nobility, and were known as the *noblesse de robe*. By virtue of a measure known as La Paulette, first introduced under Henri IV, they were allowed to transmit their office to their heir on payment of an annual tax of one-sixtieth of its value. The upper members of the *noblesse de robe* were also members of a *parlement*, of which there were eventually eight in the whole of France, and which constituted the supreme judicial assembly for its region. The *Parlement de Paris* was traditionally hostile to the attempts of the King to encroach upon its traditional privileges of registering and occasionally criticising royal edicts, and much of the appeal of Jansenism for the *parlementaires* is said to have lain in the fact that they saw it as a means of challenging the King's authority. The King could, by holding a *lit de justice*, override the refusal of the *parlement* to register a particular edict, and he could also banish recalcitrant lawyers to the provinces until they changed their minds on a particular issue. The *parlements* were also known as *Cours souveraines*, and were hereditary and not elective bodies. A *Maître des Requêtes* was also the owner of his charge, and had the task of receiving and reporting on petitions made to the King, and of presenting certain cases before the *parlements*.

INDEX

its truest representatives, 18;
linked with the social position of
the legal nobility in seventeenth-
century France, 103–41, 23, 98,
223; the three main tendencies,
55; some general characteristics,
142; the importance of the
wager, 301
Jacquard, L. J., 114 n
Jansenius, Bishop of Ypres, 84, 142,
182
Joseph, Father, 113

Kant, Immanuel, 5, 9, 11, 15, 22,
23, 33, 46, 52, 58, 67, 89, 91, 92,
98, 102, 145, 172, 195, 203, 210,
220, 224, 226, 227, 228, 247, 271,
278, 303, 332; his reaction to
Hume, 19–20; his views distorted by the neo-Kantians, 24–5,
265. For comparison of his ideas
with those of Pascal, see under
Pascal, Blaise. For page references to English translations of
his work and to the German
Academy edition see footnotes to
pp. 92, 232, 242, 262, 263, 291,
294, 299
Kierkegaard, Soren, 10, 45
Koyré, Alexandre, 25, 26, 27, 227.
241

Lafuma, Louis, value of his edition
of the *Pensées*, 201
Lamoignon, Guillaume de, 1617–
77, 132, 133, 141
Lancelot, Claude, 1615–95, 115,
117, 147
Laporte, Jean, 10, 13, 84, 230, 241,
242; his interpretation of Pascal
criticised, 193 n; assimilates Pascal's position to that of Arnauld,
203; sympathy for Hume, 207;
views of the 'Laporte school' of
Pascalian scholars, 221
Laplace, Pierre-Simon, 1749–1827,
248

La Rocheposay, Henri–Louis,
1577–1651, 112
Leconte de Lisle, 73
Leibnitz, 28, 29, 172, 223, 233
Le Maitre, Antoine, 105, 116, 121,
122, 345; effects of his withdrawal from the world in 1637,
112–15
Lenin, 187, 188
Lessing, G. E., 172, 175, 191, 210,
211, 385
Lewis, Geneviève, 221
Liancourt, duc de, 116
Longueville, Madame de, 116
Louis XI, 110, 118
Louis XIII, 113, 118, 130
Louis XIV, 8, 103, 107, 118, 157,
316, 373, 402
Lukàcs, Georg, X, 5, 12, 22, 23, 42,
49, 59, 67, 68, 71, 78, 91, 145,
168, 187, 188, 195, 214, 235, 243,
250, 252, 303, 317, 384; his
definition of tragic man, 35–9, 56;
similarity between his ideas and
those expressed in *On the Conversion of the Sinner*, 65, 70–5;
similarity with an anonymous
Jansenist text, 66; similarity with
The Mystery of Jesus, 80, 83; importance of the wager, 308; his
views on tragedy quoted in relation to *Phèdre*, 377
Luynes, duc de, 116

Maignart des Bernières, Charles,
136, 139
Malebranche, Nicolas, 23, 24, 28,
29, 31, 161, 172
Marie des Anges, Sister, 113–15
Marivaux, Pierre, 352
Marx, Karl, X, 4, 5, 15 n, 25, 40 n,
89, 96, 145, 168, 172, 175 n, 187,
188, 211, 220, 235, 236, 247, 249,
250, 347; similarity with Pascal,
278, 281; comments on Goethe's
Faust, 280
Marxism, 90, 264; goes beyond the
tragic vision by means of the

International Library of Philosophy & Scientific Method

Editor: Ted Honderich

(Demy 8vo)

Allen, R. E. (Ed.), **Studies in Plato's Metaphysics** *464 pp. 1965.*
  Plato's 'Euthyphro' and the Earlier Theory of Forms *184 pp. 1970.*
Allen, R. E. and Furley, David J. (Eds.), **Studies in Presocratic Philosophy**
  326 pp. 1970.
Armstrong, D.M., **Perception and the Physical World** *208 pp. 1961.*
  A Materialist Theory of the Mind *376 pp. 1967.*
Bambrough, Renford (Ed.), **New Essays on Plato and Aristotle**
  184 pp. 1965.
Barry, Brian, **Political Argument** *382 pp. 1965.*
Bird, Graham, **Kant's Theory of Knowledge** *220 pp. 1962.*
Bogen, James, **Wittgenstein's Philosophy of Language** *256, pp. 1972.*
Broad, C. D., **Lectures on Psychical Research** *461 pp. 1962.*
  (2nd Impression 1966.)
Crombie, I. M., **An Examination of Plato's Doctrine**
  I. Plato on Man and Society *408 pp. 1962.*
  II. Plato on Knowledge and Reality *583 pp. 1963.*
Day, John Patrick, **Inductive Probability** *352 pp. 1961.*
Dennett, D. C., **Content and Consciousness** *202 pp. 1969.*
Dretske, Fred I., **Seeing and Knowing** *270 pp. 1969.*
Ducasse, C. J., **Truth, Knowledge and Causation** *263 pp. 1969.*
Edel, Abraham, **Method in Ethical Theory** *379 pp. 1963.*
Farm, K. T. (Ed.), **Symposium on J. L. Austin** *512 pp. 1969.*
Flew, Anthony, **Hume's Philosophy of Belief** *296 pp. 1961.*
Fogelin, Robert J., **Evidence and Meaning** *200 pp. 1967.*
Franklin, R., **Freewill and Determinism** *353 pp. 1968.*
Gale, Richard, **The Language of Time** *256 pp. 1967.*
Glover, Jonathan, **Responsibility** *212 pp. 1970.*
Goldman, Lucien, **The Hidden God** *424 pp. 1964.*
Hamlyn, D. W., **Sensation and Perception** *222 pp. 1961.*
  (3rd Impression 1967.)
Husserl, Edmund, **Logical Investigations** *Vol. I: 456 pp. Vol. II: 464 pp.*
Kemp, J., **Reason, Action and Morality** *216 pp. 1964.*
Körner, Stephan, **Experience and Theory** *272 pp. 1966.*
Lazerowitz, Morris, **Studies in Metaphilosophy** *276 pp. 1964.*
Linsky, Leonard, **Referring** *152 pp. 1967.*
MacIntosh, J. J. and Coval, S. C. (Eds.), **Business of Reason** *280 pp. 1969.*
Meiland, Jack W., **Talking About Particulars** *192 pp. 1970.*
Merleau-Ponty, M., **Phenomenology of Perception** *487 pp. 1962.*
Naess, Arne, **Scepticism** *176 pp. 1969.*
Perelman, Chaim, **The Idea of Justice and the Problem of Argument**
  224 pp. 1963.
Ross, Alf, **Directives, Norms and their Logic** *192 pp. 1967.*
Schlesinger, G., **Method in the Physical Sciences** *148 pp. 1963.*
Sellars, W. F., **Science and Metaphysics** *248 pp. 1968.*
  Science, Perception and Reality *374 pp. 1963.*
Shwayder, D. S., **The Stratification of Behaviour** *428 pp. 1965.*